Tocqueville's Voyages

Tocqueville's Voyages

The Evolution of
His Ideas and Their
Journey Beyond
His Time

Edited and with an introduction by

CHRISTINE DUNN HENDERSON

Liberty Fund

Indianapolis

Amagi books are published by Liberty Fund, Inc., a foundation established to encourage study of the ideal of a society of free and responsible individuals.

𒂼𒄄

The cuneiform inscription that appears in the logo and serves as a design element in all Liberty Fund books is the earliest-known written appearance of the word "freedom" (*amagi*), or "liberty." It is taken from a clay document written about 2300 B.C. in the Sumerian city-state of Lagash.

P 10 9 8 7 6 5 4 3 2 1

Library of Congress Cataloging-in-Publication Data

Tocqueville's voyages: the evolution of his ideas and their journey beyond his time/edited and with an introduction by Christine Dunn Henderson.
     pages cm
  Includes bibliographical references and index.
  ISBN 978-0-86597-870-6 (paperback: alkaline paper)
  1. Tocqueville, Alexis de, 1805–1859—Travel. 2. Tocqueville, Alexis de, 1805–1859—Political and social views. 3. Tocqueville, Alexis de, 1805–1859—Influence. 4. Voyages and travels—History—19th century. 5. Democracy—History—19th century. I. Henderson, Christine Dunn, 1967–
DC36.98.T63T63 2014
306.2092—dc23   2014022561

LIBERTY FUND, INC.
8335 Allison Pointe Trail, Suite 300
Indianapolis, Indiana 46250-1684

Contents

Note on the Contributors

ENRIQUE AGUILAR holds a PhD in political science from Pontificia Universidad Católica in Argentina, where he presently is professor of political theory and director of the PhD program in Political Science of the Faculty of Social Sciences of the Universidad Católica Argentina. He is the author of books and articles on topics pertaining to the liberal and republican traditions.

BARBARA ALLEN is Ada M. Harrison Distinguished Teaching Professor of the Social Sciences, professor and former chair of the Department of Political Science, and director of Women's Studies at Carleton College in Northfield, Minn. She has served as a contributing editor to the Martin Luther King Jr. Papers Project at Stanford University and has written extensively on the political thought of Martin Luther King Jr. and Alexis de Tocqueville. Her book *Tocqueville, Covenant, and the Democratic Revolution: Harmonizing Earth with Heaven* examines the covenant idea in politics and its influence on American federalism. Recently, she directed the award-winning feature length documentary *Signing On: Stories of Deaf Breast Cancer Survivors, Their Families, and the Deaf Community.*

JEAN-LOUIS BENOÎT received his MA in moral and political philosophy from the Université Paris–Sorbonne (Paris IV) and his PhD from the Université de Caen. Since the 1980s, his research has focused on the life, work, and thought of Tocqueville. He initiated and co-organized the 1990 international colloquium *L'actualité de Tocqueville* and was one of the co-organizers of *Tocqueville entre l'Amérique et l'Europe,* the international colloquium honoring the bicentenary of Tocqueville's birth. He is the editor of volume 14 of Gallimard's *Oeuvres Complètes d'Alexis de Tocqueville: Correspondence familiale* (1998). His many publications include *Tocqueville moraliste* (2004); *Comprendre Tocqueville* (2004); *Tocqueville, un destin paradoxal* (2005); and *Tocqueville, notes sur le Coran et autres textes sur les religions* (2007).

JAMES W. CEASER is Harry F. Byrd Professor of Politics at the University of Virginia and a senior visiting fellow at the Hoover Institution. He is author of several books on American politics and political thought, including *Presidential Selection, Liberal Democracy and Political Science, Reconstructing America, Nature and History in American Political Development,* and *Designing a Polity.* Professor Ceaser is a frequent contributor to the popular press, and he often comments on American politics for the Voice of America.

AURELIAN CRAIUTU is professor of political science at Indiana University–Bloomington. His main research interests are modern and contemporary French political thought. His most recent book is *A Virtue for Courageous Minds: Moderation in French Political Thought, 1748–1830* (Princeton University Press, 2012). He has also edited and translated (with Jeremy Jennings) *Tocqueville on America after 1840: Letters and Other Writings* (Cambridge University Press, 2009) and coedited (with Sheldon Gellar) *Conversations with Tocqueville: The Global Democratic Revolution in the Twenty-First Century* (Rowman & Littlefield, 2009).

S. J. D. GREEN is professor of modern history at the University of Leeds and fellow of All Souls College, Oxford. His many publications include *Religion in the Age of Decline* (1996) and *The Passing of Protestant England* (2010). He is currently preparing a study of British Conservative responses to Tocqueville's *Democracy in America.*

CHRISTINE DUNN HENDERSON is senior fellow at Liberty Fund, Inc. She received her PhD in political science from Boston College. She is the contributing editor of *Seers and Judges: American Literature as Political Philosophy,* coeditor (with Mark Yellin) of *Joseph Addison's "Cato" and Selected Essays,* and cotranslator (with Henry Clark) of *Encyclopedic Liberty: Political Articles from the "Dictionary" of Diderot and D'Alembert.* Her publications include pieces on Tocqueville, Beaumont, French liberalism, and politics and literature.

JEREMY JENNINGS is professor of political theory at King's College University of London. He has published extensively on the history of political thought in France, including *Revolution and the Republic: A History of Political Ideas in France Since the Eighteenth Century* (Oxford University Press, 2012). He is now writing a book titled *Travels with Tocqueville.*

ALAN S. KAHAN is professor of British civilization at the Université de Versailles/St. Quentin-en-Yvelines. He received his PhD in history from the University of Chicago in 1987. His most recent books are *Mind vs. Money: The War between Intellectuals and Capitalism* (Transaction, 2010) and *Alexis de Tocqueville* (Continuum, 2010). He has also translated Tocqueville's *The Old Regime and the Revolution* (Chicago, 1998). His book *Tocqueville, Religion, and Democracy: Checks and Balances for Democratic Souls* will be published by Oxford University Press in 2015.

HARVEY C. MANSFIELD is the William R. Kenan Jr. Professor of Government at Harvard University, where he studies and teaches political philosophy. He has held Guggenheim and National Endowment for the Humanities fellowships, has served on the advisory council of the NEH, and is a senior fellow at the Hoover Institution at Stanford. He has written on Edmund Burke and the nature of political parties, on Machiavelli and the invention of indirect government, in defense of a defensible liberalism, and in favor of a constitutional American political science. He has also written on the discovery and development of the theory of executive power and is a translator of Machiavelli and Tocqueville. He is presently working on a book on Machiavelli, summarizing and carrying forward earlier work.

REIJI MATSUMOTO graduated from the University of Tokyo (BA in 1969, MA in 1971), started his professional career at the University of Tsukuba, and has been teaching political theory at Waseda University since 1982. He is known as a leading Tocqueville scholar in Japan for his books and articles on Tocqueville as well as for his four-volume Japanese translation of *Democracy in America* (Iwanami Bunko). Among his English publications are "Tocqueville on the Family" and "Is Democracy Peaceful? Tocqueville and Constant on War and the Army" (both in the *Tocqueville Review*), and "Tocqueville and Japan" (in *Conversations with Tocqueville*, ed. Craiutu and Gellar).

EDUARDO NOLLA is professor of political theory and rector at Universidad Camilo José Cela, Madrid. He was a visiting scholar at Yale University from 1981 to 1985 and taught there full time from 1986 to 1992. He is the author of numerous books and articles on Tocqueville and the editor of *The Historical-Critical Edition of "Democracy in America."* In 1993, he was awarded the Ordre des Arts et des

Lettres of the French Republic. He is a member of the Tocqueville Commission and the academic director of Unidad Editorial, Spain's leading media group

FILIPPO SABETTI is professor of political science at McGill University, Montreal, Quebec, Canada, and an affiliated member of the Tocqueville Program and a Senior Research Fellow of the Vincent and Elinor Ostrom Workshop in Political Theory and Policy Analysis at Indiana University–Bloomington. Much of Sabetti's work is concerned with the development of liberal and federalist thought and the practice of self-governance in Canada and Europe. His most recent book, *Civilization and Self-Government: The Political Thought of Carlo Cattaneo* (Lexington Books, 2010), reveals why the nineteenth-century pioneering analysis of Cattaneo merits a place, alongside Tocqueville, in our continuing debate about the meaning of civilization, liberty, and political economy. His current project extends that inquiry to about ten centuries of political thought and practice on the Italian peninsula in order to uncover the creative capacities of people as creators of the world in which they lived, thereby discovering the past to improve the future prospects of liberty, individual responsibility, and life in common.

JAMES T. SCHLEIFER, professor emeritus of history and former dean of Gill Library at the College of New Rochelle, received his PhD in history from Yale University. Internationally recognized as a Tocqueville scholar, he has taught as a visiting professor at Yale University and at the University of Paris and has lectured at universities in the United States and abroad. His major publications include *The Making of Tocqueville's "Democracy in America"* (University of North Carolina Press, 1980; second revised edition published by Liberty Fund, 2000); *The Chicago Companion to Tocqueville's "Democracy in America"* (University of Chicago Press, 2012); as coeditor, critical edition of *De la démocratie en Amérique*, in the Pléiade series published by Gallimard (Paris, 1992); and as translator, the complete critical edition of *Democracy in America*, edited by Eduardo Nolla and published by Liberty Fund (4 vols., 2010).

CHERYL B. WELCH is senior lecturer and director of undergraduate studies in government at Harvard University. Her teaching and research interests are in the history of political thought (especially nineteenth-century France), liberal and democratic theory, and the history of human rights. She is the author of *Liberty and Utility: The French Idéologues and the Transformation of Liberalism* (1984) and *De Tocqueville* (2001), and the editor of *Critical Issues in Social Theory* (with M. Milgate, 1989) and *The Cambridge Companion to Tocqueville* (2006). Welch has also published articles on liberalism, on utilitarianism, and on the works of Alexis de Tocqueville, and is coeditor of *The Tocqueville Review/La Revue Tocqueville*. She is currently working on two projects: a book on the history of the concept of humanity in early nineteenth-century European thought and a study of the fate of utilitarianism in nineteenth- and twentieth-century francophone thought.

CATHERINE H. ZUCKERT is Nancy Reeves Dreux Professor of Political Science at the University of Notre Dame where she also serves as editor-in-chief of the *Review of Politics*. Her books include *Natural Right and the American Imagination: Political Philosophy in Novel Form*; *Postmodern Platos: Nietzsche, Heidegger, Gadamer, Strauss, Derrida*; *Plato's Philosophers*; as well as *The Truth about Leo Strauss* and *Leo Strauss and the Problem of Political Philosophy* (both coauthored with Michael Zuckert). She has also edited two volumes of essays, *Understanding the Political Spirit: From Socrates to Nietzsche* and *Political Philosophy in the Twentieth Century: Authors and Arguments*.

Introduction

No man ever steps in the same river twice, for it is not the same
river, and he is not the same man.
—Attributed to Heraclitus

For while traveling, one is never the absolute master of one's movements.
One often does something other than one would have imagined.
—Tocqueville to Nassau Senior, November 15, 1857

I do not need to travel across heaven and earth to find a marvelous
subject full of contrast, of grandeur and infinite pettiness, of
profound obscurities and singular clarity, capable at the same time
of giving birth to pity, admiration, contempt, terror. I have only to
consider myself.
—Tocqueville, *Democracy in America*

Voyages are about change. We change as we journey and encounter
new places, ideas, and people; the place to which we journey changes
as it moves from an abstraction to a reality and as we explore, understand, and live within it; upon our return, we find our homeland
changed, for we perceive that homeland through changed eyes. Nothing is the same.

Voyages and the changes they bring are the theme of the present
volume.

On April 2, 1831, twenty-six-year-old Alexis de Tocqueville set sail for
America, accompanied by his friend Gustave de Beaumont. The official
purpose of their voyage, which lasted nine months, was to undertake
a comparative study of the U.S. penitentiary system; although the penitentiary report was published in 1833, Tocqueville confessed in an
1835 letter to his friend Louis de Kergorlay that it had merely been "a

pretext" for their journey.[1] The political situation in France had made it expedient for the two magistrates to remove themselves from the country, and they were also interested in studying the American republic, quickly forming—somewhere in the journey's early phases—plans to write a book together about the United States. With this project in mind, Tocqueville kept notebooks of his observations and thoughts, as well as notes about his various conversations and interviews with Americans. His letters to his friends and family in France also contain his reflections on his voyage and on the various aspects of American life—point of departure, religion, equality of condition, tyranny of the majority, etc.—which would emerge eventually as key themes of *Democracy in America*.

Having traveled throughout much of the United States in nine months, the two Frenchmen returned to France in March 1832. Soon after, Tocqueville settled into an apartment in Paris and began first working on the penitentiary report with Beaumont. Although that report was published with both American voyagers listed as authors, the idea of a larger, joint project on America was eventually abandoned; *Democracy in America* was written by Tocqueville, while Beaumont penned a novel about American mores entitled *Marie*. Following the publication of the penitentiary report and after a brief trip to England in the late summer and early autumn of 1833, Tocqueville began outlining and eventually writing the first two volumes of *Democracy in America*. By early 1834, his outlines had become a full draft, which he felt comfortable sending to select family and friends, to get their comments and criticisms. He took their oral and written feedback into consideration, editing, changing, and redrafting—sometimes extensively—portions of the text. By the autumn of 1834, Tocqueville had completed the final

---

1. Tocqueville writes, "The penitentiary system was a pretext; I took it only as a passport that would let me enter thoroughly into the United States. In that country, in which I encountered a thousand things beyond my expectation, I perceived several things about questions that I had often put to myself. I discovered facts that seemed useful to know. I did not go there with the idea of writing a book, but the idea for a book came to me there." Letter to Louis de Kergorlay, January 1835, in Tocqueville, *Selected Letters on Politics and Society*, ed. Roger Boesche, trans. James Toupin and Roger Boesche (Berkeley: University of California Press, 1985), 95.

versions of those two volumes, which would be published in January 1835. The last two volumes followed a similar process of outlines, drafts, redrafts, criticisms, and final drafting before their 1840 publication.

The recently translated historical-critical edition of *Democracy in America* is, in part, an effort to shed light on Tocqueville's process in composing *Democracy in America*. In creating the historical-critical edition, Eduardo Nolla painstakingly worked through the major French editions, comparing them to each other and to the manuscript. He then selected among Tocqueville's textual fragments—Tocqueville's notes and queries to himself, as well as passages and ideas he contemplated including in the final version but ultimately rejected—and incorporated these into the main text. Finally, Nolla added a series of notes to this enlarged text, consisting primarily of marginalia, draft variants, selections from Tocqueville's travel notes, as well as criticisms from the family members and friends who read the draft manuscript.

The historical-critical edition thus gives the reader unprecedented access to the development of Tocqueville's thought. We witness the text emerging out of his voyage to the United States, and we discover the many things he learned by direct observation of democracy as enacted in nineteenth-century America. The essays in the first part of this volume particularly explore the "voyage" of writing and how Tocqueville's distinctive ideas developed and found expression during the composition of *Democracy in America,* while the essays in the second part explore the "voyage" of Tocquevillian ideas beyond a nineteenth-century Franco-American context.

Early chapters by James Schleifer and Jeremy Jennings particularly touch on the question of what Tocqueville learned in the United States. Jennings reminds us that the travel notebooks and drafts allow readers to glimpse, for the first time, how Tocqueville distilled the sundry impressions of his American voyage into the key themes of *Democracy in America,* especially the significance and extent of equality of conditions; the unceasing movement and rapid pace of change throughout American society; the importance of mores, self-interest, and religion; and the various mechanisms and "habits" for moderating democracy and preserving liberty in an age of equality. Jennings also uses the new material presented in the historical-critical edition to rebut the charge that Tocqueville had made up his mind about America before he arrived, arguing that "a reading of Tocqueville's diaries, notebooks and letters reveals a mind, not closed to new experiences, but overwhelmed by the novelty and importance of what he was seeing."[2]

Schleifer's chapter, too, helps us see how the journey itself shaped Tocqueville's thought and how Tocqueville's ideas took form during his sojourn in the United States and during the process of drafting *Democracy in America.* Schleifer particularly focuses on the development of Tocqueville's thought about what he considered the greatest dangers to democracy: materialism, individualism, and above all, consolidation of power and the "chilling new form" of soft despotism accompanying administrative centralization. Schleifer also analyzes the various arts and institutions of liberty, as well as the habits and mores that Tocqueville believed supportive to a free society, and he develops the idea that part of Tocqueville's distinctiveness lies in his use of specifically democratic remedies for the problems unique to democratic times.

Through the historical-critical edition, we also learn of Tocqueville's care in drafting *Democracy in America* and of the multiple layers behind the printed text. Many of the essays in this volume touch on this topic, showing how various aspects of the final text were modified in the process of writing. Eduardo Nolla's chapter, for example, offers evidence of Tocqueville's assiduousness in crafting a message that would be palatable to his audience, showing us how the manuscript's more democratic message is moderated with an eye to its intended French audience. S. J. D. Green, too, reminds us of *Democracy in America*'s meticulous craftsmanship, noting that "[t]ime and again, careful perusal of the Nolla edition establishes how concepts, even case studies, apparently new to the second volume actually appear half and even fully formulated in the notes and drafts deployed for the earlier study."[3]

The historical-critical edition thus allows us to see also a more figurative sense of voyage, an intellectual one, as Tocqueville's ideas begin to take shape and the text emerges on the page. The present volume explores the idea of voyage in this sense as well, with chapters investigating Tocqueville's complex relationship to his primary intellectual

2. Jennings, 93, in this volume.
3. Green, 50-51, in this volume.

influences—particularly Montesquieu, Blaise Pascal, Jean-Jacques Rousseau, and to a certain extent, François Guizot—and the development of Tocqueville's own independent ideas from this intellectual formation and from his American journey. Essays by Nolla, James Ceaser, Catherine Zuckert, and Alan Kahan confront this question of influences perhaps most directly. Ceaser particularly finds Montesquieuian roots to Tocqueville's thought, most notably in Tocqueville's deployment of a "Customary History," which allows philosophic ideas to enter indirectly into political life. Zuckert, too, cites the influences especially of Montesquieu and Rousseau, but her essay focuses on how Tocqueville's political science modifies his forerunners' philosophies in several important ways. Kahan's chapter asserts that Tocqueville sought new sources of moral greatness for the new democratic age, and he contends that in Tocqueville's treatment of religion broadly understood, we find a major source of greatness in democratic eras, as well as significant modifications of his Pascalian sources. By contrast, Nolla finds more direct indebtedness to—and less modification of—Pascal in Tocqueville's tone and his teaching.

Filippo Sabetti's essay, found in the second part of the present volume, also touches on these themes of influences and beginnings, but Sabetti highlights a pre-American voyage—Tocqueville's 1827 voyage to Sicily—as the beginning of the Frenchman's intellectual journey. In his notes from that voyage, which Sabetti explores, we see the birth of Tocqueville's hallmark comparative analytic perspective, as well as his awareness of the significance of situational particularities, and many other traits associated with Tocqueville's mode of proceeding in *Democracy in America*. Not only does Sabetti remind us of the importance of Tocqueville's youthful Sicilian journey to his mature thought, but he also draws attention to the influence of Tocqueville and his method in nineteenth-century Italy and to the continued relevance of Tocquevillian modes and ideas in contemporary social science.

Having a textual window into the development of Tocqueville's thought through the historical-critical edition also invites us to a fresh consideration of *Democracy in America*. Among the many things we discover from the historical-critical edition is that the work's original opening was "The work that you are about to read is not a travelogue, <the reader can rest easy>." The passage continues, "You will also not find in this book a complete summary of all the institutions of the United States; but I flatter myself that in it, the public will find some new documentation and, from it, will gain useful knowledge about a subject that is more important for us than the fate of America and no less worthy of holding our attention."[4] What kind of a work, then, is *Democracy in America*? More broadly, what is its purpose, and what kind of useful—and new—knowledge did Tocqueville believe he was presenting?

Many of the essays collected in this volume offer responses to the question of what type of work is *Democracy in America*. For Green, Tocqueville is the philosopher of liberalism, who understood the American experiment's innovation in tempering nature with art or in combining equality of conditions with the principles of ordered liberty. At the heart of Tocqueville's famously "new political science,"[5] suggests Green, is the recognition that the principle of equality is not merely confined to the political realm, as popular sovereignty, but that it orders or shapes the world beyond politics. Moreover, one of Tocqueville's key discoveries was that equality was both the potential problem and the best hope for a solution. As Nolla observes at the end of his essay, this is a quintessentially Tocquevillian mode, of applying more of the problematic principle to remedy the problem itself.

Harvey Mansfield follows Green in casting Tocqueville as a philosopher, yet Mansfield finds Tocqueville's philosophy a "modest" one, designed not to make the world new but to adjust to the new age of democracy and to shape that new world of equality in a way supportive of liberty rather than destructive of it. According to Mansfield, Tocqueville felt the need to hide the philosophic teaching of *Democracy in America*, but that teaching is a philosophy that is a moderation of liberal foundationalism in the name of liberty itself. Ceaser as well seems to cast Tocqueville as a philosopher, and he gives us an account focusing on Tocqueville's development of a Customary History that recognizes and responds to the fixity of the human, social, and political

---

4. Alexis de Tocqueville, *Democracy in America: Historical-Critical Edition of "De la démocratie en Amérique,"* ed. Eduardo Nolla, trans. James T. Schleifer, 4 vols. (Indianapolis: Liberty Fund, 2010), 3–4. This edition is hereafter cited as *DA.*
    5. *DA,* 16.

material and that serves as a "counterdoctrine to modern philosophy." Despite its opposition to modern philosophy, however, the act of composing a customary history is a philosophic endeavor in that it constitutes a deliberate effort to school democratic society; thus, Tocqueville's own political-philosophic art consists in shaping and guiding democracy so that it can avoid falling into "one form or other of democratic despotism."[6]

By contrast with these accounts of Tocqueville explicitly as a philosopher, Zuckert and Kahan, respectively, characterize him as a political scientist and a *moraliste*. Zuckert's chapter suggests that Tocqueville's voyage to America was undertaken to learn what laws, habits, mores, and ideas could preserve liberty in an age of equality, particularly against the danger of soft despotism. *Democracy in America* details those protections; its political science is an analysis of the social state resulting from equality of conditions and an attempt to isolate and analyze the factors (geography, laws, and above all, mores) determining whether the political results of this social state would be free or despotic. Kahan characterizes Tocqueville's project less in political terms than in moral ones, and he proposes that Tocqueville's primary concern was to ensure that human greatness, rather than human degradation, was "the outcome of democracy."[7] Among the sources of greatness in democratic times Tocqueville discovered and sought to encourage were religion and spirituality broadly understood, poetry, and associative life. Kahan emphasizes the utility of religion or, more broadly, spirituality as a source of democratic grandeur, capable of doing for the majority of humans what aristocracy had only been able to do for a few.

Yet perhaps there is ultimately less opposition between these accounts of Tocqueville and the characterizations of him explicitly as a philosopher, for Mansfield, Zuckert, and Kahan all emphasize a philosophic dimension to Tocqueville, perhaps most especially in the role of knowledge and art to shape nature and to create in an age of equality societies that would be conducive to political and individual liberty.

Tocqueville concluded the 1835 edition of *Democracy in America* with a long chapter on "Some Considerations on the Present State

---

6. Ceaser, 135, in this volume.
7. Kahan, 179, in this volume.

and Probable Future of the Three Races That Inhabit the Territory of the United States." This chapter stands somewhat apart from the rest of the 1835 work, not merely because it far exceeds the other chapters in length, but because it treats rather exceptional topics, which Tocqueville notes in the chapter's opening pages "are American without being democratic."[8] The chapter is also remarkable for, as Nolla reminds us, it seems to have been rapidly composed and was not part of the material critically read by Tocqueville's family or his friends Beaumont and Kergorlay. Thus, the chapter gives us, in Jennings's words, Tocqueville in his "most unmediated form."[9] Three essays in the first half of this volume focus on this exceptional chapter and are, in their own way, a distinctive subsection to it.

Barbara Allen examines Tocqueville's treatment of the three races within the context of his greater narrative of the universalization of equality of conditions, noting that both slavery and the plight of the Native Americans invite us to reconsider the inexorability of equality's march as well as the extent to which the democratic ideal "buffers the counter-current of prejudice."[10] She notes that, on the one hand, Tocqueville's writings on race offer rich insights into the advance of democracy's equality of conditions as well as the problems of adaptation and transculturation, but on the other hand, Tocqueville's own analytic framework limited his analysis and blinded him to the potential of individuals to transcend contexts of imperialism and enslavement.

Jean-Louis Benoît's chapter focuses on the Native Americans and on the paradox of the denial of their right to self-determination within the greatest modern democracy. He sees Tocqueville's chapter on them in two lights: as a lawyerly brief of carefully documented facts, assembled by Tocqueville to denounce the Americans' injustice to the Native Americans; and as an effort to convince the French aristocracy that it must adapt to the inevitably increasing political and social democratization of the world. Like both Allen and Cheryl Welch, Benoît also emphasizes the international dimension to Tocqueville's chapter on the three races, by showing Tocqueville's application of the lessons learned

8. *DA*, 516.
9. Jennings, 105, in this volume.
10. Allen, 242-75, in this volume.

from the plight of the Native Americans to the French engagement in Algeria.

The lessons beyond France and America are indeed Welch's primary focus, and her essay allows us to see how Tocqueville's voyage to America remained with him after publication of *Democracy in America* and how the ideas developed during his American voyage and during the crafting of *Democracy in America* shaped his thinking about French involvement in Algeria. Welch's analysis of Tocqueville's writings and speeches on Algeria invites us to consider the limits within which Tocqueville endorsed imperialism and, thus, the possible limits of his own liberalism, particularly when confronted with the realities of the French political landscape of his day.

Each of the essays on the "Three Races" reminds us of how the ideas Tocqueville developed in *Democracy in America* continued to influence his thought and writings after his American experience. Situated at the division on the cusp of the first and second parts of this volume, these three chapters serve something of a transitional purpose between the first part's exploration of Tocqueville as a literal and intellectual voyager, and the second part's investigations of the "voyage" or application of Tocquevillian ideas beyond their immediate context of nineteenth-century America and France. If the essays in the first part of this volume touch on the development of Tocqueville's thought and on his indebtedness to a variety of intellectual sources, those in the second part of this volume focus on how we are indebted to him today, or the contemporary legacy of Tocquevillian ideas as they have been disseminated throughout the world.

The chapters composing part two of this volume—those by Enrique Aguilar, Aurelian Craiutu, Reiji Matsumoto, and Filippo Sabetti—thus explore Tocqueville's voyage beyond the United States and France, by investigating the application of Tocquevillian modes and concepts to contexts in Latin America, Europe, and Asia.

Aguilar takes his point of departure from Tocqueville's well-known awareness of the importance of mores to sustain political institutions and laws. Articulated with statements like "I am persuaded that the most fortunate situation and the best laws cannot maintain a constitution in spite of mores, while the latter still turn to good account the most unfavorable positions and the worst laws," the importance of mores is a crucial aspect of Tocqueville's thought. Yet the historical-critical edition reminds us of the reciprocal influence laws and mores exert upon each other, for in a fragment that was not included in Tocqueville's final text, he observes, "Laws, however, work toward producing the spirit, the mores and the character of the people," then musing, "But in what proportion? There is the great problem that we cannot think too much about."[11] Working within this context of reciprocity between laws and mores, Aguilar considers whether Argentina's present disorders are primarily due to national mores, or to political leaders' abuses. He argues that the more political signs of disorder, such as the corruption of governmental officials, are but one manifestation of widespread societal movements. Moreover, he notes parallels between Tocqueville's soft despotism and the tutelary state that has arisen in contemporary Argentina, and he suggests that any reforms that hope to find success in Argentina must engage on both legal and extra-legal levels, and that they must seek above all to generate "consensus and habits related to free institutions."[12]

Craiutu's chapter also emphasizes the importance of mores for a postcommunist Eastern Europe, because, as he observes, Tocqueville invites us to explore whether democracy can first be implanted into the political sphere, then "transplanted" into society's mores. He finds Tocqueville a particularly apt guide for understanding contemporary Eastern Europe, because of the similarities between that region's present and those faced by Tocqueville's France after the end of the Old Regime: in particular, both the France about which Tocqueville wrote and the countries of present-day Eastern Europe are societies struggling with the legacy of an "old regime" as they transition to democracy and attempt to create and strengthen institutions and culture supportive of a free society. In addition to offering Tocquevillian warnings about possible dangers—including soft despotism springing from citizens' senses of isolation and atomization—Craiutu offers a range of prescriptions for that region's countries, stressing particularly Tocquevillian concepts such as civil society, social capital, the art of association, local government, and intermediary bodies.

11. *DA,* 499 and *n*m.
12. Aguilar, 389, in this volume.

Like the explorations of Tocquevillian ideas and methods in nineteenth-century and contemporary Italy we find in Sabetti's chapter, Matsumoto's contribution to this volume focuses on Toqueville's relevance to Japan (a country he neither visited nor wrote about), during the period of the Meiji Revolution (1867–1868) and today. Matsumoto traces the manner in which some of *Democracy in America*'s key ideas, such as freedom of the press, individual rights, administrative decentralization, and voluntary associations, entered into the debates about political life in Japan as that country began to transition from a closed society to an open one and as an egalitarian era dawned. Matsumoto's discussion particularly emphasizes Tocquevillian elements in the thought of one of the period's key liberals, Fukuzawa Yukichi. The affinities between Fukuzawa's writings and Tocquevillian themes such as the role of local government to promote a spirit of independence and the dangers of democratic despotism remind us of Tocqueville's portability beyond a transatlantic context; similarly, Matsumoto's analysis of contemporary Japan reminds us of these ideas' continued application beyond their nineteenth-century articulation.

The ideas expressed by Tocqueville in *Democracy in America* have continued to move beyond their immediate contexts of time and place. Similarly, Tocqueville's own literal and figurative journeys continued beyond his time in the United States and the writing of *Democracy in America*. Although Tocqueville did not cross the Atlantic again, the remaining years of his life witnessed him traveling to England, Switzerland, Germany, France, and Algeria. When health or other reasons made travel impossible, he read travel literature, one of his favorite genres, and allowed his imagination to transport him. His intellectual interests and output continued beyond *Democracy in America* as well, and his post–*Democracy in America* writings reflect his interest in France, Algeria, and England, as well as his continued engagement with America and his desire to know more about other countries to which he would not journey, like China.

Yet the voyage to the United States remained with Tocqueville always, for it had marked him deeply. On a personal level, he continued to find it a touchstone, returning frequently to his memories of his time in America and its lessons, corresponding with his American friends until the end of his life, and calling himself "half Yankee" or "half an American citizen."[13] Intellectually, he also continued to draw upon the approach he had developed there, particularly the paired comparisons and contrasts characteristic of his analytic method, and the essential categories and conceptual framework of his philosophic mode.

This volume invites the reader to continue Tocqueville's journeys, considering not only what he discovered in the United States and how he developed his ideas during the process of composing *Democracy in America* but also how the lessons of America have been and might be carried beyond their immediate contexts of time and place.

If travel is—as Michel de Montaigne suggests and as Tocqueville certainly found his American voyage to be—a means of honing our judgment and of clarifying our vision of ourselves and the world, let our journeys begin.

Christine Dunn Henderson

13. See Tocqueville's letter to Edward Vernon Childe, December 12, 1856, and his letter to Theodore Sedgwick, December 4, 1852. Translations of both of these letters appear in *Tocqueville on America after 1840: Letters and Other Writings,* ed. and trans. Aurelian Craiutu and Jeremy Jennings (Cambridge: Cambridge University Press, 2009).

Symbols Used in the Liberty Fund Edition of *Democracy in America*[1]

[...]   Text not crossed out in the manuscript.

<...>   Text circled or surrounded in pen (this generally concerns fragments that Tocqueville wanted to delete, but the presence of a circle around a word sometimes served solely to draw the author's attention: Is the use pertinent? Does the word conflict phonetically with the one following?).

≠...≠   Word or text crossed out by one or several vertical or diagonal lines.

{...}   Word or text crossed out horizontally.

/   Sign placed at the end of the sentence to indicate that a horizontal line separates it in the manuscript from the one that follows.

[... (ed.)] Information given by the editor.

1. For a complete listing of symbols and for an explanation of the editorial method used in *DA*, see Eduardo Nolla's foreword, *DA*, xxviii–xliii.

Part One

Tocqueville as Voyager

1

Hidden from View: Tocqueville's Secrets

EDUARDO NOLLA

And now I will unclasp a secret book, And to your quick-conceiving
discontents I'll read you matter deep and dangerous.
—William Shakespeare, *Henry IV,* part 1, act 1.

Much is hidden in Tocqueville's *Democracy*[1] in the surface and under
the printed text, both literally and figuratively, so much in fact that the
book sometimes resembles more a mystery or a cryptographic novel
than a political treatise.

The tone of the text itself and the relation that it establishes between
author and reader are also closer to what can be found in literature
than in political theory.

The drafts, notes, and manuscripts of Tocqueville's *Democracy in America*[2]
form a unique palimpsest that allows researchers to discover the buried structure of the book.[3] They offer a different, and often surprising,
vision of his thought.

---

1. Alexis de Tocqueville, *Democracy in America: Historical-Critical Edition of "De
la démocratie en Amérique,"* ed. Eduardo Nolla, trans. James T. Schleifer, 4 vols.
(Indianapolis: Liberty Fund, 2010). This edition is hereafter cited as *DA.* This
edition uses the same page numbers as the two-volume English-only edition
published by Liberty Fund in 2012, and the Spanish translation in one volume
published in Madrid by Trotta in 2010.

2. For a detailed description of Tocqueville's manuscripts, see the foreword
in *DA,* xxviii–xliii.

3. These are at the Yale Tocqueville Collection, housed at Yale University's
Beinecke Rare Book and Manuscript Library, from now on quoted as YTC. All

The so-called working manuscript of *Democracy in America* is kept at Yale University, inside four boxes, under the call number C.VI. My guess is that it comprises around 1400 quarto sheets: about 650 for the 1835 volumes and 750 for the 1840 part. The large majority of them are written on both sides.

This estimate does not include his notes, drafts, correspondence, or the famous *Rubish*. The *Rubish* is kept in two boxes, under the call number C.V.g., and is by itself about 1000 pages long.

Tocqueville knew that the materials he used to write the book contained hidden gems and valuable information, and that his papers could in the future be of some use to himself or to others.

Cover page of the 1835 part: "Volume I. My manuscript."[4] With the kind permission of the Beinecke Rare Book and Manuscript Library.

Democracy in America's drafts and notes are carefully organized in bundles, according to their content and to their future use, some with revealing titles such as "Notes, documents, ideas relative to America. Good to consult if I again want to write something on this subject"[5] or "Fragments, ideas that I cannot place in the work (March 1840) (insignificant collection)."[6]

The manuscript pages for each of the chapters of the book are kept in a larger piece of paper that acts as a folder and contains the corresponding title.

Tocqueville also kept his letters and notes organized and dated.

---

unpublished texts are quoted here with the kind permission of the Beinecke Rare Book and Manuscript Library.

4. *DA*, 1.
5. *DA*, xli.
6. *DA*, xli.

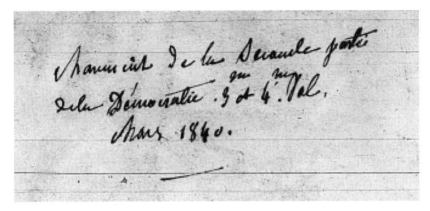

Cover page of the 1840 part: "Manuscript of the second part of Democracy. Volume III and IV. March 1840."[7] With the kind permission of the Beinecke Rare Book and Manuscript Library.

A few pages of the working manuscript are copies, made probably by the same copyist who produced the final version sent to the editor.[8] The comments made by family and friends refer sometimes to "copyist's error," which seems to point out the possible existence of a previous first complete or partial copy of Tocqueville's text.[9]

There are also a few pencil notes on the manuscript, which seem to be comments made before Tocqueville decided to give his book the final shape because some of the remarks are related to some later changes in the text.[10]

The front page of the folder containing the manuscript for the third

7. *DA,* 689.

8. See *DA,* with a reference to a Monsieur Parier. The copy sent to the editor is now lost.

9. Were this copy found, it would legally belong to Yale University.

10. There is such a note, unpublished, on the manuscript page corresponding to *DA,* 113.

In order to offer readers an easier identification, quotes made here from previously unpublished materials from Tocqueville's working manuscript of *Democracy in America* will include references to the corresponding pages of the Liberty Fund edition where the quoted texts would have been found if they had been incorporated into the edition.

chapter of the first part of the 1835 *Democracy* states: "The copy has been sent to Guerry."[11]

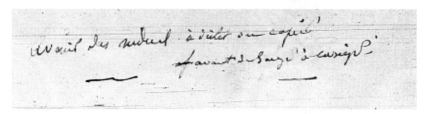

"Future of the Indians. To be dictated or copied before thinking of correcting."[12] *With the kind permission of the Beinecke Rare Book and Manuscript Library.*

Only very rarely, domestic and everyday life or, simply, boredom pierces through the seriousness of Tocqueville's purpose.[13] A couple of doodles, some figures, a portrait, a note, possibly about a loan requested by a servant; there is not much more than this out of place in the thousands of pages of his working manuscript, drafts, and notes.

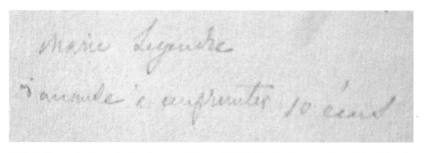

"Marie Legendre has asked to borrow 10 écus." With the kind permission of the Beinecke Rare Book and Manuscript Library.

11. This chapter is numbered fourth in the working manuscript. The figures to be found on the same cover are estimations of the sizes of American states.

André-Michel Guerry was a famous French statistician and a recipient of the Prix Montyon, as were Tocqueville and Beaumont. Cf. in *Oeuvres complètes*, Gallimard edition, tome 8, vol. 1, p. 142, a noncomplimentary comment by Tocqueville on Guerry, to whom he had sent two "detached articles."

12. Unpublished. *DA,* 522.

13. Hippolyte Wouters is a Belgian playwright author of two theater pieces on Tocqueville. *La conversation* is a fictitious dialog between Tocqueville and Madame Récamier. *L'exile* is a discussion between Tocqueville and his wife, Mary Mottley. He has recently attempted to find the humorous side of Tocqueville, in a predictably slender book, *Tocqueville humoriste* (Paris: Michel de Maule, 2011).

Doodles are very uncommon occurrences in Tocqueville's manuscripts. With the kind permission of the Beinecke Rare Book and Manuscript Library.

That Tocqueville had only faint sympathy for machinery, technology, or the practical sciences in general is well known. His ideas are expressed in terms of textual analogies and logical thought processes, almost never with the help of schemes, plots, or graphical outlines.

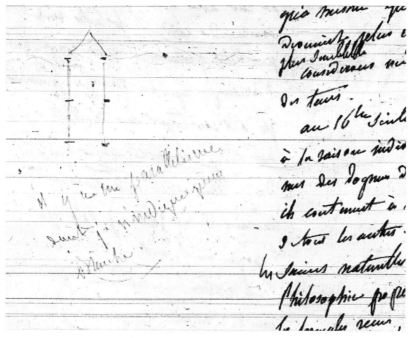

One of the very few cases when there is a graphical representation of thought processes in his manuscripts. When speaking of the relation between the growth of equality and the reliance on individual reason, Tocqueville draws two parallel lines with a common origin and notes on the margin: "There is a parallelism of which I only indicate one branch."[14] *With the kind permission of the Beinecke Rare Book and Manuscript Library.*

14. Unpublished. *DA,* 702.

Similarly, Tocqueville originally used a mathematical comparison to explain the assimilation process among the different parts of the American union, but he later removed it from the manuscript.

"≠Denominator.

Common divider.

Common measure.

Arithmetical comparison.≠"[15]

There is, however, no need to get into the reading of the manuscript itself to be able to discover that *Democracy in America* is also, in terms of its literary construction, a very special kind of book.[16]

The Author and His Reader

A careful reader of *Democracy in America* is able to find out that throughout the book, Tocqueville keeps a constant dialog with his reader. This ongoing conversation with the person facing the book is unheard-of in works of political theory, with the possible exception of Montesquieu.

The reader appears in the very first sentence of *Democracy,* later eliminated by Tocqueville: "The work that you are about to read is not a travelogue, <the reader can rest easy>."[17]

Appealing to the reader in the introduction of a work is not uncommon. Tocqueville recommends Beaumont's book,[18] begs the reader to believe him,[19] advances what he thinks will be the main criticism to his book,[20] or defends his impartiality.[21] What is less common is to prolong this dialog throughout the text. Tocqueville begs the reader to

---

15. Unpublished. *DA*, 614.

16. Tocqueville's own description of an ideal democracy needs to be read in the same terms of his own description of the painting of the ideal and his exposition about the literature of democracies in *Democracy in America* itself.

17. *DA*, 3.

18. *DA*, 29, 29n1.

19. *DA*, 30.

20. *DA*, 32, 32nu.

21. *DA*, 694, 694nm.

observe the harsh New England legislation,[22] the connection between religion and liberty,[23] and the different forms of a democratic system,[24] and to pay attention to many other circumstances.[25] Tocqueville also instructs the reader against drawing conclusions too soon,[26] has fears of being boring,[27] asks him to draw his own conclusions,[28] explains

22. *DA,* 63, 666.

23. "The reader will undoubtedly have noticed the preamble of these ordinances: in America, it is religion that leads to enlightenment; it is the observance of divine laws that brings men to liberty" (*DA,* 67).

24. "Before beginning the present chapter, I feel the need to remind the reader of what I have already pointed out several times in the course of this book.

"The political constitution of the United States seems to me one of the forms that democracy can give to its government; but I do not consider American institutions as either the only or the best that a democratic people should adopt" (*DA,* 376).

"In a thousand places in this work I have pointed out to readers what influence the enlightenment and habits of the Americans exercised on maintaining their political institutions. So now, few new things remain for me to say" (*DA,* 488–89).

"Here I recall to the reader the general sense in which I take the word mores; I understand by this word the whole of the intellectual and moral dispositions that man brings to the state of society" (*DA,* 495n8).

"If, in the course of this work, I have not succeeded in making the reader feel the importance that I attributed to the practical experience of the Americans, to their habits, to their opinions, in a word, to their mores, in maintaining their laws, I have missed the principal goal that I set for myself by writing it" (*DA,* 499–500).

It would be possible to explain Tocqueville's theory with just these quotations. They represent the most important grounds for the whole book. It is not fortuitously that Tocqueville draws the attention of the reader to them.

25. *DA,* 109 (origin of political life in the town), or in 168 (judicial power).

26. *DA,* 71.

27. *DA,* 230, with too many details on courts, for example.

Afraid the reader will find his explanations of the American local government too boring: "≠In the following chapter I will be drawn, against my own efforts, into minute details. I will be forced to travel a field that the reader may find sterile. I pray the reader to think [end]≠" (Unpublished. *DA,* 104).

Comparable worries appear not infrequently in his drafts, and many times in the comments made by Tocqueville's father and brother Édouard.

28. *DA,* 274, 583.

directly to him the difficulties of the author's task,[29] or gives several other warnings.[30]

This, as I have pointed out, makes one think of Montesquieu and how large is in many respects Tocqueville's debt to him.

In his preface to *On the Spirit of the Laws,* Montesquieu wrote:

> I request one favor, which I fear may not be granted me: do not judge the work of twenty years on the basis of a single rapid reading; approve or condemn the book as a whole, rather than by a few of its phrases. There is no better way to discover its author's design than through the design of the work he has written.[31]

Montesquieu's plea is very analogous to Tocqueville's own admonition to the reader in the introduction to the 1835 volumes:

> But the diversity of the subjects that I had to treat is very great, and whoever will undertake to contrast an isolated fact to the whole of the facts that I cite, a detached idea to the whole of the ideas, will succeed without difficulty. So I would like you to grant me the favor of reading me with the same spirit that presided over my work, and would like you to judge this book by the general impression that it leaves, as I myself came to a decision, not due to a particular reason, but due to the mass of reasons.[32]

If we jump from the first pages to the end of the book, we will find additional similarities. Montesquieu finished his preface with the celebrated phrase: "I have been able to say along with Correggio, 'And I too am a painter.'"[33]

---

29. *DA,* 351, 921. There are also comments on the reading of the book by American readers. See *DA,* 422.

30. *DA,* 360, 367*n*17, 425*n*6, 451, 465, 515, 526, 691.

31. Baron de Montesquieu, *Selected Political Writings,* trans. and ed. Melvin Richter (Indianapolis: Hackett, 1990), 107. On the influence of Montesquieu on Tocqueville's new science of politics, see Sheldon S. Wolin, *The Presence of the Past* (Baltimore: Johns Hopkins University Press, 1989), 73–74.

32. *DA,* 31.

33. Montesquieu, *Selected Political Writings,* 109.

Niccolò Machiavelli is, of course, the best well-known political painter:

In the conclusion to the 1835 part of *Democracy in America,* Tocqueville also speaks of painting:

> Now I would like to bring all of them together in a single point of view. What I will say will be less detailed, but more sure. I will see each object less distinctly; I will take up general facts with more certitude. I will be like a traveler who, while coming outside the walls of a vast city, climbs up the adjacent hill. As he moves away, the men that he has just left disappear from his view; their houses blend together; he no longer sees the public squares; he makes out the path of the streets with difficulty; but his eyes follow more easily the contours of the city, and for the first time he grasps its form. It seems to me that I too discover before me the whole future of the English race in the New World. The details of this immense tableau have remained in shadow; but my eyes take in the entire view, and I conceive a clear idea of the whole.[34]

Predictably, Tocqueville also ascribed to himself Montesquieu's understanding of writing and books.

Montesquieu wrote: "But it is not always necessary to exhaust a subject and leave the reader with nothing to do. I write, not so much to make people read, but rather to make them think."[35]

In a letter to Corcelle, analogously, Tocqueville explained:

> I believe that the books that have made men think the most and have had the greatest influence on their opinions and actions are those in which the author hasn't attempted to tell them dogmatically what had to be thought, but rather those where he has placed their

---

Neither do I wish that it be thought presumptuous if a man of low and inferior station dares to debate and to regulate the rule of princes; for, just as those who paint landscapes place themselves in a low position on the plain in order to consider the nature of the mountains and the high places and place themselves high atop mountains in order to study the plains, in like manner, to know well the nature of the people one must be a prince, and to know well the nature of princes one must be of the people.

Machiavelli, *The Prince,* in *The Portable Machiavelli,* trans. and ed. Peter Bondanella and Mark Musa (New York: Penguin Books, 1985), 78.

34. *DA,* 649.

35. Montesquieu, *Selected Political Writings,* 194.

minds on the road that goes toward the truths, and has made them find these, as if it were, by themselves.[36]

It is this understanding of the task of the writer as a type of literary author that guides the reader through a labyrinth of clues, disguises, and appearances that also singularizes *Democracy in America*. The book is much more than a rhetorical exercise; it tries to elicit an emotional response from the reader, seducing him, establishing with him an intimate and personal relation.

This form of close, almost autobiographical, dialog between reader and author based in self-scrutiny and confession is in the opposite pole of an Aristotle, a Thomas Hobbes, or a John Stuart Mill. It would be hard to find, barring to a certain degree Montesquieu, anything similar in the political theory tradition.

Hidden in Print

Alexis de Tocqueville's manuscripts offer an enormous wealth of information about the trappings behind *Democracy in America,* but there is no need to use them to find Tocqueville's obsession with the uncovering of truth. The published text itself also abounds in hidden laws, concealed passageways, and secret principles that Tocqueville attempts to unveil.[37]

Tocqueville's obsession with removing veils and bringing secrets into light is not unexpected. It associates him clearly to Jean-Jacques

36. Tocqueville, *Oeuvres complètes*, Gallimard edition, 15:80.

37. In quoting and using my critical edition, I will obviously be making references to both the originally published version and the previously unpublished texts. My point being that the idea of something hidden is common through all his work, I will in the following pages make no distinction between fragments from the original edition and quotations from the newly published. Later on, I'll concentrate myself exclusively in numerous texts published here for the first time and that have until now remained hidden from the public. Due to the limited extension of the present piece, these new fragments will come exclusively from the working manuscript. No references will be made to drafts, including the *Rubish*, notes, letters, or other materials employed to write the book.

Rousseau's ideal of transparency[38] and to the whole Enlightenment project of using reason to explain and construct the world. Very fittingly, on the frontispiece of Diderot's *Encyclopedia* drawn by Cochin, reason removes the veil of truth.

It also recalls Montesquieu's own attempt at a mechanical and see-through vision of the workings of political power.[39]

Rousseau and Montesquieu are two of the authors Tocqueville confessed he lived with every day of his life. The third, as is well known, is Blaise Pascal.

It is the Pascalian streak in Tocqueville's thought that explains his calculated skepticism at ever being capable of really discovering the complete truth and his not sharing into the idea of the Enlightenment being the end result of universal human reason.

At the heart of his explanation of the world we find Tocqueville's own approach to the problem of his two main themes, aristocracy and democracy.

The world is a book entirely closed to man.

So there is at the heart of democratic institutions a hidden tendency that carries men toward the good [v: to work toward general prosperity] despite their vices and errors; while in aristocratic institutions a secret inclination is sometimes uncovered that, despite talents and virtues, leads them to contribute to the miseries of the greatest number of their fellows.

If a hidden force independent of men did not exist in democratic institutions, it would be impossible to explain satisfactorily the peace and prosperity that reign within certain democracies.[40]

---

38. The seminal text in this regard being Jean Starobinski, *Jean-Jacques Rousseau: La transparence et l'obstacle* (Paris: Plon, 1957).

39. The *Spirit of the Laws* is an attempt to bring to light the hidden workings of political and legal structures, and the *Persian Letters* are a critique of modernity through oriental veils. Montesquieu also happened to write a short piece on the transparency of objects. He ironically died blind.

40. *DA*, 383nm.

The same Pascalian tone is also found in this often-quoted paragraph: "Of all beings, man is assuredly the one best known; and yet his prosperity or miseries are the product of unknown laws of which only a few isolated and incomplete

Tocqueville faces, consequently, his object as if struggling against a complex and multifaceted mystery. Hidden laws, secret instincts, veiled[41] relations people the pages of both his drafts and his notes, and the final printed version of the work.

Without the aim of being exhaustive or repetitive in the enunciation of the many underground processes found in the book, the reader can find the following many different mysteries.

To begin with, God's grand designs are secret to common man. Chance is the form under which God's hidden will[42] appears to the immense majority of mortals. Only the extraordinary mind of a Pascal could "have been able to summon up, as he did, all the powers of his intelligence to reveal more clearly the most hidden secrets of the Creator."[43] We do know that Providence has the secret design to divide the world between America and Russia[44] and that the movement toward equality is also divinely inspired.

If God's projects are inscrutable, so are events to come. The future is, according to Tocqueville, a hiding place for human will,[45] for the

---

fragments come into our view. Absolute truth is hidden and perhaps will always remain hidden" (*DA*, 263).

In an equivalent way: "But man is revealed enough for him to see something of himself, and hidden enough for the rest to disappear into impenetrable shadows, into which he plunges constantly and always in vain, in order finally to understand himself" (*DA*, 840).

41. The image of the veil appears frequently. For example: "The name republic given to the oligarchy of 1793 has never been anything except a bloody veil behind which was hidden the tyranny of some and the oppression of all" (*DA*, 360*n*t). Beaumont's novel hides the seriousness of his purpose behind a light veil (*DA*, 29). See, for many other veiled realities, *DA*, 90, 125, 180, 423, 627, 701, 750, 829, 1045, 1077, 1336.

42. *DA*, 90*n*k.

43. *DA*, 782.

44. "Their point of departure is different, their paths are varied; nonetheless, each one of them seems called by a secret design of Providence to hold in its hands one day the destinies of half the world" (*DA*, 656).

45. "All of man is in the will. His entire future is hidden there as in a germ that the first ray of good fortune comes to make fruitful" (*DA*, 1251*n*k).

"If God allowed me to lift the veil of the future, I would refuse to do so; I would be afraid to see the human race in the hands of clerks and soldiers" (*DA*, 746*n*d).

passions of the New World,[46] for the results of the American population moving toward the West,[47] for the forces secretly gathering in New England[48] or the American forests,[49] as well as for the unstoppable power of the majority.[50]

When we descend to the study of democratic society, we find ourselves in the midst of multiple invisible processes. Originally, national character is defined as an unseen force that struggles against time.[51] Aristocracy and democracy are themselves secret tendencies to be found under all political parties.[52] The benefits of democracy are initially hidden and will only be discovered after the passage of time.[53] It is also an unnoticed tendency that brings democracies toward prosperity.[54]

Furtive affinities exist between the Native Americans and the

46. "As for the passions of the New World, they are still hidden in the future" (*DA*, 369).

47. "The distant consequences of this migration of the Americans toward the West is still hidden from us by the future" (*DA*, 458).

48. *DA*, 37.

49. *DA*, 41–42.

50. *DA*, 277. Municipal bodies and county administrations act as "hidden reefs that slow or divide the tide of popular will" (*DA*, 429). Predictably, they also develop in secret (*DA*, 92, 102).

51. "There is indeed in the bent of the ideas and tastes of a people a hidden force that struggles with advantage against revolutions and time. This intellectual physiognomy of nations, which is called their character, is found throughout all the centuries of their history and amid the innumerable changes that take place in the social state, beliefs and laws" (*DA*, 344*n*y).

52. *DA*, 286. Jurists are a "scarcely noted" power that "works on society in secret, [and] acts constantly on society without society's knowledge and ends by shaping society according to its desires" (*DA*, 441–42, 439). A comparable idea is found in connection with the jurists' secret aristocratic habits and tastes (*DA*, 443).

53. "The vices and weaknesses of the government of democracy are easily seen; they are demonstrated by obvious facts, while its salutary influence is exerted in an imperceptible and, so to speak, hidden way. Its drawbacks are striking at first sight, but its qualities are revealed only in the long run" (*DA*, 377).

54. "So there is, at the heart of democratic institutions, a hidden tendency that often makes men work toward the general prosperity, despite their vices or errors, while in aristocratic institutions a secret inclination is sometimes uncovered that, despite talents and virtues, carries them toward contributing to the miseries of their fellows. In this way, in aristocratic governments, public men can

French,[55] as between liberty and industry,[56] or, mistakenly, between equality and revolution.[57] Surreptitious connections also exist between military mores and democratic mores,[58] democratic ideas and pantheism,[59] material enjoyment and restlessness,[60] and equality and servitude.[61]

Secret or hidden instincts abound among political factions,[62] majorities,[63] the human heart,[64] democratic governments,[65] French democra-

---

do evil without wanting to do so, and in democracies, they can produce good without thinking to do so" (*DA*, 383).

55. "Misfortune decreed that a secret affinity be found between the Indian character and theirs [the French]" (*DA*, 534*n*17). The same idea is explained on 536*n*18, speaking of Tanner.

56. "There is a hidden but very close bond between these two things: liberty and industry" (*DA*, 949).

57. *DA*, 1134.

58. "There is, moreover, a hidden connection between military mores and democratic mores that war exposes" (*DA*, 1175).

59. *DA*, 758.

60. *DA*, 944, 1120. "This tumultuous and constantly fretful life, which equality gives to men, not only diverts them from love by removing the leisure to devote themselves to it; it also turns them away by a more secret, but more certain road" (*DA*, 1058).

61. "Equality produces, in fact, two tendencies: one leads men directly to independence and can push them suddenly as far as anarchy; the other leads them by a longer, more secret, but surer road toward servitude" (*DA*, 1193).

62. "I am not saying that American parties always have as their open aim, or even as their hidden aim, making aristocracy or democracy prevail in the country. I am saying that aristocratic or democratic passions are easily found at the bottom of all the parties, and, although hidden from view, they form the tender spot and the soul of the parties" (*DA*, 286).

63. *DA*, 619.

64. *DA*, 636. "At the bottom of the human heart, there is a secret instinct that constantly calls out that the approval of the present [v: the sincere approval of contemporaries] and the admiration of posterity belong to virtue alone" (*DA*, 226*n*u).

65. "So you can say that for democratic peoples centralization is an innate idea. Not only will this monstrous concentration of all the social [v: political] powers in the same hands not shock the natural ideas of democratic peoples as regards government, but it will favor several of the secret instincts and the most lively tastes that equality [v: their social state] suggests" (*DA*, 1253*n*o).

cy,[66] the lower classes,[67] political bodies,[68] religious men,[69] or democratic citizens.[70]

Even while traveling through the wilderness, among hidden streams[71] and animals concealed in the woodland,[72] to the author of *Democracy* the noises of the American wilderness sound as a "secret warning from God."[73]

It is not surprising then that, for the Frenchman, one of the traits that best defines democracies is that these underground processes are much more complex and difficult to comprehend than in all previous forms of society.

> I am very persuaded that, among democratic nations themselves, the genius, the vices or the virtues of certain individuals delay or precipitate the natural course of the destiny of the people; but these sorts of fortuitous and secondary causes are infinitely more varied, more hidden, more complicated, less powerful, and consequently more difficult to disentangle and to trace in times of equality than in the centuries of aristocracy, when it is only a matter of analyzing, amid general facts, the particular action of a single man or of a few men.[74]

It is typical that authors of mystery novels present their cases to the reader as the most difficult and complicated ever. Tocqueville places

66. *DA*, 24.

67. *DA*, 316.

68. "The Constitution had not destroyed the individuality of the states, and all bodies, whatever they may be, have a secret instinct that carries them toward independence. This instinct is still more pronounced in a country like America, where each village forms a kind of republic accustomed to governing itself" (*DA*, 615).

69. "Men today are naturally little disposed to believe; but as soon as they have a religion, they find a hidden instinct within themselves that pushes them without their knowing toward Catholicism" (*DA*, 755).

70. *DA*, 888*ne*, 993. A hidden bond moves democratic citizens to associate (*DA*, 916, 1150), while a secret war for social position takes place among them (*DA*, 996) and even inside democratic homes (*DA*, 1019).

71. *DA*, 1328.

72. *DA*, 1339.

73. *DA*, 1357.

74. *DA*, 855.

himself *avant la lettre* in the position of the detective who will solve the tangle of democratic obscure secrets and concealments.

> I have yet to make known by what paths this power, which dominates the laws, proceeds; what its instincts, its passions are; what secret motivating forces push, slow or direct it in its irresistible march; what effects its omnipotence produces, and what future is reserved for it.[75]

Similarly, the end of a liberal form of government, which is the objective of Tocqueville's project, is also linked to the discovery of the secrecy of self-sufficiency.

> So the government [v. social power], even when it lends its support to individuals, must never discharge them entirely from the trouble of helping themselves by uniting; often it must deny them its help in order to let them find the secret of being self-sufficient, and it must withdraw its hand as they better understand the art of doing so.[76]

At almost the very end of his book, Tocqueville explains what would have been his existence if he had not written *Democracy in America*.

> I would not have written the work that you have just read; I would have limited myself to bemoaning in secret the destiny of my fellow men.[77]

Secrets, once more.

Basic Colors

It is easy to understand why many trappings of *Democracy* were kept hidden from the reader. Authors don't want their public to see their thought processes, only the final result.

---

75. *DA*, 277. In a similar vein: "It is not I who will deny that such inclinations are not invincible, since my principal goal in writing this book has been to combat them. I maintain only that, today, a secret force develops them constantly in the human heart, and that it is enough not to stop them for those inclinations to fill it up" (*DA*, 1201).
76. *DA*, 904.
77. *DA*, 1276–77.

But the meanderings of the mind and pen offer a unique opportunity to better understand the intentions and success of an author as complex as Tocqueville himself. I would like to point out in the next pages some of those hidden elements that never made it to the printed version.

Given the wealth of materials available to researchers, I will concentrate myself exclusively in some curious or outstanding texts from the working manuscript. I will make no references to any additional materials from the drafts, notes, letters, or the famous *Rubish*.

Tocqueville was aware of the newness of his project and recurrently struggled to find the language and words appropriate to this new endeavor. His new science of politics needed a new name. Democratic despotism was qualified as "soft" in the absence of a better word. Individualism was a neologism he knowingly used. His manuscript reveals these and other frequent quarrels with the written word.[78]

Problems with words and terminology concern expressions such as social state, mores, sovereignty, tolerant, rationalism, individualism, sympathy, courtesy, civility, honor, *patrie*, vulgar, industrial, civil rights, despotism, democracy, or settlers.

In writing about the positions becoming an industry, for instance, Tocqueville initially wrote: "Citizens, losing hope of improving their lot by themselves, rush tumultuously toward the power of the State." A note in the margin reads: "<I do not like this word 'power,' vague and new.>"[79] The final version will substitute the word "power" by the word "head."

Writing on poetry, he observes: "≠To idealize [*idéaliser*] isn't French. Try to find an equivalent or, in any case, only put it in italics.≠"[80] The word appears also in his drafts but will not be in the printed version.

---

78. These are found in *DA*, 74 (social state); 466, 495n8 (mores); 91na, 584no (sovereignty); 602nc (tolerant); 700–701nj (rationalism); 881nb (individualism); 989nf (sympathy); 1071nb (courtesy, civility); 1093n1 (honor); 1100n2 (*patrie*); 1121nj (vulgar); 1131ne (industrial); 1231np (civil rights); 1245nb, 1248–49 (despotism); 91na, 1283nh (democracy); 1313nh (settlers).

The topic of the changes democracy brings into language is itself fully discussed by Tocqueville in chapter 16, *DA*, 818–29.

79. *DA*, 1130nc.

80. Unpublished. *DA*, 832, 832nd.

In the margin of one page we read: "≠Tolerant indicates a virtue. A word would be needed that indicates the interested and necessary toleration of a man who needs others.≠"[81]

But most of Tocqueville's problems will come from the need to use neologisms for new social or political phenomena. "≠The thing is new [v: other], but an old word is still needed to designate it.≠"[82] This difficulty is frequently expressed in the manuscript.

Inevitably, some paragraphs required writing and rewriting before they found their way into the final version. Some never made it. The text at the start of page 68, for instance, offered several variants: "{The sun on modern civilization was already in the horizon}", read the first version. He crossed it out and started again: "≠We see the sun appear in the horizon and start lighting the mountains before casting its clarity on all the world.≠" A third variant didn't get his approval either: "<≠The top of the social edifice already received the glow of modern civilization, while the base still remained in the darkness of ignorance [v. of the Middle Ages.≠>"[83] None of these versions convinced Tocqueville, and the text was eliminated.

Frequently, Tocqueville writes notes for himself, as at the start of the chapter on the point of departure: "≠One must remember that this chapter still requires some research in the laws of New England, Massachusetts, Rhode Island. See particularly the *Town Officer.*≠"[84] He also reminds himself to complete some information: "{Know exactly the state of things on this point.}"[85] And the notes reveal Tocqueville's doubts also exist about whether to include or not or how to call his chapters: "What title should I give to this chapter?"[86]

---

81. *DA,* 602nc.

82. *DA,* 254nk. The note refers to this passage: "So a form of government, neither precisely national nor federal, is found. But here things have stopped, and the new word needed to express the new thing does not yet exist."

83. Unpublished. *DA,* 68.

84. Unpublished. *DA,* 45.

85. *DA,* 92nc.

86. Unpublished. This refers to the chapter titled "Necessity of Studying What Happens in the Individual States before Speaking about the Government of the Union." *DA,* 98.

Or: "≠Think about this. A bad inference could be drawn from it, too generalized.≠"[87]

Notes sometimes point out the need to find sources: "≠Where to find the outline of the first federation?≠"[88]

He reminds himself to ask for help on whether to add a chapter or not on what is meant by a Constitution in America and in Europe: "Ask advice here."[89] In the end, he didn't write it.

In most cases, the need for advice is from his two best readers, Louis de Kergorlay and Gustave de Beaumont.

"≠Ask L[ouis (ed.)] and B[eaumont (ed.)] if it is necessary to support these generalities with notes. Here either very minutely detailed notes are needed or nothing.≠"[90] This related to the part about the American county assembly. No more details were given in the printed book than exist in the manuscript.

There is also an unpublished remark by Tocqueville in relation to note c of page 685: "Is it necessary to enter into all this fastidious detail or would it be better to make a short and clear summary and quote the authors in support? Ask Beau.[mont]."

We know he also read the manuscript to other friends to see their reactions.[91]

This didn't always remove his doubts. "≠Is this true?≠",[92] he asks himself on a point about the French Constitution.

---

87. *DA*, 83*ny*.

88. *DA*, 186*na*.

89. *DA*, 96*nk*.

90. *DA*, 131*nr*. An analogous remark exists in *DA*, 88*ng*: "≠To sacrifice, I think, because all of that implies something more than the social state. Ask G[ustave (ed.)]. and L[ouis (ed.)].≠"

There are analogous remarks in 332*nb* and 376*nb*.

See also how Beaumont helped Tocqueville in 118*ng*, 769*ng*, 777*nc*, 801*nc*, 903*nt*, 978*nj*, 995*nb*; 1025*na*; 1073*nc*; 1223*nd*: "Read all of that to Beaumont before deleting it entirely."

Kergorlay, for his part, appears in 698*na*; 872*na*; 903*nt*; 963*nb*; 972*nb*; 1025*na*; 1156*nb*; 1214*nn*; 1281*nd*.

91. Ampère is quoted in the 1840 part manuscript. See 757*nb*; 893*nn*; 699*nd*; 715*ng*. See also *DA*, 1000*nb* and 1261*na* on Chateaubriand.

92. *DA*, 170*ne*.

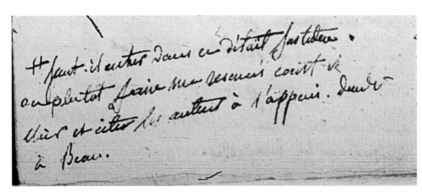

"Is it necessary to enter into all this fastidious detail or rather make a short and clear summary and quote the authors in support? Ask Beau.[mont]."[93] *With the kind permission of the Beinecke Rare Book and Manuscript Library.*

If we move from the merely stylistic to the more theoretical aspects of his book, in an effort to find what and how the hidden elements in the manuscript affect or change the vision we get from the printed work, we may find a double-sided conclusion, that Tocqueville seems to be more democratic and more aristocratic in his first, rougher version, more excited by the prospects of democracy and simultaneously more pessimistic about its results, more in admiration of the American system, and at the same time more critical. As in a painter's palette, the colors are much more vivid and raw in the manuscript than in the final painting.[94]

Let me point out some examples.

In the manuscript, Tocqueville insists on the necessary passage of humanity through a period of aristocracy in order to learn to be free, a fact that is less evident in the final printed version.

> I am persuaded that humanity owes its enlightenment to such strokes of fortune, and I {think that it is in losing their liberty that men acquired the means to reconquer it} that it is under an aristocracy or

93. Unpublished. *DA,* 685*n*c.

94. Tocqueville's work has been read as if it were a composite of pictures by artists such as Friedrich, Turner, Bierstadt, or Piranesi. See José María Lasalle, "De crepúsculos y auroras: Una lectura pictórica sobre Tocqueville," in *Alexis de Tocqueville: Libertad, igualdad, despotismo,* ed. Eduardo Nolla (Madrid: Gota a Gota, 2007), 289–304.

under a prince that men still half-savage have gathered the various notions that later would allow them to live civilized, equal, and free.[95]

Another example can be found in the famous final chapter of the 1835 volume, "Some Considerations on the Present State and Probable Future of the Three Races That Inhabit the Territory of the United States." That Tocqueville considered American slavery the most serious problem of the United States is a well-known fact. That he was so aghast at the condition of the free slaves in the Northeast that he thought they would find themselves in even worse condition in freedom than in slavery is much less evident.[96] Yet a variant of the paragraph in which Tocqueville thinks the abolition of slavery will not improve the condition of the black population reads: "≠I must admit that of all the means of accelerating the fight between the two races in the states of the South the most powerful one seems to me to be the abolition of slavery.≠"[97] The message was, he probably thought, too negative, and the fragment was definitely eliminated.

The author of *Democracy* also often suppressed expressions that could have reminded the reader of his aristocratic origins and the French aristocracy or that could have been read as too much of a critique of popular sovereignty or public opinion. "No influences except intellectual ones [{a kind of intellectual patronage}] could ever be established there."[98] *Patronage* was too much of a prerevolutionary word to be used and was removed. Similarly, he limited his criticisms of the people: "In this way, the upper classes did not incite [{implacable}] popular passions against themselves."[99]

Tocqueville also felt the need to conceal his belief that some peoples are incapable of being free, that they will never even understand the origin of their miseries and that "≠it is necessary that experience hits

---

95. *DA*, 879nf.

96. "I admit that if I had the misfortune to live in a country where slavery had been introduced and I had the liberty of the Negroes in my hand, I would keep myself from opening it" (*DA*, 578nf).

97. Unpublished. *DA*, 578.

98. *DA*, 76.

99. Unpublished. *DA*, 95.

them a thousand times with its ruthless hammer to tailor them a bit to liberty.≠"[100]

He must also have felt that putting too much emphasis on social division could be read in France as being too liberal and thus suppressed the following paragraph:

> ≠When in the same society one finds very enlightened individuals and others who are very ignorant or very rich and very poor, very strong and very weak, the second readily abdicate the use of their reason in favor of the first.≠[101]

Even a direct statement of the book's purpose seemed too risky to include in the text: "<Far from wanting to stop the development of the new society, I am trying to produce it.>"[102] This phrase, which appears in a draft, will not make it to the printing press.[103]

Nor could Tocqueville appear clearly in favor of a peaceful and well-regulated republic, as he is in his manuscript: "{For me, I will have no difficulty in saying, in all countries where the republic is practical, I will be republican.}"[104]

Many other points of Tocqueville's theory will also have stronger and clearer expression in the manuscript, only to be toned down in the final version of the book. For example, the lack of society in the West will be bluntly stated: "{There are men but there is no society.}"[105] So, too, the destructive force of the law of inheritance will be washed down in the process of drafting the final manuscript, perhaps because the idea could have had a different reading for a French audience. A first version of the phrase "The law of inheritance completed the dismantling of local influences" read "the law of inheritance completed the constitution of democracy."[106]

100. Unpublished. *DA*, 365.

101. Unpublished. *DA*, 700.

102. *DA*, 694*n*h.

103. The purpose of the book is also expressed thus: "Democracy, social state. Its effects on laws and mores. Object of the book" (Unpublished. *DA*, 481).

104. *DA*, 630.

105. Unpublished. *DA*, 86.

106. Unpublished. *DA*, 94.

Likewise, a large number of things that Tocqueville greatly admired in America appear much more clearly in the manuscript.

The practical experience of Americans and their ability to organize themselves in towns and in associations were very highly praised by Tocqueville: "≠In the political world. Equal education. Experience. Usage. Habit.≠"[107]

"Isn't doubt the final stage of the common people in everything./

Make it felt the advantages of liberty in associations for the members, and for the purpose of the association."[108]

In another note: "≠Americans undertake a multitude of initiatives on the margin of the administration, initiatives that the administration would not even have contemplated accomplishing.≠"[109]

Something similar happened with the importance of towns: "Without town institutions, a nation can pretend to have a free government, but it does not possess the spirit of liberty," wrote Tocqueville. But a first version read was more assertive: "≠[W]ithout town institutions, a nation can pretend to have free institutions but it will not have the spirit of liberty.≠"[110]

The same admiration for American improvement appears in other places:

≠Nothing prevents him from innovating.
Everything leads him to innovate.
He has the energy to innovate.≠[111]

Equally, Tocqueville probably thought that his wholehearted praise of innovation and entrepreneurship in America were not going to be well received in Europe. To give but one example, he leaves out of the final version the following phrase: "So the idea of the new, ≠which in

---

107. Unpublished. *DA*, 87. This text is written to the side of the one before the last in the page.

In another part: "≠They don't see that in killing the association one does not only kill the association but society itself≠" (Unpublished. *DA*, 902).

108. Unpublished. *DA*, 312.

109. Unpublished. *DA*, 160.

110. Unpublished. *DA*, 102.

111. Unpublished. *DA*, 643.

the mind of the European is so easily associated with that of the worst, is liked in his to that of the best.≠"[112]

Tocqueville's ideas of the American Indians will also be edited in the process of refining his thoughts and presentation for the final version. "Isolated in their own country, the Indians no longer formed anything except a small colony of inconvenient foreigners in the midst of a numerous and dominating people {and they discovered for themselves that they had exchanged the evils of savage life for all the miseries of civilized peoples}."[113]

Curiously, and maybe due to the influence of Gustave de Beaumont, the author of *Democracy* is initially more optimistic about their future: "[{The Indians today share the rights of those who conquered them and one day perhaps will rule over them}]."[114]

The importance of both liberty and equality for a real and well-organized democracy is also poignantly evident in the manuscript: "≠Political liberty is the great remedy against almost all the evils with which equality threatens men.≠"[115]

But this is not to despise the effectiveness of equality for the workings of a free democracy. In a thought that he later excised, probably because he found it too favorable to equality, Tocqueville states:

> ≠I have just pointed out great dangers. I add that they are not inevitable. At the same time that equality suggests the idea and the taste of social omnipotence, it provides the idea and taste of individual independence.≠[116]

A very similar idea is presented in Tocqueville's explanation of the object of the book, particularly the second volume of *Democracy,* which could not be stated as clearly in the printed version as in the preparatory notes:

> Danger of democratic peoples without liberty.
> Need of liberty greater for these peoples than for all others.

112. Unpublished. *DA*, 643.
113. Unpublished. *DA*, 540.
114. *DA*, 546.
115. Unpublished. *DA*, 1285.
116. Unpublished. *DA*, 1285.

Those who yearn for liberty in democratic centuries must not be enemies of equality but only try to take advantage of it.

That a more centralized government will be needed in those centuries more than in others. This is not only necessary but also desirable.

Means of preventing excessive centralization. Secondary bodies. Aristocratic persons.

If these means do not work, others are to be found, but some must be found in order to protect human dignity.

To find these means, to direct towards them his attention, the most general idea of the book.[117]

It would be tempting to read Tocqueville's democratic mystery novel as a modern version of the Enlightenment project of bringing into the light the hidden processes of human behavior and history.

Admittedly, the Middle Ages are frequently represented by Tocqueville, careful reader of Guizot, as a moment of darkness and barbarism.[118] "Europe left to itself managed by its own efforts to pierce the shadows of the Middle Ages,"[119] he wrote, for instance. In this regard, Tocqueville seems to follow the ideas of his time. Congruently, he also saw the period before the French Revolution as a movement forward characterized by the fact that "the peoples of Europe left the shadows and barbarism in order to advance toward civilization and enlightenment."[120]

117. Unpublished. *DA*, 1285.

118. See, for instance, this reference: "And alongside the prison, lasting monument of the mildness and enlightenment of our time, was found a dungeon that recalled the barbarism of the Middle Ages" (*DA*, 409).

"Europe, divided among so many diverse peoples; Europe, through constantly recurring wars and the barbarism of the Middle Ages" (*DA*, 654).

This idea is also manifest in this Enlightenment play of light and darkness: "[<≠The top of the social edifice already received the lights of modern civilization, while the base still remained in the darkness of ignorance [v. of the Middle Ages]≠>]" (*DA*, 68).

119. *DA*, 644. "Europe, through constantly recurring wars and the barbarism of the Middle Ages, succeeded in having four hundred ten inhabitants per square league" (*DA*, 654).

120. *DA*, 491.

But Tocqueville's *Democracy* is something else than a late product of the century of Enlightenment. It is also much more modern than the Enlightenment endeavor because modernity for Tocqueville, as first introduced by René Descartes and Francis Bacon, was not necessarily and always associated to the light. Individualism,[121] obsession with material well-being, and reliance on the state could send human beings back into darkness.[122]

> But today, when all classes are merging together, when the individual disappears more and more in the crowd and is easily lost amid the common obscurity; today, when nothing any longer sustains man above himself, because monarchical honor has nearly lost its dominion without being replaced by virtue, who can say where the exigencies of [absolute] power and the indulgences of weakness would stop?[123]

Tocqueville foresaw the very possible arrival of a new form of treacherous darkness and obscurity: "So you must not feel reassured by thinking that the barbarians are still far from us; for if there are some peoples who allow light to be wrested from their hands, there are others who trample it underfoot themselves."[124]

For Tocqueville, darkness or barbarism, as he likes to say, could exist at the end of the democratic age too.[125]

---

121. "The barbarians forced each man to think only of himself; democracy leads them by themselves to want to do so" (*DA*, 919nf).

122. This is the case in both America and Europe. "I take the European peoples such as they appear before my eyes, with their aristocratic traditions, their acquired enlightenment, their liberties, and I wonder if by becoming democratic they risk, as some would like to persuade us, falling back into a kind of barbarism" (*DA*, 769ng).

123. *DA*, 508–9.

124. *DA*, 786.

125. "The social state of these peoples also differed in several respects from what was seen in the Old World: it could have been said that they multiplied freely in their wilderness, without contact with more civilized races. So among them, you found none of those doubtful and incoherent notions of good and evil, none of that profound corruption which is usually combined with ignorance and crudeness of mores among civilized nations who have descended into barbarism again" (*DA*, 40).

In a very Tocquevillian twist of excesses being lessened by more of the thing that produces them, Tocqueville notes that the only way to avoid the problems of modernity is through enlightenment itself: "Pour out enlightenment lavishly in democratic nations in order to elevate the tendencies of the human mind. Democracy without enlightenment and liberty would lead the human species back to barbarism."[126]

The despotic form of democracy represents reason gone wrong and giving birth to a soft totalitarian democratic state. Then, it will become apparent that "[t]his time the barbarians will come not out of the frozen North; they are rising from the heart of our fields and from the very midst of our cities."[127]

Tocqueville's ability to foresee modern barbarians at the gates of democracy is also the reason why *Democracy in America* remains modern while Marx's works, which should be read as the last manifestation of a kind of unidirectional Enlightenment, have lost most of their appeal.

If for Tocqueville modernity was not necessarily a moment of unrelenting light, then the Middle Ages were not either a period defined exclusively by darkness. Rather, the Middle Ages represented a necessary step toward modernity, in the form of aristocracy.

This is the clearest expression of this idea:

Nothing is so difficult to take as the first step out of barbarism. I do not doubt that more effort is required for a savage to discover the art of writing than for a civilized man to penetrate the general laws that regulate the world. Now it is not believable that men could ever conceive the need for such an effort without having it clearly shown to them, or that they would make such an effort without grasping the result in advance. In a society of barbarians equal to each other, since the attention of each man is equally absorbed by the first needs and the most coarse interests of life, the idea of intellectual progress can come to the mind of any one of them only with difficulty, and if by chance it is born, it would soon be as if suffocated amid the nearly instructive [instinctive? (ed.)] thoughts to which the poorly satisfied

126. *DA*, 1267nj. The same idea appears in 1272nt.

127. *DA*, 514no. See in *DA*, 896nc, how barbarians interpose themselves among the people impeding associations and communication. The same is found in 898–90.

needs of the body always give birth. The savage lacks at the very same time the idea of study and the possibility of devoting himself to it.

Further along the same text, the author explains how it is by losing their liberty that nations become free.[128] In this and foremost, Tocqueville was not in tune with the typical Enlightenment position.

His argument was that because democracies instinctively reject everything that comes from aristocratic times, they find themselves at risk of falling into despotism. Tocqueville warns: "They [democracies] will suffer poverty, enslavement, barbarism, but they will not suffer aristocracy."[129]

Not by chance, the very idea of an open two-pronged future finds its way into the very last sentence of the book: "The nations of today cannot make conditions among them not be equal; but it depends on them whether equality leads them to servitude or liberty, to enlightenment or barbarism, to prosperity or misery."[130]

Despite the fact that the future held dark possibilities as well as bright ones, Tocqueville remained an optimist at heart, a son of his own era: "In the middle of this impenetrable obscurity of the future, however, the eye sees some shafts of light."[131]

128. *DA*, 879nf.
129. *DA*, 878.
130. *DA*, 1285.
131. *DA*, 12nr.

2

Tocqueville's Voyages:
To and from America?

S. J. D. GREEN

It seems almost pointless to praise Tocqueville these days. His fame has probably never been greater nor, indeed, his standing higher than now. This is true on both sides of the Atlantic. In America, putative statesmen, ambitious journalists, and even eccentric philanthropists vie to associate their names with his cause. During the summer of 1996, both Bill Clinton and Newt Gingrich cited him in speeches to their respective party conventions.[1] Two years later, the television company C-SPAN beamed a reenacted version of his great occidental journey into seventy million domestic households, devoting sixty-five hours of live programming to the description, analysis, and celebration of nine months of nineteenth-century travel.[2] All the while, anyone willing to donate $10,000 or more to the charitable conglomeration United Way anywhere in the United States is automatically entitled to membership of the National Alexis de Tocqueville Society: ostensibly in honor of their practical corroboration of "Tocqueville's most important

---

1. Isaac Kramnick, introduction to Tocqueville, *"Democracy in America" and Two Essays on America,* trans. Gerald Bevan (London: Penguin, 2003), ix. Cheryl B. Welch, "Introduction: Tocqueville in the Twenty-First Century," in *The Cambridge Companion to Tocqueville,* ed. Cheryl B. Welch (Cambridge: Cambridge University Press, 2006), 1–20, furnishes the essential context. Hugh Brogan, *Alexis de Tocqueville: Prophet of Democracy in the Age of Revolution* (London: Profile Books, 2008), is now the standard biography in English.

2. Eventually published by Anne Bentzel as *Traveling Tocqueville's America: Retracing the 17-State Tour That Inspired Alexis de Tocqueville's Political Classic "Democracy in America"* (Baltimore: Published for C-SPAN by the Johns Hopkins University Press, 1998).

observation . . . that Americans help . . . each other in time of need."[3]
Not entirely coincidentally, at least four new translations of *Democracy in America* have been published within the last ten years.[4]

Of course, Tocqueville was always popular in America. He has been positively fêted there for the last fifty years. Every president since Eisenhower has quoted him to preferred, that is, to generally self-regarding, effect. But this was not true until recently in France. Lauded in his own lifetime, and still an acknowledged prophet down to the end of the nineteenth century, Tocqueville's francophone reputation faded precipitously during the first third of the twentieth century.[5] This was so much so that when Gallimard eventually launched the project for an *Oeuvres complètes* in 1939, it invited a German Marxian specialist, J. P. Mayer, to act as editor, for there were no suitable French scholars willing to undertake the task.[6] For perhaps another generation, what little Gallic kudos Tocqueville still enjoyed was owed mainly to those lasting literary qualities his countrymen acknowledged in the otherwise ephemeral *Souvenirs*.[7] Today, all that is changed. As Françoise Mélonio has recently put it:

> Tocqueville is [now] the object of a kind of consensus [associated] with the emergence of a new democratic bible. [The family] château

3. United Way, National Alexis de Tocqueville Society Awards. I owe this reference to Kramnick's introduction to the Bevan translation of *Democracy in America,* cited in *n1,* above, xi.

4. Tocqueville, *Democracy in America,* trans. Bevan; Tocqueville, *Democracy in America,* trans. and ed. Harvey C. Mansfield and Delba Winthrop (Chicago: University of Chicago Press, 2000); Tocqueville, *Democracy in America,* trans. Arthur Goldhammer, ed. Olivier Zunz (New York: Library of America, 2004); finally, Tocqueville, *Democracy in America: Historical-Critical Edition of "De la démocratie en Amérique,"* ed. Eduardo Nolla, trans. James T. Schleifer, 4 vols. (Indianapolis: Liberty Fund, 2010). This edition is hereafter cited as *DA.*

5. Françoise Mélonio, *Tocqueville and the French,* trans. Beth G. Raps (Charlottesville: University of Virginia Press, 1998), chap. 6 passim.

6. Mélonio, *Tocqueville and the French,* 190. Mayer's significance is generously acknowledged in Jack Lively, *The Social and Political Thought of Alexis de Tocqueville* (Oxford: Clarendon Press, 1962), 216.

7. Tocqueville, *Recollections,* trans. George Lawrence (London: Doubleday, 1970). The introduction to this edition of *Souvenirs/Recollections* gives a good account of its publishing history and subsequent reputation; see xii–xxi.

is a pilgrimage site for . . . French presidents and ministers. The highest authorities in the land participate in Tocqueville Prize ceremonies. . . . He is cited in ministry meetings.[8]

With renewed fame has come enhanced respect. Tocqueville, the philosopher of liberalism, is now widely admired in his own country. Indeed, through the writings of Pierre Manent especially, he has achieved a certain priority there among the great political scientists of the early nineteenth century.[9] More remarkably still, he is now revered by serious indigenous scholars as the principal interpreter of France's world-historical moment. Turn to Mona Ozouf's monumental edition of François Furet's collected writings on *La Revolution Française*. Consult the index. There you will find the most cited actors and commentators in (or concerning) this great event as: Robespierre, Tocqueville, and Louis XVI, in that order. Napoleon comes a poor fourth.[10]

Yet to apprehend the true, *philosophical* significance of Eduardo Nolla's newly translated critical edition of *Democracy in America* is, paradoxically, to confront a great thinker still seriously underrated. Worse still, it is to meet a philosopher even now insufficiently appreciated by those very philosophers and scholars of philosophy who should otherwise appreciate him most. It is almost as if two generations of intellectual revisionism have left us reeling—anyway uncomprehending—before a great political metaphysician. Some take an original democratic theorist for a "messy . . . social scientist." Others confound a great contemporary historian with an aristocratic itinerant, blind to most of what

8. Mélonio, *Tocqueville and the French*, 189.

9. See, among others, Pierre Manent, *Tocqueville et la nature de la démocratie* (Paris: Fayard, 1993), esp. "Preface de la présente edition"; Manent, "Tocqueville philosophe politique," in *Enquête sur la démocratie: Etudes de philosophe politique* (Paris: Gallimard, 2007), chap. xix, and the remarks in Manent, *Le Regard Politique: Entretiens avec Bénédicte Delorme-Montini* (Paris: Flammarion, 2010), esp. 130–36.

10. François Furet, *La Révolution Francaise: Penser la Révolution Française; La Révolution, de Turgot à Jules Ferry, 1770–1880; Portraits; Débats au Tour de la Révolution; L'Avenir d'une passion*, preface de Mona Ozouf (Paris: Gallimard, 2007), 1033–53; the actual figures were Robespierre 97, Tocqueville 94, Louis XVI 92, and Napoleon 75. Given what follows, it might also be of interest to note that Guizot clocks in at 68.

was actually in place in Jacksonian America.[11] How could this be? How could Tocqueville be at once so famous yet curiously little known? Similarly, why is he so widely praised yet also unjustly belittled? Is it because he remains, as Russell Baker once shrewdly remarked, "the most widely quoted...of all the great unread writers"?[12] Or do even those who take the trouble continue to construe him badly? If so, does Nolla's edition enable us to read him aright—and judge him properly—for the first time?

There are, I shall suggest here, powerful reasons for thinking that this might be so. True, Tocqueville's first book brought him instant recognition both in France and beyond. If it did nothing else, Reeve's virtually simultaneous, though often sloppy, translation saw to that. But it also brought immediate confusion (for which, read multiple interpretation) in both the domestic and the foreign understanding of his work.[13] Not all of this can be blamed on Tocqueville's hapless translator. Some part of the difficulty must also be traced to the author's elusive, almost aphoristic, prose style. But it owed still more to the detached, seemingly anonymous, method of *Democracy*'s organization and presentation. For Tocqueville's "new political science" was, as Harvey Mansfield has wisely observed, a great theoretical departure that barely bothered to explain itself.[14] It was also, as Jeremy Jennings notes, a scholarly treatise that

11. The phrase "messy" comes from Jon Elster, "Tocqueville on 1789," in Welch, *Cambridge Companion,* 64; see also Harvey C. Mansfield, "Intimations of Philosophy in Tocqueville's *Democracy in America,*" XX, in this volume. Indigenous histories, from Arthur M. Schlesinger Jr., *The Age of Jackson* (New York: Little, Brown, 1945) to Daniel Walker Howe, *What Hath God Wrought: The Transformation of America, 1815–1848* (New York: Oxford University Press, 2007), make strikingly few references to Tocqueville for just that reason.

12. Russell Baker, *New York Times,* November 23, 1976.

13. Tocqueville, *Democracy in America,* trans. Henry Reeve (London: Saunders and Otley, 1835); see the translator's preface, xi–xii, esp. xi. For some of the problems this caused, see Tocqueville, *Democracy in America,* the Henry Reeve Text, as revised by Francis Brown, now further corrected by Phillip Bradley (New York: Knopf, 1948), esp. vol. 2, app. 2, 370–84.

14. Mansfield, "Intimations of Philosophy in Tocqueville's *Democracy in America,*" XX–XX; also in Tocqueville, *Democracy in America,* trans. and ed. Mansfield and Winthrop, editors' introduction, xliiiff.

largely obscured its sources.[15] More still: it was a work cast in a curious relationship, with both its author's youthful past and what became of a mature statesman's future. The Tocqueville who wrote *Democracy* barely appears in its pages. No less strikingly still, the celebrated public figure he quickly became interjected himself only rarely into subsequent editions of the text. Perhaps as a result, Tocqueville is still widely misconceived, either as a theoretical ideologue or as an aristocratic dupe, in America. To these ways of thinking, he was alternatively a Parisian intellectual who brought too much continental conceptual baggage and too little unprejudiced observation to his American travels, or a European grandee, characteristically compromised by the testimony of local notables barely better informed about what was actually going on in that country themselves. Whatever, and for all his undoubted intelligence and perspicacity, he remained (so the argument goes) a typical man of the old world—rural, agricultural, and traditional—simply unable to appreciate the dynamic realities of a new order—at once, urban, industrial, and democratic.[16]

This is nonsense. To be sure, Tocqueville never pretended to have written a mere travelogue. As he said himself, "I admit that in America I saw more than America."[17] Even at the time, he acknowledged that he was "think[ing] about Europe" all along.[18] Later, he would make it quite clear, in a letter to Louis de Kergorlay, that while "he rarely spoke of France in the book, he rarely wrote so much as a page without... having it in front of his eyes."[19] Yet, as James Schleifer has properly observed, it would have been quite extraordinary—actually, it would have been

15. Jennings, "Tocqueville's Journey into America," XX–XX, in this volume.

16. Jennings, "Tocqueville's Journey," XX–XX, in this volume, catalogs many of these criticisms. For a few more, for the most part, similarly unjustified, see Brogan, *Tocqueville: Prophet of Democracy*, chap. 12. James T. Schleifer, *The Making of Tocqueville's "Democracy in America,"* 2nd ed. (Indianapolis: Liberty Fund, 2000), chaps. 1 and 2, deals with many of these problems.

17. *DA*, 28.

18. *DA*, 28no. "While I had my eyes fixed on America, I thought about Europe."

19. Tocqueville, *Oeuvres complètes,* vol. 13, *Correspondance d'Alexis de Tocqueville et de Louis de Kergorlay,* ed. André Jardin (Paris: Gallimard, 1977), 209; lettre 220, Tocqueville à L. de Kergorlay, 18 Octobre 1847. Author's own translation.

somewhat disturbing—if Tocqueville had *not* "touched the shores of America carrying much of the historic and intellectual baggage of early-nineteenth-century France" with him.[20] Of course, he was a young man when he visited America. But he was not especially young; within living memory Pitt had been prime minister of England at two years his junior and Napoleon became first Consul barely four years older.[21]

More to the point, Tocqueville had been the beneficiary of a quite remarkable political education before his arrival in the United States in May 1831. Its purely formal aspects have been quite satisfactorily considered elsewhere.[22] We might simply note in passing three of its most important, informal dimensions. First, there was the significance of his birth. This was aristocratic, but it was not simply aristocratic. Tocqueville was also a member of a quite distinct *second* generation; he was among those men and women who did not make the Revolution at first hand but who grew up under its influence, by way of the Napoleonic Empire and then the restoration—only to become victims of the "great ennui" of the 1820s.[23] Second, he was the product of a legitimist upbringing and yet also of deep liberal connections. This was true at the outset, during the years of reaction under Charles X, and then in the wake of the July Revolution and the reign of Louis-Philippe.[24]

20. James T. Schleifer, "Tocqueville's Journey Revisited: What Was Striking and New in America," *Tocqueville Review* 37 (2006): 404, cited in Jennings, "Tocqueville's Journey," XX–XX, in this volume.

21. William Pitt, 1759–1806, prime minister of England from 1783; Napoleon Bonaparte, 1769–1821, 1st Consul of France from 1799.

22. See, for instance, Brogan, *Tocqueville: Prophet of Democracy,* chap. 3, and André Jardin, *Tocqueville: A Biography,* trans. Lydia Davis (London: Farrar, Straus and Giroux, 1988), chap. 3.

23. An argument first developed by Alan B. Spitzer in *The French Generation of 1820* (Princeton, N.J.: Princeton University Press, 1987), esp. 3–34, subsequently developed into something of a general theory of postrevolutionary France—he insists upon the identifiable existence of five such generations—by Robert Gildea in *Children of the Revolution: The French, 1799–1914* (London: Allen Lane, 2008), chap. 1; see esp. 6–9. The notion of the "grand ennui" is discussed at length in Roger Boesche, *The Strange Liberalism of Alexis de Tocqueville* (Ithaca, N.Y.: Cornell University Press, 1987), chap. 1.

24. Brogan, *Tocqueville: Prophet of Democracy,* chaps. 1, 2, and 4, offers a general account; see also the very helpful remarks in Eduardo Nolla's editor's introduction, in *DA,* xlviii–lxiv.

Finally, he had *immersed* himself—no other word will do—in the lectures and the writings of François Guizot: about France, on the historic course of European civilization, and concerning the nature of modernity itself.[25]

The political breadth and moral depth of the intellectual grounding so gained should go without saying. It also enables us to appreciate, without in any way belittling his subsequent achievement, how:

> [a]ll the themes which Tocqueville developed (in *Democracy in America*) were being discussed, indeed were already well known, when he published [his first great book]; the notion of the "social state," pretty well everywhere; the difference between the two kinds of centralisation (administrative and political), commonly so in the legitimist milieu. The tyranny of public opinion under democracy (normal in certain American circles, and perhaps also from Fenimore Cooper), the religious dimension of democracy (Lamenais, Leroux), the irresistible march of equality (Constant, Guizot, Royer-Collard, Chateaubriand) even the inherent opposition of democratic and aristocratic literature (Mme de Staël)—these were recurrent, contemporary ideas; so too finally... was the idea of democracy in Restoration and post-1830 France.[26]

Certainly, what was at least initially significant about Tocqueville's *Democracy* was not that he had such ideas. These were common currency in contemporary, thinking, French circles. Rather, it was that he chose to test them—and that he eventually came to insist that their full implications could only be properly understood—in an *American* context. Put another way, his fundamental presupposition about America was that it was the country from which he (and others) had most (that was positive) to learn. We underestimate the importance of that conceptual breakthrough at our peril.[27]

---

25. Brogan, *Tocqueville: Prophet of Democracy*, 90–94, 108, 115–17, 269; more subtly, Aurelian Craiutu, *Liberalism under Siege: The Political Thoughts of the French Doctrinaires* (Lanham, Md.: Lexington Books, 2003), chap. 4, esp. 88–100.

26. Lucien Jaume, *Tocqueville; les sources aristocratiques de la liberté: Biographie intellectuelle* (Paris: Fayard, 2008), 15–16. Author's own translation.

27. Brogan, *Tocqueville: Prophet of Democracy*, chaps. 8 and 9; *DA*, lxiv–lxxiv; Jardin, *Tocqueville*, chaps. 6 and 7, offer varying accounts of his motives. Perhaps the most interesting remains that of François Furet, "The Intellectual Origins of

True, he was not the first to insist upon the importance of this idea. Hegel had famously celebrated—if scarcely elucidated—the great possibilities of America long before.[28] But Tocqueville was highly unusual in postrevolutionary France, and perhaps particularly during the early years of the July Monarchy, in looking to America (as opposed to England) as the vital model for his country's political salvation and indeed civilization's broader future. It cannot be stated too often that most European visitors to early nineteenth-century America came with no such intention. Still less did they ordinarily leave with so portentous a thought. Most did little more than gawp at Niagara Falls and sneer in New York society.[29] Of course, there were serious travelers to the United States at the time. By no means the least observant was Edward Stanley, subsequently 14th Earl of Derby, and thrice Conservative prime minister of England. He visited North America between July 1824 and March 1825, saw everyone who mattered from President Adams downward, and kept an impressive private journal, in which he tempered a damning judgment of democratic politics and an unambiguous condemnation of southern slavery with surprisingly sympathetic accounts of material well-being and moral decorum among the natives. Still, to Stanley, America was for

Tocqueville's Thought," *Tocqueville Review* 7 (1985–86): 117–27. The very different and very powerful, contemporary and contrary, view that they had much more to learn from the British example is exhaustively set out in J. A. W. Gunn, *When the French Tried to Be British: Party, Opposition and the Quest for Civil Disagreement, 1814–1848* (Montreal: McGill-Queen's University Press, 2009), esp. chaps. 5–7. There is precisely one reference to Tocqueville in this book, on p. 464.

28. G. W. F. Hegel, *The Philosophy of History*, trans. J. Sibree (New York: Dover, 2004), 83–87, esp. 86–87; for a very thoughtful discussion of both extent (and limits) of this insight, see James W. Ceaser, *Reconstructing America: The Symbol of America in Modern Thought* (New Haven, Conn.: Yale University Press, 1997), 165–67. On France and Britain, see Gunn, *When the French Tried,* esp. chaps. 1–4.

29. Most famously, perhaps, Frances Trollope, *Domestic Manners of the Americans,* 2nd ed. (London: Whittaker, Treacher, 1832), vol. 2, chaps. 30–34. For a general account, see Peter Conrad, *Imagining America* (New York: Oxford University Press, 1980), chaps. 1 and 2.

the most part an example of what best to avoid.[30] This was a view of the United States that (sympathetic) Tory interpreters of Tocqueville subsequently commended in what they took to be a fellow skeptic's account.[31]

French observers were generally more disposed to be favorable. The very year that Stanley journeyed (almost incognito) around America, Lafayette toured the United States at the (very public) invitation of President Monroe. Visiting twenty-four states in twelve months, ostentatiously paying homage at the tomb of Washington, even embracing his old friend Jefferson at Monticello, he was finally feted at a banquet in the capital where he declared how delighted he was to "see the American people daily more attached to the liberal institutions which they have made such a success, while in Europe they were touched by a withering hand."[32] Still, this was in a sense the point. Tocqueville may never have had much time for Lafayette, whom he considered a "vain and dangerous demagogue." But he went to America with the highest opinion of Guizot. And Guizot believed that America had become a successful republic precisely because it had never degenerated into a pure democracy. That had been the fate of revolutionary France.[33] The United States, by contrast, had been led into independence by a landed élite; more specifically, by "les classes indépendants et éclairs,"

30. Angus Hawkins, *The Forgotten Prime Minister: The Fourteenth Earl of Derby* (New York: Oxford University Press, 2007), 33–34. Edward Stanley's *Journal of a Tour of North America, 1824–1825*, was (eventually) privately printed in 1930.

31. [Basil Hall], "Tocqueville on the State of America," *Quarterly Review* 57 (September 1836): 132–62; [M. O'Donnell], "Democracy in America," *Blackwood's Magazine* 57, no. 235 (May 1875): 758–66; also note Robert Peel's very favorable remarks collected in *A Correct Account of Sir Robert Peel's Speech at Glasgow, January 1837* (London, 1837). For a general interpretation, see D. P. Crook, *American Democracy in English Politics, 1815–1850* (Oxford: Oxford University Press, 1965), 191–98.

32. Auguste Lerasseur, *Lafayette en Amérique en 1824 et 1825* (Paris: Baudoin, 1829), 1:463–75, 2:163–73, 2:602. Author's own translation.

33. For Tocqueville on Lafayette, see the remarks cited in George Wilson Pierson, *Tocqueville and Beaumont in America* (Oxford: Oxford University Press, 1938), 36; on Guizot and French democratic degeneration, see François Guizot, *De la démocratie en France* (Paris: Victor Masson, 1849), 16ff.

who had subsequently established precisely that balance of aristocracy and democracy in its constitution that had averted those class struggles in its society that had so disfigured France during the 1790s.[34] As a result, 1787 had proved to be America's (similarly fortunate) 1688.[35]

This was precisely the understanding of America that Tocqueville came to reject in his study of *Democracy in America*. Hence the peculiar significance of his very first words: "Amongst the new objects that attracted my attention during my stay in the United States, none struck me more vividly than the equality of conditions."[36] Note: new objects, striking him. But how had he reached such a startling conclusion? For if it was just a presupposition, then it was also a very remarkable insight. Certainly, little in his previous reading would have prepared him for what he subsequently claimed to have seen. We know that Tocqueville had Guizot's *History of Civilisation* sent to him from France during the week after he arrived in New York.[37] Aurelian Craiutu, in an important interpretation of this episode, suggests that Tocqueville "adapted creatively" from Guizot's theory during his time in America. Yet the old master's account of the triumph of the Third Estate had been concerned more with Europe generally, and France particularly.[38] Indeed, he insisted upon a—shall we call it, certain Anglo-Saxon—difference in this broader development. That, he believed, not only survived, but strikingly, indeed contrarily, postdated Tocqueville's account of America.[39] So if Tocqueville was ostensibly "adapting," he was in reality transforming Guizot's thoughts in this matter. In other words, his journey

34. François Guizot, *Washington* (London: Nutt, 1841), xx–xxi; see also Guizot, "Washington: Etude Historique," in Cornelius de Witt, *Histoire de Washington et de la foundation de la République des États-Unis* (Paris: Didier, 1868), xxii–xxvii, xlv–xlvi, lvii–lix.

35. François Guizot, *Discours sur l'histoire de la Révolution d'Angleterre,* ed. H. W. Eve (Cambridge: Cambridge University Press, 1894), 101–3. For a broader discussion, see Gunn, *When the French Tried,* chap. 7, esp. 433–57.

36. *DA,* 4.

37. François Guizot, *The History of Civilisation: From the Fall of the Roman Empire to the French Revolution,* 3 vols., trans. William Hazlitt (London: H. G. Bohn); see esp. vol. 3, lectures 16–19.

38. Craiutu, *Liberalism under Siege,* 93ff.

39. Guizot, *Discours,* chap. 10; Guizot, *De la démocratie,* chap. 3, 37ff.

to America marked a critical intellectual breaking point between the two men.[40] What caused it?

It may be, of course, that reading Guizot in situ stimulated such thoughts.[41] It may even have been the case that, having come specifically to study one—progressive—American institution, Tocqueville was suitably inspired to learn about others, and that the cumulative effect bore fruit in his truly radical conclusions. The one thing we can say with some degree of certainty is that Tocqueville seems to have been genuinely surprised by much of what he saw in America.[42] Professor Schleifer long ago noted just how often Tocqueville recorded a sense of amazement at his discoveries, whether in his notes or in the final published text itself. There is no reason to doubt the sincerity of these remarks. To the contrary, given what he had previously read and given what he subsequently saw, there is every reason to take him largely at his ingenuous word in this respect. Put another way, Tocqueville's continued enlightenment *by* America was the product of time very well spent *in* America. Whatever he may subsequently have come to insist, the penitentiary project was no mere pretext.[43] It produced a major study.[44] In constructing it, Tocqueville and Beaumont traveled a great deal. As a result, they saw many parts of the country. They never made the mistake—all too common among European travelers to America well into the second half of the twentieth century—of defining the

40. For a more conventional account, see Brogan, *Tocqueville: Prophet of Democracy,* 379–85, and for another variation, Craiutu, *Liberalism under Siege,* 92–100.

41. Craiutu, *Liberalism under Siege,* 93.

42. Craiutu, *Liberalism under Siege,* 95.

43. Tocqueville, *Selected Letters on Politics and Society,* ed. Roger Boesche, trans. James Toupin and Roger Boesche (Berkeley: University of California Press, 1985), 95, Tocqueville to Louis de Kergorlay, June 17, 1835: "The Penitentiary system was a pretext. The passport that would let me enter thoroughly into the United States."

44. Gustave de Beaumont and Alexis de Tocqueville, *On the Penitentiary System in the United States and Its Application to France,* trans. Francis Lieber (Philadelphia: Carey, 1833). For a full account of the conception, construction, and consequences of this work, see Thorsten Sellin, "Tocqueville and Beaumont and Prison Reform in France," the important introduction to the 1964 edition of this text, published by Southern Illinois University Press, xv–xxi.

United States solely through superficial experience of the Northeastern seaboard and (perhaps) its southern alternative. Few, in fact, seem to have understood quicker the novel historical significance of so much new settlement in and beyond the Mississippi valley: similarly, to have appreciated more fully the novelty of the society that was emerging in the new cities of the Midwest. Here, indeed, was the new epicenter of America, of democracy in America and of the wholly novel society—related only to Europe by language—that was being created there. In our time, it has only moved a bit further west still.[45]

This is all very well. It still leaves us with a problem. If Tocqueville understood that much, why did he make so little of contemporary American industrial-urbanization? Compare him to Michel Chevalier in this respect and it seems almost as if the aristocrat was stuck in a Jeffersonian dream while the engineer had taken full measure of America's great leap forward.[46] But this is just a superficial impression. Not the least of the great merits of the Nolla edition is that it makes absolutely clear just how inadequate a judgment that is. Tocqueville may not have visited Lowell or spent much time in Pittsburgh.[47] He spoke relatively little about the banking crises of the early 1830s in the pages of *Democracy in America*.[48] There is not much concerning the bourgeoisie and the proletariat in his American writings, tout court.[49] But as his notebooks make clear, he was fully aware of all these phenomena.[50] Professor Jennings offers one very important reason why he

45. See, among others, *DA*, 458ff, 582–648, esp. 608: "In thirty or forty years' time, the Mississippi basin will have taken its natural rank" (i.e., at the head of American civilization). Hence, perhaps, the true significance of the multivolume *History of California* currently being written by Professor Kevin Starr.

46. Michel Chevalier, *Society, Manners and Politics in the United States: Being a Series of Letters on North America*, trans. Thomas Bradford (Boston: Weeks, Jordan, 1879); see esp. letters 3–5, 7–8, 11–12, 15, 20–21, 23–24, 38–41.

47. Jennings, "Tocqueville's Journey," XX–XX, in this volume; on Chevalier and Lowell, see *Society, Manners and Politics*, letters 11–12; and on Pittsburg [*sic*], letter 15.

48. Though see *DA*, 618ff.; cf. Chevalier, *Society, Manners and Politics*, letters 4–5, 8, 13, 23, 24.

49. Though note *DA*, 981–85 passim; cf. Chevalier, *Society, Manners and Politics*, letters 31–33.

50. Jennings, "Tocqueville's Journey," XX–XX, in this volume; also

may have made relatively little use of them in the published text.[51] But there might be another. Before he completed *Democracy,* he had also been to England.

The significance of Tocqueville's English journey of 1833—its significance, that is, for what would eventually become *Democracy in America*—is easily overlooked. Indeed, it is all too easily caricatured in much the same way as his American sojourn. His extensive trip across the Channel in 1833 apparently took in not one industrial town.[52] This is not proof that he was indifferent to the "great social problems" of his day. To the contrary, the England that Tocqueville visited was a nation in which the "great social problems" of the day issued mainly out of the countryside and largely concerned its rural, agricultural population. He even wrote—actually quite extensively—about them.[53] Industrial-urban England remained comparatively peaceful until the economic downturn of 1838.[54] Moreover, Tocqueville knew well enough about the phenomena of large, sprawling towns and new factory practices in the northern and midland regions of England.[55] This told him something about their development in contemporary America too. That was while they were new *in* America around 1831–32, they were

Tocqueville, *Journey to America,* trans. George Lawrence, ed. J. P. Mayer (London, 1959), 68, 75, 94, 96, 103, 110–12, 112–18, 165, 178–81, 204, 235–52.

51. Namely, that they were so blindingly obvious; see Jennings, "Tocqueville's Journey," XX–XX, in this volume.

52. Jennings, "Tocqueville's Journey," XX, n.X, in this volume; for Tocqueville's own account, see Tocqueville, *Journeys to England and Ireland,* trans. George Lawrence (London: Faber and Faber, 1958), chap. 2. For an interpretation of Tocqueville and English industrialists, see Seymour Drescher, *Tocqueville and England* (Cambridge, Mass.: Harvard University Press, 1964), chap. 7.

53. Tocqueville, *Memoir on Pauperism,* trans. Seymour Drescher, with an introduction by Gertrude Himmelfarb (London: Civitas, 1997). For an important, broader consideration of this aspect of Tocqueville's thoughts, see Michael Drolet, *Tocqueville, Democracy and Social Reform* (Basingstoke: Palgrave Macmillan, 2003), chap. 6.

54. Boyd Hilton, *A Mad, Bad and Dangerous People? England 1783–1846* (New York: Oxford University Press, 2006), 612–22; Norman Gash, *Aristocracy and People: Britain, 1815–1865* (Cambridge, Mass.: Harvard University Press, 1979), chap. 7; Asa Briggs, *The Age of Improvement, 1783–1867* (London: Longmans, 1959), chap. 6.

55. Tocqueville, *Journeys to England and Ireland,* 94–111.

not new *to* America in the early nineteenth century. Industrial Massachusetts loomed small by comparison with industrial Lancashire at the time.[56] Mexico City remained the largest city in North America during the age of Jackson (it still is).[57] Industrial activities flowed from "democracy." Tocqueville knew that much.[58] But they were not unique to it. His experience in England told him so: quite definitively.[59]

I

What was *truly* novel about America—what differentiated it from the rest of the world—was its equality of conditions. What was—increasingly—remarkable about the American republic was the ordered liberty it still enjoyed. The fundamental problem of democracy, as Tocqueville's contemporaries understood it, lay in its innate tendency to destroy authority. This was true of all hitherto existing authority, whether of rank, tradition, or even revelation. The modern world had wrought what Tocqueville himself characterized as "a carnage of all authorities . . . in all hierarchies, in the family, in the political [sphere]."[60] Revolutionary France furnished powerful corroboration of that proposition. The superficial evidence of American history pointed to a similar catalog of catastrophic vandalism, ruthlessly pursued down precisely that path. The American nation had rid itself at birth of both monarchical rule and aristocratic right. Its constituent states subsequently spent much of the next generation divesting themselves of established churches. Nineteenth-century property law dissolved traditional family bonds. But above all, equality of conditions destroyed intellectual authority, including the authority of priests, whom no good Protestant acknowledged, or the authority of history, which no

56. For an excellent analysis, with much comparative material, see François Crouzet, *The Victorian Economy,* trans. A. S. Forster (London: Methuen, 1982), 1–11, and chap. 7.

57. Howe, *What Hath God Wrought,* 19.

58. *DA,* 972–78 passim; cf. Chevalier, *Society, Manners and Politics,* letter 27.

59. Tocqueville, *Journeys to England and Ireland,* 94–103, 110–13, 115–16; Drescher, *Tocqueville and England,* chap. 7.

60. Tocqueville, "Idée des discours," *Oeuvres complètes,* vol. 3, *Écrits et discours politiques,* ed. André Jardin (Paris: Gallimard, 1985), 551.

self-respecting American recognized. The Americans' peculiar point of departure enabled them not only to ignore the Church but also to forget their own past as well. This was how America had become "one of the countries in the world where the precepts of Descartes are least studied and best followed."[61]

Yet the expected outcome—perfectly well demonstrated by France's continuing nightmare of alternating anarchy and tyranny—had not eventuated in America. That Western-most republic was, by now, self-evidently a land of stable government. This was characterized not by "weakness" but by almost "irresistible strength," its administration served by a lawful people, themselves subject to strict moral codes.[62] Indeed, firsthand examination of American society suggested that its fundamental underlying problem was defined not by any tendency toward disorder but rather in a surreptitious slide to "soft despotism."[63] If this was true—if what his eyes revealed to him was indeed so—then all hitherto existing accounts of the fundamental basis of political order were wrong. At the same time, America, for all its inherent propensities to facilitate the consolidation of power, was visibly a land of liberty: blessed by freedom of religion, of the press, even of association. Just as revolution had not entailed social dissolution, so social order did not preclude freedom. All of which meant that neither democracy in general nor this democracy in particular was especially well understood. A "new political science" was going to be needed to understand "a world altogether new." *Democracy in America* set out to furnish it.[64]

That declaration, as Nolla rightly insists, is the pivotal moment in the book. But it is also easily misunderstood. This was true for one obvious reason. Tocqueville may have dramatically announced the necessity for change, yet he scarcely proceeded to describe any detailed content of the matter.[65] Indeed, there is not much in the way of a conceptu-

---

61. *DA,* 699.

62. As it had been from the moment of its birth; *DA,* vol. 1, pt. 1, chap. 2, esp. 57–70.

63. *DA,* 402–26 passim.

64. *DA,* 16.

65. Mansfield, "Intimations of Philosophy in Tocqueville's *Democracy in America,*" XX–XX; see also Tocqueville, *Democracy in America,* trans. and ed. Mansfield and Winthrop, editor's introduction, xliii.

ally explicit, methodologically precise, still less empirically grounded analysis—for which read recognizable political science—at work in the chapters of *Democracy in America*. As such, it is a good deal easier to describe what Tocqueville's political science is not rather than what it is. Few would doubt that it bears little obvious relation to received wisdom of the ancients in this respect. It effectively denied the priority of the régime. It dismissed even the possibility of a mixed government and generally derided Greek concepts of justice.[66] Yet, as Harvey Mansfield has noted elsewhere, it offered little comfort to modern prejudices either. It spurned any prepolitical state of nature. Then it eschewed the social contract.[67] Most strikingly of all, it rejected Federalist political science.[68]

There is no need to exaggerate the full force of this departure in order to appreciate its vital significance. Certainly, there is little to be gained in contrasting supposedly backward-looking Americans with a future-orientated Frenchman. The once fashionable image of the framers as classical republicans, determinedly devoted to an agrarian ideal, has long since faded. All of them—from Hamilton to Jefferson— were committed to a liberal republicanism rooted in the improving

66. *DA,* 411–12, 732–35.

67. Tocqueville, *Democracy in America,* trans. and ed. Mansfield and Winthrop, editor's introduction, xliv–xlv.

68. Alexander Hamilton, James Madison, and John Jay, *The Federalist,* ed. Benjamin Fletcher Wright (Cambridge, Mass.: Harvard University Press, 1961), a collection of eighty-five newspaper articles (each cited as *Federalist* hereafter in this chapter). The articles, written individually and severally by the above authors under the collective pseudonym Publius as part of the war of words that raged in 1787–88 over the proposed constitution, were first published in book form as the *Federalist* in the spring of 1788. At the time of their first permanent publication, the general standing of the essays was so low that only Hamilton helped prepare the edition for the press, and he (alone) added the (first) preface. Still worse, two authors—Hamilton and Madison—failed to preserve their original drafts, with the effect that respective responsibility (and relative kudos) remained uncertain as late as 1964. Far from coincidentally, perhaps, Guizot was a profound early admirer of the *Federalist,* describing it as "the greatest work known to man on the application of elementary principles of government to political administration." Whether Tocqueville first acquired his own, whether initial or subsequent, opinion from that source remains unclear; see Craiutu, *Liberalism under Siege,* 147.

possibilities of a commercial society.[69] The Federalist Papers served, inter alia, to outline that new, improved political science appropriate for the new, improved order of the ages that the American founding had inaugurated.[70] Tocqueville was properly respectful of the insights that these studies afforded into the American political scene, even as late as 1831. Nonetheless, he doubted that they had achieved this wider aim.[71] That was not because the Federalists repudiated the doc-

69. Most famously advanced in J. G. A. Pocock, *The Machiavellian Moment: Florentine Political Thought and the Atlantic Republican Tradition* (Princeton, N.J.: Princeton University Press, 1975), see esp. 518, 521–27, and 546. More subtly developed in Gordon S. Wood, *The Creation of the American Republic, 1776–1787* (Chapel Hill: University of North Carolina Press, 1969), chaps. 1 and 2. Progressively demolished in Forrest MacDonald, *Novus Ordo Seclorum: The Intellectual Origins of the Constitution* (Lawrence: University of Kansas Press, 1985), chaps. 2–4; Thomas L. Pangle, *The Spirit of Modern Republicanism: The Moral Vision of the American Founders and the Philosophy of Locke* (Chicago: University of Chicago Press, 1988), pt. 1, chap. 4, and pt. 2 passim, and Jerome Huyler, *Locke in America: The Moral Philosophy of the Founding Era* (Lawrence: University of Kansas Press, 1995), chaps. 7–9. Some of the postrevisionist possibilities are explored in Andreas Kalyvas and Ira Katznelson, *Liberal Beginnings: Making a Republic for the Moderns* (Cambridge: Cambridge University Press, 2008), chap. 4.

70. *Federalist* No. 9, 125: "The science of politics . . . like other sciences, has received general improvement"; see also *Federalist* No. 1, 89: "It seems . . . to have been reserved for the people of this country . . . to decide . . . whether societies of men are fully capable of . . . establishing good government from reflection and choice." For the most searching modern accounts, see David F. Epstein, *The Political Theory of the Federalists* (Chicago: University of Chicago Press, 1984), esp. chaps. 1 and 5–7; the essays collected in Charles R. Kesler, ed., *Saving the Revolution: The Federalist Papers and the American Founding* (New York: Free Press, 1987), esp. chaps. 1, 5, 8, 11, and 13; and, more generally, William A. Schambra, ed., *As Far as Republican Principles Will Admit: Essays by Martin Diamond* (Washington, D.C.: AEI Press, 1992), esp. chaps. 2–4 and 6–9. Finally, much can still be gained from the unexhausted insights in Trevor Colbourn, ed., *Fame and the Founding Fathers: Essays by Douglass Adair* (New York: Norton, 1974), esp. chaps. 3–5.

71. *DA*, 193n8. "I will often have the occasion to cite the *Federalist* in this work. . . . The *Federalist* is a fine book, that though particular to America, should be familiar to statesmen of all countries." Yet, ironically, Tocqueville may, in fact, have contributed to the subsequent neglect of that classic of political science, common in European intellectual circles up to very recent times; see Ceaser, *Reconstructing America,* 268n6.

trine of the sovereignty of the people, as Guizot did.[72] To the contrary, they openly acknowledged it. However, in recognizing its just claims, they did not grasp the broader results seriously enough. They afforded proper due only to what they took to be popular sovereignty as a political norm. They failed to appreciate that this creed defined the whole social state over which they were attempting to preside. They had not realized just how radical a rupture was entailed in the events of 1776 and their aftermath.[73]

This was, perhaps, scarcely remarkable. For all their intellectual progressivism, the framers remained the aristocrats that Adams (among their number) and Guizot (among their admirers) took them to be. As such, they believed it was possible to regulate a popular democracy by just rule: in a government of laws, not men.[74] They also presumed it was desirable to lead it with wisdom rather than through whim, that is, by representative methods of administration and legislation. This was the political science the Federalist Papers were supposed to describe.[75] But Tocqueville's journey through Jacksonian America proved to him that such aspirations were—in truth, had always been—forlorn hopes. What he discovered was that in a democracy, in the final analysis, the majority observed only those laws it chose to honor. That was why Negroes

72. *Federalist* No. 39, 280–86, esp. 281. "It is essential to [republican] government that it be served from the great body of society, not from an inconsiderable proportion of it.... It is *sufficient* for such a government that the persons administering it be appointed, either directly or indirectly, by the people." On Guizot and the explicit repudiation of the doctrine of the sovereignty of the people, see François Guizot, *Du gouvernement de la France depuis la Restauration et du ministère actuel* (Paris: Ladvocat, 1820), 201; also, Guizot, *Mémoires pour servir à l'histoire de mon temps* (Paris: Michel Lévy frères, 1858), 167.

73. *DA,* 91–97 passim, but note esp. 92–94: "The American Revolution broke out. The dogma of the sovereignty of the people emerged from the town and took over the government.... A change almost as rapid was carried out within the interior of society."

74. On Adams and the uses of a political élite, see John Adams, *A Defence of the Constitutions of Government of the United States of America* (London, 1787), 3 vols.

75. See *Federalist* No. 14, 150–54; also *Federalist* No. 63, 413–19. What they did is best set out in Gordon S. Wood, "Interests and Disinterestedness in the Making of the Constitution," in *The Idea of America: Reflections on the Birth of the United States* (New York: Penguin, 2011), chap. 4.

never got to vote in Pennsylvania.[76] Not that Americans were often confronted by legislation of which they disapproved. This was because in the United States, the people increasingly elected congressmen only like themselves: "for the most part, village lawyers, businessmen, or even men from the lowest classes."[77] As a result, the tyranny of the majority was an ever-present threat in American society.[78] Tocqueville has often been accused of overstating the contemporary importance of this malevolent possibility. In truth, he did no more than state its stark potential.[79] The "planned extinction of the American native" and the "slavery of the African Americans" bore grim witness to what proved all too easily realizable under its sway. Abraham Lincoln knew that much; so too, in a very different way, did Stephen Douglas.[80]

But if the tyranny of the majority was such a threat to liberty, how could its sway be sufficiently tempered, if not by law and representation? Tocqueville found the answer to this critical question in his subtle reworking of the doctrine of the "democratic social state." His argument went like this. Equality of conditions destroyed the historical basis of authority. But they failed to preclude the passion for rule.[81] At the same time, they diminished the sense of individual responsibility and elevated the aura of personal vulnerability. This was because in extending the "doctrine ... of equality" wholesale, even to personal intelligence, democracy "attacked the pride of men in its last refuge." The result was not a republic of autonomous selves but rather a state of fearful similars (*semblables*).[82] Such men, so placed, still occasionally sought to lord it over each other. But what they most desperately

76. *DA*, 414*n*4.

77. *DA*, 320.

78. *DA*, pt. 2, chap. 7 passim.

79. On the accusation that Tocqueville overstated the threat of the tyranny of the majority, see the remarks in Jennings, "Tocqueville's Journey," 8, 16.

80. On the argument about slavery and "popular sovereignty," see, above all, Harold Holzer, ed., *The Lincoln-Douglas Debates* (New York: Harpercollins, 1993), esp. 40–85, and, for a recent interpretation, see Thomas L. Krannawitter, *Vindicating Lincoln: Defending the Politics of Our Greatest President* (Lanham, Md.: Rowman & Littlefield, 2008), chaps. 1 and 2.

81. I owe this very important point to Tocqueville, *Democracy in America*, trans. and ed. Mansfield and Winthrop, editors' introduction, xlvi.

82. *DA*, 1, 404–5.

desired was the mutual protection of common authority. They found it in America, as "democratic man" qua democratic man can only find it, in the "moral empire of the majority."[83] What this meant was that men in the "democratic social state" were governed, at least in the first instance, by extrapolitical common custom, or mores, that is, by those broad-ranging attitudes and feelings that informed the whole rather than by specific laws, which instituted individual rights. If this was true in general, it is especially so of Jacksonian America. There, the vital instrument of this amorphous empire was found in "public opinion."[84]

It is easy to miss the true significance of this, characteristically Tocquevillian, formulation, or rather, reformulation. For, in drawing such attention to the significance of "public opinion" in the social and political organization of early nineteenth-century American life, Tocqueville deployed a concept seemingly well known to his contemporaries. But he surreptitiously redefined it. This was "public opinion" conceived not as that "sentiment on any given subject which is entertained by the best informed, most intelligent and most moral persons in the community," as William MacKinnon's famous rendering theoretically had it.[85] Rather, it was "public opinion" laid bare, as Tocqueville had actually seen the phenomenon, at work in America.

> Mass opinion . . . common opinion . . . ready-made opinion . . . covering . . . a great number of theories in matters of philosophy, morality and politics [even including] religion itself . . . which reigns there

83. *DA,* 405.

84. Tocqueville, *Democracy in America,* trans. and ed. Mansfield and Winthrop, editors' introduction, xlv.

85. William A. MacKinnon, *On the Rise, Progress and Present State of Public Opinion in Great Britain and Other Parts of the World* (London: Saunders and Otley, 1828), 16. Deploying that definition of the phenomenon, MacKinnon went on to insist that "public opinion" was "all-powerful" in the United States of America at the time; and, as a result, "liberty fully-established" there. In fairness, he also admitted to having "no personal knowledge of America." Rather, so it seemed to him, "the broad and general principles already mentioned" seemed to apply there "with sufficient accuracy" to justify such a "clear statement" of the impact of "public opinion" in that state. MacKinnon, *On the Rise,* 306.

less as revealed doctrine [and more] as adopted in this way by each person without examination...on the faith of the public.[86]

In that way, he disclosed an entirely new form of authority. This was democratic, social authority. Just as Tocqueville said it must, "the [new] social world" had created new forms of "intellectual and moral authority" out of the carnage democracy had wrought in the old [social] order.[87] The authority of such "mass...opinion" would extend, progressively, to the whole of the world. It was already "infinitely greater than any other power." Indeed, it was all the more effective for wielding such sway silently, that is, without ostentatious action.[88] This was how republican democracies "immaterialisent le despotisme." It explained why the freest society on earth boasted virtually no variety of views about any question that really mattered.[89]

But that was not a justification for nostalgic fatalism. Rather, it explained an essential task of Tocqueville's political science. This was, as James Schleifer so arrestingly puts it, "to speak for liberty," under conditions of equality.[90] It was a goal specifically defined. This necessarily determined much of the resultant method. For, just as Tocqueville dismissed long-standing liberal hopes vested in representative democracy, so he also derided those new scientific pretensions entailed by purely regulative, political organization. Practical wisdom rather began in appreciating the possibilities that critical observation established between the nature and arts of democracy.[91] Nowhere were these more

86. *DA,* 718–20.

87. Tocqueville, "Idée des discours," *Oeuvres complètes,* vol. 3, *Écrits et discours politiques,* ed. André Jardin (Paris: Gallimard, 1985), 551.

88. *DA,* 716–17.

89. Quoted in Jaume, *Tocqueville,* 22; itself citing Tocqueville, *Démocratie,* 1:352, in the Garnier-Flammarion edition. It seems best to leave those words untranslated.

90. Schleifer, "Democratic Dangers," 80.

91. *DA,* vol. 4, pt. 4, chap. 7 passim. For a very important discussion of this distinction, see Pierre Manent, "Democratic Man, Aristocratic Man, and Man Simply: Some Remarks on an Equivocation in Tocqueville's Thought," in Pierre Manent, *Modern Liberty and Its Discontents,* ed. and trans. Daniel J. Mahoney and Paul Seaton (Lanham, Md.: Rowman & Littlefield, 1998), 65–77, esp. at 70–73.

apparent than in America. Its nature always tended toward equality. But its art sometimes allowed for liberty. Such artificial freedom was achieved not just, nor even primarily, through the application of rules as in the performance of duties. That was why Tocqueville began his analysis of American liberty in American associations. It was also why the fruits of that association ended, for Tocqueville, not just in recip-rocation but in self-knowledge. Recall his understanding of the social function of the jury system. Moreover, liberty, in America, was nurtured both through its own arts, which he called the "legal, constitutional and institutional mechanisms" that make a society, and in habits, by which Tocqueville meant those mores that sustained them. Schleifer lists some of these:

> The spirit of industry, the spirit of association, the spirit of religion, political experience, general enlightenment, public and private morality, a sense of justice, respect for the law, public spirit, sensitiv-ity to the rights of others, and a grasp of interest, well-understood.[92]

All of this made for what Harvey Mansfield has called an "instruc-tional political science."[93] It was concerned, quite specifically, "to instruct democracy... to revive its beliefs, to regulate its movements, to substitute... the science of public affairs for its inexperience (and) knowledge of its true interests for its blind instincts."[94] It was forged by means of a treatise conceived less as a compendium of profound abstractions and invariable laws than through a description of contin-gent truths and admirable practices: put simply, by means of a useful guide, replete with examples. Thus *Democracy* begins with a historical moment—the American point of departure—and moves on to a con-tinuing model—the New England township.[95] And it goes on, and on, in that fashion. Moreover, this is true for the whole book. Time and again, careful perusal of the Nolla edition establishes how concepts, even case studies, apparently new to the second volume, actually appear half and even fully formulated in the notes and drafts deployed for the

---

92. Schleifer, "Democratic Dangers," XX–XX and XX–XX, in this volume.
93. Mansfield, "Intimations of Philosophy," XX–XX.
94. *DA*, 9.
95. *DA*, pt. 1, chaps. 2, 3, 5.

earlier study. In that way, the intellectual unity of the work is demonstrated as never before. These—seeming—distinctions, between the supposedly empirical first and allegedly abstract second volume, similarly between a consideration first of the political then of the social state of the Americans, even between an optimistic departure and a pessimistic arrival, turn out to be more superficial than profound on closer inspection.[96]

This is not to say that there are no differences between the two *Democracies*. It is to suggest that such divergences as emerge were cumulative and contingent rather than clear-cut and crucial. Moreover, there may have been important reasons behind such apparent messiness. For if Tocqueville wrote an instructional book—put simply, an exposition to a French audience of how the Americans did so many things so much better—his brother Édouard believed that he also authored something of an insinuating account. Stated in another way, it was a subtle work, one which, in Lucien Jaume's words, surreptitiously attempted to "guide the reader" toward certain critical conclusions. On the surface, it seemingly left him free to "forge his own opinion," as if he had "devised that [judgment] all by himself."[97] Underneath, he was actually being persuaded by a gentle but persistent philosopher of one course of action rather than another.[98]

How did Tocqueville achieve that ulterior end? He did so, at least in part, by posing as a detached arbiter between the aristocratic and the democratic way of doing things. He was a curious arbiter, to be sure: one who, after all, always insisted that the (historic) aristocratic dispensation was dead.[99] But he was an insistent one too, one whose genuine ambivalence about our democratic fate—think of Tocqueville on human dignity, sociability, and well-being against individualism,

96. A point well made in Schleifer, "Democratic Dangers," esp. XX–XX, in this volume. See also the remarks in Arthur Kaledin, *Tocqueville and His America: A Darker Horizon* (New Haven, Conn.: Yale University Press, 2011), 279–87.

97. Jaume, *Tocqueville*, 11; cf. the correspondence between Édouard and Alexis de Tocqueville, June 15, 1834. Author's own translation.

98. Jaume, *Tocqueville*, 10–11.

99. *DA*, 10–12: "So the gradual development of equality of conditions is a providential fact; . . . [I]t is universal, it is lasting, it escapes every day from human power; all events, like all men, serve its development."

materialism, and mediocrity—always pointed toward other, tantalizing, possibilities.[100] This element in Tocqueville's persuasive purposes may have increased in scope as the chapters of his analysis unfolded. For all that, Craiutu's ingenious division of *Democracy* into two voyages—one literal, one intellectual—is, perhaps, best resisted.[101] It is not as if Tocqueville revealed himself as unconcerned to preserve those (surreptitious) aspects of aristocracy that governed in Jacksonian America. Think of his account of the lawyers in volume 1.[102] Nor can his increasing concern for the preservation of the aristocratic sources of liberty in democracies beyond America be unrelated to his all too obviously enraptured description of those extrademocratic bulwarks for liberty—above all else, its Puritan religious heritage—that America had historically enjoyed.[103]

Still, we might reasonably ask, instruction in what? Similarly, we might profitably demand, insinuation with what end in mind? It seems scarcely sufficient to answer "liberty." For that simply begs further questions. What kind of liberty? And to what purpose? As Harvey Mansfield observes, Tocqueville acknowledged no notion of a prepolitical state of liberty.[104] Yet he also denied the autonomy of politics. For all that, he never reduced the political to the social. And he became a protosociologist only in the very broadest sense. Even in its strange novelty, his was still a *political* science. And it remained political freedom that he was trying to defend. Still, Tocqueville's text points to no specific goal. It contains no obvious end state of freedom. Perhaps, in the final analysis, the reader really was left to do his own thinking in this respect. That possibility compels the present author to conclude that in so explicitly

100. Jaume, *Tocqueville*, 10.

101. Craiutu, *Liberalism under Siege*, 95.

102. *DA*, vol. 2, pt. 2, chap. 8, esp. 433. "So you find, hidden at the bottom of the souls of jurists, a portion of the tastes and habits of an aristocracy. Like the aristocracy, they have an instinctive propensity for order and a natural love of forms; [similarly] they conceive a deep distaste for the actions of the multitude and secretly despise the government of the people."

103. *DA*, vol. 1, pt. 1, chap. 2 passim, and note the important discussions in Schleifer, "Democratic Dangers," XX–XX, in this volume; and Mansfield, "Intimations of Philosophy," XX–XX.

104. Mansfield, "Intimations of Philosophy," XX.

differentiating human nature, rightly understood, from the merely material sum of things, Tocqueville surely also intended to distinguish what makes a man free from what merely renders us all the same.[105]

II

But what about Tocqueville *after* America? Did he change his mind, not just about the future for freedom in America, but also concerning the possibility of liberty, within democracy, tout court? Did he, in other words, make one final—melancholy—moral voyage, after 1848? If so, what are we to make of his lasting intellectual achievement? Many readers have noted a difference in tone between even some of the more pessimistic remarks of volume 2 in *Democracy* and many, if not most, of the substantive conclusions of *L'ancien régime et la révolution*.[106] Confronted by such evidence, some have concluded that Tocqueville's rhetorical remarks in the *Avant-propos*—defending what he then described as an unfashionable cause—cut little conceptual ice.[107] There can be no doubt that Tocqueville intended *Democracy* to be a book for the ages: timely only for its obvious connotations, more genuinely timeless in its deeper significance.[108] The suggestion is that experience eventually disillusioned him. The implication is that his teaching was flawed.

We might note in passing that if Tocqueville had particular reasons to be bitter after 1851, other contemporary "aristocratic liberals" passed through a chronologically concurrent path from simple hope to complex anguish.[109] John Stuart Mill, Tocqueville's English champion, struck a notably bullish tone during the early years of Whig government after 1830. Yet *On Liberty,* his best-known later work, often reads like a nostalgic memoir. Much of it pointed to the possibility of a drearily conformist—read illiberal—future that would have struck

105. *DA,* 39–40; cf. Mansfield, "Intimations of Philosophy," XX.

106. Brogan, *Tocqueville: Prophet of Democracy,* chaps. 15, 21.

107. Brogan, *Tocqueville: Prophet of Democracy,* 569ff is only the most recent.

108. Jaume, *Tocqueville,* 11–12.

109. I owe the term to Alan Kahan, *Aristocratic Liberalism: The Social and Political Thought of Jacob Burckhardt, John Stuart Mill, and Alexis de Tocqueville* (New York: Oxford University Press, 1992); see esp. 119–25.

a definite chord with his recently deceased friend.[110] In a different way, Tocqueville's own observations about America after 1840 often hinted at an increasingly uncertain future—even there—for the ends he had long espoused for the whole world. But then again, he had every reason to be uncertain about America after the passing of the Kansas-Nebraska Act. In addition, he was unlucky enough to die before the promulgation of the Fourteenth Amendment. A careful reading of his subsequent writings on America reveals a man properly concerned for the future but not fatalistic about the possibilities of freedom, either there or elsewhere.[111]

What is less clear is whether anything linked these concerns. He certainly did fear the concentration of power, for which the whole of recent French history—ancien régime as well as the revolutionary era—so powerfully attested.[112] But if America was moving in the same direction, it was doing so in a rather different way.[113] This is not to minimize the crisis of the 1850s. Rather, it is to emphasize the significance of Tocqueville's abiding insight that American liberty was sustained, in America, as much by what was American as by what was democratic. This mattered more generally because it pointed to how the future of liberty there depended in no small measure on what was permanent, as opposed to purely transitory, in the American "democratic experiment." That was what Tocqueville had discovered on his voyage to America. He never forgot that lesson, however much he subsequently journeyed (literally and figuratively) beyond America. So it is surely not fanciful to assert that, for Tocqueville, a true apprehension of these

110. On the optimistic Mill, see above and "The Spirit of the Age" (1831), most recently anthologized in Gertrude Himmelfarb, ed., *The Spirit of the Age: Victorian Essays* (New Haven, Conn.: Yale University Press, 2007), 50–79; for the later pessimist, see John Stuart Mill, *On Liberty*, ed. Gertrude Himmelfarb (London: Penguin, 1974), 62–68, and esp. 72–74, also 131ff.

111. Jeremy Jennings and Aurelian Craiutu, "Interpretative Essay: Tocqueville's Views of America after 1840," in *Tocqueville on America after 1840: Letters and Other Writings*, ed. and trans. Aurelian Craiutu and Jeremy Jennings (Cambridge: Cambridge University Press, 2009), 1–39, offers an account. For Tocqueville's understanding of Kansas-Nebraska, see letters 97 (pp. 154–57), 102 (pp. 161–62), and 131 (pp. 199–201).

112. Tocqueville, *L'ancien régime*, book 2, 107–14.

113. *DA*, vol. 3, pt. 2, chap. 20.

permanent things will determine liberty's place in the origins, course, and consequences of those many "democratic experiments" that he anticipated and that have eventuated far beyond America's shores. If this is true, then we still have much reason to praise him in our own time, after all.

3

Democratic Dangers, Democratic Remedies, and the Democratic Character

JAMES T. SCHLEIFER

This essay is a brief reconsideration of the genesis and development of some of the important themes of Alexis de Tocqueville's *Democracy in America*, especially his description of democratic dangers, democratic remedies, and the democratic character. To reexamine these key ideas, this paper draws largely upon Liberty Fund's four-volume, bilingual version of his masterpiece, which presents a very broad and extensive selection of materials relating to the writing of *Democracy in America*, including early outlines, drafts, manuscript variants, marginalia, unpublished fragments, and the autograph working manuscript.[1] The Liberty Fund edition also includes editorial notes, a selection of important appendices, excerpts from and/or cross-references to Tocqueville's travel notebooks, his correspondence, and his printed sources, as well as significant excerpts from the critical commentary of family and friends, written in response to their readings of Tocqueville's manuscript. In short, the edition re-creates much of Tocqueville's long process of thinking (and rethinking) and writing (and rewriting), and allows the interested reader to follow along, from 1832 to 1840, as Tocqueville's ideas developed and as *Democracy* took shape.

1. Alexis de Tocqueville, *Democracy in America: Historical-Critical Edition of "De la démocratie en Amérique,"* ed. Eduardo Nolla, trans. James T. Schleifer, 4 vols. (Indianapolis: Liberty Fund, 2010). This edition is hereafter cited as *DA*.

The Dangers

Tocqueville's deepest passion was for liberty, which he considered at risk in democratic times. In large part his book is an exploration of democratic dangers (How does equality threaten freedom?) and democratic remedies (How best to protect liberty in the face of advancing equality?).

What were the essential dangers? Tocqueville warned his readers about three in particular: materialism, individualism (or excessive privatism), and consolidated power. We will touch very briefly on the first two and then elaborate on the third.

In democratic times, people were increasingly concerned with their material comfort, and with the order and public tranquility needed to further this ease and prosperity. Their ceaseless striving toward physical well-being narrowed their hearts and minds, and diverted them from public affairs.

Advancing equality also led people toward a growing sense of isolation and noninvolvement; they ended by withdrawing from public life and by focusing almost exclusively on personal and family well-being. By 1840, Tocqueville would name this phenomenon *individualism*. But the message was clear in the 1835 text and even in the working papers for the first part of his book. One passage from the 1835 *Democracy* declared:

> There are such nations in Europe where the inhabitant considers himself a sort of settler, indifferent to the destiny of the place where he lives. The greatest changes occur in his country without his participation.... Even more, the fortune of his village, the policing of his street, the fate of his church and his presbytery have nothing to do with him; he thinks that all these things are of no concern to him whatsoever.... When nations have reached this point, they must modify their laws and mores or perish, for the source of public virtues has dried up; subjects are still found there, but citizens are seen no more.[2]

2. *DA,* 157.

And in a draft for the 1835 portion, Tocqueville described the moral costs of despotism and lamented men who became

> indifferent to their interests and enemies of their own rights. Then they wrongly persuade themselves that by losing in this way all the privileges of civilized man, they escape all his burdens and evade all his duties. So they feel free and count in society like a lackey in the house of his master, and think that they have only to eat the bread that is left for them, without concerning themselves about the cares of the harvest. When a man has reached this point, I will call him, if you want, a peaceful inhabitant, an honest settler, a good family man. I am ready for everything, provided that you do not force me to give him the name of citizen.[3]

Both materialism and individualism led therefore to the erosion of public participation and the collapse of civic life, diminishing human beings morally. More specifically, materialism and individualism encouraged people to allow the state or the presumed representatives of the people to gather power and take control of society; they opened the door to the third great danger: power consolidated in the hands of some despot or despotic force.

In *Democracy,* Tocqueville cataloged and carefully examined the variety of possible democratic despotisms that might arise from the consolidated power that threatened to emerge from modern democratic societies. In the 1835 part of his book, he described legislative tyranny (Tocqueville was thinking particularly of the National Convention), executive tyranny, military despotism, or rule by one man (in these cases, he was thinking especially of Napoleon and the worst of the Caesars), and tyranny of the majority (here, the American republic was the dangerous example).[4]

Still another possible democratic despotism was administrative

---

3. *DA,* 386–87nr. On *individualism,* see James T. Schleifer, *The Making of Tocqueville's "Democracy in America,"* 2nd ed. (Indianapolis: Liberty Fund, 2000), chaps. 17 and 18; hereafter cited as Schleifer, *Making.* Also consult Jean-Claude Lamberti, *La notion d'individualisme chez Tocqueville* (Paris: Presses Universitaires de France, 1970).

4. On the variety of democratic despotisms described in Tocqueville's *Democracy,* see Schleifer, *Making,* chaps. 11–13.

centralization. Tocqueville's basic views about centralization are familiar and can be summarized in a few sentences. In the 1835 *Democracy* he made a well-known distinction between governmental and administrative centralization, praising the first as necessary for national strength and condemning the second as enervating politically, socially, and morally. He described the American republic as highly centralized governmentally but remarkably decentralized administratively, a trait that he saw as one of the key reasons for the social and political health and the material prosperity of the United States.

It is important to note that in the 1835 portion of his book, he already recognized that democracy led to centralization and that this tendency was one of the great dangers facing democratic societies. "I am convinced," he wrote, "that there are no nations more at risk of falling under the yoke of centralized administration than those whose social state is democratic."[5] In a draft of the 1835 portion he declared: "Moreover we must not be mistaken about this. It is democratic governments that arrive most quickly at administrative centralization while losing their political liberty."[6]

By 1840 he even more emphatically warned that democracy tended almost inevitably toward centralization. In one of his most famous and powerful passages, he offered readers a terrible portrait of the new, "soft" democratic despotism of the centralized state.[7] We should note, however, that when he sketched this chilling picture, he was thinking primarily of Europe, in general, and of France, in particular. America, with its particular laws, circumstances, and mores, especially its local liberties, federal structure, associational habits, and doctrine of interest well understood, escaped the danger at that time. The long-term implications of his warnings about administrative centralization have chilled the hearts of many American readers, however, especially during the past half century.

But Tocqueville's views about centralization are far more complicated than this brief summary. First, his distinction between governmental and administrative centralization was weak and never worked

5. *DA*, 162.
6. *DA*, 164*ne*.
7. *DA*, 1249–52.

effectively.[8] Tocqueville himself knew this and wrote: "The permanent tendency of [nations whose social state is democratic] is to concentrate all governmental power in the hands of the single power that directly represents the people.... Now, when the same power is already vested with all the attributes of government, it is highly difficult for it not to try to get into the details of administration ... and it hardly ever fails to find eventually the opportunity to do so."[9] So the two centralizations were really inseparable; when an instrument or branch of government, claiming to represent the people, has sufficient power, it cannot resist the temptation to apply it more widely and in more precise ways. After 1835, as he drafted the second part of his book, the distinction disappeared from Tocqueville's thinking and writing.

Second, Tocqueville was not opposed to centralization as such. On the contrary, in *Democracy* and elsewhere, he argued forcefully for the benefits of centralization for certain purposes. In some of his working papers, he asserted that administrative centralization, within limits, is a necessary fact in modern societies, arguing that great national enterprises, essential to the public good, required a centralized state. He called on the state actively to support, and even to fund, academic and scientific societies; such support would assure continuing research in the theoretical sciences and in other fields not attractive to the immediate, often shortsighted interests of democratic society. The Americans, he noted, were so decentralized administratively and so afraid of centralization that they did not know some of the advantages of centralization.[10]

In one draft fragment, with the title "Unity, centralization" and dated March 7, 1838, he wrote: "However animated you are against unity and the governmental unity that is called centralization, you cannot nonetheless deny that unity and centralization are the most powerful means to do quickly, energetically, and in a given place, very

8. Concerning this point about centralization, see Françoise Mélonio, *Tocqueville and the French*, trans. Beth G. Raps (Charlottesville: University of Virginia Press, 1998), 23–24, 49–50, and esp. 146–48, 211.

9. *DA*, 162–63.

10. See, on the American fear of centralization, *DA*, 584–85*n*o, 587*n*q, 612–13; on necessary governmental support for academies and research, 775*n*a, 869–70*n*h; on centralization and the appropriate role of government, 796*n*c, 902*n*s, 903–4, 978–79*n*j; 1206–15.

great things. That reveals one of the reasons why in democratic centuries centralization and unity are loved so much."[11] In another draft, he declared: "Contained within certain limits, centralization is a necessary fact, and I add that it is a fact about which we must be glad. A strong and intelligent central power is one of the first political necessities in centuries of equality. Acknowledge it boldly."[12]

Of course, he also warned that the state or central power must not act alone. Tocqueville had noticed that in the United States "internal improvements" often combined private and governmental (local, state, and federal) support. The Americans, Tocqueville realized, had developed a mixed system for major economic undertakings.[13] By combining public and private involvement, they accomplished wonders.[14] In his drafts, he argued that if the administration in France became deeply involved in great industrial enterprises, it had to be checked by the legislature and by the courts. A system of balance was required.[15] The real issue, according to Tocqueville, is not how to bar state participation but where and how to draw the limits of state participation.[16]

In the 1840 text he forcefully declared: "It is at the very same time necessary and desirable that the central power that directs a democratic people be active and powerful. It is not a matter of making it weak or indolent, but only of preventing it from abusing its agility and strength."[17]

11. *DA*, 1201–2*n*c.

12. *DA*, 1255*n*p.

13. Tocqueville, *Alexis de Tocqueville and Gustave de Beaumont in America: Their Friendship and Their Travels*, ed. Olivier Zunz, trans. Arthur Goldhammer (Charlottesville: University of Virginia Press, 2010), Notebook E, "Means of Increasing the Public Prosperity," 364–65; hereafter cited as Tocqueville, *Tocqueville and Beaumont;* or see Tocqueville, *Journey to America*, trans. George Lawrence, ed. J. P. Mayer (New Haven: Yale University Press, 1960), 272; hereafter cited as Tocqueville, *Journey to America.*

14. See *DA*, 902*n*s, 903–4, 1215*n*p, 1232–41. Also see 558*n*36.

15. See *DA*, 1226–27*n*k, 1228–29*n*o, 1230-31*nn*p and 4, 1234–37*nn*5 and y.

16. See for example, *DA*, 1235–37*n*y. On the larger matter of Tocqueville's moderation and rejection of absolutes, see especially Aurelian Craiutu, "Tocqueville's Paradoxical Moderation," *Review of Politics* 64, no. 4 (Fall 2005): 599–629.

17. *DA*, 1265.

Excessive focus on the dangers of centralization as such, and especially on administrative centralization, has often blinded readers not only to Tocqueville's praise for what he described as the benefits of centralization but also to his more fundamental concern about democratic societies. Although Tocqueville harshly condemned bureaucratic centralization, his broader message involved the danger of any consolidated power. In his book, he described a long series of possible democratic tyrannies: the majority, the mass, public opinion, the legislature, the military leader, one man alone, the bureaucracy, the state, or even the manufacturing aristocracy or some faction. By claiming and attempting to exercise concentrated and unchecked power, each threatened liberty. Here was the heart of his warnings about democratic despotisms.

In the 1835 text he declared:

So I think that a social power superior to all others must always be placed somewhere, but I believe liberty is in danger when this power encounters no obstacle that can check its course and give it time to moderate itself.

Omnipotence in itself seems to me something bad and dangerous. Its exercise seems to me beyond the power of man, whoever he may be; and I see only God who can, without danger, be all powerful, because his wisdom and his justice are always equal to his power. So there is no authority on earth so respectable in itself, or vested with a right so sacred, that I would want to allow it to act without control or to dominate without obstacles. So when I see the right and the ability to do everything granted to whatever power, whether called people or king, democracy or aristocracy, whether exercised in a monarchy or a republic, I say: the seed of tyranny is there and I try to go and live under other laws.[18]

---

18. *DA*, 412–13; and see also the discussion in Roger Boesche, "Tocqueville and *Le Commerce*: A Newspaper Expressing His Unusual Liberalism," *Journal of the History of Ideas* 44, no. 2 (April–June 1983): 288–90. Also consult Schleifer, *Making*, chaps. 11–13. Note that the chapters that present the famous portrait of the new democratic despotism are really focused on the concentration of power; see *DA*, 1221–44 and 1245–61.

To preserve liberty in democratic societies, Tocqueville believed strongly that all power has to be limited or hedged in by various restraints, both formal and informal. Unchecked power was dangerous no matter where it was located. For Tocqueville, decentralization was simply one of the ways to spread power as widely as possible.

Even this brief overview demonstrates that beneath the major democratic dangers that worried Tocqueville was an underlying moral concern. Tocqueville was most troubled by the potential moral impact of materialism, individualism, and consolidated power. As a moralist, Tocqueville believed that the worst democratic dangers undermined human responsibility, shrank the human spirit, and diminished the human soul.

The Remedies

For this trinity of dangers—materialism, individualism, and consolidated or unchecked power—what were the remedies? The continuity of remedies for democratic ills that Tocqueville offered his readers in 1835 and 1840 is one of the great evidences of the unity between the two halves of *Democracy*. Tocqueville wrote about the *art* and the *habits* of liberty. By the *art* of liberty, he meant primarily the legal, constitutional, and institutional mechanisms that mark a society. A people and their lawmakers can shape laws and institutions in ways that lessen democratic dangers and foster liberty. One of the features that Tocqueville admired most about the United States, for example, was the way in which power was scattered or spread about; he often used the word *éparpiller* when describing American institutional and legal arrangements. In particular, he had in mind decentralization (especially local liberties and associations); the federal system (including checks and balances among the branches of government); liberty of the press; and individual civil and political rights. Many of the most important lessons learned by Tocqueville in the New World republic involved key legal and structural mechanisms for moderating democracy and avoiding its worst dangers.

By the *habits* of liberty, Tocqueville meant something closely related to mores of a certain kind, especially inherited ideas, behaviors, habits, and values, such as the spirit of association, the spirit of religion, a sense of justice, and a grasp of interest well understood. In his book, he consistently stressed the restraints on power that arose from mores in America as well as from legal and institutional arrangements. He also insisted that the *habits* of liberty were more powerful and enduring, more essential and reliable, than the *art* of liberty.

Nonetheless, the *art* and *habits* of liberty were, for Tocqueville, intimately intertwined. Lawmakers practicing the *art* of liberty can establish laws and institutions that counteract the worst dangers of democracy. But according to Tocqueville, it is the *habits* of liberty that give real life to those laws and institutions and that make them more than empty legal and institutional structures. For example, the spirit of locality makes town government come alive, the spirit of association prompts individuals to gather together to address and solve problems, and long practical political experience makes the conceptual intricacies of American federalism possible.

From another perspective, the core of Tocqueville's program of remedies is civic involvement or public participation; his solutions—by *art* and by *habits*—to democratic dangers were related to his concept of citizenship and public life. For Tocqueville, citizenship assumed such basic liberties as the rights to vote; to participate in local self-government; to write, speak, and associate; and to trial by jury. These freedoms, essentially political and civil rights, are related to the *art* of liberty and make public participation *possible.*

But the most essential dimension of citizenship for Tocqueville is *actual* public participation. Ongoing, habitual involvement in public affairs, particularly at the local level, fosters practical political experience and knowledge, a concept of the larger public good, respect for the rights of others, and a comprehension of interest well understood. Note that these elements of genuine citizenship are related to *mores* and to the *habits* of liberty.

Activity in the American town served for Tocqueville as a particularly powerful example of citizenship. In the drafts and working manuscript of the 1835 *Democracy,* he repeatedly emphasized the importance of public life in the town. "The town puts liberty and government within the grasp of the people; it gives them an education....A town system is made only with the support of mores, laws, circumstances and time. Town liberty is the most difficult to suppress, the most difficult to create. It is in the town that nearly all the strength of free peoples resides."[19] Again later: "Town institutions not only give the *art of using great political liberty,* but they bring about the *true taste* for liberty. Without them, the taste for political liberty comes over peoples like childish desires or the hotheadedness of a young man that the first obstacle extinguishes and calms."[20]

Civic involvement, especially in the localities, helps therefore to overcome the major dangers of modern democratic society. Involvement on the local level limits any tendency toward the consolidation of power, especially in the hands of a centralized bureaucracy; it supports the scattering of power in the society. Participation in public life brings people out of their own private or narrow spheres of interest, and it teaches them to care about the wider public good, about something other than material goals.

This brief consideration of the *art* and *habits* of liberty and of the necessary framework for citizenship should remind us that Tocqueville spoke not only for *liberty* in the abstract but also for *liberties,* for the specific list of political and civil rights noted above. Individual liberties protected the individual in the face of all the possible democratic despotisms, especially the majority, the mass, the state, or society as a whole. Liberties made individual independence possible and supported genuine civic participation and true public life.[21] As Tocqueville wrote in the 1840 *Democracy*:

[It] is above all in the democratic times in which we find ourselves that the true friends of liberty and of human grandeur must, constantly, stand up and be ready to prevent the social power from sacrificing lightly the particular rights of some individuals to the general execution of its designs. In those times no citizen is so obscure that it is not very dangerous to allow him to be oppressed, or individual rights of so little importance that you can surrender to arbitrariness

19. *DA,* 101nd.

20. *DA,* 162nb, Tocqueville's emphasis.

21. For a similar insistence that true liberty must be understood as promotion of the broadest possible participation in public life, consult Stephen G. Breyer, *Active Liberty: Interpreting Our Democratic Constitution* (New York: Knopf, 2005).

with impunity.... [To] violate [the particular right of an individual] today is to corrupt the national mores profoundly and to put the entire society at risk.[22]

He summarized:

The political world is changing; from now on we must seek new remedies for new evils. To fix for the social power extensive, but visible and immobile limits; to give to individuals certain rights and to guarantee to them the uncontested enjoyment of these rights; to preserve for the individual the little of independence, of strength, and of originality that remain to him; to raise him up beside society and sustain him in the face of it: such seems to me to be the first goal of the legislator in the age we are entering.[23]

For Tocqueville, particular *liberties* made *liberty* real.

Among all of these remedies of *art* and *habits* proposed by Tocqueville, let us focus now on one of the most well known, the doctrine of interest well understood. Tocqueville's concept of *interest well understood* developed gradually from 1831, when he was in America, to the late 1830s, when he was completing the 1840 *Democracy*.[24] But the idea clearly emerged from what he had learned as he traveled in the United States.

Very quickly Tocqueville discovered what he would call the bedrock principle of American society, "[the] maxim that the individual is the best as well as the only judge of his particular interest.... This doctrine is universally accepted in the United States." It served as the foundation of town liberty, but it also exercised a general influence over "even the ordinary acts of life."[25] Even more striking was the way that Americans blended private and public interest. As early as May 1831, Tocqueville realized that what he was seeing in the New World put some familiar theories in doubt.

In his travel notebooks he wrote:

---

22. *DA,* 1272.

23. *DA,* 1275 and 1276*nz*. See also 718*nm* and 389, where Tocqueville declares, "There are no great men without virtue; without respect for rights, there is no great people."

24. For a full discussion, consult Schleifer, *Making,* chaps. 17 and 18.

25. *DA,* 108; and see also 598–601, 600*nb*.

The principle of the ancient republics was the sacrifice of particular interest to the general good. In this sense, you can say that they were *virtuous*. The principle of this one appears to me to be to make particular interest part of the general interest. A kind of *refined and intelligent egoism* seems the pivot on which the whole machine turns. These people do not trouble themselves to find out if public virtue is good, but they claim to prove that it is useful. If this last point is true, as I think it is in part, this society can pass for enlightened, but not virtuous. But to what degree can the two principles of individual good and general good in fact be merged? To what point will a conscience that you could call a conscience of reflection and calculation be able to control the political passions that have not yet arisen, but which will not fail to arise? That is what the future alone will show us.[26]

By the time he was drafting the 1835 *Democracy*, he realized that the American example required a revision or recasting of Montesquieu:

Of virtue in republics—The Americans are not a virtuous people and yet they are free. This does not absolutely prove that virtue, as Montesquieu thought, is not essential to the existence of republics. The idea of Montesquieu must not be taken in a narrow sense. What this great man meant is that republics could subsist only by the action of society over itself. What he means by virtue is the moral power that each individual exercises over himself and that prevents him from violating the rights of others.

When this triumph of man over temptation is the result of the weakness of the temptation or of a calculation of personal interest, it does not constitute virtue in the eyes of the moralist; but it is included in the idea of Montesquieu who spoke of the effect much more than of the cause. In America it is not virtue that is great, it is temptation that is small, which comes to the same thing. It is not disinterestedness that is great, it is interest that is well understood, which again comes back to almost the same thing. So Montesquieu was right although he spoke about ancient virtue, and what he says of the Greeks and Romans is still applicable to the Americans.[27]

26. *DA*, 509na (second part), my emphasis: *refined and intelligent egoism.*
27. *DA*, 509na (first part).

In another draft, Tocqueville listed some of the key intellectual bonds that tied Americans together: "Shared ideas. *Philosophical and general ideas.* That interest well understood is sufficient to lead men to do good. That each man has the ability to govern himself."[28]

Note that in these (and other) drafts for the 1835 volumes, long before he began to write the 1840 *Democracy,* Tocqueville was already using the term *interest well understood* and developing the idea. The seeds appear in the 1835 text. In his discussion of public spirit in the United States, Tocqueville remarked on a "more rational" love of country that he had witnessed in America and that "arises from enlightenment; it develops with the help of laws; it grows with the exercise of rights; and it ends up merging, in a way, with personal interest. A man understands the influence that the well-being of the country has on his own." But how did the Americans "unite . . . individual interest and the interest of the country"? "[H]ow is it," Tocqueville asked, "that each person [in the New World republic] is involved in the affairs of his town, of his district, of the entire State as his very own?" "Today," he declared, "civic spirit seems to me inseparable from the exercise of political rights."[29]

Tocqueville carried this argument as well into his discussions of the idea of rights and the respect for law in the United States.[30] In both cases, the exercise of political rights was the key to linking personal interest and the larger public interest. When he presented the social benefits of the jury in America, he described how the jury spread the idea of rights to all classes, taught responsibility, and increased the enlightenment of the people. Once again, Tocqueville saw an instrument that linked personal and public interest. "By forcing men to get involved in something other than their own affairs, it combats individual egoism, which is like the rust of societies."[31]

In his 1840 text, Tocqueville would call the *refined and intelligent egoism,* the new kind of virtue that he had described in his travel notebooks

---

28. *DA,* 598–99*nz*, 600*nb*.
29. *DA,* 384–89, esp. 385 and 387.
30. *DA,* 389–95.
31. *DA,* 448.

and in the drafts for 1835, the *doctrine of interest well understood*. For him it served as a major remedy for democratic individualism.[32]

> I have already shown, in several places in this work, how the inhabitants of the United States almost always knew how to combine their own well-being with that of their fellow citizens. What I want to note here is the general theory by the aid of which they succeed in doing so. . . .
>
> I will not be afraid to say that the doctrine of interest well understood seems to me, of all philosophical theories, the most appropriate to the needs of the men of our time, and that I see in it the most powerful guarantee remaining to them against themselves. So it is principally toward this doctrine that the mind of the moralists of today should turn. Even if they were to judge it as imperfect, it would still have to be adopted as necessary.
>
> I do not believe, everything considered, that there is more egoism among us than in America; the only difference is that there it is enlightened and here it is not. Each American knows how to sacrifice a portion of his particular interests in order to save the rest. We want to keep everything, and often everything escapes us.[33]

"[The] Americans," he remarked elsewhere in his text, "have so to speak reduced egoism to a social and philosophical theory."[34] What is important for us to recognize are the American roots of this doctrine of interest well understood, one of the most famous and original elements of Tocqueville's thinking and writing. But where and how did the Americans learn to combine private and public interest and to understand individual and general interests in such a strikingly new way?

In a brilliant discussion, James Kloppenberg has described the concept of interest well understood, discovered by Tocqueville in America, as an expression of an "ethic of reciprocity" and has argued that reciprocity is fundamental to the healthy habits of liberty that Tocqueville witnessed in the United States, especially the spirit of locality and the

32. See *DA*, 918–25.
33. *DA*, 919 and 922.
34. *DA*, 993.

spirit of association. The ethic of reciprocity casts the idea of interest well understood in a new light.[35]

Kloppenberg defines this ethic as fruitful interaction among individuals engaged in a shared enterprise, as awareness of and respect for others, and as the "practice of deliberation," or the experience of expressing, listening to, and respectfully considering the viewpoints and opinions of others in order to arrive at a mutually acceptable and beneficial conclusion. This mutual consideration, shared involvement, and respectful deliberation rested upon a deep sense of "reciprocal obligation." It described how Americans (at their best) behaved in their towns and associations and defined what Tocqueville meant by the spirit of locality and the spirit of association. Kloppenberg has argued that the ideal of reciprocity was a fundamental characteristic of American mores. Tocqueville also understood reciprocity as a key solution to democratic dangers. "Sentiments and ideas are renewed," he declared in *Democracy,* "the heart grows larger and the human mind develops only by the reciprocal action of men on each other."[36]

What was the deeper source of such an ethic of reciprocity in America? Kloppenberg has located the source in the American religious heritage and has reminded us once again of Tocqueville's insistence on the Puritan experience as the essential point of departure for the American republic.[37] This argument has been taken up in much greater detail by Barbara Allen in a recent book in which she underscores the importance of the Puritan concept of covenant.[38] To "own the covenant" in Puritan terms was to take profound moral and religious responsibility for sustaining the relationship between the individual and the community. Its most immediate and direct expressions were in the Puritan congregation and congregational meeting, but it also shaped the mores of the earliest town meetings that took

35. See James T. Kloppenberg, "Life Everlasting: Tocqueville in America," chap. 5 in *The Virtues of Liberalism* (New York: Oxford University Press, 1998), esp. 76–81.

36. *DA,* 900.

37. See *DA,* 45–73, esp. 52–70.

38. Consult Barbara Allen, *Tocqueville, Covenant, and the Democratic Revolution: Harmonizing Earth with Heaven* (Lanham, Md.: Rowman & Littlefield, 2005).

place in the "meetinghouse" (as the church building was called) and that reflected Puritan covenantal theology. According to her analysis, covenant brought forth what Tocqueville described as the American habits of liberty, including such basic political mores as assuming and expressing a voice in communal deliberations, feeling a sense of obligation toward political participation, sharing a commitment to the larger public good, and grasping what Tocqueville labeled as interest well understood.

For the Puritans, covenant, as a social and political concept, defined the relationship between the individual and the church or congregation, and between the individual and the larger society. It required the mutual moral responsibilities of the individual and the group for sustaining the larger community, for balancing the good of the individual and the good of the community, and for avoiding any definitive break in communal bonds. It called for mutual commitment, active participation, and respectful deliberation—the very behavioral characteristics included in Kloppenberg's ethic of reciprocity.

Tocqueville did not specifically locate the source of the concept of interest well understood in the Puritan religious heritage of the American republic. But a case can be made that the concept of covenant, by shaping the mores of American social and political culture, also produced the social and philosophical theory that Tocqueville found so new and so special in the New World republic and that he called the doctrine of interest well understood. Interest well understood involved the essential covenantal principle: the assumption that the fundamental good of the individual and the good of the community were in fact compatible and even mutually supportive, that private and public interest could be harmonized in surprising ways, given the right religious and moral traditions.

This argument underscores the defining role in American society of religion in general and of the dissenting Protestant and Puritan traditions in particular. It reaffirms the brilliance of Tocqueville's insights about the centrality of religion in shaping American politics, society, and culture, and about the unique way in which Americans blended the spirit of religion and the spirit of liberty. If the ultimate root of the doctrine of interest well understood is the Puritan concept of covenant, we need to recognize the fundamental, if hidden, moral dimension of the doctrine of interest well understood. Most commentators treat the doctrine as essentially utilitarian and amoral; some even treat it negatively, as unworthy of the highest moral dimensions of humanity. But if covenant plays a defining role, we need to acknowledge the profound moral dimension of this innovative American social and philosophical theory.

This quick review of remedies emphasizes three fundamental features of Tocqueville's intellectual journey. It demonstrates once again how Tocqueville's ideas, as he envisioned and wrote *Democracy* between 1831 and 1840, were shaped by American lessons. The American experience was, in many ways, transformative; it significantly inspired, deflected, and renewed Tocqueville's thinking. This summary also illustrates a fixed principle of Tocqueville's thought. For him, remedies based on *habits* were more important than those based on *art*. *Mores*, as Tocqueville insisted so eloquently, are more crucial to the health and success of democracies than are laws, institutions, or circumstances. Finally, this survey reveals that hidden beneath Tocqueville's remedies for democratic ills was the goal of a vigorous civic life. As Tocqueville wrote, the best cure for democracy was more democracy, understood as the broadest possible public participation.

The Democratic Character

Tocqueville believed that a new, emerging society would call forth a new man: the "democratic man," who would exhibit characteristic habits, attitudes, beliefs, and ideas (mores). The story of Tocqueville's developing understanding of the democratic character is complex; what follows is only a summary treatment of the topic. Once again, we must begin in America, where, as he traveled, he carefully observed those around him and gradually developed a full picture of the American character.

Throughout the writing of his book, Tocqueville's concept of national character remained vague and elusive. But in an early version of the manuscript of *Democracy*, he offered a tentative definition.

There is indeed in the bent of the ideas and tastes of a people a hidden force that struggles with advantage against revolutions and time. This intellectual physiognomy of nations, which is called their character, is found throughout all the centuries of their history and amid the innumerable changes that take place in the social state, beliefs and laws. A strange thing! What is least perceptible and most difficult to define among a people is at the same time what you find most enduring among them.[39]

For him, national character really meant the mores of a particular nation.

What was the *bent of the ideas and tastes,* or the *intellectual physiognomy* of the Americans? Among the features of the American character that Tocqueville noted and praised in his travel notes and in the working papers and text of *Democracy* were:

- Religious faith and a high regard for religion;
- Good morals and a positive attitude toward women;
- Abundant energy, hard work, and relentless activity;
- Practical political experience and general knowledge and intelligence;
- Good sense and steadiness of habits or "habits of restraint";
- Fixity of certain fundamental principles;
- Public spirit and a drive to participate in public life;
- A sentiment or feeling of equality with fellow citizens;
- Respect for law and for the rights of others;
- Willingness to help others, or a benevolent attitude; and
- An intelligent and refined egoism, or a remarkably different understanding of how private and public interest were linked.

Among American traits that Tocqueville observed and criticized were:

- Love of money and passion for wealth and material well-being;
- Commercial passions and habits of business;
- Greediness to acquire material goods and to dominate the continent;

39. *DA,* 344*ny.* And see also 45–49.

- Lack of general ideas and interest in practice rather than theory;
- Restlessness and constant movement;
- Tendency to follow momentary passions;
- Passion for change and expectation of constant improvement;
- Nearly universal ambition and drive to advance in society;
- Exaggerated seriousness or coldness;
- Inability to enjoy life;
- Tendency to conform to the majority and to follow public opinion;
- Discontent and frustration despite prosperity and success;
- Envy;
- Deep anxiety; insecurity about status and well-being;
- National self-absorption and pride;
- Racist attitudes toward blacks and Native Americans; and
- Fanatical spiritualism (at times).

Even these two short lists underscore several significant features of Tocqueville's portrait of the American character. Remarkably, Tocqueville's portrayal began to emerge quickly during the first days of his American journey and can be found throughout the working papers and final text of the 1835 *Democracy*. Yet his depiction is complex and extraordinarily perceptive, containing both high praise and severe criticism. It particularly highlights certain fundamental American traits, such as religious faith, practical political experience, constant activity, and the ability to understand private and public interests in a new way.

But Tocqueville's portrait is also limited in several respects. First, it focuses on the Anglo-American man; women and the other two races of North America are largely considered apart. Second, it is a description even more specifically of the Northerner (even of the New England Yankee); in the pages of *Democracy*, Tocqueville offers us a separate picture of the Southerner that differs in several important ways from the general image. Third, and finally, we should note that much of his portrayal, especially the features that he most disliked, is a description of middle-class habits and characteristics. To some extent, Tocqueville saw the Americans through the preexisting lens of his profoundly unfavorable conception of the middle class and of middle-class society.

Among Tocqueville's catalog of American characteristics, the psychological features offer arguably the most brilliant insights of his analysis. Again we need to remember that these psychological traits as well are already present in Tocqueville's travel notes and in the drafts and manuscripts of the 1835 *Democracy*. His journey notebooks, for example, describe an American who has a profound sentiment or feeling of equality with his fellows.[40] In the working papers of the 1835 portion of *Democracy*, Tocqueville observes that, in a society without the traditional markers of caste and class, the Anglo-American is constantly anxious about his status in society, and in a society where the primary distinction is wealth, he is constantly worried about his material well-being.[41]

Tocqueville also describes an American who, despite great prosperity, remains restless and profoundly disappointed because the two key goals that he is always pursuing inevitably elude him. Full equality can never be attained. Paradoxically, as equality comes closer, the small remaining inequalities become more irritating and frustrating. The passion for equality can never be satisfied.[42] Tocqueville even remarks on a pervasive envy and on what he calls the principle of "relative justice," which means that small inequalities among those most similar to you are harder to endure than the vast inequalities between castes or classes.[43] A satisfying material success also eludes the American; he always wants more, and ultimately he runs out of the time needed to acquire all that he desires.[44]

Despite the sad realization that his desires would never be fully achieved, the American, according to Tocqueville, lives with his eyes fixed on a better tomorrow; he assumes that change is improvement and expects the future to surpass the present.[45] This assumption also

---

40. Tocqueville, *Tocqueville and Beaumont*, Notebook E, "On Equality in America," 354–56; or see Tocqueville, *Journey to America*, 258–61.

41. For example, see Tocqueville, *Tocqueville and Beaumont*, Notebook E, "On Equality in America," 355–56; or Tocqueville, *Journey to America*, 260; also see *DA*, 943–46.

42. See, for example, *DA*, 316, 942–47.

43. On the concept of "relative justice," see *DA*, 2:571.

44. See, for example, *DA*, 2:460, 503–4; and compare 935–36*n*b and 1317–19.

45. See, for example, *DA*, 3:935–36*n*b.

feeds both his discontent with his current situation and his unrelenting drive forward.

Out of this image of the Anglo-American came Tocqueville's parallel portrait of the "democratic man." Certain striking differences between his depiction of the American and that of the "democratic man" must be noted, however, especially the latter's lack of sufficient religious faith to counterbalance materialistic passions and his impulse to withdraw from public life (individualism). These twin tendencies of "democratic man" toward unchecked or unrestrained materialism and toward noninvolvement or nonparticipation in civic affairs were, for Tocqueville, two of the most troubling features of the democratic character.

But Tocqueville's psychological sketch of "democratic man" (fully presented in 1840) closely mirrored his portrayal of the Anglo-American (already apparent between 1831 and 1835). The democratic psychology was marked by the same envy, anxiety, frustration, discontent, and restlessness that Tocqueville had observed among the Americans.

Another significant question remains. How is the character of "democratic man" related more broadly to the theme of democratic dangers and remedies? Tocqueville's sketch of the democratic character is deeply critical. The impulses and psychological traits of "democratic man" exacerbate the democratic threats that so worried Tocqueville, especially the dangers of materialism and individualism that have been discussed above.

If, however, the democratic character largely heightened Tocqueville's worries, he also found among American characteristics some features of democratic mores that served—at least potentially—as possible remedies for democratic dangers. Precisely where the American character differed from that of "democratic man," Tocqueville found habits, ideas, and attitudes—most notably religious faith, the drive toward participation in public life, and the sense of interest well understood—that could correct some of the worst flaws and weakness of the democratic character.

From one perspective, Tocqueville offered readers two possible democratic scenarios: one, healthy; the other, toxic. As we have seen, his portrayal of the democratic character was largely anticipated by and even modeled on his depiction of the American character. But where the mores of "democratic man" seemed especially toxic, Tocqueville looked to what was distinctive about the American example in order to find healthy corrections. For him, the peculiar features of the American character served as important remedies for particular dangers presented by democratic mores. Once again Tocqueville found in the American experience reasons for hope about the democratic future.

This brief discussion of democratic dangers, democratic remedies, and the democratic character serves once again as a powerful demonstration of the unity between the 1835 and the 1840 portions of *Democracy*. Not only does Tocqueville's political program—his suggested remedies for democratic dangers—remain constant, but also we have seen several important examples of how chapters in the 1840 text grew out of a few sentences or paragraphs in the 1835 *Democracy*, including such important concepts as individualism and interest well understood, and such psychological features of democratic man as envy, discontent, restlessness, and anxiety. A careful reading of the Liberty Fund edition, with its rich presentation of materials from the drafts and other working papers of Tocqueville's masterpiece, reveals the way in which the 1840 volume grew almost organically out of the seeds first put down in 1835 (or earlier). This characteristic of *Democracy* reflects Tocqueville's habit of constantly turning and returning ideas in his mind: an inescapable feature of his method of thinking and writing.

We have also repeatedly followed the ideas of Tocqueville, the moralist. If the fundamental threat from democratic dangers is the narrowing of the human heart (due to materialism, excessive privatism, and withdrawal from public life), the most basic benefit of democratic remedies is its feeding and expansion (due to reciprocity, involvement with others, and focus on the larger public good). Tocqueville's effort to grasp the democratic character was essentially an attempt to understand democratic *mores*. We have already noted that his primary concern as a political analyst was mores rather than laws, institutions, or circumstances. As a moralist, Tocqueville believed that *mores*—ideas, beliefs, attitudes, and behaviors—ultimately held the key to liberty and to the future of democratic societies.

Finally, our discussion showed Tocqueville drawing on American lessons to teach his readers how to use the *habits* of liberty and particular democratic *mores* to counteract the dangers in modern societies, or, if the necessary *habits* were weak or absent, how to use the *art* of liberty—the establishment of proper laws and institutions—to address those dangers. Here at its most basic is the new science of politics that Tocqueville urged upon the citizens and legislators of the new democratic world.[46]

46. Many of the themes and arguments of this essay, originally written in 2008, are developed more fully in various chapters of James T. Schleifer, *The Chicago Companion to Tocqueville's "Democracy in America"* (Chicago: University of Chicago Press, 2012).

4

Tocqueville's Journey into America

JEREMY JENNINGS

All Tocqueville scholars are familiar with Garry Wills's charge that Tocqueville did not "get" America.[1] "A fact usually omitted in discussions of Tocqueville," Wills contends, "is the shallow empirical basis of his study." "It is," he continues, "as if [Tocqueville] ghosted his way directly into the American spirit, bypassing the body of the nation." In Tocqueville's account, Wills further reminds us, there is virtually nothing about American capitalism, manufactures, banking, or technology. During their nine months in America, Tocqueville and his companion Gustave de Beaumont spent around two months "narrowly focused on prison life." In addition, they devoted time on trips "only remotely connected, or not connected at all, with what went into *Democracy*." These included a trip to Lower Canada, where, as Tocqueville wrote to the Abbé Lesueur, "we felt as if we were at home, and everywhere we were received like compatriots,"[2] and the now-famous "Two Weeks in the Wilderness," where he and Beaumont saw only "the still empty cradle of a great nation."[3] Most of the remaining seven months, Wills tells us, were spent in the North, where "almost all of *Democracy*'s conclusions" were "formed while Tocqueville was fresh in the country and seemed particularly impressionable." Wills further contends that Tocqueville was also extremely selective—not to say snobbish—about those with

1. Garry Wills, "Did Tocqueville 'Get' America?" *New York Review of Books,* April 29, 2004, 52–56.

2. Quoted in George Wilson Pierson, *Tocqueville in America* (Baltimore, Md.: Johns Hopkins University Press, 1996), 314.

3. See Pierson, *Tocqueville in America,* 229–89.

whom he chose to converse, showing little interest in "ordinary people."[4] Wills is likewise less than charitable in his assessment of the impact of these meetings with the superior minds of the East Coast. "Tocqueville," he writes, "took many of his views from the last remnants of the Federalists, who supplied him with what he thought necessary to democracy, a moderating counter to extreme egalitarianism." Accordingly, Wills affirms, Tocqueville "parroted" the views of the Federalists in his "scathing" comments on Andrew Jackson and upon populist leaders such as Sam Houston and Davy Crockett. The implication of Wills's comments is that not only were these views of dubious worth—damned, as they were, by their lofty social origin—but also Tocqueville would have discovered an altogether different America had he chosen occasionally to mix with his social inferiors.

The criticism does not cease there. "In his erratic traversing of the country," Wills writes, "what Tocqueville did not see is often more interesting than what he did." Tocqueville, it seems, never visited a New England town meeting. He never saw an American university. He made no efforts to become familiar with American intellectual life. The only state capital he visited was Albany.[5] His journey through the South to New Orleans was hasty in the extreme and diminished as a source of potential information by Tocqueville's debilitating illness.

The conclusion is clear. Tocqueville "would probably not have benefited by a longer stay in America." His ideas were formed upon the basis of first encounters and rarely changed afterward. He had a propensity to form "instant judgments." He "concluded things about America because of the prejudices he brought with him from France." He was not seeking to write "an objective account of what he saw in America." His pronouncements were made "*de haut en bas.*" The whole book, like

4. In his article Wills, somewhat misleadingly, makes use of the following quotation: "To acquire information about institutions and public establishments, etc., etc., we really have to see people, and the most enlightened people are in the best society." Contrary to the impression given, this is in fact a quotation from a letter written not by Tocqueville but by Beaumont to his brother on May 26, 1831; see Pierson, *Tocqueville in America,* 86.

5. Wills makes a subtle distinction here between visiting and "passed through." For example, on his definition, Tocqueville passed through, rather than visited, Hartford, Connecticut.

Tocqueville's work in general, was characterized by "the taste for grand simplification."

The surprise is that these conclusions find an echo in what would normally be regarded among Tocqueville scholars as a friendly source, namely, George Wilson Pierson's reconstruction of Tocqueville's stay in America. At the end of his magisterial volume, Pierson devoted a set of four chapters to a consideration of the overall character of Tocqueville's achievement.[6] Let us first be clear that Pierson was of the opinion that Tocqueville drew "some useful conclusions" from his American experiences. In particular, Pierson wrote, Tocqueville saw that "there seemed to exist in the United States certain habits, certain institutional practices, that increased the good effects obtainable from self-government at the same time that they mitigated or even altogether eliminated the dangers inherent in mass control."[7] Second, Pierson acknowledged that Tocqueville "had carried some prejudices to America," but he countered this by asserting that "the Americans themselves had again and again supplied the corroborating information." To take but one example, Tocqueville no longer saw the Native American "through the romantic haze of a tale by Chateaubriand, but in terms of personal contact and experience."[8]

Yet Pierson did not seek to disguise or hide the "defects" to be found in *Democracy in America*. Of these, Pierson suggested, the principal deficiency was to be found in Tocqueville's philosophical method. Tocqueville was "neither a historian nor a scientist but a philosopher, and a philosopher whose concepts and whose habits were not well calculated, if he wanted, rigorously, to find the truth." It was this, Pierson concluded, that "injected into his classic the strong dose of mortality that it undoubtedly contains."[9] We might further note that Pierson was also of the view that Tocqueville was "unscientific in his use, or rather in his failure to use, contemporary literature" and that he was "not sufficiently inquisitive."[10]

6. Pierson, *Tocqueville in America*, 718–77.

7. Pierson, *Tocqueville in America*, 723.

8. Pierson, *Tocqueville in America*, 724.

9. Pierson, *Tocqueville in America*, 756.

10. Pierson, *Tocqueville in America*, 758–59.

So, too, Tocqueville was guilty of "errors of observation."[11] Here is a shortened version of the lengthy list highlighted by Pierson. Tocqueville misread the American inheritance laws. He neglected American material development, in the process ignoring "the one great factor that was going to transform his chosen civilization almost overnight." He failed properly to acknowledge the nationalizing influence of American commerce and underestimated the centralizing tendency in American politics. He did not foresee the rise of American cities and therefore did not appreciate the strain that would be placed upon institutions of local self-government. In his appraisal of American institutions, he failed to obtain "sufficient knowledge of their historical background," and so he was unable correctly to discuss the dispute over slavery and the bitterness between North and South. In the field of politics, he made "two considerable errors of omission": he failed to notice the growth of a two-party system and he neglected the intermediate unit of American politics, the state, thus closing his eyes to "its significant possibilities as a balancing force and experimental laboratory." "Both of these mistakes," Pierson concluded, "can be traced to his visit to Albany and his failures of observation there."[12] More than this, because of his experience with Andrew Jackson, Tocqueville "underestimated the power of the executive branch in American government." Most alarming of all given its centrality to the argument of the text and its subsequent notoriety, Tocqueville "perhaps overestimated the tendency of democracy, at least as practiced in the United States, to degenerate into tyranny by the majority."

Having got this far, we might pause to consider the justice and substance of some of the critical remarks cited above. There is, indeed, no shortage of evidence to support the view that Tocqueville quickly made up his mind about what he saw in America. Letters to his two close friends Ernest de Chabrol and Louis de Kergorlay, written shortly after his arrival, gave a strong intimation of what would in due course form the content of his famous book.[13] Likewise, Tocqueville's chosen

11. Pierson, *Tocqueville in America*, 764–67.
12. Pierson, *Tocqueville in America*, 766.
13. Tocqueville, *The Tocqueville Reader: A Life in Letters and Politics*, ed. Olivier Zunz and Alan S. Kahan (Oxford: Blackwell, 2002), 40–49.

pattern of social interaction was also quickly evident. Once on dry land, Tocqueville and Beaumont soon found themselves the toast of New York society and later found the doors of the Bostonian elite opened to them. A reading of Tocqueville's notebooks reveals just how much he learned from his eminent acquaintances. It was, for example, Alexander Everett who informed Tocqueville one evening that "[t]he point of departure for a people is of immense importance."[14] It was this idea, as Tocqueville was later to inform readers of *Democracy in America,* that provided "the key to nearly the whole book."[15]

But what of the more serious, and most often repeated, charge that Tocqueville showed no interest in and failed to perceive the growing industrialization of the American economy? This assertion can often figure as part of a broader argument alleging that Tocqueville knew nothing of economics and displayed a near total indifference to the social issues and problems of his day. That this general contention is largely false has been amply shown by the recent work of Michael Drolet and Richard Swedberg,[16] but does it hold true for the specifics of Tocqueville's examination of America? This is the manner in which the evidence has been presented by one of the most perceptive of commentators upon Tocqueville's work, Seymour Drescher. Tocqueville and Beaumont, he writes,

> visited prisons until they felt themselves imprisoned by their own mission. They sacrificed comfort, and almost their lives, to view the American West at first hand. But though they knew of the world famous industrial experiment at Lowell, Massachusetts, they simply

14. Tocqueville, *Alexis de Tocqueville and Gustave de Beaumont in America: Their Friendship and Their Travels,* ed. Olivier Zunz, trans. Arthur Goldhammer (Charlottesville: University of Virginia Press, 2010), 241. In the course of his stay in Boston, Tocqueville recorded a similar remark from Jared Sparks to the effect that "I believe that our government and mores are best explained by our origins," *Tocqueville and Beaumont,* 242.

15. Alexis de Tocqueville, *Democracy in America: Historical-Critical Edition of "De la démocratie en Amérique,"* ed. Eduardo Nolla, trans. James T. Schleifer, 4 vols. (Indianapolis: Liberty Fund, 2010), 49. This edition is hereafter cited as *DA.*

16. Michael Drolet, *Tocqueville, Democracy and Social Reform* (Houndmills: Palgrave Macmillan, 2003), and Richard Swedberg, *Tocqueville's Political Economy* (Princeton, N.J.: Princeton University Press, 2009).

passed it by. Their one hour in Pittsburgh . . . was spent catching up on correspondence. They were deeply impressed by Cincinnati's throbbing industry but spent their extremely rationed time there with its lawyers rather than its industrial classes.[17]

How, on Tocqueville's behalf, might we respond?

The failure to visit Lowell was undoubtedly a notable omission. Despite its recent creation, after 1821 it had already achieved notoriety as a purpose-built mill town and regularly received foreign visitors, including some from France. Among these was Michel Chevalier, who devoted considerable space to Lowell and its factory girls in his own account of his journey across America.[18] Chevalier also discoursed at some length on the towns of Pittsburgh and Cincinnati, both cities evoking his admiration and enthusiasm.[19] With regard to Tocqueville's visit to Pittsburgh, however, Drescher is perhaps unfair. Beaumont and Tocqueville arrived there only after an arduous journey fraught with considerable difficulty and in blizzard conditions. Moreover, following a request from the French Ministry of Justice, they were obliged to cut short their visit to America and were now hurrying in order to return to France within a year.[20]

A similar observation might be made about their four-day stay in Cincinnati. While it is undeniably true that Tocqueville used his letters of recommendation in order to secure interviews with lawyers—and also Supreme Court Justice John McLean—these conversations were wide ranging and led Tocqueville to reflect extensively upon the character of the rapidly expanding American West. "More than any other part of the Union," Tocqueville confided to his notebook, "Ohio strikes me as a society totally occupied with its own affairs, and, through work, with

17. Seymour Drescher, *Dilemmas of Democracy: Tocqueville and Moderation* (Pittsburgh: University of Pittsburgh Press, 1968), 52–53.

18. Michel Chevalier, *Society, Manners and Politics in the United States: Being a Series of Letters on North America* (Boston, 1839), 125–44.

19. Chevalier, *Society, Manners and Politics*, 166–75, 190–209.

20. Tocqueville, *Oeuvres complètes,* vol. 13, *Correspondance familiale* (Paris, 1998), 147. Selections from Tocqueville's letters are now available in translation in *Alexis de Tocqueville: Letters from America*, ed. Frederick Brown (New Haven, Conn.: Yale University Press, 2010), and Tocqueville, *Tocqueville and Beaumont*, 7–208.

rapid growth."[21] The whole of society, he observed, is an industry, and everyone has come there to make money. Of Cincinnati, in particular, Tocqueville remarked:

> It is always difficult to know exactly why cities develop and grow. Chance always plays a part. Cincinnati is situated in one of the most fertile plains of the New World, and because of this it began to attract settlers. Factories were built to supply the needs of these settlers and before long the whole of the region of the West, and the success of these industries attracted new industries and more settlers than ever. Cincinnati was, and I believe still is, a transit point for many shipments to and from the Mississippi and Missouri valleys to Europe and for trade between New York, and the northern states and Louisiana.[22]

From this, and other similar observations in his notebooks, it would be difficult to conclude that Tocqueville did not either observe or appreciate the importance of the rapid industrial and commercial progress that was transforming America and pushing its population ever westward.

Nevertheless, this does not appear in *Democracy in America*. Indeed, in his printed text, this part of Tocqueville's journey into America figured largely as the occasion for him to reflect upon how, when traveling down the Ohio River, the "traveller...navigates so to speak between liberty and servitude." "The white on the right bank," Tocqueville commented, "obliged to live by his own efforts, made material well-being the principal goal of his existence.... The American on the left bank scorns not only work, but all the enterprises that work brings to success. ...So slavery not only prevents whites from making a fortune; it turns them from wanting to do so."[23] These remarks were anticipated in his notebooks and in a letter to his father.[24] Yet, if one looks a little closer at the printed text, one also sees a curious footnote in which Tocqueville

---

21. Tocqueville, *Tocqueville and Beaumont*, 356.

22. Tocqueville, *Tocqueville and Beaumont*, 359–60.

23. *DA*, 560.

24. See the letter to his father, dated December 20, 1831: Tocqueville, *Oeuvres complètes*, vol. 14, *Correspondance familiale* (Paris, 1998), 154–57.

makes reference to the efforts of the state of Ohio to ensure the building of a canal between Lake Erie and the Ohio River, thanks to which
"the merchandise of Europe that arrives in New York can descend by
water as far as New Orleans, across more than five hundred leagues of
the continent."[25] This observation is also prefigured in his travel notes.

I draw particular attention to this reference to the American canal
network because, when comparisons are made between the accounts
provided by Tocqueville and the Saint-Simonian Michel Chevalier,
it is usually to suggest that Tocqueville ignored the transport revolution that was turning an agrarian society into an entirely different
kind of economic order. According to Wills, for example, Tocqueville
"rides around on steamboats without noticing how crucially they were
changing American life. . . . He also ignores the infant railroad industry and the burgeoning canal systems." It is undoubtedly true that
Chevalier devoted a larger proportion of his efforts to detailing the
routes of transportation across the North American continent, but
just as Tocqueville and Beaumont were commissioned to report on the
American penitentiary system, Chevalier was assigned a similar task
with regard to the new nation's railway network.

The fact of the matter is that Tocqueville was not unfamiliar with
these aspects of the American economic infrastructure. In his Notebook E, the section recording his impressions of Cincinnati and Ohio
is followed almost immediately by a section titled "Means of Increasing
the Public Prosperity." "Roads, canals and the mails," Tocqueville there
wrote, "play a prodigious part in the prosperity of the Union." America,
he continued, not only enjoyed a greater sum of prosperity than any
other country but also had "done more to provide for . . . free communications." One of the first things done in a new state was to create a
postal service such that "there is no cabin so isolated, no valley so wild
that letters and newspapers are not delivered at least once a week."
Main roads are built in the middle of a wilderness and almost always
before the arrival of those whom they were meant to serve. America,
Tocqueville further observed, "has planned and built immense canals.
It already has more railways than France. Everyone recognizes that the
discovery of steam immeasurably increased the strength and prosperity

25. *DA*, 558*n*36.

of the Union by facilitating rapid communications among the various parts of this vast country." Moreover, because Americans were not a sedentary people, they felt the need for means of communication with a liveliness and zeal unknown in France. As to the means employed to open up communications in America, Tocqueville saw that, while "the American government does not involve itself in everything," when it came to "projects of great public utility," they were seldom left to the care of "private individuals." The states led the way.[26]

Why did Tocqueville not include these observations in *Democracy in America*? Wills has a simple answer. "Tocqueville," he tells us in a footnote, "took some notes on these matters, but did not consider them important enough to reflect on in *Democracy*." There might be another explanation. Tocqueville himself made the following remark: "To return to the subject of roads and other means of rapidly transporting the products of industry and thought from one place to another, I do not claim to have made the discovery that these promote prosperity, for this is a universally accepted truth."[27] As far as Tocqueville was concerned, in other words, these conclusions were so blindingly obvious that they did not merit comment or inclusion in his text.

There is a further, and equally compelling, reason why Tocqueville chose to exclude these issues from his account. This is found in the first paragraph of the critical edition of *Democracy in America* provided by Eduardo Nolla. It reads as follows: "The work you are about to read is not a travelogue, the reader can rest easy. I do not want him to be concerned with me. You will also not find in this book a complete summary of all the institutions of the United States; but I flatter myself that, in it, the public will find new documentation and, from it, will gain useful knowledge about a subject that is more important for us than the fate of America and no less worthy of holding our attention."[28] Tocqueville therefore intended quite explicitly to distance his own inquiry from

---

26. Tocqueville, *Tocqueville and Beaumont,* 363–64.

27. Tocqueville, *Tocqueville and Beaumont,* 365.

28. *DA,* 3–4. This part of the text was the subject of discussion between Tocqueville and Kergorlay. See Toqueville, *Oeuvres complètes,* 12:364–68, 12:373–75. The two letters date from October 1834 and January 1835. Kergorlay commented: "Your idea is clearly to show that you are going to concern yourself with more important objects than the existence of a single individual. . . . You wish to

the extensive travel literature that had flourished in France from the 1780s onward and that, for the most part, had focused its attention upon the flora and fauna of the American continent, its majestic landscape, and the rude manners of its people.[29] To continue in this vein was no part of Tocqueville's purpose. Again his perspective is clarified by the Nolla critical edition. In a first version of the drafts, Tocqueville wrote: "I have not said everything that I saw, but I have said everything that I believed at the same time true and useful [v: profitable] to make known, and without wanting to write a treatise on America, I thought only to help my fellow citizens resolve a question that must interest us more deeply."[30] He went on to add the following remark: "I see around me facts without number, but I notice one of them that dominates all the others: it is old; it is stronger than laws, more powerful than men; it seems to be a direct product of the divine will; it is the gradual development of democracy in the Christian world."[31] This was the subject of Tocqueville's *Democracy in America,* and this was so, as he declared in the opening lines of the published version, because "[a]mong the new objects that attracted my attention during my stay in the United States, none struck me more vividly than the equality of conditions."[32]

This aspect of American society was so striking and so novel that it came progressively to displace all other considerations in Tocqueville's mind.[33] Again, the process by which this occurred can be seen by consulting the Tocqueville material held at Yale University's Beinecke Library and assembled by Eduardo Nolla. In brief, if on Tocqueville's

----

show that you have considered something more serious than the satisfaction of personal vanity."

29. See Durand Echeverria, *Mirage of the West: A History of the French Image of American Society to 1815* (Princeton, N.J.: Princeton University Press, 1957), 190. See also René Rémond, *Les Etats-Unis devant l'opinion française, 1815–1852* (Paris, 1962), and Philippe Roger, *L'Ennemi Américain: Généalogie de l'antiaméricanisme français* (Paris, 2002).

30. *DA,* 4nc.

31. *DA,* 4.

32. *DA,* 4.

33. Cheryl B. Welch speaks of Tocqueville's "single-minded focus on his own subject—the social, political and psychological manifestation of a democratic condition of life"; see *De Tocqueville* (New York: Oxford University Press, 2001), 70.

part there was no lack of interest in the commercial aspects of American society, as he came to reflect upon what he wanted to say in his own study, they were not integral to the argument that he wished to develop. As Tocqueville made plain in his letter to Beaumont of November 4, 1836, in which he asked his friend specifically for commentary on Chevalier's rival text, his own study was intended to be an *"ouvrage philosophique-politique."*[34]

It was accordingly in light of the impact of industrialization upon the workings of democracy that, in volume 2 of the *Democracy in America*, Tocqueville considered the question of "What Makes Nearly All Americans Tend toward Industrial Professions."[35] Recognizing that "no people on earth who has made as rapid progress as the Americans in commerce and industry" and that, although they had "arrived only yesterday," the Americans had "overturned the whole natural order to their profit," Tocqueville drew three conclusions of substance and not inconsiderable importance from these "industrial passions": commercial crises would be endemic to industrial capitalism; industrialization would produce a new kind of capitalist aristocracy; and a version of state capitalism would engender a new form of soft despotism. It was, however, never Tocqueville's intention to publish a detailed description of America's transport infrastructure.

The second substantive criticism—and one that might be deemed to be fatal to his entire enterprise—is that Tocqueville overestimated the potential of American democracy to degenerate into the tyranny of the majority. For example, when Tocqueville's good friend Jean-Jacques Ampère visited America in the early 1850s, he recorded that Americans were almost universally agreed that, on one thing, Tocqueville had been mistaken: the possibility of a tyranny of the majority was unfounded. The most intriguing of Ampère's encounters, therefore, was with John C. Spencer, author of a preface to the first American edition of *Democracy in America*. According to Spencer, the ever-changing nature of majority opinion ensured that no "lasting tyranny" could

---

34. Tocqueville to Beaumont, November 4, 1836, in Tocqueville, *Oeuvres complètes*, vol. 8, *Correspondance d'Alexis de Tocqueville et de Gustave de Beaumont* (Paris, 1967), 177.

35. *DA*, 972–79.

be established. Spencer himself attributed Tocqueville's error to the peculiar political circumstances pertaining during his stay: namely, the support of the overwhelming majority for General Jackson's populist measures, which might have given the impression that the minority was "crushed" and without the power to protect itself.[36]

A very similar charge was made by Tocqueville's American friend Jared Sparks, the man who in 1833 told Tocqueville that in his forthcoming book he anticipated "a more accurate and judicious account of the United States than has yet appeared from the pen of any European traveller"[37] and who, after its publication and in the face of objections in America to Tocqueville's remarks on "the defects of Democratic institutions," assured his colleague that "all the intelligent persons among us who have read your treatise have applauded its ability and candour."[38] In a letter to another of Tocqueville's critics, Guillaume-Tell Poussin,[39] of February 1841, he wrote:

> Your criticisms of M. de Tocqueville's work also accord for the most part with my own sentiments. Notwithstanding the great ability with which his book is written, the extent of his intelligence, and his profound discussions of many important topics, I am persuaded that his theories, particularly, when applied to the United States, sometimes lead him astray. For instance, in what he says of the tyranny of the majority, I think, he is entirely mistaken. His ideas are not verified by experience. The tyranny of the majority, if exercised at all, must be in the making of laws; and any evil arising from this source operates in precisely the same manner on the majority itself as on the minority. Besides, if the majority passes an oppressive law, or a law which the people generally disapprove, this majority will certainly be changed at the next election, and be composed of different elements. M. de Tocqueville's theory can only be true where

36. J.-J. Ampère, *Promenade en Amérique* (Paris, 1856), 1:337–41.

37. Quoted in Richmond Laurin Hawkins, "Unpublished Letters of Alexis de Tocqueville," *Romanic Review* 19 (1928): 195.

38. Quoted in Herbert B. Adams, *Jared Sparks and Alexis de Tocqueville* (Baltimore, 1898), 39.

39. See Guillaume-Tell Poussin, *Considérations sur le Principe démocratique qui régit l'Union Américaine et d'autres états* (Paris, 1841).

the majority is an unchangeable body and where it acts exclusively on the minority, as distinct from itself—a state of things which can never occur where the elections are frequent and every man has a voice in choosing the legislators.[40]

It should be noted that Ampère himself was not convinced by these criticisms and that, on Tocqueville's behalf, he provided a response that is not without merit or cogency. That the oppressed could themselves in turn become the oppressors, he countered, was no safeguard for personal liberty. Moreover, the new majority might simply continue to voice many of the "common passions" and "prejudices" of the previous majority, thus continuing the oppression of "a persistent minority." This was especially true in the states of the South where freedom of expression on the subject of slavery did not exist and where, on this issue, it mattered not whether the Whigs or the Democrats were in power. Moreover, that the excesses of Jacksonian democracy no longer existed did not prove that they had been completely cured and that they could not return. Tocqueville, he consequently affirmed, had been right to diagnose the existence of a "radical infirmity" existing at the heart of American society: "the possible tyranny of number where numbers counted for everything."[41] Nor, it should be added, was it the case that everyone shared the view that Tocqueville had failed to observe America in an accurate and impartial fashion. In a lengthy article written for the *North American Review*,[42] Edward Everett, while not denying that Tocqueville was sometimes "led away by the desire to generalize," affirmed that Tocqueville's work was "by far the most philosophical, ingenious and instructive, which has been produced in Europe on the subject of America."

Be that as it may, it is not easy to dislodge the criticism that errors in central aspects of Tocqueville's analysis arose because of both the brevity of his stay and the fact that he could not escape his own inherited prejudices. Here let us remember that Tocqueville was an outsider in America not only because he was French and aristocratic but also

40. Quoted in Adams, *Jared Sparks*, 43–44.
41. Ampère, *Promenade en Amérique*, 1:337–41.
42. Edward Everett, *North American Review* 43 (1836): 178–206.

because he was a Catholic.[43] In short, on this view, the odds were well and truly stacked against Tocqueville ever producing an account of America that rose above shallow empiricism and vague theoretical generalization. Indeed, this was the view of no less an authority than François Furet, who asserted that "when Tocqueville went to the United States in the spring of 1831, he had already formed his own hypothesis for comparing the French Revolution and the American Republic."[44] Thus forewarned, it might be argued, are we not better placed to make sense of Tocqueville's well-known remark that "in America I saw more than America," for was he not really only interested in France all along? Moreover, is this not substantiated by Tocqueville's statement that "[w]hile I had my eyes fixed on America, I thought about Europe."[45]

Is this then not evidence enough to dispel any lingering doubt as to the lack of utility and purpose in Tocqueville's voyage? First, we would do well to remember James T. Schleifer's observation that it would have been remarkable had Tocqueville not "reached the shores of America carrying much of the historical and intellectual baggage of early 19th century France." Could it have been imagined that he would have arrived with a completely empty mind, without "a variety of preconceptions about the fundamental nature and direction of modern society"?[46] Next, Tocqueville was only too aware of his own prejudices and of the difficulties involved in freeing himself from them. In his *Two Weeks in the Wilderness,* we find the following remark: "[A]s for me, in my traveler's illusions—and what class of men does not have its own—I imagined something entirely different." America, he had believed, would be bound to exhibit "all the transformations that the social state imposed on man and in which it was possible to see those transformations like a vast chain." Nothing of this picture, he confirmed, had any truth. Indeed, America was "the least appropriate

43. Michael Novak, *The Universal Hunger for Liberty* (New York: Basic Books, 2004), 141.

44. François Furet, "The Passions of Tocqueville," *New York Review of Books,* June 27, 1985, 23–26.

45. *DA,* 28no.

46. James T. Schleifer, "Tocqueville's Journey Revisited: What Was Striking and New in America," *Tocqueville Review* 27 (2006): 404.

for providing the spectacle that I was coming to find."[47] For his part, Tocqueville was in turn utterly damning in his attitude toward those of his fellow countrymen who had not bothered themselves with doing anything other than observing America from a lofty and disdainful distance. In a letter to the Abbé Lesueur, for example, he warned that his compatriot, a man called Scherer, "will paint you an unfavourable picture of America: the fact is that he has made the most stupid journey in the world. He came here without any other end than to stroll about, knowing nothing about either the language or the customs of the country."[48] He later repeated the advice to his mother, condemning what was probably the same person for deriving all he knew of the country from a "particular class of Frenchmen whom he saw exclusively."[49] Moreover, all of this accords with Gustave de Beaumont's own description of Tocqueville as a traveler. Contrasting his friend with those visitors to North America "who passed through, seeing nothing and looking for nothing, not even wild ducks," he remarked that, for Tocqueville, "everything was subject to observation."[50]

Accordingly, a reading of Tocqueville's diaries, notebooks, and letters reveals a mind, not closed to new experiences, but overwhelmed by the novelty and importance of what he was seeing. For example, having told us that the penitentiary system was a pretext for his visit to America, a letter to Kergorlay continues as follows: "In that country, in which I encountered a thousand things beyond my expectation, I perceived several things about questions that I had often put to myself. I discovered facts that seemed useful to know. I did not go there with the idea of writing a book, but the idea for a book came to me there."

Nor is it easy to unravel the complex relationship between Tocqueville's impressions of America and his thoughts on the future of European civilization. Even his earliest reviewers realized that this was not merely a book about America, and the fact that it is not so explains why we continue to read it for instruction and enlightenment (unlike the vast

---

47. *DA*, 1309.
48. Tocqueville, *Oeuvres complètes*, 14:112.
49. Tocqueville, *Oeuvres complètes*, 14:143.
50. "Notice sur Alexis de Tocqueville," *Oeuvres et correspondance inédites d'Alexis de Tocqueville* (Paris, 1861), 1:22.

majority of nineteenth-century accounts of America that, if read at all, are done so for entertainment and amusement alone). Again, a letter to Kergorlay clarifies his intentions:

> Although I rarely spoke of France in this book, I did not write a page without thinking of her and without always having her, so to speak, before my eyes. And above all what I tried to highlight in the United States and to make understood was less a complete picture of this foreign country but the contrasts and resemblances with our own. It was always, either through opposition or analogy with the one, that I endeavoured to present a fair and, above all, interesting idea of the other. In my opinion, the permanent return that I made, without making it known, to France was one of the main causes of the success of the book.[51]

But this does not reduce the journey itself to insignificance. A letter to his father reported that since their arrival, Tocqueville and Beaumont had had, "in truth, only one idea...this idea is to understand the country through which we are travelling."[52] He similarly told his brother: "In my opinion, one must be truly blind to want to compare this country to Europe and to impose on one what works in the other. I believed this before I left France; I believe it more and more in examining the country in the midst of which I now live."[53]

Moreover, Tocqueville was under no illusions as to the limits of his knowledge and acquaintance with the United States. Writing from Washington, D.C., as his time in America reached its end, he confided in separate letters to his father and to his brother Édouard that he had only a "superficial" knowledge of the South and that a minimum stay of two years was required to prepare a "complete and accurate picture" of the whole country. To attempt to take in the whole, he continued, would be madness, because he had simply not seen enough. In any case,

51. Tocqueville to Kergorlay, October 18, 1847, in Tocqueville, *Oeuvres complètes*, vol. 9, *Correspondance d'Alexis de Tocqueville et de Louis de Kergorlay* (Paris, 1977), 209; in *Tocqueville on America after 1840: Letters and Other Writings*, ed. and trans. Aurelian Craiutu and Jeremy Jennings (Cambridge: Cambridge University Press, 2009), 321–22.

52. Tocqueville, *Oeuvres complètes*, 14:99–100.

53. Tocqueville, *Oeuvres complètes*, 14:92.

such a work would be as "boring as it was instructive." Nevertheless, Tocqueville recorded, his time had been spent usefully and he had collected many documents and spoken with many people. Furthermore, he felt that he knew more about America than was generally known in France and some of what he knew might be of "great interest." "I believe," Tocqueville wrote modestly, "that if, upon my return I have the leisure, I might write something passable on the United States."[54] Less than four years later, the first volume of *Democracy in America* was published to instant acclaim.

Furthermore, the Nolla critical edition of *Democracy in America* provides an unprecedented insight into how Tocqueville's text was written and how its content evolved over time. Tocqueville began with the notebooks and letters he had written while in America. He worked his way through the extensive collection of printed material he had accumulated. He continued to communicate and interrogate his American acquaintances by mail. To help him to complete his research, he employed two young Americans, Francis Lippitt and Theodore Sedgwick, as his assistants. The manuscript was passed on to his family, to Gustave de Beaumont, and to Louis de Kergorlay, and in turn received extensive, expert comment. Certain sections were read out to close friends. Given this thoroughness, it is difficult to know what to make of the charge that Tocqueville was not sufficiently inquisitive and was unscientific in his use of contemporary sources. That aside, we know that his long reflection upon his investigation of America convinced Tocqueville that "[a] new political science is needed for a world entirely new."[55] Later Tocqueville was to sketch out in greater detail what he took the "science of politics" to be, distinguishing it in the process from the "art of government."[56]

Why was a new science of politics required? For the simple reason, as Tocqueville pointed out in his own introduction, that "a great democratic revolution is taking place," and this was a revolution where "the generating fact from which each particular fact seemed to derive" was

54. Tocqueville, *Oeuvres complètes*, 14:165, 166.

55. *DA*, 16.

56. Tocqueville, "The Art and the Science of Politics: An Unpublished Speech," *Encounter* 36 (January 1971): 27–35.

revealed in American society. The corollary to this, as James T. Schleifer
has observed, is that Tocqueville discounted "the traditional inclination to draw lessons about democracy from ancient and Renaissance
texts."[57] The entire book, Tocqueville confided, was written "under
the impression of a sort of religious terror" produced "by the sight of
this irresistible revolution that has marched for so many centuries over
all obstacles."[58] To wish to stop it was to act against God himself. The
best we could do was to accommodate ourselves to the social state that
Providence wished to impose upon us.

There is much that might be said about the merits and character
of this avowedly new political science. To what extent was it genuinely
new and innovative? Was it to be value free? Did it possess predictive
power? To what extent was it philosophically and empirically flawed?
Whatever the answer to these questions, there can be no doubt that
Tocqueville did not imagine that his new political science amounted (as
Sheldon Wolin has recently suggested)[59] to a form of political impres-
sionism. The guiding assumption was that, sooner or later, Europe
would also arrive at something near to the equality of conditions. This
did not mean that Europe would be obliged to draw the same political conclusions from this social state as had been done in America or
that democracy would produce only one form of government. It had
therefore been no part of Tocqueville's purpose to write a "panegyric"
on America or to advocate "any particular form of government in general." Rather, his hypothesis was that, beyond a legitimate curiosity,
one could "find lessons there from which we would be able to profit."[60]

This was achieved with a level of methodological self-awareness and
sophistication that was unusual for the age and certainly unusual for
the subject matter. In both the printed text and his notes, Tocqueville
acknowledged that nothing would be easier than to criticize his book.
It would be sufficient, he acknowledged, only "to contrast an isolated

57. James T. Schleifer, "Tocqueville's *Democracy in America* Reconsidered," ed.
Cheryl B. Welch, *The Cambridge Companion to Tocqueville* (Cambridge: Cambridge
University Press, 2006), 124.

58. *DA*, 14.

59. Sheldon S. Wolin, *Tocqueville between Two Worlds: The Making of a Political
and Theoretical Life* (Princeton, N.J.: Princeton University Press, 2001), 140–41.

60. *DA*, 27–28.

fact to the whole of the facts," "a detached idea to the whole of the ideas." Yet, he remained adamant that he had "never yielded, except unknowingly, to the need to adapt facts to ideas, instead of subjecting ideas to facts."[61] To this disclaimer, he added a clear statement of his methodology. "When a point could be established with the help of written documents," Tocqueville explained, "I have taken care to turn to original texts and to the most authentic and respected works. I have indicated my sources in notes, and everyone will be able to verify them. When it was a matter of opinions, of political customs, of observations of mores, I sought to consult the most enlightened men. If something happened to be important or doubtful, I was not content with one witness, but decided only on the basis of the body of testimonies."[62] To an extent, Tocqueville conceded, this had to be taken on trust, because it needed not to be forgotten that "the author who wants to make himself understood is obliged to push each of his ideas to all of their theoretical consequences, and often to the limits of what is false and impractical."[63] Tocqueville therefore, and not without some justification, made a plea for generosity on the part of the reader. "I would like you," he remarked, "to grant me the favor of reading me with the same spirit that presided over my work, and would like you to judge this book by the general impression that it leaves, as I myself came to a decision, not due to a particular reason but due to a mass of reasons."[64] In his unpublished notes, he added the following remark: "To whoever will do that and then does not agree with me, I am ready to submit. For if I am sure of having sincerely sought the truth, I am far from considering myself as certain to have found it."[65] Tocqueville's modesty in this and (as we have seen) with regard to other elements of his inquiry on America seems frequently to have been overlooked by his critics.

What of the voyage itself and how did Tocqueville come to understand his journey into America?[66] We have to acknowledge, with François

61. *DA,* 30.
62. *DA,* 30.
63. *DA,* 31.
64. *DA,* 31.
65. *DA,* 3.
66. See Leo Damrosch, *Tocqueville's Discovery of America* (New York: Farrar, Straus and Giroux, 2010).

Furet, that "the genesis of Tocqueville's visit to America is shrouded in mystery."[67] When and why he decided to undertake this hazardous enterprise is difficult, if not impossible, to gauge. Next, we should begin by remembering that Tocqueville was only one of many French men and women who, throughout the nineteenth century, crossed the Atlantic to witness the New World at first hand. We should then add that his journey was in many ways not dissimilar from that of substantial numbers of his compatriots. Most arrived by way of New York and were immediately overwhelmed by its sense of fervent and perpetual activity. Educated visitors tended to make their way to Boston. Substantial numbers visited Canada and the Great Lakes (and, like Tocqueville, saw and wondered at the startling beauty of Niagara Falls),[68] but few ventured to the South, preferring rather to satisfy their curiosity on the Eastern Seaboard. Typically people came for an extended stay, but it was unusual for it to last longer than between three and six months. Rarely did the French come alone—characteristically they came with a friend or member of the family—and even more rarely did they decide not to return home. But for all of them, America began the moment they boarded ship and set sail, most often (as in Tocqueville's case) from Le Havre.

With the advent of the steam ship, the journey time was reduced to between one and two weeks, and it could be undertaken in relative comfort. In Tocqueville's day, a journey time of between six and seven weeks was quite normal, and it was not without hazard or hardship.[69] As Jacques Portes recounts, travelers used their enforced leisure to read books about the United States, to meet Americans, and to improve their often very poor English.[70] Tocqueville was no exception.[71] Armed with a copy of Basil Hall's *Travels in North America* and Volney's *Tableau du climat et du sol des Etats-Unis d'Amérique*, Tocqueville embarked on

67. François Furet, "The Conceptual System of *Democracy in America*," in *In the Workshop of History* (Chicago: 1984), 166.

68. Tocqueville, *Oeuvres complètes*, 14:126–27.

69. Tocqueville informed his father that he had met an American whose voyage had taken sixty-six days; see Tocqueville, *Oeuvres complètes*, 14:88.

70. Jacques Portes, *Fascination and Misgivings: The United States and French Opinion, 1870–1914* (Cambridge: Cambridge University Press, 2000), 21–25.

71. Tocqueville, *Oeuvres complètes*, 14:82–83.

April 2, 1831, and, with the ship's provisions almost exhausted, landed at Newport, Rhode Island, on May 9. A day later he and Beaumont arrived in New York. A long letter to his mother, written on board ship and dated April 26,[72] vividly portrays what reads as an almost existential experience. No sooner was he out of sight of the French coast and laid low by seasickness than Tocqueville began to doubt that he would see dry land again. He quickly came to see his world as "a kind of narrow circle upon which play heavy clouds." To this he added that "the solitude of the ocean is a very remarkable thing to experience." His vessel came to take on the form of a separate universe, with its own rituals and codes of behavior. Noah's ark, he told his mother, did not contain a greater variety of animals. Although tightly confined, everyone acted as if they were completely alone and enjoyed a level of freedom unknown elsewhere. "Everyone," he wrote, "drinks, laughs, eats or cries as the fancy takes him." Privacy was almost nonexistent, leading Tocqueville to conclude that they were living in the public space like the ancients. Weather permitting, he and Beaumont tried to work as normal. After dinner they spoke English to "all those prepared to listen." Their first sense of coming within reach of America came when an injured, sky-blue bird became trapped in the ship's rigging. You could not imagine, he told his mother, the joy caused by such a small animal, which "seemed to have been sent with the express intent of announcing the approach of land." Later came more birds and fish and, finally, marine vegetation. Then came the first sighting of land and the "delicious spectacle" of grass and trees. Soon after they dropped anchor and went ashore. Never, he wrote, had people been so happy: "[W]e leapt onto land and each of us took a dozen unsteady steps before coming to stand solidly on our feet." Tocqueville had arrived, and the journey into America had begun.

It is at this point that Tocqueville's journey can be read as a travelogue, his letters bristling with detail, his mood never less than one of fascination. A new world passed before him, he told one of his sisters-in-law, as if it were seen through a magic lantern.[73] The houses along the coast were small and clean, like "chicken coops." The coastline

---

72. Tocqueville, *Oeuvres complètes*, 14:75–86.

73. Tocqueville, *Oeuvres complètes*, 14:102.

was low and lacking in beauty. No description was adequate to portray the "immense" steamship that conveyed them over sixty leagues in only eighteen hours. New York was greeted with "cries of admiration." Its external aspect was "bizarre and not very agreeable." It was possible to call on a lady at nine in the morning without impropriety. No wine was drunk at meals, although American eating habits left much to be desired, with Americans consuming copious amounts in conditions of "complete barbarism." Americans smoked, chewed tobacco, and spat in public. Generally speaking, they lacked grace and elegance; but this did not mean that they were not a "quite remarkable race of men."[74] The navigation of rivers and canals meant that distance was regarded with "unbelievable contempt." The speed at which journeys were completed never ceased to astound him, especially when his steamship unexpectedly raced past West Point on its way to Albany. To his brother Édouard, he reported that he was now living in "another world," where political passions were superficial and the desire to acquire wealth prevailed. Moreover, there were a thousand ways of doing this without troubling the state.[75] The cost of living was less than in Paris, although the price of manufactured goods (Tocqueville was especially concerned about the price of much-needed gloves) was exorbitant. Nothing was more delicious than the spectacle offered by the banks of the Hudson, disappearing as the river did in the high, blue mountains to the north, nor anything as sublime as the "perfect calm" and "complete tranquillity" of the wilderness around the Oneida Lake.[76] Autumn, with its great variety of colors and its "pure and sparkling sky," was "the moment when America appeared in all her glory."[77] Even the flies that lit up the nighttime sky were a source of fascination. Nothing, however, had quite prepared him for the extraordinary Shaker ceremony he witnessed in the woods not far from Albany or for the Fourth of July celebrations the day after, all carried out in "perfect order."[78] Nor could he but be

---

74. Tocqueville, *Oeuvres complètes*, 14:144.

75. Tocqueville, *Oeuvres complètes*, 14:91–92.

76. Tocqueville, *Oeuvres complètes*, 14:118–21; "Voyage au Lac Onéida," in *De la démocratie*, 2:287–90; *DA*, 1295–1302.

77. Tocqueville, *Oeuvres complètes*, 14:143.

78. Details of the Fourth of July ceremony are found in a letter to Ernest

moved by the lamentable and mournful sight of the Choctaw Indians being transported from their homeland to probable oblivion.

Above all, it was the sheer newness and novelty of America that came increasingly to press itself upon him. Writing to his mother from Louisville in December 1831,[79] Tocqueville recorded his impressions of the society he was seeing emerging in the new cities of the Midwest. The Europeans who had first arrived in America, he wrote, had built a society that was analogous to that of Europe but which "at bottom" was radically different. Since then, a new "swarm" of immigrants had poured westward, creating in the valleys of the Mississippi "a new society which bore no comparison with the past and was connected to Europe only by language." It was here that "a people absolutely without precedents, without traditions, without customs," which ignored the wisdom of others and of the past, were carving out institutions, as they were roads, in the forests where they had just arrived, sure in the knowledge that they faced neither obstacles nor limits. With time, their job done, they would uproot themselves again, pushing headlong ever westward toward yet more virgin soil and new challenges. Phrased in the terminology of Tocqueville's published text, this sense of constant movement reappeared in his conclusion that "there is something precipitous, I could almost say revolutionary, in the progress society makes in America."[80]

The mistake is to believe (primarily on the basis of the letters written to Chabrol and Kergorlay in June 1831) that Tocqueville quickly settled his mind on what he had seen of American society. This was not the case because it is clear that his journey across the continent forced him to rethink his impressions and conclusions on an almost daily basis. To his father, in early June, he wrote that he could not tell him what most struck him about America, "a whole volume would be necessary to tell you; and, in any case, I would perhaps not think the same tomorrow."[81] In September, writing from Boston, he told his

---

de Chabrol, July 16, 1831; see *Tocqueville: Lettres choisies, souvenirs*, ed. Françoise Mélonio and Laurence Guellec (Paris, 2002), 203–6.

79. Tocqueville, *Oeuvres complètes*, 14:152–54.

80. *DA*, 610.

81. Tocqueville, *Oeuvres complètes*, 14:100.

mother that "[e]verything I see, everything that I hear, everything that I see from a distance, forms a confused mass in my brain which I will perhaps never have the time nor the strength to unravel. It would be an immense undertaking to present a picture of a society that is as large and as lacking in homogeneity as this one."[82] A month later, this time writing from Hartford, he reaffirmed the observation earlier passed on to his father. "I will know what I think of America only when I am no longer here," he wrote: "One has to give up any idea of studying things deeply when one sees so many things, when one impression drives out the one that preceded it; at best there remain a few general ideas, a few general conclusions, which much later can enable you to understand details when one has the time to study them."[83] From Philadelphia in November, he told his mother that the clearest outcome of his trip would be that, upon leaving America, he would be in a position to understand the documents that he had collected but not yet studied. "For the rest," he continued, "on this country I have only disordered and disconnected notes, disjointed ideas to which only I hold the key, isolated facts which recall a mass of others." The only general ideas he had expressed on America, he confided, were to be found in letters to his family and a few friends in France, and these were written in haste, on a steamboat or in a corner, with his knees serving as a desk. Would he ever write a book on this country? he asked himself. In truth, he did not know. "It seems to me," he concluded, "that I have a few good ideas, but I still do not know how to arrange them."[84]

How these various ideas emerged is captured vividly in Tocqueville's letters and notebooks. To his father, he explained that, despite his mental confusion, two ideas had already come to him. The first was that the American people were the happiest in the world. The second was that America owed its prosperity less to its own virtues and even less to a form of government that was superior to all others than to the particular circumstances in which it found itself. This in turn told him that political institutions were neither good nor bad in themselves and that everything depended upon the physical conditions and social

82. Tocqueville, *Oeuvres complètes*, 14:137.
83. Tocqueville, *Oeuvres complètes*, 14:139.
84. Tocqueville, *Oeuvres complètes*, 14:144.

state of the people where they applied. What might work in America, might not work in France and vice versa.[85] An altogether different set of conclusions was listed in a note titled "First Impressions," dated May 15, 1831. The Americans were a prey to national pride and small-town pettiness. They seemed a religious people, but how far religion regulated their conduct was unclear. The whole of society seemed to be composed of one enormous middle class. Elegant manners and polite refinement were lacking, but all Americans, "right down to the simple shop assistant," seemed to have had a good education and to possess sober manners. Betraying what was to be one of his abiding preoccupations, Tocqueville also commented upon the way women dressed and the causes of chaste morals.

By dint of considerable effort and imaginative intuition, Tocqueville came, in fits and starts, to make sense of these confused and diverse impressions. Yet, as George Wilson Pierson observed long ago, their very tone "prophesized the book that one day would result."[86] Tocqueville showed himself not to be interested in individuals. There were no descriptions of domestic interiors. His subject from the beginning was "the real character of the American people," and with that came necessarily a fascination with the patterns of behavior and institutions of a democratic society.

What Tocqueville came to observe and to learn from his journey through America has best been summarized by James T. Schleifer.[87] Tocqueville, he contends, learned first of all of the equality of conditions in all its assorted forms. He came to appreciate the pace of change and mobility of American society. He discovered some of the key mechanisms for moderating democracy. These included the federal system and the independence of the judiciary. He noticed the importance of administrative decentralization. He understood the significance of the habit of association. Perhaps most important, he saw the centrality to American mores of the doctrine of self-interest rightly understood

85. Tocqueville, *Oeuvres complètes,* 14:100–101.

86. Pierson, *Tocqueville in America,* 77.

87. In addition to James T. Schleifer, *The Making of Tocqueville's "Democracy in America,"* 2nd ed. (Indianapolis: Liberty Fund, 2000), see Schleifer, "Tocqueville's Journey Revisited," 404–19.

and of religion as a guarantor of liberty and democracy. To his obvious delight, he discovered fresh ways of thinking about Catholicism and saw that it might be on the new continent that it would achieve its most authentic expression.

In highlighting these and other themes, Schleifer has also drawn our attention to the language used by Tocqueville to indicate moments of surprise in his journey. He specifically refers us to the numerous occasions when Tocqueville admits that he found something to be "striking." The best example of this occurs in the very first sentence of the published text, where Tocqueville states: "Among the new objects that attracted my attention during my stay in the United States, none struck me more vividly than the equality of conditions."[88] By extending this analysis of the actual words used by Tocqueville in his account, we gain a further insight into the importance of Tocqueville's journey and the manner in which it shaped the content of his argument about America. If, for example, we limit ourselves only to chapters 9 and 10 of part 2 of volume 1, we read such phrases as: "I sometimes encountered in the United States," "While I was in America," "I saw Americans associating," "I encountered wealthy inhabitants of New England," and "As I prolonged my stay, I perceived the great political consequences that flowed from these new facts"; "I saw with my own eyes"; "During my stay in America I did not encounter a single man, priest or layman, who did not come to accord on this point"; "I remember when traveling through the forests"; "I learned with surprise that"; "I discovered that"; "I heard them"; "I wondered how it could happen that"; "I lived much with the people of the United States"; "I met men in New England"; "What I have seen among the Anglo-Americans brings me to believe that." Many more similar phrases and expressions can be found that testify to the impact upon Tocqueville of his voyage, but to confirm the point we might care to consider the following short paragraph:

> Thus *I found* in the United States the restlessness of heart that is natural to men when, all conditions being more or less nearly equal, each sees the same chances to rise. *There I encountered* the democratic sentiment of envy expressed in a thousand different ways. *I observed*

88. *DA*, 4.

that the people often showed, in the conduct of affairs, a great blend of presumption and ignorance, and *I concluded* that in America, as among us, men were subject to the same imperfections and exposed to the same miseries.[89]

With the emphases added, we see clearly how Tocqueville combined a series of observations and reflections drawn directly from experience in order to reach a substantive conclusion.

In closing, I wish to make the suggestion that it is in the final two chapters of volume 1 of *Democracy in America* that the impact of Tocqueville's journey appears in its most unmediated form. As Eduardo Nolla informs us, these parts of the book were written as late as the spring or summer of 1834, and they were not the subject of commentary from either Tocqueville's friends or family. There were few drafts, and there are no great differences between the manuscript and the published version.[90] Tocqueville himself also recognized their distinctiveness within the book as a whole. Issues relating to the future and permanence of the Republic, he commented, "touch on my subject, but do not enter into it; they are American without being democratic, and above all I wanted to portray democracy. So I had to put them aside at first: but I must return to them as I finish."[91] In short, given that there was no clear or obvious parallel between the situation of the slave and Indian populations and conditions then pertaining in Europe, there were no conclusions to be drawn for France. These were specifically American issues and had to be addressed as such.

There can be no doubt that Tocqueville was deeply moved by the plight of the Native Americans. Denying that the picture he had drawn was "exaggerating," he added, referring to the incident so vividly recalled in a letter to his mother: "I have gazed upon evils that would be impossible for me to recount."[92] But these evils, he believed, were irredeemable, as it seemed inevitable that the "Indian race of North America is condemned to perish."[93] Whether they continued to wander

89. *DA*, 503.
90. *DA*, 515*n*a.
91. *DA*, 516.
92. *DA*, 526.
93. *DA*, 529.

through the wilderness or decided to settle made no difference to their prospects. The relentless and prodigious advance of the European settler population condemned them to destruction and extinction. If the individual states sought their complete expulsion, the Union, exuding the spirit of philanthropy and respect for the law, made it possible.

If then the Native American was fated to live on only in our memories, the same could not be said of the slave population of the South. Here was "the most formidable of all the evils that threaten the future of the United States."[94] Again, Tocqueville's description of their situation and his deep sense of foreboding about the future were structured around his own experience of traveling down the Ohio River to the mouth of the Mississippi. He also drew upon the numerous conversations he had had on the subject while in America. From this he could see how slavery penetrated into the souls of the masters and, therefore, how to the tyranny of laws had to be appended the intolerance of mores. The acute dilemmas and difficulties of this situation did not escape Tocqueville. Slavery neither could nor should endure. It defied economic reason. It denoted a reversal of the order of nature. It was attacked as unjust by Christianity. But, as a deleted passage from the original manuscript reveals, it also told us something profound about American society. "The Americans," we read in the Nolla edition,

> are, of all modern peoples, those who have pushed equality and inequality furthest among men. They have combined universal suffrage with servitude. They seem to have wanted to prove in this way the advantages of equality by opposite arguments. It is claimed that the Americans, by establishing universal suffrage and the dogma of sovereignty have made clear to the world the advantages of equality. As for me, I think that they have above all proved this by establishing servitude, and I find that they establish the advantages of equality much less by democracy than by slavery.[95]

The prospects of a resolution to this terrible question, in Tocqueville's view, were slim indeed. Either the Negroes in the South

94. *DA*, 549.
95. *DA*, 561.

would seize their own freedom (by violent means if necessary) or, if freedom were granted to them, they would undoubtedly abuse it. This, in turn, raised the question of the future viability of the Union itself. In his lengthy meditation on this subject, we see clearly the extent to which Tocqueville had taken note of the key political questions agitating America at the time of his stay. He commented, at some considerable length, not only upon the character of President Andrew Jackson but also upon the intense debates over the renewal of the charter of the Second Bank of the United States, tariff reform, and the nullification crisis engineered by Calhoun and his supporters in South Carolina. Jackson, he concluded, was "a slave of the majority" who "tramples underfoot his personal enemies…with an ease that no President has found."[96]

Yet, as ever, Tocqueville's preoccupation was not with the fleeting questions of today but with the future. His focus remained upon the long-term trends that would decide and determine the course of American history. He saw the threats to the Union that came from the slave-owning interests of the South but believed (incorrectly, as it turned out) that all Americans recognized the commercial and political incentives to remain united. Americans, "from Maine to Florida, from the Missouri to the Atlantic Ocean," agreed about the general principles which should govern society and about the sources of moral authority. The greatest threat to the Union, therefore, came from expansion and what Tocqueville termed "the continual displacement of forces that take place within it."[97] The rapidity and extent of this internal movement, driven forward by the search for material prosperity, only accentuated the danger. Countering these tendencies toward dissolution, however, were the forces of greater economic integration— the civilization of the North, Tocqueville contended, would become the norm—and the Constitution itself. The principles of the Republic had deep roots in American society, and he believed therefore that it could only be with extreme difficulty that the principles of monarchy and aristocracy could be received into American customs. Again

96. *DA*, 625.
97. *DA*, 605.

misjudging the situation, he believed that federal power was weakening rather than strengthening, and thus that talk of presidential despotism was unfounded. His position, then, was one of relative optimism.

It was at the very end of these reflections that Tocqueville provided a glimpse of what he clearly perceived as the forces likely to transform America in the decades to come. He first turned his attention to the causes of America's commercial greatness. And here he captured something of the all-conquering spirit of American capitalism. "I cannot better express my thoughts," Tocqueville wrote, "than by saying that Americans put a kind of heroism in their way of doing commerce."[98] They constantly adapted their labors to satisfy their needs and were never hampered by old methods and old attitudes. They lived in "a land of wonders" where everything was in motion and where change was seen as a step forward. Newness was associated with improvement. Americans lived in a "sort of feverish agitation," keeping them above "the common level of humanity." "For an American," Tocqueville wrote, "all of life happens like a game of chance, a time of revolution, a day of battle."[99]

In consequence, America was destined to become a major maritime power. It would, as a matter of course, gain dominance over South America. Inescapably, commercial greatness would soon generate military power. Moreover, America would drag the whole North American continent into its orbit. He saw that the United States would soon break its treaty obligations with Mexico. Its people would "penetrate these uninhabited areas," intent on snatching ownership of the land from its rightful owners. Texas, although still under Mexican rule, was day by day being infiltrated by Americans, imposing their language and way of life. The same was happening wherever the "Anglo-Americans" came into contact with other peoples. "So it must not be believed," Tocqueville concluded, "that it is possible to stop the expansion of the English race of the New World," for such was its "destiny."[100]

Moreover, the mistake has been to imagine that Tocqueville, having completed the second volume of *Democracy in America*, turned his

98. *DA*, 641.
99. *DA*, 643.
100. *DA*, 651.

back for good upon the country that had so contributed to his fame
and renown. This fits in well with the opinion that derides the value
and significance of his journey to America. Nothing could be further
from the truth. Not only did Tocqueville keep in touch with many of
those he had met on his travels across the North American continent,
but, time upon time, he referred to America in his published writings
and parliamentary speeches, always reminding his readers and listen-
ers of what there was to learn from the American experience. More
intriguing still, as time passed by, Tocqueville focused his attention
ever more upon the issues he had raised in the final chapters of volume 1. As the institution of slavery was extended westward, he saw
that it risked securing a new lease of life with fateful consequences
for the Union. He saw a heroic commerce turning into a rapacious
capitalism, led by a breed of men not before seen in the world and
fueled by an unbridled materialism. He saw America needlessly and
dangerously expanding its territory, constantly running the risk of
war with its neighbors on land and sea. He saw a decline in law and
order and in political morals. America, he wrote in 1856, was such
as now to "distress all the friends of democratic liberty and delight
all of its opponents."[101]

Nevertheless, the memories of Tocqueville's visit to America never
lost their power to move him. Writing to Gustave de Beaumont from
Compiègne during the harsh winter of 1855, he reminisced as follows:

> [F]or the last week I have not stopped from going, once a day, for a
> walk of an hour or more in the forest. These enormous trees, seen
> through the snow, remind me of the woods of Tennessee that we
> travelled through, almost 25 years ago, in weather still more severe.[102]
> What was most different in the picture was myself. . . . This little ret-
> rospective review put me back in good humour and, to finish the job
> of cheering me up again, I thought how I had kept to this day the
> same friend with whom I had hunted the parrots of Memphis and

101. See *Tocqueville on America after 1840,* ed. Craiutu and Jennings, 142–308.
102. Tocqueville and Beaumont arrived in Memphis on December 17, 1831,
bound for New Orleans. Because the river was frozen, they could not depart and
spent their time walking and shooting in the woods: see Pierson, *Tocqueville in
America,* 593–99, and Damrosch, *Tocqueville's Discovery,* 149–53.

that the passing of time had only strengthened the ties of trust and of friendship which then existed between us. This thought seemed to me more heartening to reflect upon than all the others.[103]

To imagine that Tocqueville might just as well have stayed at home is simply mistaken.

103. Tocqueville, *Oeuvres complètes*, vol. 8, *Correspondance d'Alexis de Tocqueville et de Gustave de Beaumont* (Paris, 1967) 3:271–72. The same episode is recounted in a letter by Beaumont to his brother Achille, dated December 5, 1831: see Gustave de Beaumont, *Lettres d'Amérique, 1831–32* (Paris, 1973), 203.

5

Alexis de Tocqueville and the Two-Founding Thesis

JAMES W. CEASER

Alexis de Tocqueville was one of the first thinkers in the nineteenth century to challenge the prevailing historical account of the American founding. According to that account, America's polity was established in the period that began with the Revolutionary War and ended with the ratification of the Constitution. The principal leaders, referred to as "founders" or "fathers," were celebrated for creating the political order and decisively shaping the character of America's way of life.[1] Tocqueville, by contrast, presents an account of the founding that identifies not one but two formative moments. For Tocqueville the Puritan–New England tradition was every bit as consequential in constituting America as the founding of 1775–1789. From the Puritan colonies, he wrote, come "the two or three principal ideas that today form the foundations of the social theory of the United States." New England's "civilization"—Tocqueville helped introduce this sense of the term to America—was like one of those "fires kindled on the hilltops

---

1. For an overview of the historiography of the early period, related to the founding, see Lester Cohen, *Revolutionary Histories* (Ithaca, N.Y.: Cornell University Press, 1980). Typical is the widely read history of Timothy Pitkin, *A Political and Civil History of the United States,* published in 1828, where the author begins by promising his readers "a more intimate knowledge and recollection of the difficulties which their political fathers had to overcome," so that they might better appreciate the "great charter of their union, as their best and only security against domestic discord and foreign force" (New Haven, Conn.: Hezekiah Howe and Durrie and Peck, 1828), 1:3.

that, after spreading warmth around them, light the farthest bounds of the horizon with their brightness."[2]

These two interpretations of America's origins are strikingly different. Although one could envision them being brought more closely together, perhaps by refining the meaning of founding, Tocqueville notably made no effort to do so. Without either acknowledging or criticizing the prevailing view, he proceeded simply to sketch his own account of the founding, with the apparent aim of having it replace the existing one. Tocqueville's version, which will be referred to here as the "two-founding thesis," is introduced in an early chapter of *Democracy in America* titled "Of the Point of Departure and Its Importance for the Future of the Anglo-Americans."[3] The chapter at first reads as if it is offering a straightforward historical explanation of how America developed. Yet further analysis clearly shows that something else, something more important, was also at stake: Tocqueville promulgated the two-founding thesis in order to promote a new political foundation for modern liberal democratic government.

Enlightenment thought held that a political foundation should rest on a public doctrine of philosophy, most notably, as in the case of America's Declaration of Independence (1776) and France's Declaration of the Rights of Man (1789), on the theory of natural rights. Foundations based on this kind of appeal to philosophy, Tocqueville thought, endangered the cause of liberty. His alternative was a foundation based on "Customary History."[4] The two-founding thesis presents his version of Customary History crafted specifically for America. By offering this account, Tocqueville was furthering a theoretical project inaugurated by Montesquieu, his chief intellectual mentor, that sought to alter the way in which political philosophy entered into political life.

The argument developed in this chapter requires treating a number of interlocking issues. I begin by identifying the major implications

2. Alexis de Tocqueville, *Democracy in America: Historical-Critical Edition of "De la démocratie en Amérique,"* ed. Eduardo Nolla, trans. James T. Schleifer, 4 vols. (Indianapolis: Liberty Fund, 2010), 52, 53. This edition is hereafter cited as *DA*.

3. This term was coined by Michael Zuckert, *The Natural Rights Republic* (Notre Dame, Ind.: Notre Dame University Press, 1996), 119, 121.

4. This term is derived from J. G. A. Pocock, *The Ancient Constitution and the Feudal Law* (New York: Norton, 1957), 36, 37.

that flow from adopting the two-founding thesis. Following a presentation of the concept of a political foundation, I turn to Montesquieu's development of the idea of Customary History as a rival to the Enlightenment idea of a philosophical foundation of natural rights. Finally, I consider Tocqueville's adaptation of Montesquieu's theory to America before examining some of the questions and problems it poses.

The Theoretical Premises of the Two-Founding Thesis

The two-founding thesis is linked to a number of arguments or conclusions that become evident when considered against the backdrop of the prevailing view of a single founding. Five points are worth mentioning.

First, the idea of two founding moments has the inevitable effect of diminishing the founders' status. The reason is that they are no longer simply *the* founders. To be sure, Tocqueville speaks of the men of 1775–1789 with great admiration. He praises them both for their "patriotism" in coming to the nation's aid at a critical moment and for their "courage" in instructing the public, somewhat against its inclinations, about the best ways for protecting and maintaining freedom.[5]

His comments nevertheless display a certain reserve concerning the magnitude of their accomplishment. Tocqueville ascribes the victory in the Revolutionary War more to America's geographical position "than to the merit of their armies or to the patriotism of their citizens"; he lauds the Constitutional Convention for including "the best minds and most noble characters that had ever appeared *in the New World*"; and he describes the *Federalist* as a "fine book . . . though peculiar to America."[6] These judgments seem to fall short of seeking to create an aura

---

5. *DA,* 247. Tocqueville lauds the character of the founders, who were "remarkable by their enlightenment, more remarkable by their patriotism," and he judges the framework they produced to be "superior to all the state constitutions" (247). His greatest praise of the founders' originality comes in his account of their invention of what we know as federalism: "This constitution . . . rests as a matter of fact on an entirely new theory that must stand out as a great discovery in the political science of today" (252).

6. *DA,* 189, 190 (emphasis added), 193.

of greatness around the founders. Tocqueville never ranks them with the famous lawgivers of antiquity, such as Lycurgus or Numa, which is a comparison that the founders themselves invited.[7] Indeed, Tocqueville never directly refers to them as "founders," reserving that term for New England's leaders ("first founders").[8]

Second, the two-founding thesis fits with Tocqueville's cultural or sociological approach that considers "mores," which derive mostly from inherited dispositions and customs, to be more important in the formation of a regime than are constitutional forms and arrangements.[9] This approach also has the effect of reducing the founders' status by assigning more weight to tradition—in this case, to the practices deriving from the New England colonies—than to the Constitution. Tocqueville directly addresses his readers to tell them that they will "find in the present chapter [Of the Point of Departure] the germ [*germe*] of what must follow and the key to nearly the whole work."[10] The two-founding thesis thus challenges an implicit premise of the standard historical account that divides American history into the colonial and the current eras, where the former is relegated to being a kind of prehistory. For Tocqueville, by contrast, colonial history is every bit as important as what has occurred since the Revolution. His presentation likewise directs attention away from the founders' handiwork—the Constitution—to the practices within the states: "There can be no doubt that the great political principles that govern American society today arose and developed in the state. So to have the key to all the rest, the state must be understood."[11]

Third, and following directly from the last point, the two-founding thesis diminishes the importance of the doctrine of natural rights, what the *Federalist* refers to as the "transcendent law of nature and

---

7. *Federalist* No. 38.

8. *DA*, 692.

9. *DA*, 499. "I am persuaded that the most fortunate situation and the best laws cannot maintain a constitution in spite of mores, while the latter still turn to good account the most unfavorable positions and the worst laws" (499).

10. *DA*, 49. I include the term *germe*, translated variously as "germ," "seed," or "kernel," because of its importance in other accounts of Customary History.

11. *DA*, 99.

nature's god."[12] This doctrine was the theoretical basis that the founders adopted to justify the Revolution and to supply the criteria for the fundamental ends of legitimate government. In Tocqueville's account, the preexisting mores, not this theoretical foundation, are the key to the development of republican government in America.

Fourth, the two-founding thesis depreciates the understanding of founding as a conscious act of "making," or construction, that draws on models conceived by reason. "Making" according to reason best expresses what was usually meant in the eighteenth century by the term "natural," as in the expression of establishing a government in accord with laws of nature. Tocqueville introduced another understanding of the meaning of natural; it is based on the notion of organic development, as in his account of the growth of a nation: "Peoples always feel the effects of their origins. The circumstances that accompanied their birth and were useful to their development influence all the rest of their course"; these origins are the "first cause" of a people's "prejudices, habits [and] dominant passions," and comprise a "national character" that continues to evolve partly on its own.[13]

Present-day political theorists often stress the connection between the idea of organic development and reactionary thought, as found in such writers as Joseph de Maistre, who mistrusted the use of science or reason in political affairs.[14] But as Tocqueville's case makes clear, this connection does not hold across the board. There were many organic liberals who were fully open to reason. Tocqueville, in fact, was renowned for his advocacy of a "new political science" that was meant to "instruct democracy" and "substitute little by little the science of public affairs for its inexperience."[15] What is noteworthy about this science, however, is that it subjects the role of rationalism in public life to critical inquiry. This inquiry goes to the very bottom, asking whether the cause of liberty is best promoted by a public understanding of founding as a wholesale remaking on the basis of a theoretical model.

12. *The Federalist* No. 43.

13. *DA,* 46.

14. *DA,* 16.

15. For one of the early treatments of these thinkers, see Isaiah Berlin, *Against the Current,* ed. Henry Hardy and Roger Hausheer (New York: Viking, 1980), chap. 1.

Whatever Tocqueville's answer to this scientific question, his two-founding version of American history clearly removes the period of 1775 to 1787 from consideration as an example of a full-blown rationalist founding. He presents this long decade more as a reform than a founding: "The form of the federal government in the United States appeared last; it was only a modification of the republic, a summary of political principles spread throughout the entire society before the federal government existed, and subsisting there independently of it."[16]

Fifth and finally, the two-founding thesis seems to have been calculated to influence what Tocqueville calls people's "mental habits," which includes the epistemological premises that people use to process reality. A nation's mental habits are influenced by how citizens conceive of their origins. In the measure that Americans embraced the two-founding thesis, they would abandon thinking primarily in terms of abstract models of politics and would concentrate somewhat more on the content of their tradition, exploring the question "Who are we?" This approach fits well with Tocqueville's understanding of how best to introduce standards of right or good into society, including aspects of "natural right," that is, the idea that certain things are just by nature and accessible to human reason. The idea of natural right, Tocqueville thought, is best made palpable not through promulgating public philosophical doctrines, which can lead to extremes and promote utopian notions, but by being presented inside of analysis of concrete historical experience. The task of instructing people about natural right is best undertaken by the analytical historian (like Tocqueville), who sifts through a tradition, indicates the practices of wrong and right, and offers corrections to specific aspects of the national character.

Tocqueville's Intention

These five points taken together add up to what looks to be a full theoretical position on the character of founding. But did Tocqueville intend to set forth a general theory, or is what looks like one just a by-product of his effort to recount America's historical origins? There

16. *DA*, 98.

are certainly grounds for favoring the last position. *Democracy in America,* after all, does not proceed in the manner of a theoretical treatise that sets out different possible conceptions of origins and then weighs their respective merits. Furthermore, Tocqueville makes clear his interest in historical explanation, announcing that one of the reasons for writing the book is to understand the rise of the democratic revolution by studying the American case. At the same time, however, it must not be forgotten that Tocqueville presents *Democracy in America* first and foremost as a work of political science intended to promote free government. The question therefore becomes whether, in the event that these two aims diverge, Tocqueville would somehow have "adjusted" his historical explanations to promote an objective commanded by political science.

Tocqueville unfortunately never directly commented on this issue, either in his published works or in his notes. A judgment can accordingly only be reached by inference. In an important article published two decades ago, Thomas West identified what he called a major "flaw" in *Democracy in America*: its omission of any mention of the doctrine of natural rights in the context of the founding. Tocqueville, according to West, failed to note the decisive fact that "in our founding we Americans understood ourselves to be dedicated to the truth that all men are created equal, and that this dedication, and this truth, are what justified the break with Britain and made us a nation."[17] Indeed, as West points out, Tocqueville never so much as mentions America's seminal document, the Declaration of Independence.

Setting aside for the moment the question of whether this omission was a "flaw," West's observation is striking. Classic accounts of America written in a comparative perspective have often characterized the

17. Thomas West, "Misunderstanding the American Founding," in *Interpreting Tocqueville's "Democracy in America,"* ed. Ken Masugi (Lanham, Md.: Rowman & Littlefield, 1991), 155–77. Although careful to point out that Tocqueville eloquently defends the importance of individual rights, West notes that he does not do so by reference to the standard of natural rights. One of Tocqueville's longest passages on individual rights occurs in a subsection of volume 1, chapter 6, and is titled "Of the Idea of Rights in the United States" (389–93). Parts of this section are highly reminiscent of John Locke's treatment of teaching the idea of rights in *Some Thoughts concerning Education,* especially in the references to children.

United States as a "propositional" or a "creedal" nation, referring to Americans' core belief in rights and equality grounded in the laws of nature. G. K. Chesterton, one of the first to develop this theme, argued that Americans were bound by the "creed...set forth with dogmatic and even theological lucidity in the Declaration of Independence."[18] Gunnar Myrdal followed in the same path in *The American Dilemma,* in which he speaks of American history as "the gradual realization of the American Creed." Finally, Samuel Huntington, whose book *Who Are We?* restates Tocqueville's two-founding thesis, felt obliged to contrast his position with what he acknowledged is a widely held "creedal" understanding of the American polity, a position to which he himself had previously subscribed in an earlier work.

If Tocqueville intended *Democracy in America* to provide a comprehensive historical account of America's origins, it is fair to ask how a thinker of his rank could have missed so fundamental a point. Was his omission of the Declaration an oversight of some kind—an instance of Homer nodding—or must it be explained as a deliberate act undertaken with a "strategic" purpose in mind? Published scholarship on Tocqueville only touches on this question.[19] Turning for help to historians, two possible responses can be drawn. One, relying on arguments of the "republican" school of historiography, might almost excuse Tocqueville's oversight on the grounds that—contrary to what most have long thought—the doctrine of natural rights was not very significant at the time of the founding; indeed, one historian, John Philip Reid, has gone so far as to entitle an article "The Irrelevance of the Declaration of Independence."[20] Only with Abraham Lincoln and the rise of the Republican

18. G. K. Chesterton, *What I Saw in America* (London: Hodder and Stoughton, 1922), 7.

19. In addition to West, "Misunderstanding," see Paul Rahe, *Soft Despotism, Democracy's Drift: Montesquieu, Rousseau, Tocqueville, and the Modern Prospect* (New Haven, Conn.: Yale University Press, 2009).

20. John Phillip Reid, "The Irrelevance of the Declaration," in *Law in the American Revolution and the Revolution in the Law,* ed. Hendrik Hartog (New York: New York University Press, 1981), 46–89. Reid's view is that "natural law principles played a relatively minor role...in motivating Americans to support the Whig cause" (48). For a summary of the republican school's position, see Alan Gibson, *Interpreting the Founding* (Lawrence: University Press of Kansas, 2006),

Party in the 1850s, this argument continues, did the foundation of natural rights become central to American political life, after which historians made the mistake of reading its importance back into the founding era.

The other response, based on the views of many recent historians, makes it inconceivable that Tocqueville could have overlooked the doctrine of natural rights. Perhaps, say these historians, the doctrine was not quite as central as older historians, such as Carl Becker, claimed. But it was still very important.[21] No one of competence could have overlooked it. In addition, the doctrine of natural rights had reemerged as a major topic of debate in the 1820s, just before Tocqueville arrived in America, in conflicts about property rights and labor issues.[22] In addition, the Declaration had become even more prominent as a result of the extensive commemorations of its fiftieth anniversary in 1826, which coincided with Thomas Jefferson's death. Taking all these facts into account, Tocqueville's omission of any reference to natural right must have been intentional; something besides pure history was going on in his developmental account in *Democracy in America*.

Other considerations lend further support to this position. From an examination of Tocqueville's correspondence from the period of his visit, it is clear that he was acutely aware of the Declaration and of its importance. In one letter, written to his friend Ernest de Chabrol,

------

22–36, and Thomas Pangle, *The Spirit of Modern Republicanism* (Chicago: University of Chicago Press, 1988).

21. See Daniel Rodgers, "Republicanism: The Career of a Concept," *Journal of American History* 79, no. 1 (1992): 11–38, and Gibson, *Interpreting the Founding*. Carl Becker's *The Declaration of Independence* (New York: Harcourt Brace, 1922) was for many years considered the major work in this area. It stressed the centrality of the ideas of the Declaration, in particular the importance of the natural rights doctrine.

22. Daniel Rodgers develops this point in his survey of discourse on political concepts in early America in *Contested Truths* (Cambridge, Mass.: Harvard University Press, 1987). Rodgers explains (69–71) that natural right discourse, having served in a perfunctory way in the early decades of the century, had been revived by the late 1820s, not only because of the celebrations attached to the fiftieth anniversary of the Declaration in 1826, but also because elements of the Jacksonian movement had begun to employ natural rights claims in political debates relating to economic issues.

Tocqueville movingly describes a July 4 celebration that he attended in Albany at which the Declaration of Independence was read in full. The ceremony made a deep impression on him: "[T]here was in all of this something deeply felt and truly great."[23] Could Tocqueville have forgotten this "great" moment when he wrote *Democracy in America* a few years later? Even more compelling is the fact that Tocqueville was a close reader of Jefferson's writings. *Democracy in America* includes more citations to Jefferson than to any other source. Tocqueville's judgment of the importance of Jefferson's thought speaks for itself: "I consider him the most powerful apostle democracy has ever had."[24] As much as anyone else, Tocqueville knew the central place that Jefferson gave to the foundation of natural rights as an "expression of the American mind."[25] Can his omission, then, have been anything other than deliberate?

Yet if one is to charge Tocqueville with the crime of being selective in his historical account, it is necessary to supply a motive. Tocqueville, it may be surmised, sought to make America's success appear less dependent on a foundation of abstract natural right than most claimed, because of the dangerous effects of "public philosophy." He developed his objections to philosophical foundations in his book *The Old Regime and the Revolution*, when discussing the disastrous role that intellectuals played in preparing the way for the French Revolution. "The men of

23. Tocquevillle to Ernest de Chabrol, July 16, 1831, in *Lettres choisies, souvenirs*, ed. Françoise Mélonio and Laurence Guellec (Paris: Gallimard, 2003), 205–6. In the letter, Tocqueville commented that the reading of the Declaration was "really a fine spectacle.... [I]t seemed that an electric current made the hearts [of the audience] vibrate." For further discussion of this event, see George Wilson Pierson, *Tocqueville in America* (Baltimore: Johns Hopkins University Press, 1996), 179–84, and Rahe, *Soft Despotism*, 195–96.

24. *DA*, 426. See also Tocqueville's characterization of Jefferson as "the greatest democrat who has yet emerged from within the American democracy" (*DA*, 323). In addition, there are whole passages of *Democracy in America*, especially in the chapter "Some Considerations on ... The Three Races That Inhabit the Territory of the United States," in which Jefferson's analysis lies in the background, though it is not explicitly cited.

25. Jefferson to Richard Henry Lee, May 8, 1825, in *The Writings of Thomas Jefferson*, ed. Andrew Lipscomb and Albert Ellery Bergh (Washington, D.C.: Thomas Jefferson Memorial Association, 1903), 16:118.

letters," as he called them, all began their thought from the same "point of departure": "they all think that it would be good to substitute basic and simple principles, derived from reason and natural law, for the complicated and traditional customs which ruled the society of their time."[26] According to Tocqueville, theorizing in this way leads to excess and encourages mental habits that abstract and simplify, when what is needed to promote liberty are habits that recognize particularities and complexity. Tocqueville expressed the same concern about "general ideas in political matters" in *Democracy in America,* though without explicitly mentioning natural rights doctrine.[27]

The Concept of Political Foundation

The contemporary term "political foundation" is not one that Tocqueville used, but his analysis of what transforms a collection of discrete individuals into a political community treats the same concept. A community, by Tocqueville's account, only comes into being where certain ideas are shared: "without common ideas, there is no common action, and, without common action, there are still men, but not a social body."[28] Scattered throughout his work are examples of the kinds of ideas that perform this function. Three types stand out.

First, in a well-known passage on patriotism, Tocqueville identifies customary thinking as the traditional source of attachment to the nation. Whereas the modern concept of patriotism stresses the individual's rational calculation of a stake in the community, the older form rested on an "instinctive love" of country. This mode of attachment, which once dominated in Europe, was based on what Tocqueville described as "a taste for ancient customs, with respect for ancestors and the memory of the past." Traditional patriotism, he emphasized, had nothing philosophical about it. Neither was it essentially religious,

26. Tocqueville, *The Old Regime and the Revolution,* trans. Alan S. Kahan (Chicago: University of Chicago Press, 1998), 196.
27. *DA,* 737.
28. *DA,* 713. He goes on: "for society to exist...all the minds of the citizens must always be brought and held together by some principal ideas" (737).

though in some nations custom contained elements of Christianity. Rather, traditional patriotism was "itself a kind of religion, it does not reason, it believes; it feels; it acts."[29]

Second, Tocqueville identified a genuinely religious basis of solidarity. The prime example he cites was found in the original New England communities. These were formed by their devotion to "*an idea*" (his emphasis) to fulfill a sacred mission.[30] There was nothing customary in this idea, which called for a clear and active commitment of ongoing faith. Tocqueville also identified another dimension of Christian thought: the doctrine of providence, which could contribute to forming a common belief in a society guided by God's benevolent hand.

Third, Tocqueville spoke of plans to make philosophical doctrines the basis of community. He noted the efforts by intellectuals in the eighteenth century to introduce ideas of natural law as the main political foundation of the new order, and he identified in his own time another philosophical idea, pantheism, that combined the laws of the natural physical processes with a vague progressive historical movement. These instances illustrate the central role that modern thinkers ascribed to philosophical doctrines in politics, which would become active as a political force in the name of philosophy (or science) and supply the bond to hold modern societies together. Philosophy also held out the hope of providing an impartial and objective standard of political right that might eventually supersede the disparate standards deriving from particular histories, partisan views of justice, or different religious beliefs.

America's founders were deeply influenced by the general philosophical ideas of the eighteenth century, even though, as men of great practical experience, most had tempered expectations about how far or how quickly this project could succeed in the world at large. Still, the major leaders were fully conscious of the "revolutionary" step they were

---

29. *DA*, 385. In another passage, Tocqueville expresses some doubts about whether the modern theoretical basis of solidarity can ever work entirely: "What maintains a great number of people under the same government is much less the reasoned will to remain united than the instinctive and in a way involuntary accord that results from similarity of sentiments and resemblance of opinions" (598).

30. *DA*, 54.

taking by offering this new ground of political solidarity. John Adams, for example, recorded a seminal debate in the Continental Congress in 1774, where the issue in question was the "*foundation* of right" to be used to justify American policy: "We very deliberately considered and debated...whether we should recur to the law of nature" along with the historical foundations of the tradition, such as the "common law" and "the charters" or "the rights of British subjects."[31] Americans were the first to bring a theoretical doctrine down from the tracts of philosophy and insert it into the city. The claim that modern polities rest on theoretical doctrines later received one of its clearest statements from Abraham Lincoln: "No policy that does not rest upon some philosophical public opinion can be permanently maintained."[32]

"Political foundation" is the term used here to designate the central idea (or set of ideas) that is proposed to supply the commonality of a political community, assuming that there is some such core idea. A foundation, as noted in the last section, refers to a general idea, whether explicit or implicit, of right or good, and ultimately to the source or authority that sanctions that idea. By this account, there are many specific political foundations, nearly as many as there are different communities (nearly, because some communities may adopt virtually the same foundation as others, as was the case, for example, in various Communist regimes). For purposes of analysis, foundations can best be categorized on the basis of their respective sources for the understanding of right. Reorganizing Tocqueville's list, these sources may be located in religion, nature, and History (capitalized here to distinguish it from ordinary narrative accounts). In the case of religion, God or scripture fixes a standard of right, or shows where history is going; in the case of nature, right is found in a permanent or eternal standard discovered by philosophical (or scientific) investigation; in the case of History, right is known from something that occurs in time, whether from what is old or ancestral (Customary History) or from

31. *The Works of John Adams* (Boston: Little, Brown, 1850), 2:371 (emphasis added).

32. Abraham Lincoln, speech at New Haven, March 6, 1860, in Abraham Lincoln, *Complete Works of Abraham Lincoln*, ed. John G. Nicolay and John Hay (New York: Century, 1894), 2:619.

knowledge of where history is going (Philosophy of History). These sources are parallel to categories used in philosophy or theology, but as political foundations they have special reference to ideas that are capable of moving large numbers of people and supplying the solidarity for what Tocqueville called a "social body."

The Theory of Customary History

With the help of the concept of political foundations, the theoretical project embedded in Tocqueville's two-founding thesis can now be more fully described. Tocqueville sought to replace the theoretical foundation preferred by modern philosophers with a foundation in Customary History. The revival of this historical approach, associated today most often with David Hume, Edmund Burke, and François Guizot, originated with Montesquieu, and it is in his thought that the character of this project comes most clearly to sight.[33]

The fact that Customary History had to be revived in the modern era meant that its properties had to change. In a world already altered by the introduction of philosophy, it could not assume the form of the naive and unconscious "instinctive patriotism" that Tocqueville described. Customary History required something new and more rational. For one thing, its premises needed to be elaborated theoretically, if not for a general audience, then at least for those who would be engaged in the project of bringing it back. For another, the modern mind could no longer readily accept legend and fable. Customary History had to

33. The interpretation that follows develops one aspect of Montesquieu's thought, not the whole of it. More than perhaps any other political theorist, Montesquieu articulated his thought in different "parts," the harmony among which has long been a subject of debate. For example, certain chapters of the work indicate that Montesquieu also favored a public doctrine of natural law. He should perhaps be seen as providing a number of alternative foundations, the choice (or mixing) among which must be at the discretion of the legislator, as context would dictate. For arguments on the importance of history as a standard along with or in place of natural law, see James Stoner, *Common Law and Liberal Theory* (Lawrence: University Press of Kansas, 1992), 154, and Pierre Manent, *The City of Man* (Princeton, N.J.: Princeton University Press, 1998), passim.

appear to meet the standard of genuine history, in Edward Gibbon's sense of "apply[ing] the science of philosophy to the study of facts."[34]

Montesquieu began the task of creating modern Customary History in his famous chapter on the English constitution, the longest in *The Spirit of the Laws* (11.6).[35] The English constitution, which had political liberty as "its direct end," was Montesquieu's preferred regime for his time (11.5). Most of the chapter is taken up with a description of the constitution's animating structural principle of the separation of powers. Near the end, however, Montesquieu abruptly shifts focus and turns to the question of the origins of this constitution. From Tacitus's work on "the mores of the Germans," Montesquieu observes, it becomes clear that "it is from them [the Germans] that the English took their idea of political government. This beautiful system was founded in the woods" (11.6).

The discovery of the origin of modern liberty in the "forests of Germany" was the basis of the celebrated Gothic (or barbarian) thesis, which was subsequently embraced in one form or another by so many thinkers, including Gibbon, Guizot, and Tocqueville (30.18). For Montesquieu, it was the Goths, those "valiant people," who taught men the worth of liberty (17.5). The Gothic thesis remained a major theme of historiography until the world wars of the twentieth century, when the German forests lost much of their luster along with their foliage. Most of the American historians who established the professional discipline of history in the latter part of the nineteenth century embraced this thesis.[36]

The challenge that the Gothic thesis posed for modern political philosophy could not have been greater. Instead of locating liberty in the philosophical abstraction of the state of nature, Montesquieu traced

34. Edward Gibbon, *The Decline and Fall of the Roman Empire*, ed. Hans-Friedrich Mueller (New York: Modern Library, 1995), 167.

35. Because readers use different editions of *The Spirit of the Laws*, references here are to book and chapter number. The edition used is Montesquieu, *The Spirit of the Laws*, trans. Anne M. Cohler, Basia Carolyn Miller, and Harold Samuel Stone (Cambridge: Cambridge University Press, 1989).

36. For an account of "Gothic history" and its use in America, see Trevor Colbourn, *The Lamp of Experience* (Chapel Hill: University of North Carolina Press, 1965), passim.

it back to "our ancestors" in their ancient historical condition. What a remarkable slight to philosophy, and, for that matter, to theology! According to Montesquieu, the principles of liberty did not originate with philosophy or, indeed, with rationalist thought of any kind. Liberty derived from the mores of a barbarian people who originally knew neither philosophy nor Christianity. Montesquieu here also initiated a new method for investigating political right: not deductive or geometric reasoning from abstract premises, but locating an origin or "germ" of the phenomenon and observing its subsequent development. The mental habits encouraged by this approach also differ from those that flow from rationalist philosophy. Individuals develop a disposition to look to the past with appreciation, rather than to dismiss everything that is old as a "prejudice." With this explanation, the modern idea of Customary History was born.

Following his treatment of the English constitution, Montesquieu turns in the next chapter to the "monarchies we are acquainted with," meaning the earlier monarchies found on the Continent (11.7). This form of government differs slightly from the English constitution in that it had honor or glory rather than liberty as its direct end—a fact that did not, however, make it less able to secure liberty. It is result, not intention, that matters, and in the world of politics, the two often differ. These older monarchies also derived from the German forests, making them cousins of the English regime, and Montesquieu here takes the occasion to develop further the Gothic thesis by tracing their development (11.8). Originally, the German tribes were each able to assemble in pure republican fashion, in the manner that Tacitus recounted. But after they conquered much of Europe, the process of popular consultation could only continue by developing a system of representation. In addition, having initially enslaved those whom they conquered, which created ranks in society, the rulers eventually took steps to grant certain civil liberties to all.

At the end of this process, the old-style European monarchy emerged—the "gothic government among us"—with its institutions of representation, its different orders, and its complex balances. Montesquieu pronounces his judgment on this system: "I do not believe there has ever been on earth a government so well tempered." He concludes the chapter: "[I]t is remarkable that the corruption of the government of a conquering people formed the best kind of government that men could imagine" (11.8).

It is unclear whether Montesquieu is asserting that the Gothic monarchy is the best regime simply, that is, forever, or whether it was the best that men could imagine until that time. No matter. If the main question of political theory is the character of the best regime, Montesquieu in this brief chapter—indeed, in three sentences—provides his response to classical political philosophy. The contrast is striking, even more in the method recommended for investigating how to determine the best regime than in the exact character of that regime itself. For the classics, the best regime is discovered by reason and has the form of an eternal model. For Montesquieu, the best regime is a gift of historical accident that is tied to a particular context, not a product of something intentionally constructed by thought. The best regime is a product of unconscious development inside of actual history, in this case even of a falling away (a "corruption") from an original form. Before the best regime came to be, it could not have been known.

This difference accounts for the otherwise curious placement of the next chapter (11.9), titled "Aristotle's Manner of Thinking." Montesquieu faults Aristotle for the incompleteness of his treatment of the different kinds of monarchy, one form of which, absolute kingship of the best person, arguably represents Aristotle's conception of the best regime. Montesquieu's deepest criticism of Aristotle is not that he erred in constructing the best regime that reason could discern but that he held that reason had the capacity to construct the best regime in the first place. The "ancients"—this would include Plato—"who did not know about the distribution of powers in the government by one, could not form a just idea of monarchy." They could not form this idea, because monarchy in its best form had not yet come into being. The classics' "manner of thinking" overestimated what pure theory can know.

In Montesquieu's presentation of Customary History—I will refer to it now as his doctrine—reason plays a role in political life, but its scope is limited in comparison to what modern political philosophy envisaged. (In comparison to classical political philosophy, Montesquieu, as just noted, also offers a more modest view of what theorizing about politics can discover—although classical political philosophy, unlike its modern counterpart, stops short of embracing the project of trying to actualize the best regime.) Under Montesquieu's doctrine, political philosophy would enter into political life in a new way, abjuring the modern approach of openly proclaiming the authority of philosophical doctrines and of encouraging people to think of starting society anew. Political philosophy should instead be introduced more indirectly. It should be inserted into society by thinkers who engage in concrete political analysis and by a certain kind of historian. These historians will look for the good in what has come to be, extracting and refining ideas of right in the process of their analysis. The good, contained in part in the original germ, carries with it a measure of authority deriving from the disposition, perhaps created or perhaps innate, to respect the original, the old, and one's own. Cultivating and encouraging the "historical sense," as distinct from the "metaphysical sense," in turn promotes the weight of the customary within society.[37] Finally, historically minded thinkers, unlike Enlightenment theorists, will not try to usurp the role of political actors, but will appear to defer to them, serving as their counselors. Political philosophy will encourage moderation.

Underlying this view of history is a premise for which Montesquieu perhaps never fully accounted. It is the idea that what unfolds or develops on its own, without imposition by vast rational plans, tends to work out well (19.5,6). This process of unfolding is not teleological, in the sense of development toward a single known end (and ultimately toward a perfect and universal model). It is "organic" or "natural," in a sense reminiscent of biological beings that follow a slow and not perfectly defined process of growth, with each particular being having its own "genius," or "spirit." Montesquieu's insertion of this premise into Customary History did as much as anything else to define and shape the alternative to the Enlightenment concept of rationality within modern political thought.

Montesquieu helped invent the idea of what we today call "tradition," referring to that which grows insensibly and which is worthy of respect. Tradition is the antidote to the modern philosophic animus against the

37. The term "historical sense" comes from the German historian Friedrich Carl von Savigny, *Vom Beruf unserer Zeit für Gesetzgebung und Rechtswissenschaft* (Hildesheim: Georg Olms Verlagsbuchhandlung, 1967), 5.

past. A tradition is presented as something already there, as a natural fact that all recognize; but it may in fact be something that the artful poet or historian must find and articulate. Authors who discover a tradition would of course be reluctant to announce their invention, because a claim of originality would undermine the purpose of the project. Montesquieu presents the Gothic thesis as the real, that is, the factually historical, path of evolution in Europe, a proposition he labors to prove in the second half of *The Spirit of the Laws* by detailing the development of European constitutions and jurisprudence. (Tocqueville proceeds in a similar manner, claiming no act of invention in articulating the Puritan tradition.) Still, it would be hard for scholars today to acknowledge the Gothic thesis as fully historical. There seems to be more than a touch of artifice in Montesquieu's discovery of it as "our" tradition.

Customary History envisages a new way of introducing natural right into the political world. Right is brought in piecemeal and judged in specific contexts, because these can be examined in the unfolding of history. As practices enter history, the "historian" (Montesquieu) selects them and pronounces on their worth. This approach is the forerunner of Burke's concept of "prescription," where the historian modestly judges what has proven its merit, calling on history to serve as the lead witness. Montesquieu's wish, by his own account, was to promote "moderation," which he praises as a great virtue (29.1). Moderation is arguably the best emulator of prudence, the classical political virtue par excellence. But moderation is not prudence, which on occasion demands boldness and immoderation. This consideration prompts one to ask whether Montesquieu's doctrine represents the best way to introduce right in the political world, or the best way to do so now, even with its limitations, in an era in which all viable positions must be offered as doctrines, even one as seemingly antidoctrinal as Customary History. Prudence no longer has the resources it once had to stand on its own, but it needs the backing of a doctrine to provide the space within which it can operate.

Classical political philosophy was modest in its political aims, urging great caution in the political application of philosophy. It was maintained that philosophy should never be introduced in an unmediated fashion as public doctrine or foundation. The limited role that political philosophy prescribed for itself was for the purpose, first, of promoting the political good, because philosophical teachings about right were too complicated to be made into doctrines, and, second, of protecting philosophy itself, because philosophy might be endangered by becoming directly embroiled as a claimant to authority. By Montesquieu's day, however, the classical approach was effectively foreclosed, in large part because of a new path that philosophy had chosen. Philosophy was now engaged in a project of wholesale reconstruction of the political world. Whatever the reasons or motives for this new disposition—whether to rescue the world from theology, to serve the interests of the many rather than the few, to construct a new defense for free inquiry, or to make use of philosophy's new powers of control (perhaps for the sheer pride of exercising power)—the consequence, for Montesquieu, was not in doubt. Philosophy had become unfriendly to the cause of political liberty and was serving as chief supporter of a new absolutism known as "enlightened despotism."

Customary History was a counterdoctrine to modern philosophy. It was believed that in a contest with the philosophic idea of nature, tradition would be more than able to hold its own. Customary History also offered some powerful new theoretical arguments. It emphasized the fact—making it perhaps more of a fact than it was—of an existent substance: the "spirit" of a nation or a civilization. The staying power of this "spirit," above all its resistance to being altered or engineered, encouraged a kind of moderation. Respecting what has developed, correcting or reforming its ways without attempting to begin anew, is not only the milder and wiser policy but also the one in accord with how things are. It is "realistic." Montesquieu answers Machiavellian (and philosophical) realism by a realism of his own making. Modern philosophy overestimated the plasticity of political matter and thus exaggerated philosophy's capacity to shape political life. It was "utopian."

On a theoretical plane, the doctrine of Customary History introduced a new and rival understanding of nature. What is natural is what is unique to each being, with a "being" in politics now referring not only to an individual person, but also—and especially—to collectivities, such as nations and civilizations. Each unit lives and unfolds on its own in interaction with an environment. Each nation develops its own "general spirit" (19.4), or what Tocqueville called a "national character." This view of the natural contrasted with the most common view of modern philosophy, where the natural meant the human discovery or construction of laws that account for the movement and properties of the things around us. Customary History also promised great appeal as a rival political doctrine, because people have generally displayed a strong inclination to look back to the past with veneration.

Two final observations may be offered about Montesquieu's doctrine. The first is that "tradition" is, of course, a general idea or an abstraction. There are only particular traditions—unless there would develop a universal tradition that applied to the whole world, which is the basis for Hegel's concept of "spirit." While Montesquieu counsels respect for tradition as such, he shows along the way that there are many cases in which a prevailing tradition has little to recommend it. In such instances, a full-scale attempt at renewal might not be unreasonable, even if the chances that it will occur are unlikely and the chances that it will succeed are less likely still. For the sake of his doctrine, however, he does not take his general bearings from these cases, but he presents the normal course of development as tending to work in a salutary direction. This approach serves to bolster moderation and to dampen the impulse to remodel societies.

Second, although Montesquieu adopts a rather "traditional" stance in politics, it does not follow that he held to a traditional view of philosophy. He opposed one doctrine (that philosophy should direct and control politics by the introduction of theoretical models) with another (that Customary History should be society's point of departure). His doctrine was a philosophical innovation that was as bold, and as much of a construction, as anything that modern philosophy had ever attempted; or, as he obliquely acknowledged, "And I too am a painter" (preface).

Montesquieu's political goal was to foster a disposition to moderation, which in his age required a new theoretical doctrine. No act of theoretical intervention, he taught, is ever without unforeseen consequences. This law of unforeseen consequences would obviously apply to his own doctrine. Whatever the risks involved, Montesquieu must have concluded that they were worth running, given the destructive consequences of prevailing theoretical views. It remains an open question whether the project he launched ultimately produced the moderation that he hoped for.

Tocqueville's Application of Customary History to America

Tocqueville cited three thinkers—Blaise Pascal, Montesquieu, and Jean-Jacques Rousseau—who were most influential for him while writing *Democracy in America*, of whom Montesquieu seems to have been the most important.[38] Tocqueville continued Montesquieu's theoretical project, though with major innovations, by fashioning a Customary History for America. Insofar as he intended America as a model for the modern world, akin to Montesquieu's presentation of England in the previous century, his account was also meant to offer instruction for how to establish and maintain liberal democratic government. Europeans, of course, would have a different Customary History from Americans, but the example of the American case, as Tocqueville presented it, might provide a template for how Europeans could treat their own past.

It is reasonable to ask why Tocqueville chose to anchor his Customary History in Puritan New England rather than in some other tradition in America. Other options were open. New England, in fact, was not the first English colony—Virginia was—but Tocqueville quickly dismissed the southern tradition, with its slave regime, from the center of the America he wanted to discuss. *Democracy in America* was, above all, a book meant "to instruct democracy."[39] Tocqueville might also have chosen the same Customary History as Montesquieu, tracing American liberty back to the Goths. Strange as it sounds, many Americans before Tocqueville (including, for a time, Jefferson) adopted this approach, and in a development that would certainly have surprised Tocqueville, the Gothic thesis enjoyed a huge revival among American intellectuals

---

38. In a letter to his friend Louis de Kergorlay, November 10, 1836, Tocqueville spoke of the three thinkers who influenced him most ("the three men with whom I live a bit every day"): Pascal, Montesquieu, and Rousseau, in *Oeuvres complètes*, ed. André Jardin and Jean-Alain Lesourd (Paris: Gallimard, 1977), 13:418. Scholars have disputed the degree of influence among the three, but I follow Raymond Aron and Jean Claude Lamberti in assigning the prize to Montesquieu.

39. *DA*, 16. Virginia helped to form the general mores of a romantic and more aristocratic slave nation in the South. Although the book's central theme is democracy, Tocqueville provides extensive treatment of the South's national character.

following his visit. For his part, Tocqueville subscribed to this thesis, explicitly at least, only for Europe. He referred to Tacitus and the "political institutions of our fathers, the Teutons," although he hinted that these ideas, which may well have constituted the "fertile seed (*germe*) of free institutions [that] had already entered deeply into English habits," helped to form the colonists' idea of liberty.[40] But Tocqueville went no further along these lines, thinking it unlikely that those who left the Old World for the New would be interested in connecting themselves to the forests of Germany.[41] To be effective in the modern age, Tocqueville argued, Customary History could not be fanciful or mythic. It had to appear as fully rational. This possibility could be realized in America, indeed only in America, because its history was visible from the beginning. It is the "only country...where it has been possible to clarify the influence that the point of departure exercised on the future of States."[42] Tocqueville could rely on documents and known sources, avoiding the manifold stories and inventions that opened the Gothic thesis to serious questions.

Most of the historians whom Tocqueville met in America were from New England, and the greater part of historical work in America at that time concentrated on that region.[43] Locating the essential point of departure in New England thus had the advantage of being accurate, or at least plausible, on historical grounds: "The principles of New England first spread into neighboring states; then, one by one, they reached the most distant states and finished...by penetrating the

---

40. *DA*, 532, 49–50.

41. The only connection Tocqueville makes between America and the Goths is between not the Goths and the European settlers but between the Goths and the Indians. Tocqueville speaks of the "similarity that exists between the political institutions of our fathers, the Teutons, and those of the wandering tribes of North America, between the customs recounted by Tacitus and those that I was sometimes able to witness" (532).

42. *DA*, 47.

43. His is the first fully rational Customary History. As for other options—for example, treating Pennsylvania as the most influential colony (as George Bancroft would shortly do)—Tocqueville either did not know enough about these possibilities or found the arguments unconvincing. The greater part of historical work in America at that time concentrated on New England.

entire confederation."[44] But historical considerations aside, Tocqueville found in New England the kernel of the principles of right needed to sustain modern democracy. New England history contained three fundamental components of free government and liberty: self-regulating individuals, political liberty (civic participation), and, after a time, private rights.

Developing self-regulating individuals depended on sound mores, which Tocqueville believed were best cultivated by religion. New England was prized for combining *"the spirit of religion* and *the spirit of liberty."*[45] Religion was rejected in modern philosophical doctrines of right. It was also absent in Gothic Customary History, which is another reason why Tocqueville found New England to be a more attractive point of departure than the forests of Germany. Tocqueville modified Montesquieu's account by substituting the Puritans for the Goths and by welcoming religion into the equation.[46] New England demonstrated the reciprocal and reinforcing relationship between Christianity and democracy. To be sure, the original Puritan theocratic community had to undergo profound change before it could become compatible with modern liberty. Its "tyrannical" excesses—laws that entered into the realm of conscience and that punished all forms of allegedly immoral behavior—had to be purged. Tocqueville intrudes himself into the narrative by declaiming against "such errors that undoubtedly shame the human spirit."[47] Like Montesquieu, Tocqueville elected to introduce his natural right teachings piecemeal, inside a historical account, rather than to offer a sweeping philosophical doctrine to remodel the entire society.

Political liberty is a second essential element of a modern liberal democratic regime. Those living in democratic times, Tocqueville

44. *DA,* 52–53. This is a point many historians today might dispute and was also called into question in George Bancroft's famous nineteenth-century history, which develops the thesis of multiple traditions in the American colonial period.

45. *DA,* 69.

46. Montesquieu appeared quite content to omit religion from the principal narrative of the early development of liberty. But when he directly takes up the theme of religion, especially in book 10 of *Spirit of the Laws,* he supports a moderate form of Christianity.

47. *DA,* 64.

stressed, need to learn the habits of taking part in governing, not only to protect themselves from the growth of an all-encompassing central state but also to promote their personal development as human beings. The roots of participatory theory, which were largely absent from modern philosophical doctrines, could be found in New England. Puritanism "was almost as much a political theory as a religious doctrine.... Democracy, such as antiquity had not dared dream it, burst forth fully grown and fully armed" in New England.[48] In the New England communities, Americans learned the skills of self-government, becoming citizens in a meaningful sense.

Finally, the third element of liberty—private rights—developed in the course of time in New England. This idea held that man "is free and is accountable for his actions only to God."[49] Private rights were undeniably promoted by the modern philosophical doctrine of natural rights, although the Puritan idea of being accountable before God contains a seed of this individualism. Tocqueville also made clear that the sentiments and energy that supported securing private rights depended heavily on cultivating the first two forms of liberty. Liberty, for Tocqueville, consisted in a combination of different principles that are arrayed in a complex and uneasy balance.

Nothing in Tocqueville's account suggests that he was a proponent of a progressive view of the movement of history, according to which matters tend to evolve for the good. His muted account of "growth" in New England is not part of a general theory of development. As for his overall view of history, Tocqueville invoked "Providence" to seal the argument for the movement of modernity to a stage of equality, which he thought held the potential to be the most just era man had known. But he saw nothing in this dispensation that assured a beneficial result. His argument rather was in the other direction: left on its own, modernity was trending to one form or other of democratic despotism. To forestall this outcome, he emphasized the need to employ "art." Reason was required to help shape and guide society, but it was reason of a different kind from the model of rationalist reconstruction developed by modern philosophy. It was instead the reason of "political science."

48. *DA*, 58–59.
49. *DA*, 108. See also 389–93.

Likewise, in cautioning against establishing political foundations based on modern natural law doctrines, Tocqueville was not rejecting natural right. He referred often to what is "by nature" or according to "the order of nature."[50] In a reversal of the modern philosophical view, however, his understanding of what was right by nature made him wary of general philosophical doctrines of right, because these inevitably entail oversimplifications. Natural right is best grasped when it is expressed in particular cases and seen in different and shifting notions of conventional right. In the course of recounting a historical narrative, the theorist-historian can make the necessary corrections and improvements along the way, purging national character of its excesses while still assuring that its core remains intact. This is precisely what Tocqueville does in his account of Puritan history.

Other thinkers at the time, especially in the Whig Party, were engaged in a similar project of creating an American Customary History. Their aim was to combat the materialism and easy progressivism of modern philosophical doctrines, which they often attributed, rightly or wrongly, to the philosophy of John Locke. Customary History offered in combination with a natural rights teaching was seen as a way to curb the defects in the philosophical foundation of the founding. One of the most thoughtful writers in this school was the New England Whig leader Rufus Choate. In a series of orations in the 1830s and 1840s, including one titled "The Age of the Pilgrims, Our Heroic Period," Choate called for new histories to celebrate the resolute qualities of our earliest "fathers."[51] Choate sought to cultivate the historical sense of looking back with reverence to what is old and one's own. This disposition was being threatened by a rationalist mind-set that led each individual, in Tocqueville's description, to "take tradition only as information . . . [and] to appeal only on the individual effort of his reason."[52] For Choate, this way of thinking was insufficient to hold a society together and promote the necessary virtues of a free people.

50. Tocqueville never offers a full, discursive treatment of his understanding of natural right, which must be pieced together from various portions of his work.

51. Rufus Choate, *The Works of Rufus Choate with a Memoir of His Life*, ed. Samuel Gilman Brown, vol. 1 (Boston: Little, Brown, 1862).

52. *DA*, 699.

Statesmanship and Political Foundations

How should Tocqueville's two-founding thesis be judged? Thomas West, in the article referenced earlier, does not hesitate to provide an answer. His concern, it turns out, is less with Tocqueville's historical error of omitting the Declaration of Independence than with his theoretical error of downplaying natural rights. For West, that doctrine is the fundamental source of protection for liberty in America. Contrary to what many others contend, fundamental flaws that may have developed in American politics since the founding are not, in West's view, attributable to natural rights thought, but owe their origins to other, and unrelated, theoretical sources. Nor would it make sense, by West's reasoning, to close the door to all philosophical doctrines in order to block the dangerous ones: the good would then only be thrown out with the bad. However admirable *Democracy in America* may be in other respects, West regards it as defective on the central point of mistaking America's political foundation.

Tocqueville's silence about the doctrine of natural rights has been explained by noting that his audience was chiefly European, not American. According to Paul Rahe, the omission of the Declaration would be odd if *Democracy in America* were in fact a book about the American founding or about America; but if, as Rahe clearly holds, "it is a book of political science about democracy focused mainly on France with an eye to American institutions and American practices as they might be useful to the French, then his silence on the Declaration is utterly meaningless and of no significance whatsoever."[53] Indeed, attempts to promote natural rights theory with moderate Europeans at that time would have proven counterproductive to the cause of liberty, because the lesson they had drawn from the French Revolution was that its excesses resulted from its philosophical foundations. Any effort to distinguish a moderate, Lockean version of natural law from a more

---

53. Paul Rahe, comments at a symposium, "Soft Despotism, Democracy's Drift: What Tocqueville Teaches Today," September 2, 2009, at the Heritage Foundation, Washington, D.C. Available online at http://www.heritage .org/research/reports/2009/09/soft-despotism-democracys-drift-what -tocqueville-teaches-today. See also Rahe, *Soft Despotism*, 195.

radical variant—supposing even that Tocqueville had been inclined to make such a distinction—was arguably too refined a position to make headway in public. In France, going back to 1776, many had interpreted the American Revolution and its doctrine of natural law as giving full license to the radical project of remaking society: "The Americans... gave substantial reality to what we were dreaming about."[54] The practical choice in Europe was therefore between a foundation that was based on philosophical doctrine and one that relied on Customary History.

This argument about audience, if correct, still leaves unanswered the question of what effect the two-founding thesis might have on Americans. After all, as Tocqueville knew full well, his book would surely be read here. If his concern was only with his European audience, he might be charged with an act of irresponsibility: endangering the cause of good government in America in order to promote good government in Europe. Under a more charitable interpretation, he arguably thought he found a way of threading the needle by helping Europe while doing no harm to America. Americans would never abandon their cherished founding principles just because a well-intentioned Frenchman failed to assign the Declaration of Independence the credit it deserved.

An alternative reading is that Tocqueville intended *Democracy in America* to instruct all readers, Americans as well as Europeans. His warnings about the danger of theoretical doctrines in political life were meant to have an effect within the American context, bolstering efforts to tone down the Lockean natural rights doctrine and promoting an admixture of natural law and Customary History. In fact, versions of the two-founding thesis became a major theme of American historiography in the years that followed.[55] Other thinkers in America, while rejecting the specific New England–Puritan narrative, followed Tocqueville's theoretical position and offered alternative versions of Customary History that were more national in scope than the Puritan account, which some judged to be too narrow and local to appeal to the whole nation. The main approach along these lines sought to locate the "germ" of liberty

54. Tocqueville, *Old Regime*, 201.

55. Other accounts of the two-founding thesis were already under discussion, as found, for example, in Rufus Choate's writing. One of the first statements of this position was Daniel Webster's Plymouth Oration, December 22, 1820.

within the founding era (1775–1787), although now based as much on customary as on philosophical grounds. James Madison had already foreshadowed this kind of admixture of foundations in *Federalist* No. 49 by suggesting that the "prejudices of the community" be placed on the side of law and that "reverence" and "veneration" be inculcated for the Constitution and the founding. Rufus Choate came around to this more national approach by 1845 in his celebrated speech to the Harvard Law School, which commemorated the general idea of law and credited the constitutions of the founding era, national and state, with being the source of American liberty.[56] Earlier, a young and unknown Whig politician from Illinois, Abraham Lincoln, proposed making obedience to the laws, attached to the memory of the founding, into "the political religion of the nation."[57]

Tocqueville's argument for Customary History connects *Democracy in America* with the general approach of many Whig thinkers in America who sought to develop a synthesis of natural rights theory and Customary History. Tocqueville, of course, differed from these writers by his silence about the founders' natural rights doctrine. He nevertheless at one point appeared to acknowledge the existence of this doctrine when he noted that Americans never displayed "so blind a faith [as the French] in the goodness and in the absolute truth of any theory."[58] Americans could make this philosophical foundation work because they pursued it less theoretically and applied it with a large dose of prudence. A theoretical foundation so hedged might satisfy the requirements of good government.

If Tocqueville intended his theory of the founding to instruct Americans as well as Europeans, the result for Thomas West would be to strengthen his general objection to *Democracy in America*. Tocqueville now could be charged with a sin of commission rather than of omission. For West, any approach that veils or qualifies "the abstract principle" at the core of the founding undermines the cause of liberty and threatens the American political order. There remains, therefore, an

56. Choate, *Works*, 1:414–38.

57. Abraham Lincoln, Address before the Young Men's Lyceum of Springfield, January 27, 1838, in Lincoln, *Complete Works*, 1:12.

58. *DA*, 738.

unresolved issue, not only of intellectual history, but also of political theory and of American political thought. What political foundation is best for America, and how does one even approach trying to answer a question of this kind? It may be, in fact, that searching for a simple determination of the "one best foundation" goes beyond what political philosophy can furnish. An alternative is to proceed in a more "political" fashion by considering the merit of foundational ideas as judged in part by their effects in different contexts. This approach recognizes a role for what amounts to "statesmanship" in determining the proper application of political ideas. Statesmanship, as Tocqueville explains, involves making judgments that abjure a strict adherence to laws or formulas on the grounds that the changing character of political life demands varying methods to achieve certain fixed ends. The form in which political foundations are expressed must therefore take account of different circumstances, not in the sense of ordinary mutations in the political situation, but because fundamental ideas generally outlast such situations, in the broader sense of great changes of context that bear on the character of the nation.

The historical experience of the United States since Tocqueville's visit obviously provides new material for judging the question of the best presentation of foundational ideas. The slavery crisis of the 1850s made it evident that the "general spirit of the nation" could not be expressed without acknowledging the centrality of the foundation of natural rights. Tocqueville himself, in his responses both in public and in private to the slavery crisis—he died in 1859—appeared already to be moving in the direction of searching for a clear doctrinal expression of right to oppose slavery and its expansion.[59] In any case, following the Civil War and Abraham Lincoln's refounding of America's polity, the context of American political life changed in a way that any viable

---

59. See especially Tocqueville's letters to Theodore Sedgwick, Edward Childe, and Jared Sparks from 1857 in *Tocqueville on America after 1840: Letters and Other Writings*, ed. and trans. Aurelian Craiutu and Jeremy Jennings (Cambridge: Cambridge University Press, 2009), 224, 226, 240. In addition, Tocqueville took the (for him) unprecedented step of publishing a public testimony in America against slavery in 1855, which appeared first in the *Liberty Bell* and was reprinted elsewhere. In this testimony he inches toward a natural law position, though the final source he cites is God's conception of man.

Customary History would have to recognize. It became impossible—it would be an absurdity—to think any longer of veiling the foundation of natural rights doctrine as expressed in the words of one of America's greatest statesman at its most critical moment.

If the essence of the doctrine of natural rights is to state a truth, then it must be asserted in this form, that is, as a truth, and not merely as a useful idea for its day, much less as a helpful myth. To say, however, that it is a truth does not deny that it may be less than the whole truth. Its incompleteness in certain circumstances can lead to distortion and error. This possibility suggests the need for an ongoing process of adjustment or supplementation of the modern philosophical doctrine of natural rights, which can take place through creative interpretation of its sources or by introducing other foundational principles to qualify and complement it. Tocqueville's *Democracy in America* remains the indispensable text for guiding us in this difficult task.

6

Tocqueville's "New Political Science"

CATHERINE H. ZUCKERT

As the critical edition shows, Alexis de Tocqueville considered beginning *Democracy in America* with a disclaimer: "The work that you are about to read is not a travelogue. . . . You will also not find in this book a complete summary of all the institutions of the United States."[1] Had he retained this disclaimer, later admirers of his work might not have been tempted to "update" it merely by retracing his steps.[2] Eduardo Nolla notes that "criticism has too generally put the accent on Tocqueville as a traveler, observer of mores and institutions, historian foreshadowing the sociologist." Tocqueville understood himself to be a political scientist. His understanding of political science was very different, however, from that now taught in most American colleges and universities. In a lecture he gave to the annual meeting of the Academy of Moral and Political Sciences in 1852, he explained: "Among all civilized peoples, the political sciences give birth or at least give form to general ideas, from which then follow particular facts, in the middle of which politicians agitate, and the laws that they think they invent."[3] As Tocqueville

---

1. Alexis de Tocqueville, *Democracy in America: Historical-Critical Edition of "De la démocratie en Amérique,"* ed. Eduardo Nolla, trans. James T. Schleifer, 4 vols. (Indianapolis: Liberty Fund, 2010), 3. This edition is hereafter cited as *DA*.

2. For example, Anne Bentzel, *Traveling Tocqueville's America: Retracing the 17-State Tour That Inspired Alexis de Tocqueville's Political Classic "Democracy in America"* (Baltimore: Published for C-SPAN by the Johns Hopkins University Press, 1998); Eugene McCarthy, *America Revisited: 150 Years after Tocqueville* (Garden City, N.Y.: Doubleday, 1978); Richard Reeves, *American Journey: Traveling with Tocqueville in Search of Democracy in America* (New York: Simon and Schuster, 1982).

3. *DA*, 16–17nx.

understood it, political science does not consist merely in an objective and essentially passive observation and analysis of institutions, laws, and behaviors; the political scientist articulates and thus shapes the general ideas on the basis of which people act.[4]

In his introduction to *Democracy in America,* Tocqueville explained that he had become convinced that "a great democratic revolution" was occurring in Europe. He traveled to America to study the people among whom this revolution had "reached the most complete and most peaceful development, in order to discern clearly its natural consequences and, if possible, to see the means to make it profitable to man."[5] Tocqueville had evidently formed his ideas or theories about the general causes, character, and consequences of the democratic revolution he thought was occurring in Europe before he set out for America. In formulating those general ideas, he drew on the works of his great predecessors, Montesquieu and Jean-Jacques Rousseau.[6] He rarely mentioned either by name, however, partly because he modified their theories in significant ways on the basis of what he found in America and partly because he thought that a description of the facts would persuade his French readers of their true future possibilities more than mere speculations or "theories."[7]

4. These general ideas are precisely the parts of Tocqueville's work that Jon Elster, *Alexis de Tocqueville: The First Social Scientist* (Cambridge: Cambridge University Press, 2009), dismisses as vague and incoherent.

5. *DA,* 28.

6. In a well-known letter to Louis de Kergorlay, November 10, 1836, in *Oeuvres, papiers et correspondances* (Paris: Gallimard, 1951), 13:418, Tocqueville says that there were three men with whom he lived a little bit each day—Pascal, Montesquieu, and Rousseau. Because I am emphasizing Tocqueville's political ideas, I have looked particularly at what he took and what he changed from Montesquieu and Rousseau, whose works he first read in his father's library when he was in school in Metz. See Paul Rahe, *Soft Despotism, Democracy's Drift: Montesquieu, Rousseau, Tocqueville, and the Modern Prospect* (New Haven, Conn.: Yale University Press, 2009), 154.

7. Tocqueville explicitly mentions Montesquieu in the text only to disagree with him about the strength of despotism (*DA,* 159) and the authority of a prince who follows a republic (*DA,* 635) although virtually all readers see that he is disagreeing with Montesquieu without naming him about England's being a mixed regime (*DA,* 412) and the effect of climate on the morals of women (*DA,* 1052).

Tocqueville explicitly announced that he did not go to America simply or even primarily to study America. On the contrary, he admitted, "In America I saw more than America. I sought there an image of democracy itself, its tendencies, its character, its prejudices, its passions."[8] That "democracy" did not consist in a political regime or popular form of government so much as an unprecedented equality of conditions.[9] In addition, Tocqueville thought, "a new political science" was needed to understand the character and implications of this equality of conditions, developing on both sides of the Atlantic.[10] As exemplified by *Democracy in America,* his new political science had three basic elements or parts.[11] The first consisted in an account of the way in which a variety of different events and inventions in Europe over the last seven hundred years had contributed, unintentionally but progressively, to an ever-increasing equality of condition. This history both drew from and in important respects modified the more explicitly

---

As Rahe, *Soft Despotism,* 168, observes, Tocqueville does not mention Rousseau in the published text of *Democracy in America.* As the critical edition shows, at one point he had explicitly referred to the *Social Contract.* One of the many virtues of the critical edition is that it includes Tocqueville's notes, which show that he was thinking in dialogue with a great many other political philosophers, including Thomas Hobbes, David Hume, and Niccolò Machiavelli.

8. *DA,* 28.

9. Pierre Manent, *Tocqueville and the Nature of Democracy,* trans. John Waggoner (Lanham, Md.: Rowman & Littlefield, 1996), ix. By emphasizing the similarities between Tocqueville's political science and Aristotle's, Harvey C. Mansfield Jr. and Delba Winthrop, "Tocqueville's New Political Science," in *The Cambridge Companion to Tocqueville,* ed. Cheryl B. Welch (Cambridge: Cambridge University Press, 2006), 81–120, blur the difference between the democratic social state and democratic government. Tocqueville considered all ancient "democracies" to be aristocracies, in fact, because they were based on slavery (*DA,* 732–33). In a letter to F. Corcelle, Paris, 6 juillet 1836, *Correspondance d'Alexis de Tocqueville et de Francisque de Corcelle,* 2 vols., in *Oeuvres complètes* (Paris: Gallimard, 1951–), 15(1):65, he wrote that even though they had been admired for three thousand years, he found Greek philosophers too antiquated to be of interest to modern readers.

10. *DA,* 16.

11. Mansfield and Winthrop, "New Political Science," 81, suggest that Tocqueville never delivered the "new political science" he promised. I contend that he demonstrated what he meant by that "new political science" in his own work.

speculative account of human development Rousseau presented in his *Second Discourse*. The second part or major element of Tocqueville's new science consisted in an empirically based, but essentially deductive description of the results of what he described as a "providential" historical development, not as a primarily political phenomenon, but as "the material and intellectual condition in which a people finds itself in a given period," which Tocqueville called its "social state."[12] Similar to, but in important respects different from, Montesquieu's concept of the "spirit" of the laws, Tocqueville's concept of "social state" was arguably his most original contribution to the study of politics.[13] His new political science was not exhausted or entirely completed by the articulation of the varied characteristics and consequences of the new egalitarian or "democratic" social state, however, because Tocqueville saw that the political results of that social state could be radically different. The third part of his new science thus consisted in an attempt to isolate and explain the operation of the factors that determined whether the political outcome of this new social condition would be free or despotic. The three most important factors, Tocqueville concluded, were geography, laws, and mores. In arguing that mores were the most decisive, Tocqueville again incorporated, but also modified, insights he took from Montesquieu and Rousseau.

Tocqueville's History

In his introduction to *Democracy in America*, Tocqueville gives a brief summary of the events and inventions that have constituted an

12. *DA*, 74.

13. Michael P. Zuckert, "On Social State," in *Tocqueville's Defense of Human Liberty*, ed. Peter Augustine Lawler and Joseph Alulis (New York: Garland, 1993), 3–20. Aurelian Craiutu, *Liberalism under Siege: The Political Thought of the French Doctrinaires* (Lanham, Md.: Lexington Books, 2003), 106–8, contests M. Zuckert's claim by tracing the concept back to Pierre-Paul Royer-Collard and François Guizot. Craiutu also emphasizes the influence of Guizot's *Historie de la civilisation en Europe* on Tocqueville's introduction. Tocqueville had both heard and read Guizot's lectures shortly before he left for America; shortly after he arrived in America, he also asked a friend to send him a copy of Guizot's *Historie*.

"irresistible" movement toward greater equality of conditions in Europe over the last seven hundred years. Emphasizing the Christian origin of the movement, Tocqueville observes that the first step away from a society ruled on the basis of force by a few who owned all the property occurred when the clergy acquired political power. Because "Christianity... made all men equal before God,"[14] the clergy opened its ranks to all; from the Church equality began to penetrate the government. As civil society became more stable and relations among people more complex, the clergy were joined at court by jurists, whose knowledge of an increasingly complicated set of civil laws provided them with status and influence. Because both groups represented powers separate from the nobility, both served as political checks on the nobility's power. In addition to these religious and legal sources, Tocqueville shows, political and economic interests and activities also contributed to the ever-increasing equality of condition. As kings and nobles impoverished themselves in attempts to expand their power militarily, commoners became wealthier; the power of money began to be felt in affairs of state. Once money, as opposed to land, became a source of power, a great many new paths to influence and status were opened. Knowledge of many different kinds became valuable, a taste for literature and the arts arose, and enlightenment spread. With enlightenment came not merely science but inventions that, like the printing press and firearms, served to equalize the capabilities of human beings even further. Indeed, Tocqueville concludes, "[T]here is not a single event among Christians that has not turned to the profit of democracy."[15]

In France, Tocqueville observed, the democratic revolution had taken place "in the material aspect of society without happening in the laws, ideas, habits and mores, the change that would have been necessary to make this revolution useful."[16] The French had thus lost the advantages of their old aristocratic order or "social state" without gleaning the advantages of the new. "The prestige of royal power has vanished, without being replaced by the majesty of laws." The "individual existences"—families, corporations, or noblemen—that could

14. *DA*, 24.
15. *DA*, 10.
16. *DA*, 18.

struggle separately against tyranny have been destroyed. "The division of fortunes has reduced the distance that separated the poor from the rich; but by coming closer together, they seem to have found new reasons to hate each other; . . . the idea of rights does not exist, and force appears to them both as the only reason for the present and the sole guarantee of the future."[17]

Tocqueville could, however, imagine a better outcome. That would be a society where all, seeing the law as their work, would love it and would submit to it without difficulty; where since the authority of the government is respected as necessary and not as divine, the love that is felt for the head of state would not be a passion, but a reasoned and calm sentiment. Since each person has rights and is assured of preserving his rights, a manly confidence and a kind of reciprocal condescension, as far from pride as from servility, would be established among all classes. Instructed in their true interests, the people would understand that, in order to take advantage of the good things of society, you must submit to its burdens. The free association of citizens would then be able to replace the individual power of the nobles, and the state would be sheltered from tyranny and from license.[18]

Such a democratic state would not be without its disadvantages or faults. One would find less brilliance there than within an aristocracy, but also less misery. Pleasures would be less extreme, but well-being more general. Knowledge would not be as great, but ignorance would be rare. With sentiments less energetic and habits more mild, one would "notice more vices and fewer crimes."[19]

Tocqueville traveled to America to see what kinds of laws, ideas, habits, and mores could preserve liberty in democratic social conditions. He insisted, however, that he did not think that the French were "necessarily called to draw from such a social state the political consequences that the Americans have drawn from it." Indeed, he was "very far from believing that they have found the only form of government that democracy may take." He insisted only that "in the two countries the generating cause of laws and mores is the same" and that he and

17. *DA*, 22.
18. *DA*, 20.
19. *DA*, 21.

his readers had an immense interest, therefore, "in knowing what that generating cause has produced in each."[20]

Two features of Tocqueville's history are particularly noteworthy. The first is Tocqueville's insistence that the unintentional, but nevertheless inexorable, march toward ever-greater equality of conditions in modern European history is not the product of any single factor or cause. There is nothing like Hegel's *Geist* or Marx's dialectical materialism at work here.[21] Tocqueville insists not only on the multiplicity but also on the interactions of a plurality of different kinds of causes — religious, legal, political, intellectual, and economic. He does claim that the universality of the result makes it a "providential fact."[22] However, although he attributes a seminal role to the Christian religion, he explicitly denies that his account of this "providential" history has its source in revelation. On the contrary, he assures his readers that "it isn't necessary for God himself to speak in order for us to discover sure signs of his will; it is enough to examine the regular march of nature and the continuous tendency of events."[23]

The second remarkable feature of Tocqueville's history is that although it moves in one direction, it does not have an entirely determined end or result. Like Rousseau in the *Second Discourse*, Tocqueville identifies the beginning of "civilization" with the coercive rule of a few who seize and claim ownership of the land. Further like Rousseau, Tocqueville sees that by making each individual ever more dependent on the assistance of others, a progressive division of labor undermines the independence of each and so threatens the liberty of all. Most important, like Rousseau, Tocqueville emphasizes the ways in which particular forms and organization of economic activity affect human

20. *DA,* 27.

21. Tocqueville explicitly criticized Hegel and his influence in a letter to R. Corcelle, Bonn, 22 juillet 1854, *Correspondance,* in *Oeuvres complètes,* 15(2):107–9. For a more extensive discussion of the differences, see Catherine H. Zuckert, "Political Sociology versus Speculative Philosophy," in *Interpreting Tocqueville's "Democracy in America,"* ed. Ken Masugi (Savage, Md.: Rowman & Littlefield, 1993), 121–52.

22. *DA,* 10.

23. *DA,* 14.

emotions and beliefs, and the ways in which these beliefs as well as their material resources, in turn, affect political behavior. Unlike Rousseau, however, Tocqueville does not think that human beings have to allow themselves to fall prey to a complete despotism in order to rebel against it. Nor does he think that it is possible to institute a new form of political order, explicitly based on the recognition that human beings are equal by nature, only in a few small, isolated places like Geneva. Indeed, in the most fundamental respect, Rousseau's and Tocqueville's histories move in opposite directions. Whereas Rousseau presents an explicitly speculative account of the origins of inequality, Tocqueville traces the development of an ever-increasing equality of condition. Although he emphasizes the desirability of maintaining a certain set of religious beliefs in *Emile* and *The Social Contract,* in his *Second Discourse* Rousseau remains completely silent about the role of religion. Tocqueville emphasizes the Christian origins and "God-given" character of the inexorable movement toward greater equality of condition in order to persuade his contemporaries not to try to resist it.[24] Because that movement is the result of the interaction of a variety of different factors, Tocqueville does not think that its political consequences are completely determined or entirely predictable. Ever-increasing equality of conditions will make it impossible to revive or reinstate a feudal monarchy or aristocracy in the civilized world for the foreseeable future. Nor (contra Guizot) did Tocqueville think that the growing middle class or bourgeoisie could stem the rising egalitarian tide by instituting a mixed form of government. The only political options are a republic, in which everyone participates equally as a citizen and shares the same rights, or an unprecedented form of despotism, to which all are equally subject, without any intermediary powers or limits. Whether the people of any particular nation will be equally free or equally subject depends upon what laws, institutions, beliefs, habits, and mores they adopt.

24. Marvin Zetterbaum, *Tocqueville and the Problem of Democracy* (Stanford: Stanford University Press, 1967), 19, goes too far, however, when he declares that Tocqueville's inevitability thesis is a salutary myth. For a fuller critique of Zetterbaum's thesis, see Catherine H. Zuckert, "Not by Preaching: Tocqueville on the Role of Religion in America," *Review of Politics* 43, no. 2 (1981): 259–80.

Social State

Tocqueville called the "fact" of the relative equality of condition he found among the people of both Europe and America a democratic "social state." By "social state," he wrote in an earlier draft of *Democracy in America*, he meant "the material and intellectual condition in which a people finds itself in a given period." In the published text, he merely explains that a "social state is ordinarily the result of a fact, sometimes of laws, most often of these two causes together. But once it exists, it can itself be considered the first cause of most of the laws, customs and ideas that regulate the conduct of nations; what it does not produce, it modifies. So to know the legislation and the mores of a people, it is necessary to begin by studying its social state."[25]

The egalitarian social state Tocqueville saw around him in France had developed gradually over centuries. By way of contrast, Tocqueville observed that Americans had been living under such equal conditions almost from the beginning. This equality was the product of the two factors he identified that usually worked together to produce a social state—the "facts" of the "exterior configuration" of the land that he describes in chapter 1 and the "laws and mores" the Puritans brought with them to America that he describes as "the point of departure" in chapter 2.

In beginning his account of the factors that combine to constitute the national character of a people with the terrain and its inhabitants, Tocqueville follows the example set by Montesquieu in his mammoth study of the spirit of the laws. However, although he gives a detailed description of the geography of the Americas, Tocqueville attributes much less importance than Montesquieu did to the locale and climate. He notes that the tropical beauties of South America seemed to offer a paradise but that they hid lethal diseases. His one bow in the direction of climatic effects consists in a single comment on the enervating influence of the air, attaching men to the present and making them unmindful of the future. Underlining the extent to which the terrain per se did not shape the character of the people who settled there,

25. *DA,* 74. The following discussion of Tocqueville's conception of "social state" owes a great deal to M. Zuckert, "Social State."

Tocqueville also observes that the North American wilderness was not entirely without people. "A few small tribes wandered in the shade of the forest or across the prairie lands."[26]

Tocqueville's description of the "social state" (material and intellectual condition) of these tribes has reminded many readers of Rousseau's depiction of the "noble savage." Although they were ignorant and poor, Tocqueville notes, the Indians were all equal and free. Indeed, he goes so far as to affirm that "the most famous republics of antiquity never admired firmer courage, prouder souls, a more uncompromising love of independence than what was then hidden in the wild forests of the New World."[27] He nevertheless concludes that the vast continent was "at the time of discovery...still only a wilderness. The Indians occupied, but did not possess it. Man appropriates the soil by agriculture, and the first inhabitants of North America lived by the hunt."[28] Like what Rousseau dubbed the "sweetest and most durable" stage in human development, the Indians and their way of life were extinguished by an external "accident": in America that extrinsic "accident" was the emigration and settlement of the New World by already civilized people from Europe.

The development of a democratic social state in America was not unrelated to, or independent of, the European history Tocqueville had sketched in his introduction. On the contrary, he emphasizes the ways in which the emigrants were products of that history. Because they were civilized, they were literate. They thus left records of their trials and errors as well as their intentions and achievements. The development of democracy in America makes such a good and enlightening "case study" precisely because, unlike the histories of virtually all other European peoples, its beginning or "point of departure" is known.

"All the new European colonies contained, if not the development, at least the germ, of a complete democracy" for two reasons. The first was simply that they were all populated by emigrants. The happy and the powerful do not go into exile, Tocqueville reminds his readers; poverty along with misfortune tends to equalize human beings. Second,

26. *DA*, 39.
27. *DA*, 41–42.
28. *DA*, 43.

when great lords who had emigrated as a result of political or religious quarrels did try to establish a hierarchy of rank by law, "the American soil absolutely rejected territorial aristocracy. To clear that intractable land nothing less was required than the constant and interested efforts of the proprietor himself. . . . So the land was naturally divided into small estates that the proprietor cultivated alone."[29] Tocqueville acknowledges that there were attempts to establish a landed aristocracy on the basis of slave labor in the South and that "the great landholders formed a superior class, with its own ideas and tastes," which generally monopolized political activity; but "it was a kind of aristocracy not much different from the mass of the people."[30] So little did these aristocrats consider themselves to be essentially different from and superior to the people, they provided the greatest leaders of the insurrection of the colonies against the mother country in the name of the rights of all.[31]

The ideas the English emigrants brought with them were even more important than the land in establishing equality of condition in America. The pilgrims who settled New England were unusual colonists. Coming from the middle class and educated, they emigrated to the New World, not because of their material needs, but for the sake of their ideas; and these ideas included not only a religious doctrine but also some very democratic and republican theories. Having received a practical political education in England, where the struggle of parties had led the factions, one after another, to seek protection of the laws, they had acquired a firmer notion of rights than most of the other peoples of Europe as well as experience in town government, "the fertile seed of free institutions," which had become ingrained in English habits even under the Tudor monarchy. "Without denying the supremacy of the home country," the colonists "did not draw on it as the source

---

29. *DA*, 50.

30. *DA*, 77.

31. When he comes to discuss the conditions of the three races he considers peculiar to America (i.e., not particularly relevant to the future of European nations) in *DA*, 600–27, however, Tocqueville predicts that the attitudes and habits southern whites have developed as a result of the institution of slavery will lead to a dissolution of the union.

of powers; they incorporated themselves."[32] They founded their community on the basis of an agreement that Tocqueville described in an earlier draft of *Democracy* as "the social contract ... that Rousseau [only] dreamed of."[33] Although they took much of the substance and even the language of the strict moral regulations they imposed by law directly from scripture, Tocqueville emphasizes that "these bizarre or tyrannical laws were not at all imposed; they were voted by the free participation of all those concerned." By legally establishing "the intervention of the people in public affairs, the free vote of taxes, the responsibility of the agents of power, individual liberty, and jury trial," the Puritans recognized "the general principles on which modern constitutions rest"[34] before most Europeans understood them. Puritanical moral legislation was not adopted in the other colonies and was later challenged and eventually abolished in New England as well. But the combination "of two perfectly distinct elements that elsewhere are often at odds ... , the *spirit of religion* and the *spirit of liberty*," became the core of "Anglo-American civilization."[35]

The physical circumstances or requirements of cultivating the land and the ideas, laws, and mores of the Puritans that gradually spread to the other colonies contributed greatly to establishing equality of condition in America; but, Tocqueville explains, these two factors alone did not produce the completely democratic social state he observed when he arrived. It took a political event—the American Revolution—to arouse a desire in the people, in whose name the struggle had been waged, to govern themselves. As a result of this newly awakened desire for popular independence, individuals lost much of the political influence they had exerted before the war as intellectual leaders in the North and plantation owners in the South. However, the social revolution that established complete equality of condition in America had not been effected simply by the political revolution that made the dogma of popular sovereignty *the* political law of the United States, mandating a democratic form of government at all levels. It was a particular kind

32. *DA*, 61.
33. *DA*, 58.
34. *DA*, 64–65.
35. *DA*, 69.

or piece of legislation, "the law of inheritance that pushed equality to its last stage."[36] As in Europe, so in America, the democratic social state was thus a product of a combination of religious, economic, and political factors.

Tocqueville emphasizes both the originality and the importance of his analysis of the effects of the laws of inheritance on the creation of a democratic "social state" that shapes the ideas and noneconomic behavior of the people concerned even more than the character and extent of their real estate holdings:

> I am astonished that ancient and modern political writers have not attributed a greater influence on the course of human affairs to the laws of landed inheritance. These laws belong, it is true, to the civil order; but they should be placed at the head of all political institutions, for they have an incredible influence on the social state of peoples, political laws being just the expression of the social state.[37]

In brief, Tocqueville argues, the laws of inheritance determine whether a people will be ruled by an aristocracy or a democracy, and the effects of these laws extend far beyond the distribution of property to shape the self-understandings of all the inhabitants. If land holdings are concentrated in the hands of a few families and must be passed on to a single heir, those few also become dominant in politics. If the law requires an equal division of the father's property among all his children, however, there are two different sorts of effects. First, as a result of the progressive division of the land with the death of each owner, the large holdings and the political power that goes with them gradually disappear. That is the direct effect of laws that abolish primogeniture. But, Tocqueville urges, the indirect effects of the progressive division of estates on the souls of their owners are even greater and more significant. So long as estates are divided among two or possibly three children, the holdings of each individual will not change much in value or quantity, because they will be dividing an inheritance deriving from both their father and their mother. When estates are no longer entailed, the attitude of the holders and heirs changes not only toward

36. *DA*, 78.
37. *DA*, 79.

the land but also toward their family. When landed estates pass from generation to generation without being divided, the land comes to represent the family—their name, origin, glory, power, and virtues. Where the inheritance law mandates equal division, each part inevitably diminishes in extent and value. In order to maintain the level of wealth and influence of his father, each heir must find another source of revenue. "The small landholder gains proportionately more revenue from his field than the large landholder; so he sells it at a much higher price." Once they are "divided, great landed estates are never reassembled."[38] Thus, the connection between land and family—as well as the self-understanding of the owners—is broken. A small landholder does not try to immortalize himself by willing his entire estate to a single heir in order to perpetuate the family name. "Since the family [separated from its embodiment in the land] no longer enters the mind except as something vague, indeterminate, and uncertain, each concentrates on his own immediate convenience and concerns himself only about the generation that follows him directly."[39]

Tocqueville admits that the effects of the division of family holdings among heirs have only begun to become visible in France, where many "memories, opinions, and habits" present obstacles. The effects can be observed in the United States, however, where laws impeding the free circulation of property have been almost completely abolished. There are still very rich people, but, instead of residing on their family estates, these men and their sons have become businessmen, lawyers, and doctors. Every trace of hereditary rank and distinction has been destroyed. The equality of fortunes in America extends, moreover, to a certain extent to an equality of intellect. Partly as a result of the ideas that spread from the Puritan settlements to the other colonies, primary education is available to everyone, but it is almost impossible for anyone to acquire higher education. Because there is little inherited wealth, "nearly all Americans need to have an occupation" and "every occupation requires an apprenticeship. So Americans can devote only the first years of life to general cultivation of the mind; at age fifteen, they

38. *DA,* 82.
39. *DA,* 83.

begin a career."[40] If pursued further, their education is directed toward acquiring knowledge that will prove useful in a specialized, lucrative field like law. "In America a certain middling level of human knowledge [has thus been] established.... Intellectual inequality [which] comes directly from God" has not been abolished, but in America unequal minds find equal means of developing. As a result, in America one encounters a great number of individuals with basically the same ideas about "religion, history, the sciences, political economy, legislation, and government."[41]

This intellectual as well as economic and political equality is what Tocqueville means by "democracy" or a democratic social state. It is the result of a fact—in the case of America the vast continent waiting to be settled and cultivated—and laws, not only the democratic agreements and strict moral regulations instituted by the Puritans, but also and more important by the laws of inheritance that abolished primogeniture right after the revolution. But "once it exists," Tocqueville insists, this social state "can itself be considered the first cause of most of the laws, customs and ideas that regulate the conduct of nations."

Tocqueville might appear to contradict himself by maintaining first that anyone who studies the history of America and examines its political and social state will see that "there is not an opinion, not a habit, not a law, ... not an event, that the point of departure does not easily explain," and then claiming that the social state "may be considered the first cause of most of the laws, customs and ideas." But Tocqueville makes it clear that the point of departure explains nineteenth-century American opinions, customs, and laws, because it contributed to the ideas, habits, laws, and mores that led the American colonies eventually to rebel against the mother country and to institute a popular form of government that quickly passed laws abolishing primogeniture. The ideas and laws the Puritans promulgated were not passed on in their original form to later generations and other colonies. The Puritans' ideas and institutions were adapted and then adopted to fit the needs of other European emigrants who came not only to secure religious liberty but also to acquire an economic stake, if not a fortune.

40. *DA*, 87.
41. *DA*, 88.

Tocqueville might also seem to be using "democracy" ambiguously to refer, on the one hand, to the "social state" of which political laws are merely an expression and, on the other hand, to a form of government based on the sovereignty for the people, which he characterizes as "a legal and omnipotent fact that rules the entire society."[42] Readers are prompted to ask which is primary. "Popular sovereignty" might appear to be; it was, after all, the popularly elected legislatures that passed the laws abolishing primogeniture and so completed the establishment of a democratic social state in America after the revolution. Tocqueville admits that the two forms of "democracy" are closely related, but he just as clearly insists that they are not the same and that the democratic social state is fundamental. The people cannot and do not actually rule, where a few are obviously far richer, better educated, and hence more powerful than the majority. For the dogma of the "sovereignty of the people" to be realized in fact, there must be a democratic social state in which people are basically equal. However, a democratic social state does not in and by itself necessarily produce a democratic form of government. On the contrary, Tocqueville reminds his readers, "democracy is even more compatible with despotism than with liberty."[43]

Once a people has a democratic social state, Tocqueville insists, there are two, but only two, possible political outcomes: "rights must either be given to each citizen or given to no one." It will not be possible to maintain a mixed regime of the kind Montesquieu and François Guizot hoped would protect liberty, because, as conditions become more and more equal, the last remnants of aristocracy are destroyed. The problem or danger is that even when citizens are granted equal rights, "it becomes difficult for them to defend their independence against the aggression of power. Since none among them is then strong enough to struggle alone . . . , it is only the combination of the strength of all that can guarantee liberty."[44] What Tocqueville most sought to learn from the Americans was how they had been able to retain their liberty in a democratic social state.

42. *DA*, 92.
43. *DA*, 76.
44. *DA*, 90.

How Human Beings Can Retain Their Liberty in a Democratic Social State

Tocqueville's understanding of the sort of despotism that people living in a democratic social state could develop changed somewhat in the course of his writing about what he saw in America. In reaction to the recent history of France, he began by worrying simply that everyone could be made equally subject to a central authority—a hierarchically organized bureaucracy headed by a single man. Americans had avoided that fate, he saw, not merely by making the people sovereign, but by dividing government into layers—town, county, state, and nation.

A NEW FORM OF FEDERATION

Tocqueville did not "profess a blind faith in legal prescriptions"or agree with [those] "who think that it is sufficient to change the laws of a people in order to modify easily their social and political state," but he thought that "no country on earth more than America has ever given a greater example of the power of laws on the life of political society."[45] Montesquieu and Rousseau had both argued that it was impossible to maintain a republic in a large territory, but the Americans had proven them wrong in fact. The framers of the Constitution of the United States had shown how it is possible to combine the advantages of small and large states on the basis of "an entirely new theory that must stand out as a great discovery in the political science of today."[46] They had created a new form of federation that was not merely a league that depended upon the cooperation of the member states to enforce its laws but a mixture, partly national and partly federal, in which the national government could act directly on individual citizens.

Popular acceptance, understanding, and operation of this complex form of government depended, however, on the existence of a set of pre-conditions peculiar to America that could not be duplicated elsewhere, especially in Europe. The union of the states was made possible by the fact that Americans shared a common civilization and language. Their political opinions and habits had been formed by their experience in

45. *DA*, 187–88.
46. *DA*, 252.

town governments that the English colonists had brought with them. These little direct democracies had taught people to get together to discuss common problems, devise solutions, and select officials to carry out their decisions.

Because the resources of a single town are too scant to supply all the needs of a people, the Americans, again following the English model, also created larger political jurisdictions called counties, which have primarily judicial functions. And above the counties, they created sovereign states with representative governments composed of bicameral legislatures, elected executives, and quasi-independent judiciaries. But observers should not be fooled by their written constitutions into thinking that the powers of these state governments are limited. On the contrary, the representatives elected for short terms to both houses of the legislature and the executive are all responsible, and thus responsive, to the desires of the same majority. Because state governments are not merely able, but anxious to do whatever a majority wants, their powers are both plenary and centralized. However, these governments apply the maxim upon which popular sovereignty is based to administration. Just as the individual is the best as well as the only judge of his particular interest and society has the right to direct his actions only when it feels harmed by them, or when it needs to call for his support,[47] they reason, local officials familiar with local conditions ought to carry out state policies. Instead of a centralized, hierarchical bureaucracy, administration in the United States is thus diffused to a large number of people working independently of one another. The administration of state policies is often less expert than it would be if it were centralized under a single authority; but the participation of a large number of citizens in the process of governing not only ties them to the state by making them feel that it is their own. It also encourages them to undertake projects on their own initiative. It teaches people how to organize in order to protect and promote their own interests rather than looking to the state to do so.

The design of the national government is superior to that of the states, because it grants both the elective executive and the appointed judiciary more independence from the pressure of immediate popular

47. *DA*, 108.

desires and whims, although these officials, too, are ultimately responsible to a popular majority. But, Tocqueville nevertheless concludes that the U.S. Constitution will not work in Europe; its operation depends too much on the relative geographical isolation of the nation that minimizes its defensive needs and the political experience of its inhabitants. Only a people long used to governing itself will be able to understand such a complicated system. The cooperation of state governments and their citizens in carrying out national policy is a product of their common civilization and habits; the national government does not have sufficient power to coerce them. Even in the area of foreign affairs, where the national government has exclusive jurisdiction, the powers of the American executive are not sufficient to lead a nation faced by the threat of foreign conquest; the army and navy he has to command are too small.

DECENTRALIZED ADMINISTRATION AND
PRACTICAL POPULAR POLITICAL EDUCATION

Tocqueville did not look to America, therefore, for a model of constitutional design or legislation. He sought to discover the effects of popular sovereignty particularly in the states, where majorities ruled with little or no resistance, in order to determine its advantages, disadvantages, and dangers. This was the knowledge he thought his French readers would find most useful in contemplating their own future.

The results of the institution of complete popular sovereignty in the U.S. were not what many had expected. Where people see themselves to be equal, everyone is granted a right to vote.[48] Merit is supposed to be the only qualification for office; but in America the results of universal suffrage are not what some had imagined. Democratic peoples do not necessarily elect the best or most virtuous individuals among them; on the contrary, people who believe that they are equal tend to be envious. They admit the superiority of others only grudgingly and when they think that it is absolutely necessary; they will, therefore, elect outstanding individuals in a crisis. Men of refined tastes are not willing

---

48. Tocqueville recognized, of course, that these rights were not extended to nonwhites or women (but argued that the confinement of married women to the private sphere was a beneficial exception, as will be discussed below).

to put themselves forward as candidates, moreover, because they are not willing to pander to the vulgar opinions of the crowd. Those who seek to advance their interests through legislation or by holding political office do form associations and parties; but these parties do not represent great principles or fundamental divisions. Tocqueville observes that "two great parties... have divided men since free societies have existed," those who want to limit popular power and those who want to expand it indefinitely. But in a democratic social state, the popular party easily wins; as a result, the rich and the highly educated tend to withdraw from politics. The need to garner the support of the majority nevertheless reduces the dangers posed by the freedom of the press and freedom of association, both of which are necessary conditions for meaningful competitive elections. Because the majority is the source of all political power, all parties and associations have to seek to obtain the support of a majority. Unless they win an openly contested election, they cannot credibly claim to represent the will of the people. Parties and associations thus use the press to attack the individuals and party in office as well as to put forward their own favored policies in order to gather support. Because it is easy and relatively inexpensive to publish a newsletter, there are many outlets. No opinion goes unchallenged or becomes authoritative unless and until it can demonstrate that it has majority support in an election. No association can claim to be acting on behalf of the people by seizing power with force; all associations have to try to persuade a majority of the voters to agree with them in order to acquire power peacefully.

Tocqueville's observations of "democracy at work" in the American states led him to modify his understanding of the kind of tyranny people living in a democratic social state had to fear. The great advantage of popular government is that it necessarily aims at serving the interests of the majority. The great disadvantage of such government is that it often lacks knowledge of the best means of achieving its end. Frequent elections and mediocre candidates combine to produce instability in the laws and inexpert administration of them. The greatest danger posed by popular government is not, however, its ineptitude or consequent weakness. On the contrary, the powers of a popular government tend to become ever more expansive.

Universal suffrage, in effect, puts government in the hands of the "poor," those who have to work for a living or possess only a small amount of property. Such people do not have the leisure to acquire a great deal of education. They are, however, quite capable of thinking of ever-new ways government can further their material interests — by building schools, roads, and ports or new trade regulations. Such people form associations and create parties to elect friendly representatives. These representatives, when elected, continually expand the powers and policies of the government in order to please their constituents.

Because all branches and levels of a popular government are controlled by the majority, the majority has the power to do what it wishes; dissenting minorities and individuals have no effective legal protection. At most, dissenters can hope to persuade a majority of their fellow citizens in the next election to support, if not to agree with, them. Tocqueville admits that where popular sovereignty is established, a majority is not apt to use its effectively unlimited political power to oppress those who disagree with or challenge its policies openly or directly. On the contrary, believing that each individual is the best judge of his own interests — the maxim at the root of popular sovereignty itself—a popular majority will not try to force dissenting individuals or minorities to accept its opinions or policies unless they deem such agreement to be necessary to maintain social order or promote the prosperity of all. But, Tocqueville observes, under conditions of popular sovereignty, majority opinion tends to exercise a kind of tyranny that is more insidious and difficult to oppose, precisely because it is indirect and intellectual. In the United States, he observes, the popular sovereign does not command citizens to cease criticizing its decrees or opinions with threats of death or prison. People are free to debate and discuss questions until a majority has formed and spoken; even after it has formed, the majority does not prohibit dissenters from continuing to think, say, or write what they want. The majority merely refuses to listen to or associate with those whose views do not conform to their own. As a result, the dissenter finds himself without an audience. He is silenced more effectively by his isolation than by any official censor.

Americans have escaped much of the potential tyranny of the majority, Tocqueville observes, because of their decentralized system of administration. Different majorities form around the different levels of government, and their participation in local governments teaches those who disagree with the majority how to associate with others to defend their own views and to increase their impact. The complex structure of American popular government helps protect the liberty of individuals in another way as well. By making knowledge of the law both difficult to acquire and yet necessary in so many daily interactions, complex government elevates the status and influence of "jurists" (or lawyers). As a result of their training (especially in case-based Anglo-American law with its reliance on precedents), lawyers acquire a taste for order and distaste for continual change, especially in the law. Legalistic ways of thought are diffused throughout the population by the requirement that everyone granted a right to vote must also serve on a jury, if called. Jurors do not merely receive a practical education in equity. Few may fear that they will be prosecuted for a crime, but most see that they may be liable to a civil procedure. Especially in civil cases, jurors thus tend to decide cases with the thought that they themselves may be judged in the future. Because civil laws are so complicated, moreover, civil trials give judges an opportunity to educate jurors about the law and the importance of rights. The only political options in a democratic social state, Tocqueville insists, are to grant rights to everyone or deny them to all. Jury service has persuaded a large number of Americans of the desirability of the former. It is primarily by participating in free government that Americans learn to appreciate its advantages.

MORES

Tocqueville concludes his reflections on the effects of popular sovereignty in the United States by arguing that the Americans have been able to maintain a large democratic republic for three reasons: their physical circumstances, their laws, and their mores. Their relative geographical isolation allowed the North Americans to establish a federation that retains the advantages of local government. Having a vast, effectively unpopulated continent ready to cultivate with their own industry has helped them prosper, and this prosperity has made them relatively content. However, Tocqueville points out, if the physical circumstances were sufficient, democratic republics would also have been established in South America. There Spanish settlers were confronted by a native population they had to subdue and then rule; they did not bring habits of local government like the English colonists to their north. Absent such habits and experience, the Mexicans who tried to copy the constitutional design of the U.S. could not do so successfully. The laws were thus more important than the physical circumstances in enabling the North Americans to establish and maintain a large democratic republic. Indeed, Tocqueville states that the main purpose of the first volume of *Democracy in America* was to inform his French readers of what the laws of the U.S. were. However, in describing the federation, town institutions, and constitution of the judicial power that he thought had enabled the Americans to preserve their liberties in a democratic social state, Tocqueville had shown that the laws of the U.S. worked not directly, because of their wisdom or goodness, so much as indirectly, by shaping the experience, education, opinions, habits, and sentiments of the people who lived under them. He thus concludes that, of the three causes that made it possible to maintain a democratic republic in the U.S., the laws were more important than the circumstances, but the mores these laws fostered were even more crucial.

In emphasizing the importance of "mores," Tocqueville once again followed Montesquieu and Rousseau, although he defined the term (and hence the phenomenon) somewhat differently. According to Montesquieu, "mores and manners are usages that laws have not established, or that they have not been able, or have not wanted, to establish."[49] Tocqueville applied the term more broadly "not only to mores strictly speaking, which could be called habits of the heart, but to the different notions that men possess, to the diverse opinions that are current among them, and to the ensemble of ideas from which the habits of the mind are formed."[50]

Like Montesquieu, Tocqueville recognized that these habits of mind and feeling could not be implanted, shaped, or destroyed directly by legislation. People may voice opinions they are required to express on pain of punishment, but they do not think or feel on command. Habits

49. Charles de Secondat de Montesquieu, *The Spirit of the Laws*, trans. and ed. Anne M. Cohler, Basia Carolyn Miller, and Harold Samuel Stone (Cambridge: Cambridge University Press, 1989), pt. 3, bk. 19, chap. 16, 317.
50. *DA*, 466.

and sentiments can be fostered or changed indirectly, however, by the example a ruler set for his people, as Montesquieu observed,[51] or, as Tocqueville argued, by the practical experience people had living under a certain set of institutions or laws. Just as it is difficult for a reader to determine exactly how and in what proportions the "climate, religion, laws, maxims of the government, examples of past things, mores, and manners" work together to form the general spirit of a nation that, in turn, determines the character of its laws, according to Montesquieu, because he shows that the various factors interact with one another, it is difficult to distinguish the way Tocqueville thinks that circumstances and laws combine to produce a "social state," which determines the legislation and mores of a people, from the way in which he thinks that mores, pre-sumably of a different origin, work with the circumstances and laws to determine whether a people in a democratic social state will live under a free or a despotic government.[52] Tocqueville himself thought that distin-guishing the effect of the democratic social state itself from the effects of the particular "point of departure" on specifically American mores was so important that he devoted the entire second volume of *Democracy in America* to the effort. He knew that his French readers would have to deal with the first without the advantages of the second.

Montesquieu emphasized the softening effects of commerce on mores. He observed that nations that traded with one another tended to have more peaceful relations, not only because it was in their eco-nomic interest but also because the knowledge of foreign ways they acquired by means of trade made them more tolerant. Commerce did not have the same unifying effect on the citizens of a particular nation, however; it tended to lead them to compete more than to cooperate. Montesquieu saw both effects in England, which had built an empire

51. *Spirit of the Laws*, bk. 19, chap. 14, 315.

52. Nolla (*DA*, 466*n*v) is thus correct to object to the claim made by Melvin Richter, "The Uses of Theory: Tocqueville's Adaptation of Montesquieu," *Essays in Theory and History* (Cambridge, Mass.: Harvard University Press, 1970), 90–91, that by the term *mores*, Tocqueville designates all that Montesquieu understood by *general spirit* with the exception of laws. Whereas Montesquieu seeks to identify the various factors that go into producing the "spirit" that determines the laws of particular nations, Tocqueville analyzes the component factors and effects of two general "social states," aristocracy and democracy, shared by many nations.

by means of navigation and trade rather than military conquest like Rome but where the classes as well as individual citizens competed at home for wealth and influence.

Tocqueville also observed the effects of commerce on American habits, but the effects he emphasized were somewhat different. He saw that the Americans "carry into politics the habits of business. They love order, without which business cannot prosper, and they particularly prize regularity of mores, which lays the foundation of good business establishments."[53] But in America, Tocqueville emphasized, these commercial habits had been combined with religious beliefs to create a new form of democratic family life. As a result, Tocqueville argued, the concern with commerce that Rousseau had argued (in his *First Discourse*) was undermining all virtue and public-spiritedness in modern nations did not have that effect in America.

Tocqueville did not attribute the gentler mores of modern nations to the effects of commerce, however, so much as to an increasing equality of condition.[54] Like Rousseau, Tocqueville thought that human beings feel a natural sympathy for the suffering of other sentient beings, so long as their self-interest does not intervene. Like Rousseau, Tocqueville thus thought that human beings spontaneously form small communities to which they feel strong sentimental ties.[55] Also like Rousseau, Tocqueville saw that these sentimental ties to the local community were easily and frequently destroyed by the ineptitude of the government and/or foreign conquest. Once the sentimental ties were broken, the connection between the interest of the individual and the good of the community could be revived only on the basis of reason. Without understanding, much less seeking to apply Rousseau's abstract formal theory concerning the general will, Tocqueville observed, Americans had learned to see the connection between their

53. *DA*, 463.

54. See "How Mores Become Milder as Conditions Become Equal," *DA*, 987–94. In his notes, Tocqueville observed that *sympathy* "is a democratic word. You have real sympathy only for those similar to you and your equals" (*DA*, 989nf).

55. "The town is the only association that is so much a part of nature that wherever men are gathered together, a town takes shape by itself. Town society exists therefore among all peoples no matter what their customs and their laws" (*DA*, 101).

own material interests and the prosperity of the community by participating in local government. As a result, the Americans had acquired
a kind of calculation-based public-spiritedness.

Tocqueville did not think that the public spirit Americans formed
by participating in local government sufficed, however, to prevent local
majorities from imposing their policies and opinions on minorities or
individuals. At all levels of government, the majority not only retained
complete political power. Democratic majorities were able to exercise
greater tyranny over the minds of individuals, informally and without
coercion, than any previous despot had been able to imagine merely
by isolating those who dissented or disagreed. In America, Tocqueville
concluded, the majority did not enforce its will directly on minorities
or individuals, because it did not believe that it should.

> Nature and circumstances had made out of the inhabitant of the
> United States an audacious man.... If the mind of the Americans
> were free of all hindrances, you would soon find among them the
> boldest innovators and the most implacable logicians in the world.
> But the revolutionaries of America are obliged to profess publicly a
> certain respect for Christian morality and equity that does not allow
> them to violate laws easily.... Until now no one has been found in the
> United States who has dared to advance this maxim: that everything
> is allowed in the interest of society.

Tocqueville thus thought that "religion, which among the Americans
never directly takes part in the government of society, must be considered as the first of their political institutions."[56]

Tocqueville's argument concerning the effect of American religious
beliefs on their political practice was, to say the least, paradoxical. He
was contending, in effect, that Americans were able to maintain a free
government, because their minds and imaginations were confined by
the tyranny of the majority exercised informally with regard to religion
and morality. The first Puritan settlers had brought a combination of
strict religious dogma and morality with democratic political institutions with them from England. Once they were joined by colonists representing different Christian sects, however, each of these sects became

56. *DA*, 475.

a minority. Because each of these sects was a minority, even Catholics came to accept the Protestant belief that each individual should be left free to decide the best way of achieving his own salvation on the basis of his own conscience—at least so far as the law was concerned. Each sect was permitted to worship God in its own way, but because they all preached the same morality in the name of God, a large majority of the Americans had come to accept the same basic set of moral principles. No religious institution or set of beliefs was imposed by law on any individual or group—or was resisted because it was externally imposed. Because it was necessary to acquire the support of a majority in order to obtain political action on behalf of any particular interest or opinion, people seeking to enhance their material interests through political action did not find it expedient to question these moral principles in public.

Like Rousseau, Tocqueville thought that it was necessary for a people to subscribe to a limited set of religious beliefs—in the existence of God, an immortal soul, and punishment in the afterlife—in order to maintain a free government. Rousseau had argued that such beliefs should, therefore, be mandated by law. But Tocqueville observed in America that a majority continued to hold such Christian beliefs precisely because they were not required or enforced by law.

Like Rousseau, Tocqueville also recognized that beliefs alone were not sufficient to check or direct human action; the passions had to be enlisted. Even in America,

> religion . . . is often powerless to restrain the man amid the innumerable temptations presented by fortune. It cannot moderate in him the ardor to grow rich that comes to goad everyone, but it rules with sovereign power over the soul of the woman, and it is the woman who shapes the mores. America is assuredly the country in the world in which the marriage bond is most respected, and in which the highest and most sound idea of conjugal happiness has been conceived. In Europe, nearly all of the disorders of society are born around the domestic hearth and not far from the marital bed.[57]

57. *DA,* 473. On the role Rousseau attributed to women in shaping and controlling the mores of men, see "Dedication to Geneva," *Second Discourse; Letter to D'Alembert; Emile,* chap. 5.

Tocqueville thus concluded that one "cannot say that in the United States religion exercises an influence on laws or on the detail of political opinions, but it directs mores, and it is by regulating the family that it works to regulate the State."[58]

Five years later in volume 2 of *Democracy in America*, Tocqueville sought to distinguish what was of commercial, English, and Puritan origin in America from what was purely democratic (and thus applicable to the nations of continental Europe).[59] He came, as a result, to a somewhat different understanding of "the type of despotism democratic nations have to fear"[60] and the primary means of forestalling it.

Tocqueville's observations of the democratic social state in the U.S. had initially made him worry that everyone might become equally subject to a single tyrant, as the people of the Roman Empire had become subject to the Caesars. Acknowledging that it might still be possible for a man of extraordinary boldness and ambition to seize absolute power with popular support (as Napoleon had in France), Tocqueville continued to emphasize the importance of establishing constitutional restrictions on the power of any office or individual. Further reflection had nevertheless led him to conclude that it would become increasingly difficult in a democratic social state for any individual to mobilize and lead a popular movement to overthrow the existing government.

Seeing how similar they were to each other, people living in conditions of equality are not apt to grant the intellectual or other superiority of another. On the contrary, each tries to think for himself. When he discovers that he is not able to settle an issue for himself satisfactorily, he tends to accept the opinion of the majority, reasoning that if all human beings are essentially equal in intelligence, the opinion of the majority must be best. But even this potential tyranny of majority opinion, which Tocqueville had observed in the United States particularly with regard to religion, was not the source of the despotism he thought people living in a democratic social state had most to fear. The power of religion in America was a product of its peculiar Puritan "point of departure" and the fact that equality of condition there had not been

58. *DA,* 473.
59. See *DA,* 689na.
60. *DA,* 1246–48.

established by means of a violent revolution.[61] During a violent revolution, all ideas are brought into question along with all traditions and existing institutions.[62] His French contemporaries' fear that the coming of democracy would bring extreme instability of government, if not anarchy, is thus a result of their revolutionary experience.[63] Once the people had ousted the aristocracy, Tocqueville predicted, they would, like the Americans, begin concentrating on improving their own material conditions as individuals. The danger was not that they would be constantly or even sporadically agitating for political change. Small property holders attempting to improve their own position and economic resources love order and dislike commotion. They would not be apt to follow a demagogue, much less engage in popular uprisings or violent revolutions. Rather, the danger was that individuals, mistakenly thinking that they were independent, would voluntarily isolate themselves by withdrawing from public activity to concentrate on their own business and family, leaving the conduct of state affairs to officials elected or appointed to do so. Because isolated individuals (or families) are weak and unable to protect themselves from others, in a democratic social state, as in nature, they will, in fact, need help. Where they have not learned the art of association from participating in local government, they will look primarily to the central government to provide the assistance they need. By becoming increasingly

61. Tocqueville considered the American "revolution" to have been a war waged against a foreign "mother country" rather than against a native aristocracy.

62. The fact that Americans so emphatically preferred practice to theory did not mean, therefore, that there could be no great ideas or poetry produced in democratic nations. There was an accidental (particular) reason the Americans had not produced any great literature—their familiarity with and dependency upon the English. Likewise, Tocqueville thought that the similarities among individuals in equal conditions made them prefer general, abstract theories. He thus worried that historians writing under democratic conditions would downplay the importance of individuals and emphasize general causes and developments (as he himself had).

63. Tocqueville also argued that the experience of the small ancient democracies (which were not truly democratic, because they were based on slavery) and the cities of Renaissance Italy (which had no middle class) were not relevant to the large nations of modern Europe (DA, 1142–43nnn, p).

dependent upon the services of a central authority, they will become less and less able to act—or to think—for themselves. In a word, they will be less and less free.

Tocqueville did not think that there was any "power on earth that can prevent the growing equality of conditions from leading the human mind toward the search for what is useful, and from disposing each citizen to become enclosed within himself." He predicted, therefore, that "individual interest [would] become more than ever the principal, if not the sole motivating force of the actions of men."[64] What was crucial, therefore, was to see and affect how individuals understood their self-interest.

As a result of their experience in local government, he observed, Americans had formulated and propagated a doctrine of "interest well-understood." They had learned and told others that it is in the interest of a man not merely to be honest, but to sacrifice some immediate benefits in order to help others, so that they will, in turn, help him in the future. Unlike the specifically Christian moral precepts that constituted American "religion," Tocqueville thought the doctrine of "interest well-understood" could be propagated in France. "Since the doctrine is within reach of all minds, each man grasps it easily and retains it without difficulty. Accommodating itself marvelously to the weaknesses of men, it easily gains great dominion and it is not difficult for it to preserve that dominion, because the doctrine turns personal interest back against itself and, to direct passions, uses the incentive that excites them."[65] Indeed, he concluded "that the doctrine of interest well-understood seems... of all philosophical theories, the most appropriate to the needs of the men of our time, and... the most powerful guarantee remaining to them against themselves."[66]

In order to justify some of the sacrifices necessary to sustain a free government, for example, of lives in war, Tocqueville saw the understanding an individual held of his self-interest would need to be extended from this world to the next. He observed, however, "that

64. *DA,* 923.
65. *DA,* 921.
66. *DA,* 922.

interest is the principal means that religions themselves use to lead men,... take hold of the crowd and become popular."[67] Since human beings naturally hope their life will extend beyond death, it is not difficult to encourage them to believe that it may be possible. It is only necessary to see that this hope is not eradicated by the propagation or enforcement of materialistic doctrines that deny the immortality of the soul. Although human beings living in equal conditions tend to seek their immediate material prosperity above all else, they are so constituted that they are never completely satisfied by the pursuit of purely material enjoyments. That was the reason he thought one saw short-lived but extreme spiritualistic movements in the U.S. periodically arise in reaction to the pervasive concern with material well-being.

In explaining why the majority did not use its unlimited power despotically in the United States, Tocqueville had attributed the restraint of the Americans not simply to their religious beliefs but particularly to the way those religious beliefs shaped family life, because of the effect of these beliefs on women. Looking specifically at "the influence of democracy on mores properly so called" (i.e., "the habits of the heart") in volume 2, Tocqueville argued that equality of conditions would lead to easier, more affectionate relations between fathers and sons as well as brother and brother. "When the social state becomes democratic, and men adopt as [sic] general principle that it is good and legitimate to judge everything for yourself..., the power of opinion exercised by the father over the sons, as well as his legal power, becomes less great." The division of patrimonies into ever smaller parcels that results from the abolition of the law of primogeniture contributes even more to closer, more egalitarian relations, because "when the father of the family has little property, his son and he live constantly in the same place and are busy together with the same work. Habit and need draw them closer and force them to communicate with each other at every moment; so a sort of familial intimacy cannot fail to be established between them, which makes authority less absolute, and which is badly adapted to external forms of respect."[68] An analogous change occurs in the relations of brothers, when the elder son no longer inherits the

67. *DA*, 927.
68. *DA*, 1036–38.

whole estate and the power that goes with it. "Under democratic laws, the children are perfectly equal, consequently independent; nothing necessarily draws them closer together, but also nothing pushes them apart; and since they have a common origin, grow up under the same roof, are the object of the same concerns, and since no particular prerogative differentiates or separates them, you see arising easily among them the sweet and youthful intimacy of childhood."[69]

Democracy does not have the same effects on the lives of women, however, as it does on men. In America, Tocqueville observed, young girls are allowed to move freely in society; that is the only way they can learn enough about the characters (and possible deceptiveness) of other individuals to choose a mate for themselves. Once an American woman chooses a husband, however, "the independence of the woman becomes irretrievably lost amid the bonds of marriage.... Religious peoples and industrial nations have a particularly serious idea of marriage. The first consider the regularity of the life of a woman as the best guarantee and most certain sign of the purity of her morals. The others see in it the sure proof of the order and the prosperity of the house."[70] An American woman does not accept her confinement merely because she is required to do so by the tyrannous pressure of public opinion, however. She accepts it because she freely chooses it. Unlike some Europeans, "Americans do not believe that man and woman have the duty or the right to do the same things." Recognizing "nature had established such a great variation between the physical and moral constitution of the man and that of the woman," they have "applied to the two sexes the great principle of political economy that dominates industry today" and carefully divided the functions allotted to the two sexes. They "have allowed the [natural] inferiority of the woman to continue to exist in society," but by allowing her to develop the intelligence to choose her own fate and requiring her to practice the self-control necessary to honor the marriage contract, they have raised her to the intellectual and moral level of man. Tocqueville thought that these arrangements constituted "the true notion of democratic progress." Indeed, he went so far as to suggest that "the singular prosperity and growing strength

69. *DA,* 1039.
70. *DA,* 1048.

of this people must be principally attributed... to the superiority of their women."[71] He did not think that the American attempt to elevate women to become the moral and intellectual equals of men would be duplicated soon in France, however; the French were too accustomed to treating women as objects of desire but essentially inferior to men because of the obvious differences in their physical constitutions.

More relevant, the intelligence and self-control, if not self-sacrifice, of American women might show that individuals living in a commercial republic could be virtuous. But if the sort of despotism people living in a democratic social state most had to fear arose from their tendency to withdraw into private life, the pleasures associated with family life only served to enhance the problem. When Tocqueville imagined "under what new features despotism could present itself to the world," he saw "an innumerable crowd of similar and equal men who spin around restlessly, in order to gain small and vulgar pleasures.... Each one of them, withdrawn apart, is like a stranger to the destiny of all the others; his children and his particular friends form for him the entire human species; as for the remainder of his fellow citizens, he is next to them, but he does not see them..., and if he still has a family, you can say that at least he no longer has a country."[72]

Tocqueville recognized that the "equality, which makes men independent of each other, makes them contract the habit and the taste to follow only their will in their personal actions."[73] Believing that all people are equal, they resist the imposition of authority and seek to establish free political institutions. Unfortunately, however, Tocqueville saw that these same independent individuals would be led—unintentionally, gradually, but inexorably—to establish a huge, central political power. Because people living in a democratic social state seek to improve their material condition, they are industrious and favor the development of industry. But the expansion of industry brings needs for more government regulation of finance, commerce, and manufacturing along with more schools, canals, ports, and taxes. The habits of thought of people

71. *DA*, 1067.
72. *DA*, 1049–50.
73. *DA*, 1191.

living in conditions of equality lead them to look to a unitary central power to satisfy their needs. Simple ideas are more easily understood and thus appeal more to people than do complicated ones. People who regard themselves as basically the equals of others also think that justice requires that everyone be treated the same way. They thus favor uniform standards administered by a single organization. People may think that they retain control of a centralized administration if they elect representatives to a national assembly to oversee its operation; but, Tocqueville observes, they exercise that control for a single day. A democratically elected and responsive government will try to serve the material interests of the people. By making them ever more dependent upon it, however, this government saps the source of individual enterprise and so eradicates the source of their prosperity along with their liberty.

Tocqueville's primary purpose in writing was to convince his readers that it was possible to forestall the development of this soft form of despotism. It was possible to disperse power among a variety of different officials and make them independent of their superiors by having them elected locally. It was possible to maintain a judicial check on elected officials and to educate people in the importance of rights by retaining jury trials. It was possible to maintain the freedom of the press that enables journalists to expose the malfeasance of governmental officials and facilitates the formation of associations through which people can promote their own interests instead of relying on government to act for them. Laws do not work so much directly by commanding citizens to do or not to do certain things. Laws work even more effectively by structuring the experiences people have and thus shaping the opinions and feelings, that is, the "mores," as Tocqueville defined them, on the basis of which they act. That was the primary lesson he took from Montesquieu and Rousseau, but he extended it much further in arguing that such an indirect form and understanding of government is especially appropriate for a people who want to be both equal and free.

By warning them of the danger they faced, Tocqueville hoped to persuade his readers to act in ways that would preserve their liberty—both as individuals and as nations. The Americans had discovered ways of preserving popular sovereignty and political liberty primarily, although not exclusively, as a result of their fortunate geographical location and distinctive historical "point of departure." Neither their laws nor their mores could or should simply be replicated elsewhere. With instruction from Tocqueville, however, legislators could learn from the American experience how to preserve liberty elsewhere as well.

7

Democratic Grandeur: How Tocqueville Constructed His New Moral Science in America

ALAN S. KAHAN

Tocqueville the Moralist

Alexis de Tocqueville was in some respects a political scientist by necessity, rather than by intention. His intent was often that of a moralist, one who studied politics as a means to moral ends. As a moralist, what interested him most was describing human character, rather than describing political or social systems; instead of searching for the ideal form of government, he sought to encourage the development of certain kinds of human beings. What blurs the distinction between Tocqueville the political scientist and Tocqueville the moralist was that for Tocqueville political freedom was essential to the full development of moral character. Freedom was both the precondition for and an essential component of human grandeur. Vice flourished in the absence of freedom. Virtue was encouraged by its presence. In its highest form, virtue was only possible for free human beings living in a free society. If Tocqueville invented a "new science of politics," as the well-known quotation goes, it was alongside a new moral science. He belongs to a long French tradition of moralists, stretching back to Michel de Montaigne, Jean de la Bruyère (one of his favorite authors as a high school student), and François de La Rochefoucauld.[1]

1. For other discussions of Tocqueville the moralist, see L. E. Shiner, *The Secret Mirror: Literary Form and History in Tocqueville's Recollections* (Ithaca, N.Y.: Cornell University Press, 1988). In my review of Shiner, I wrote that "for Shiner, the

His discoveries in America were as much moral as political. What he learned about the democratic character and its characteristic forms of greatness[2] are at the heart of *Democracy in America.*

That Tocqueville intended to communicate a new moral science to his readers—readers more attuned to moral concerns than many of the twentieth-century political scientists who have discussed Tocqueville's "new political science"—is shown by the Introduction to *Democracy in America.* It opens with a discussion of the history of the growth of democracy, defined as "equality of conditions." In the course of that discussion, Tocqueville suggests that the spread of knowledge and education put "into relief the natural grandeur of man." A few paragraphs after this remark the secular history[3] of equality ends. The rise of equality is then redescribed in religious terms, through a parallel sacred history in which the rise of equality is revealed to be a "Providential fact." The mission statement of *Democracy in America* follows this double history and is addressed to "those who lead society." It includes both a moral (and in part religious) component and a political component. The mission is "to instruct democracy, to revive its beliefs if possible, to purify its mores, to regulate its movements, to substitute little by little the science of public affairs for its inexperience, knowledge of its true interests for its blind instincts; to adapt its government to times and places; to modify it according to circumstances and men."[4]

In the central portion of the Introduction, Tocqueville proposes to aid these democratic leaders in accomplishing their mission through his "new political science," a striking phrase that has monopolized many

---

moral, not the political, is the key reference for Tocqueville; this book might well have been subtitled 'Tocqueville the Moralist.'" Jean-Louis Benôit did just that, in French, in *Tocqueville moraliste* (Paris: Champion, 2004), passim. The latter discussion, however, uses the term "moralist" in a different sense than found here.

2. The Schleifer translation of *Democracy in America* translates *grandeur* as "grandeur." I use "grandeur" and "greatness" interchangeably. Alexis de Tocqueville, *Democracy in America: Historical-Critical Edition of "De la démocratie en Amérique,"* ed. Eduardo Nolla, trans. James T. Schleifer, 4 vols. (Indianapolis: Liberty Fund, 2010). This edition is hereafter cited as *DA.*

3. A history largely derived from the standard Scottish Enlightenment account of the four stages of human history, that is, savage, pastoral, feudal, and, finally, commercial (and egalitarian).

4. *DA,* 9–10, 16.

readers' attention. But what follows is not a set of political prescriptions. Instead, Tocqueville calls on the "most powerful, most intelligent and *most moral* classes of the nation" (emphasis added) to take democracy in hand. They must act to avert social damage, which Tocqueville describes in moral terms, damage incurred when the wrong kind of democracy, "abandoned to its wild instincts," breeds "servility," idolatry (democracy "adored as the image of strength"), and excess. Democratic peoples and people are threatened by a new evil, one from which aristocratic society, for all its faults, had preserved them: their souls risked being degraded.[5]

The Introduction thus creates a moral problematic in which the alternative outcomes of democracy are human degradation or human greatness, just as it sets up the political alternatives of democratic freedom or democratic despotism. Tocqueville the moralist aimed to teach society's leaders how to avoid the one and encourage the other. This was also the purpose of his new political science, a fundamentally moral purpose, one that aimed at ensuring that human greatness was the outcome of democracy. Tocqueville's political science, like his moral science, supported "human liberty, source of all moral grandeur."[6]

Some will argue that what Tocqueville sought in America was not moral grandeur or virtue, and that in fact he did not find it there. This misperception is excused by the fact that Tocqueville himself wrote that the Americans were *not* virtuous, at least in the way traditionally expected of the citizens of free republics, and that those who had contempt for material well-being and valued glory and great accomplishments should not choose democracy. But *Democracy in America* is a book designed to show readers how they can have their cake and eat it too, that is, how democracy can lead to even greater freedom, and thus in its own way to as much or more human greatness as aristocracy.

Tocqueville recognized from the beginning of his trip that modern democracies would not be, could not be, as virtuous as the Romans of the Republic, the traditional paragons of virtue, had been. As he wrote in his travel notebooks, America was not like the ancient republics, in which individuals sacrificed their private interests for the general good.

5. *DA*, 17–18, 20.
6. *DA*, 24.

He mused that America proved wrong the long tradition that identified virtue as a prerequisite for freedom. In America, it was a "sort of refined and intelligent selfishness" that produced freedom. "Americans are not more virtuous than others; but they are infinitely more enlightened (I speak of the mass) than any other people I know; I don't mean only that there are more people there who know how to read and write . . . , but that the number of people who understand public affairs, know laws and precedents, have a feeling for national interests and the ability to understand them, is greater there than anywhere else on earth."[7]

Tocqueville found in the self-interest well understood of the Americans a democratic substitute for virtue. But this ersatz quality, for all its many virtues, did not produce the taste for human grandeur that Tocqueville sought and which was in his view necessary for freedom to endure. Religion (as well as other, secular mechanisms) was necessary for building moral character in democratic society because the doctrine of enlightened self-interest could only go so far and no farther. Interest "*succeeds in fact in making society proceed comfortably, but without grandeur*" (emphasis original). Enlightened self-interest, necessary and useful though it is in a democratic society, can produce only the lesser virtues, not grandeur. Surely Tocqueville was speaking for himself when he wrote that "great souls for whom this doctrine cannot be enough, pass in a way through it and go beyond it, while ordinary souls stop there."[8]

How could one encourage the formation of great souls in democratic society? How could people in such societies be led to look beyond self-interest? The problem was that, as Tocqueville wrote, "Do you want to give the human spirit a certain nobility, a generous fashion of envisioning the things of this world? Do you want to inspire in men a sort of contempt for material goods? Do you desire to bring about or to maintain profound convictions and prepare great devotions. . . . If such . . . is the principal object that men must propose for themselves in society, do not opt for the government of democracy; it would not lead you surely to the goal." But if democracy did not lead "surely" to the

7. Tocqueville, *Oeuvres complètes* (Paris: Gallimard, 1951–), 5:234, 278.
8. *DA,* 922nk, 923nn, 925.

moral perfections Tocqueville sought, it could still lead there, just as democracy did not inevitably bring freedom, but it could and should. Tocqueville never renounced the aristocratic goal of moral perfection.[9]

Indeed, it is not certain that Tocqueville considered aristocracies superior to democracies even in virtue: "I doubt that men were more virtuous in aristocratic centuries than in others." The real difference with regard to virtue between aristocracies and democracies was that "it is certain that [aristocracies] talked constantly about the beauties of virtue; they only studied in secret how it was useful. But as [in democracies] imagination soars less and as each person concentrates on himself, moralists become afraid of this idea of sacrifice, and they no longer dare to offer it to the human mind; so they are reduced to trying to find out if the individual advantage of citizens would not be to work toward the happiness of all...what was only an isolated remark becomes a general doctrine," that is, the doctrine of enlightened self-interest. If one wanted to have virtue, it was useful to talk about it. But there was one place where people still talked about the beauties of virtue in democratic societies: in church (even if they also spoke of interest there). Religion is a back door through which the pursuit of greatness enters democratic societies.[10]

At the foundation of American greatness and American freedom, Tocqueville found American religion. It must be noted at the outset, however, that there are two roughly parallel accounts of the origins of democratic moral greatness in Tocqueville. Tocqueville's study of America revealed that democratic moral grandeur had a dual basis, both secular and spiritual, or to put it in overly narrow but more familiar terms, both political and religious (the secular basis of democratic moral greatness includes aspects of civil society that are not strictly political, such as the habit of association, and Tocqueville's perspective on democratic spirituality is not limited to formal religion, e.g., his discussion of poetry). The secular sphere could and must, in Tocqueville's view, also encourage the development of the highest aspects of human character through association and political participation.

9. *DA*, 400.
10. *DA*, 919.

Politics, however, was in a sense a more aristocratic means to the end of freedom, whereas religion was a more democratic one.[11] For Tocqueville, "Political liberty, from time to time, gives sublime pleasures to a certain number of citizens."[12] The restricted number of those who felt this sublime pleasure made it harder for political freedom to struggle against the bad aspects of "equality [that] provides a multitude of small enjoyments at every moment." Religion, unlike politics, had the advantage of naturally appealing to all human beings. Religion was inextricably associated with that universal human trait, hope, because all people inevitably desired a life after death. Thus, "Unbelief is an accident; faith alone is the permanent state of humanity."[13] Faith was part of human nature, and thus religion was in a better position than was political freedom to fight the constant temptation of egalitarian pettiness and materialism. The tactic of using a democratic phenomenon, like religion, to counterbalance democracy's flaws is classic Tocqueville: "Use democracy to moderate democracy. That is the sole path of salvation open to us."[14] The role of religion in political education and in encouraging democratic greatness was crucial for Tocqueville.[15]

11. Comparison between Tocqueville's ideas and those expressed by Benjamin Constant in his essay on ancient and modern freedom is almost unavoidable here. Constant, too, thinks politics less natural to modern people than religion. But the comparison is deceptive. From Constant's perspective, modern greatness should not have a political origin at all; it should be purely private. For Tocqueville, a purely private human greatness is not possible, and modern democratic greatness has a *different* political source and expression than ancient freedom, as well as a private origin in democratic religion.

12. *DA*, 876. Tocqueville is ambivalent about whether all people have a natural desire for freedom, among other desires, or whether only some people take particular pleasure from it, as in the citation above. He is certain, however, that religion is natural to all people, though the taste for it will vary and circumstances will make some people reject it.

13. *DA*, 482.

14. *DA*, 1279nn. As Antoine notes, for Tocqueville, religion in democratic society never has a weight equal to democracy itself; it can only be a sort of therapeutic counterweight. See Agnès Antoine, *L'impensé de la démocratie: Tocqueville, la citoyenneté et la religion* (Paris: Fayard, 2003), 152.

15. A point emphasized by Antoine, *L'impensé*, 130.

The rest of this essay emphasizes how, in Tocqueville's account, religion contributes to democratic moral greatness, and hence to freedom. This emphasis is in line with Tocqueville's own tactics. For Tocqueville, the religious origin of democratic grandeur needed to be stressed for a nineteenth-century French audience accustomed to seeing a contradiction between religion (e.g., Catholicism) and democracy.[16] Today many perceive the same contradiction between religion and freedom, whether with respect to Catholicism, Islam, or other religious traditions, and the subject is thus of contemporary importance.

Tocqueville discussed religion in *Democracy in America* in two ways.[17] He discussed the effect of democracy on religion, and the effect of religion on democracy. As an example of the former, he argued that aristocratic religion, like aristocratic society, emphasized intermediate powers, in this case between humans and God (e.g., angels, saints, and devils). Democracy banished or diminished these intermediate beings, as it did all aristocratic intermediate powers between the people and the Sovereign. "God reveals himself more and more to the human mind in his full and entire majesty." Democratic religion thus naturally emphasizes the greatness of God, "Providentially," as Tocqueville would doubtless say, precisely when human beings are most in need of greatness to contemplate.[18]

It is on the influence of religion on democracy that Tocqueville put his chief emphasis, however. He wanted to "say more oratorically how [religion] is indispensable in democracies in order to immaterialize man." For Tocqueville, there was a spiritual, immaterial component to human nature that was an essential part of human greatness. Faced with what he considered the decline of the "feeling for the great" in his time, Tocqueville turned to religion for help.[19] To understand the

16. Tocqueville was far from alone in associating religion with democracy, and contemporary French thinkers from François Guizot to the socialists argued along the same lines. The reason Tocqueville had to repeat it was that numerous Frenchmen, on both the Left and the Right, saw Church and freedom as opposed.

17. As he himself distinguished. See *DA*, 742*n*b.

18. *DA*, 838.

19. *DA*, 742–43*n*b; Tocqueville to P.-P. Royer-Collard, April 6, 1838, Tocqueville, *Oeuvres complètes*, 11:61.

role religion plays in fostering human greatness in democratic societies, we must understand two things: (1) Tocqueville's view of human nature and human greatness in general, and (2) Tocqueville's view of how democracy affects human nature. Only then can the role religion plays in creating great democratic souls be understood.

Tocqueville and Pascal

Tocqueville's understanding of human nature was developed, as was so much of Tocqueville's thought, in dialogue with certain privileged partners. With respect to religion, these were Blaise Pascal, Jean-Jacques Rousseau, and François-René de Châteaubriand (which is not to say that others, as diverse as Louis Bossuet, Montesquieu, Voltaire, and Hugues-Félicité Robert de Lamennais, did not influence him as well).[20] It is his dialogue with Pascal that is most relevant to Tocqueville's views of human greatness. Tocqueville often expressed himself about human nature in imagery and language borrowed from Pascal. However, Tocqueville gave these terms a very different meaning. Tocqueville's definition of human greatness, and thus of the manner in which religion may help human beings attain moral perfection, is very different from Pascal's. Contrasting the pair's divergent use of some of the same terms helps to highlight Tocqueville's own position.

Many commentators have argued that Tocqueville owed much more to Pascal than just a few striking phrases. That Tocqueville read Pascal assiduously there can be no doubt. As his oft-cited letter to his friend Louis de Kergorlay states, there were three authors to whom he constantly referred: Pascal, Montesquieu, and Rousseau.[21] References overt and covert to Pascal abound in *Democracy in America* and elsewhere in Tocqueville's writings. Nevertheless, it aroused much surprise when in 1965 Luis Diez del Corral informed a session of the French Académie des Sciences Morales et Politiques of Pascal's influence on

---

20. On Lamennais's hitherto underestimated influence on Tocqueville, see Lucien Jaume, *Tocqueville. Les sources aristocratiques de la liberté. Biographie intellectuelle* (Paris: Fayard, 2008).

21. Tocqueville to Kergorlay, Tocqueville, *Oeuvres complètes*, vol. 13, tome 1:418.

Tocqueville. Since Diez del Corral's seminal work, Doris Goldstein, Peter Lawler, Joshua Mitchell, and Eduardo Nolla have taken up the case for Pascal's influence, particularly with regard to Tocqueville's religious thought.[22]

Against the argument that Tocqueville and Pascal held similar substantive views, we have the evidence of two other sources. One is Louis de Kergorlay, Tocqueville's correspondent, cousin, and close friend. The other, still weightier, is Tocqueville's writings themselves.

Tocqueville died in 1859. Not long after, in 1867, Kergorlay published what he described as a "literary study" of Tocqueville. In it, he noted the fact that has seduced so many readers into overestimating Pascal's influence on Tocqueville: his influence on Tocqueville's literary style. Once he reached maturity, Kergorlay writes, Tocqueville attached himself by preference "to no one more than to Pascal for the very basis of his language, and to Voltaire for ease and the art of making one's style light. He demanded of the former above all to help him perfect the qualities which were natural to him, and of the other to teach him something of those with which he felt himself less naturally gifted." This is similar to a remark made by Tocqueville's other great friend, Gustave de Beaumont, that "these two minds [Tocqueville and Pascal] were made for one another. For Tocqueville the constant obligation to think that Pascal inflicts on you was full of charm."[23]

However, no one has ever suggested that Voltaire was an important intellectual influence on Tocqueville. For Kergorlay, the same can be said of Pascal: "Assuredly nothing is further from Voltaire's genre than Tocqueville, and neither is Pascal the type to which one might

22. See Luis Diez del Corral, "Tocqueville et Pascal," *Revue des Travaux de l'Académie des Sciences Morales et Politiques*, 2nd semestre 1965, 70–83; Diez del Corral, "Tocqueville et les *Pensées* de Pascal," *Philosophie*, 12–14, no. 2 (1986–88):321–32; Doris S. Goldstein, *Trial of Faith: Religion and Politics in Tocqueville's Thought* (New York: Elsevier, 1975); Peter Augustine Lawler, *The Restless Mind: Alexis de Tocqueville on the Origin and Perpetuation of Human Liberty* (Lanham, Md.: Rowman & Littlefield, 1993); Joshua Mitchell, *The Fragility of Freedom: Tocqueville on Religion, Democracy, and the American Future* (Chicago: University of Chicago Press, 1995); *DA*, 712nc.

23. Louis de Kergorlay, Tocqueville, *Oeuvres complètes*, 2:360; Gustave de Beaumont, in Diez del Corral, "Tocqueville et Pascal," vol. 13, tome 2:74.

justly compare him."[24] According to Kergorlay, Pascal's influence on Tocqueville was a matter of style, not substance. The many instances in which Tocqueville quotes, often covertly, from Pascal, or borrows his metaphors, hide an underlying gulf between the two thinkers as great as that which separates Tocqueville from Voltaire.

Tocqueville uses many images borrowed from Pascal. Often, however, he gives them a very different content. One such image in particular, that of the angel and the beast, is central to Tocqueville's understanding of human nature and its relationship to religion. It also shows us how much Tocqueville borrowed from Pascal in the matter of style and expression, while rejecting Pascal with regard to substance.

"The angel and the beast," a metaphor to describe the divergent aspects of human nature, figures prominently in Pascal's *Pensées*. Tocqueville borrowed the metaphor and used it on a number of occasions. For both Pascal and Tocqueville, the human soul was a compound of the angel and the beast, regardless of whether it was situated in an aristocratic or a democratic society. For both Pascal and Tocqueville, this compound was the fundamental source of the contradictions inherent in human nature. But this is the end of the similarity: Tocqueville and Pascal understood the angel and the beast very differently. For Pascal, speaking from a perspective that was radically Augustinian and Christian, the angel was great and the beast vile. For Pascal, all humanity's contradictions stem from this fundamental fact. Indeed, section 7 of the *Pensées*, "Contradictions," begins "Contradictions. (After showing how vile and how great man is.)."[25] But for Tocqueville, who was not Augustinian and who never once referred to the Fall of Man in his writings, the relationship between the beast and the angel was more complex. Although he occasionally refers to the *misère* of our nature, a very Pascalian term, Tocqueville is essentially a Pelagian, that is, a thinker who believes that no part of human nature is utterly vile. This is why he thinks human greatness is attainable in democratic societies. Tocqueville's *misère* stems from

---

24. Kergorlay, "Tocqueville," *Oeuvres complètes*, vol. 13, tome 2:360.

25. *Pensées*, 119. There are several different ways of numbering Pascal's *Pensées*. For convenience, I cite Blaise Pascal, *Pensées*, trans. A. J. Krailsheimer (New York: Penguin, 1966). Hereafter cited by number.

the fact that there *are* inevitably contradictions and doubts in a world where he would like there to be certainty. Pascal's *misère* stems from the fact that human nature is essentially vile and abject even in its greatest moments.

For Tocqueville, the angel represents our nonmaterial desires, or more broadly idealism, and the beast our material desires, or more broadly materialism. "Any philosophy or religion which wants to entirely ignore one or the other of these two things will produce some extraordinary individuals, but it will never have a broad effect on humanity." So far Pascal might go. But for Tocqueville the angel is not necessarily great, nor the beast necessarily vile. Both can be evil when taken to extremes, although Tocqueville claims a preference for the angel. Under certain circumstances, however, Tocqueville, unlike Pascal, prefers the things of the body. Thus, while in democratic societies the role of religion is to tear people away from the materialism natural to those societies and to lead them to higher goals, in aristocratic societies, which are naturally biased toward the ideal, a way must be found to bring people down to earth: "If I were born in an aristocratic century," in which "souls [were] as if benumbed in the contemplation of another world, I would want it to be possible for me to stimulate among such a people the sentiment of [material] needs; . . . I would try to excite the human mind in the pursuit of well-being."[26] Pascal could never have accepted this. He could only lament the inability of human beings to benumb their souls in the contemplation of Heaven while sitting quietly in a room.

For Tocqueville, the angel and the beast represent extremes between which religion, as well as the legislator, must navigate. As he put it: "All the art of the legislator consists in clearly discerning in advance these natural inclinations of human societies, in order to know where the effort of the citizens must be aided, and where . . . to slow it down. For these obligations differ according to the times. Only the end toward which humanity must always head is unchanging; the means to reach that end constantly vary." This end is unchanging even though Tocqueville refers in *Democracy in America* to aristocratic and democratic nations as being "like two distinct humanities, each of which has its

26. *DA*, 956.

particular advantages and disadvantages, its good and its evil which are its own." The elements of human character that must be checked and balanced in order to attain the desired end differ, as well as the means for doing so. "We must not aim to make ourselves similar to our fathers, but to work hard to attain the type of grandeur and happiness that is appropriate to us."[27]

Human beings were thus just as capable of moral perfection in the present as in the past, but their moral perfection, like their moral flaws, would be different, because of the differences between a modern democratic society and the people it produced, and the old aristocratic societies and the people they produced.[28] Angel and beast find very different opportunities to express themselves depending on their social situation. The fundamental truths of religion and of human nature may not be altered by time, but the functions of religion, both political and spiritual, do change over time. Religion therefore must find a way to help people balance the angel and the beast in their souls, the better to lead them toward their "unchanging end."

In their conceptions of human greatness, Tocqueville and Pascal were far apart. Their differences help us see more clearly the end Tocqueville was aiming at. For Pascal, "Man's greatness comes from knowing he is wretched. A tree does not know it is wretched. Thus it is wretched to know that one is wretched, but there is greatness in knowing that one is wretched." There is no escape from wretchedness, because such an escape would be tantamount to an escape from original sin, from the beast that is always and inevitably a part of human nature. Man's sole greatness lies in knowing that he is fallen, "recognizing that, if his nature is today like that of the animals, he must have fallen from some better state which was once his own." But knowledge of one's wretchedness is not, for Tocqueville, the foundation of human greatness—there is no hint of this view in Tocqueville. Rather, for Tocqueville there are inherent qualities in human beings, qualities that can be developed in democratic society, that are great.

27. *DA*, 955, 1282–83.

28. The one constant form of moral perfection in both societies would be political freedom.

Tocqueville's angel, with a little help from the legislator and the priest, is more powerful than Pascal's.[29]

Perhaps Tocqueville's angel is stronger because he gets more exercise than Pascal's or because his actions have more significance. Pascal wrote that "I have often said that the sole cause of man's unhappiness is that he does not know how to stay quietly in his room." Thus, "the only good thing for men is to be diverted from thinking of what they are, either by some occupation which takes their mind off it, or by some novel and agreeable passion which keeps them busy, like gambling, hunting, some absorbing show, in short by what is called diversion."[30] Pascal characterizes human action as a mere diversion from the human condition of wretchedness. Peter Lawler, attempting to create a Pascalian Tocqueville, transforms Tocqueville's political and intellectual involvement into such "diversions."[31] Tocqueville would have said that such activities, rather than being a diversion from the human condition, constitute an essential part of it, and more important, of human greatness. Pascal identifies human action with such trivial pursuits as gambling, hunting, and so on, with which he goes on to lump politics. That which is an essential aspect of human greatness for Tocqueville, political participation, is for Pascal no more important than gambling or sexual seduction. For Pascal, as for his inspiration St. Augustine, no action a person may take can lead to salvation. Tocqueville, however, was a moralist for whom politics was an essential part of morality. Salvation by faith alone was hardly a workable political strategy, nor was divine grace to be counted on.

Fundamentally, Raymond Aron was right when he rejected Diez del Corral's case for Pascal's influence on Tocqueville. As Aron said in the discussion in response to Diez del Corral, "All the multiple citations from Pascal that Tocqueville uses do not prove much.... The opinions of the same kind that one can attribute to Pascal, do not seem to

29. Pascal, *Pensées*, 114, 117. Jean-Louis Benôit speculates, on the basis of a letter Tocqueville's tutor, Abbé Lesueur, wrote to him, that Tocqueville rejected the idea of original sin entirely. His evidence is suggestive but not conclusive. See Benôit, *Tocqueville moraliste*, p. 568.

30. Pascal, *Pensées*, 136.

31. Lawler, *Restless Mind*, 110–11.

me to have contributed much to Tocqueville's intellectual or political education."[32]

Tocqueville and Human Perfection

Because we cannot rely on Pascal for help in understanding Tocqueville's view of human greatness, we must look more closely at Tocqueville's own writings, where references to human greatness abound, albeit in very scattered fashion. In what does human greatness consist for Tocqueville?[33] How can greatness be encouraged in a democratic society? From the texts, it quickly becomes clear that in response to these questions Tocqueville adopted a mix of utilitarian and perfectionist views.[34]

While "utilitarianism," that is, the greatest good for the greatest number, is a widely familiar term, "perfectionism" is not. "Perfectionism" was originally invented by Stanley Cavell to describe the ideas of the American essayist Ralph Waldo Emerson, but it has since been widely adopted and given a broader application.[35] The "perfectionist" tradition in Western thought goes back to Plato and Aristotle. Perfectionists value human excellences, variously defined, "regardless of how much a person enjoys or wants them." Some perfectionists care about

32. Diez del Corral, "Tocqueville et Pascal," 80. After Diez del Corral's presentation, there was a brief discussion recorded in the article, in which Aron took part.

33. Ralph Hancock claims that Tocqueville does not define man's true greatness, but in what follows I will argue that we have the elements of such a definition. See Hancock, "The Uses and Hazards of Christianity in Tocqueville's Attempt to Save Democratic Souls," in *Interpreting Tocqueville's "Democracy in America,"* ed. Ken Masugi (Savage, Md.: Rowman & Littlefield, 1991), 388. For Hancock's very different discussion of the theme of human greatness in Tocqueville, see 354–55 and following.

34. For a more extended discussion of Tocqueville's "perfectionism," see Kahan, "Checks and Balances for Democratic Souls," forthcoming, *American Political Thought.*

35. Stanley Cavell, *Conditions Handsome and Unhandsome: The Constitution of Emersonian Perfectionism* (Chicago: University of Chicago Press, 1981); Thomas Hurka, *Perfectionism* (Oxford: Oxford University Press, 1993).

only the perfection of a handful (Nietzsche) or of a minority (Matthew Arnold, Nietzsche in other moods). Some, such as Tocqueville, strive for the perfection of the majority.[36]

When Tocqueville talks about religion checking democracy's bad tendencies, he adopts a utilitarian perspective, and when he talks about religion encouraging democratic souls to pursue "higher" goals, he adopts a perfectionist perspective. We might add that his utilitarian viewpoint represents his recognition that democracy is more just than aristocracy, because it is for the greater good of the majority. His perfectionist perspective embodies the aristocratic aspect of his thought, devoted to the achievement of the noblest aspects of human nature—which, thanks in part to religion, democracy can also attain.[37] Religion works to improve both happiness (utility) and greatness (perfection). Tocqueville himself summarizes this dual function neatly: "If religion does not save men in the next world, it is at least very useful to their happiness and to their greatness in this one."[38]

But it would be wrong to approach Tocqueville too schematically, because he often mixes angel and beast, utility and perfection. "Who knows if, in the eyes of God, the beautiful is not the useful?"[39] More broadly, in the chapter of *Democracy in America* titled "How the Excessive Love of Well-Being Can Harm Well-Being," Tocqueville discusses the relationship between body and soul, and uses the metaphor of the angel and the beast in his own fashion. The passage deserves quotation at length:

> There is more of a connection than you think between the perfection of the soul and the improvement of the goods of the body; man...cannot separate the two entirely without finally losing sight of both of them....
>
> What makes us superior in this to animals is that we use our soul to find the material goods towards which their instinct alone leads

36. Hurka, *Perfectionism*.

37. Whether democracy can produce individuals equally perfect as those produced by aristocracy is a question that Tocqueville leaves open. See, among others, *DA*, 919, 1282.

38. *DA*, 744, 1282.

39. *DA*, 1282nf.

them. With man, the angel teaches the brute the art of satisfying himself. Man is capable of rising above the goods of the body and even of scorning life, an idea animals do not even conceive; he therefore knows how to multiply these very advantages to a degree that they also cannot imagine.

Everything that elevates, enlarges, expands the soul, makes it more capable of succeeding at even those enterprises that do not concern it.

Everything that enervates the soul, on the contrary, or lowers it, weakens it for all things, the principal ones as well as the least ones, and threatens to make it almost as powerless for the first as for the second. Thus the soul must remain great and strong, if only to be able, from time to time, to put its strength and its greatness at the service of the body.

If men ever succeed in being content with material goods, it is to be believed that they would little by little lose the art of producing them, and that they would end by enjoying them without discernment and without progress, like animals.[40]

The task of perfecting our souls' higher dimensions is therefore essential even to attaining our material desires—the angel and the beast are ultimately allies.[41]

Tocqueville nevertheless recognized the tensions between angel and beast, even within religious practice. Useful as religion was to Tocqueville's search for moral perfection, some of the most universal, democratic aspects of religion, necessary though they were to religion's appeal, could be harmful to Tocqueville's quest for human greatness. The promise of eternal bliss was, for Tocqueville, simply another form of materialism. This is why he thought Pascal's wager (that it is better to believe in God in the hope of eternal life and be wrong than not to believe in God and be damned for unbelief) unworthy of the great soul he believed Pascal to be.[42] The wager reduced religion to a bid for

40. *DA*, 964.

41. Something else Pascal would not have said. For more in this vein, see *DA*, 960–61*nj*.

42. *DA*, 928*nd*.

material well-being beyond the grave. If religion had only been this sort of higher materialism, it would have been very democratic, but useless for Tocqueville's moral science.

Tocqueville's search for balance in the larger society was thus paralleled by a search for a balanced religion. Indeed, for Tocqueville, religions must achieve this balance in order to be successful. All "positive religions," Tocqueville noted, mix material incentives, for example, eternal life, with higher ones: "In Christianity, for example, we are told that it is necessary to do good *out of love of God* (magnificent expression...) and also to gain eternal life."[43] In Tocqueville's view, religion itself must mix utilitarian and perfectionist dogmas, that is, appeal to both angel and beast, in order to have broad effect.[44]

Thus, religion's role is naturally both utilitarian and perfectionist. In its utilitarian role, religion acts as a check on the will of the majority—God acts as a kind of alternative sovereign to democratic public opinion. Religion limits the majority, preventing them from transgressing certain moral rules. Even "the revolutionaries of America are obliged to profess publicly a certain respect for Christian morality and equity which does not allow them to violate laws easily." Religion prevents American democrats from arguing that everything is permissible as long as it is done in the name of society. "Therefore, at the same time that the law allows the American people to do everything, religion prevents them from conceiving of everything and forbids them to dare everything." Americans, Tocqueville stresses, are universally convinced that these limits are useful to the maintenance of political freedom and republican institutions.[45]

That religion imposed restraints on human passions was hardly a new discovery. That the restraints it imposed helped a free society to maintain political stability was only a slightly newer application of an old principle. But God did not serve Tocqueville or America merely to

43. *DA*, 924.

44. Unfortunately, no actual religion attained this balance in Tocqueville's view, although he thinks the Gospels do. See Kahan, "Checks and Balances."

45. *DA*, 475. In this sense, it also limits, at least when performed properly, the "self-celebration" of society. Cf. Jaume, *Tocqueville*, in particular his comments on Tocqueville and Émile Durkheim.

limit the scope of human ambitions to what was morally permissible. Tocqueville added to the utilitarian function of religion a perfectionist role, no less indispensable for the preservation of freedom—that of uplifting men's souls. God served Tocqueville as the ultimate representation of grandeur, the ultimate incentive to rise above materialism and the everyday and find the taste for higher things. That religion could, did, and should serve this function even or especially in democratic societies, and that this would help them preserve their freedom while they perfected their souls, might or might not have been a new discovery in itself. Tocqueville cared little about originality. The perfectionist role of religion was crucial to Tocqueville's new moral science for democratic times.

Perfection, Politics, and Religion in Democratic Societies

As Tocqueville announced in the Introduction to *Democracy in America*, democracy was inevitable, but democratic equality did not necessarily lead to grandeur, any more than it did to freedom. The new moral and political sciences developed in *Democracy in America* were meant to show, through the American example, how democracy could lead to greatness (and freedom). Political freedom is Tocqueville's crowning virtue, but political perfection is the peak of a set of other human perfections, referred to here as human "grandeur" or "greatness." To maintain freedom in the long run, religion was necessary, because without it democratic societies risked losing any desire for perfection. Only the two working together could lift humanity to greatness: "I have never been more convinced than today," he wrote to the liberal Catholic Charles de Montalembert in 1852, "that it is only *freedom* . . . and *religion* that can, by a combined effort, lift men above the quagmire where democratic equality naturally plunges them, as soon as one of these supports is lacking them."[46]

Tocqueville posited a sort of elective affinity between religious commitment and political commitment, or rather, between the type of character that would be attracted to both of them as opposed to the

---

46. Tocqueville to Montalembert, cited in Antoine, *L'Impensé*, 130.

personality type more likely to be attracted to materialism.[47] What they had in common was perfectionism. As he wrote to Louis de Kergorlay, "[T]here exist more family ties than are supposed between political passions and religious passions. On both sides general goods, immaterial to a certain degree, are in sight, on both sides an ideal of society is pursued, a certain perfecting of the human species." Tocqueville went on to say that he could understand an individual who was motivated by both political and religious passion far better than one motivated by both religion and the desire for material well-being. For those who doubted the logical or psychological proof of the connection between religion and political freedom, Tocqueville had the American example ready to hand: "nothing shows better how useful and natural religion is to man, since the country where today it exercises the most dominion is at the same time the most enlightened and most free."[48]

Of all religious doctrines, the one Tocqueville singles out as most necessary to the perfection of the democratic individual, and in the final analysis to the maintenance of political freedom, is the doctrine of the immortality of the soul:

> The belief in a non-material and immortal principle, united for a time with matter, is so necessary for the grandeur of man, that it still produces fruitful effects even when you do not join the opinion of rewards and punishments with it. . . . It is not certain that Socrates and his school had well-fixed opinions on what must happen to man in the other life; but the sole belief on which they were settled, that the soul has nothing in common with the body and survives it, was enough to give platonic philosophy the sort of sublime impulse which distinguishes it.[49]

Yet "Socrates and his school" were not necessarily members of any religion. Could some nonreligious version of spirituality or philosophy

---

47. He recognizes, however, that this is not necessarily the case, and that no general conclusion can be drawn. See Tocqueville to Kergorlay, October 18, 1847, in Tocqueville, *Selected Letters on Politics and Society,* ed. Roger Boesche, trans. James Toupin and Roger Boesche (Berkeley: University of California Press, 1985), 191–92.

48. *Selected Letters,* 192; *DA,* 473.

49. *DA,* 958–59.

suffice to kindle the taste for greatness among a democratic people, as it had in the aristocratic world of ancient Athens? In America, Tocqueville pondered whether deism or "natural religion," as embodied by the Unitarians and William Ellery Channing, might provide a sufficient dose of spirituality. He concluded it could, at least for the upper classes.[50] But for the masses he was sure that traditional religion, that is, Christianity, was the necessary means for preaching the immortality of the soul.

The combination of the doctrine of rewards and punishments with the doctrine of the immortality of the soul in Christianity was an appeal to the mixture of the angel and the beast in the human soul. Tocqueville put even the beastly aspect of religion to work in the service of his moral science. What made religion's appeal to the natural human desire for eternal life invaluable to Tocqueville was that it paradoxically served as the foundation for religion's fight against materialism. Out of the material desire for eternal bliss, religion fashions the means to limit human desires for earthly satisfactions. "The principal business of religions is to purify, to regulate and to limit the overly ardent and overly exclusive taste for well-being that men feel in times of equality."[51] This is the crucial moral function of religion in a democratic society. Democracy:

opens souls excessively to love of material enjoyments.

The greatest advantage of religions is to inspire entirely opposite instincts. There is no religion that does not place the object of the desires of men above and beyond the good things of the earth, and that does not naturally elevate his soul toward realms very superior to those of the senses. . . .

So religious peoples are naturally strong precisely in the places where democratic peoples are weak; this makes very clear how important it is for men to keep their religion while becoming equal.[52]

This passage comes immediately after the claim that if man "does not have faith, he must serve," and "[i]f he is free, he must believe."

---

50. See the discussion of deism and Channing in Kahan, "Checks and Balances."

51. *DA,* 751.

52. *DA,* 745–46.

The claim is not that faith brings freedom or vice versa, but rather that faith is a necessary but not sufficient prerequisite for freedom, at least in the long run (and vice versa—state religions die out). For Tocqueville, spirituality has a crucial political role to play in shaping human character, to lift it above materialism and petty pleasures, and to give human beings a taste for higher things, of which the highest is political freedom.

Religion thus does for potentially all human beings what aristocracy once did for a few. Aristocratic society "readily imagines glorious enjoyments for man and sets magnificent ends for his desires. Aristocracies often undertake very tyrannical and very inhuman actions, but they rarely conceive low thoughts; and they show a certain disdain for small pleasures... that gives all souls there a very lofty tone. In aristocratic times you generally get very vast ideas about the dignity, power and grandeur of man." It is the "lofty tone" of aristocracy, in suitably democratic form, which Tocqueville hopes religion will preserve and reinject into democratic society: "[L]egislators in democracies and all honest and enlightened men who live in democracies must apply themselves without respite to lifting up souls and keeping them pointed toward heaven. It is necessary... that all in concert make continual efforts to spread within these societies the taste for the infinite, the sentiment for the grand and the love of non-material pleasures." What are these nonmaterial pleasures that Tocqueville thought men should love? As he wrote in a marginal note to *Democracy:* "Great passion of the *true,* the *beautiful,* and the *good.* Analogous things flowing from the same source, equally rare, producing great men of learning, great men of literature, and great virtues." For Tocqueville, greatness in democratic societies is always conceived in opposition to the material.[53]

Materialism, in such societies, is always the prime enemy for Tocqueville the moralist, and his religion as well as his politics is designed above all with that enemy in mind. Tocqueville sought to make democracy safe for great souls, for what one might call the noblest, that is to say most aristocratic, aspects of human nature. But he sought more than safety, he sought freedom, without which greatness could neither be attained nor endure. In order to obtain what he sought, he turned

53. *DA,* 782, 924 (emphasis original), 957.

to religion: "*Political consequences:* Extreme efforts that the legislator must make in democracies to spiritualize man. Particular necessity for religions in democracy; even dogmatic and not very reasonable religions, for lack of anything better. Show heaven even if it is through the worst instruments."[54] Religion is thus an essential part of what makes Tocqueville an aristocratic liberal. Freedom and greatness go together, and in a democratic society, religion helps preserve or create necessary elements of what otherwise would be a purely aristocratic grandeur. Democratic religion can make democracies great.[55]

The Utility of Moral Science

Religion is thus necessary to the freedom of democratic nations and to their greatness—which amounts, from a Tocquevillian perspective, to much the same thing. But is this a role that religion can play everywhere? Is religion's role in promoting human greatness really a democratic role, as Tocqueville so earnestly tried to show, or just an American one?

These questions are susceptible to different answers, depending on whether one focuses on Tocqueville's intentions or his results. Certainly Tocqueville, who, as he said, never wrote a line of *Democracy in America* without thinking of France, intended his book to be about democracy, and intended it to have lessons to teach, first to France, and then to the rest of a democratizing world. Those lessons would require translation and adaptation according to circumstances. Tocqueville was explicit that American institutions, including American religion, could not be copied verbatim in other societies. But in principle his discoveries were meant to be transferable.[56]

54. *DA,* 924*n*2. Tocqueville, however, comes close to making an exception to this rule in the case of pantheism, which he condemns as being incapable of encouraging greatness. See the chapter "What Makes the Minds of Democratic Peoples Incline toward Pantheism."

55. On aristocratic liberalism, see Alan S. Kahan, *Aristocratic Liberalism: The Social and Political Thought of Jacob Burckhardt, John Stuart Mill, and Alexis de Tocqueville* (New Brunswick, N.J.: Transaction, 2001).

56. Tocqueville to Kergorlay, October 18, 1847, in *Selected Letters,* 191; *DA,* 512–13.

In terms of results, however, the answer is far less clear. If one considers the question that mattered most to Tocqueville, "Could the American model of religion be exported to France?" then the answer Tocqueville gave was negative. Tocqueville had feared this even when writing *Democracy*. A rejected passage, rejected perhaps for its pessimism, displays his anxiety: "For me, if something could make me despair of the destiny of Europe, it is to see the strange confusion which reigns there in minds. I see pious men who would like to suffocate liberty, as if liberty, this great privilege of man, was not a nearly holy thing. Further along, I see others who think to arrive at being free by attacking all beliefs, but I do not see any who seem to notice the tight and necessary knot that ties religion to liberty." It was because he came from France that the situation of religion in America struck Tocqueville so forcefully. But if he learned that freedom and religion could be allies in America, he was not sure how to reconcile them at home. "If it is easy to see that, particularly in times of democracy, it is important to make spiritual opinions reign, it is not easy to say what those who govern democratic peoples must do for those opinions to reign." Tocqueville did not believe in "the duration of official philosophies" (perhaps a slap at the philosophy of Victor Cousin, more or less the official philosopher of the July Monarchy). Nor did he believe in State religions, which in his view were always sooner or later deadly to the Church.[57]

The course of European history after the completion of *Democracy* in 1840 gave Tocqueville little reason for optimism that religion could play in continental Europe the role it played in America. His experiences as foreign minister in 1849, when he failed in his desperate attempt to persuade the pope to permit some degree of freedom in a Rome reconquered from anticlerical revolutionaries, and in the years after he left office, when Napoleon III's coup d'etat in 1852 was greeted with hosannas by the Church, are sufficient explanation for his growing pessimism. Thus the explanation for the passage he wrote about religion and freedom to his friend Francisque de Corcelle in 1853: "You must

---

57. *DA*, 477, 961. For his own lack of influence, see his intervention in the question of religious schools through his newspaper, *Le Commerce*. See *Oeuvres complètes*, vol. 3, *Écrits et discours politiques*, 2:516–60.

pardon me a little because of the sadness, I could almost say the despair in view of what is happening, that is felt by a man who is as convinced as I am that man's true grandeur lies only in the harmony of the liberal sentiment and religious sentiment, both working simultaneously to animate and to restrain souls, and by one whose sole political passion for thirty years has been to bring about this harmony."[58] Tocqueville, when his life came to an early end in 1859, was unquestionably pessimistic about the prospects for freedom in France, not least because of the situation of French religion.

The contrast between America and France is clear, but did religion really play the role Tocqueville wanted it to play even in America, even in his own eyes? Is not Tocqueville's account of American religion in practice full of reservations and criticisms? Without recounting all of Tocqueville's descriptions of American religion, this much can be said: Tocqueville saw the universality of spirituality in America, most commonly incarnated as Protestant Christianity, and he thought it good. He thought America's faith crucial to the preservation of American freedom. He might well have said that America was great because America was good (though this famous Tocqueville "quotation," first found in a speech by President Eisenhower, is apocryphal). But more likely he would have said that what was best about America was that it showed that a democracy could be great.

Could be great—it is not clear that Tocqueville thought that the mass of Americans really did rise above petty materialism, nor that religion as actually practiced in America successfully transmitted the taste for greatness to any large number of Americans. America, it has often been noted, played the role of an ideal type for Tocqueville, a vision of democratic society pushed to the extreme. Insofar as Tocqueville thought the long-term relationship between democracy and freedom, democracy and human grandeur, an uncertain one, so he must logically have thought the same about American religion.

Any answer except ultimate uncertainty would have been objectionable to Tocqueville, who famously rejected all forms of determinism.[59] What mattered was that democracy *could* be great and *could* be free, and

58. Tocqueville to Corcelle, September 17, 1853, in *Selected Letters*, 294–95.
59. The relevant passages may be found in his *Recollections*.

that his moral science showed how spirituality *could* play a positive role in encouraging human greatness and freedom. Was what Tocqueville discovered in America transferable? In the long run, what would have mattered for Tocqueville was the possibility that this might be so, and that his reflections might help it become so. Politics, it has been said, is the art of the possible. The same is true of Tocqueville's moral science. In the end, perhaps, it comes down to faith, hope, and charity—faith that greatness and freedom can be maintained in democratic societies, hope that the moral and political science of democracy is teachable, and charity toward human beings and their ability to listen to the better angels of their nature. As Tocqueville wrote in *The Old Regime and the Revolution*: "We do not differ over whether freedom is worthwhile, but over the higher or lower opinion we have of people." It seems appropriate to apply to humanity as a whole what Tocqueville, even at his most pessimistic, could write of France: "never so free that one must despair of enslaving it, or so servile that it may not once again break the yoke."[60]

60. Tocqueville, *The Old Regime and the Revolution*, trans. Alan S. Kahan (Chicago: University of Chicago Press, 1998), 88, 246.

8

Intimations of Philosophy in Tocqueville's *Democracy in America*

HARVEY C. MANSFIELD

Americans did not need to draw their philosophic method from books; they have found it within themselves.
—*Democracy in America* (2.1.1, 701)

There is hardly any human action, no matter how particular you assume it to be, that is not born out of a very general idea that men have conceived of God, of God's relationships with the humanity, of the nature of their soul, and of their duties toward their fellows. . . . So men have an immense interest in making very fixed ideas for themselves about God, their souls, their general duties.
—*Democracy in America* (2.1.5, 743)

The debate over "foundations" in liberal theory today is hardly new, for it is featured in the early history of liberalism in the contrast between those seventeenth-century political philosophers, Hobbes, Spinoza, and Locke, who relied on the notion of the state of nature and those of the eighteenth century, Montesquieu and Hume, who did not. The "state of nature" was one in which men lived in "perfect freedom" (Locke's words), and to make it the foundation, or the beginning, of politics was to ensure that every restriction on liberty had to be argued for and had to receive the consent of those considered perfectly free. One could not assume that men have a nature, or natural inclinations, that make them receptive to such restrictions, as did preliberal philosophers. For this reason the invention of the "state of nature" can be justly considered the beginning of liberalism, even though the term "liberalism" that we now scatter so freely was not in use until Tocqueville's time.

The general issue in the early debate over foundations was not so different from the issue today, though the formulations have changed (for example, John Locke's "state of nature" has become John Rawls's "original position"). It was whether such a foundation was necessary to liberty, or was rather an infringement on liberty. A foundation in freedom would be necessary in order to demote or exclude alternatives to liberty such as virtue or salvation; or it would be an infringement because it relied too much on fear, was too individualistic, and justified restrictions on liberty too easily as necessary compromise from an impossible extreme.

Tocqueville called himself "a new kind of liberal"; where does he figure in this debate?[1] Quickly, one might say, on both sides. In the first quotation opening this chapter, we see him rejecting the bookish influence of philosophers, in the context particularly Descartes, where foundations are discovered and advanced, in favor of actual practice, where citizens grope their way forward without the help of a foundation, particularly a new foundation like that of Descartes, which brings recognition and renown to philosophers and philosophy. In the second quotation, however, we see the need stated for "very fixed ideas" that do not arise from practice but precede and guide practice. In context[2] one sees that these ideas must come from religion rather than philosophy.[3] Any society, and especially a democratic one, must take account of what most people think, and most people have recourse to the dogmas of religion for guidance because they have neither the time nor the capacity for philosophizing. Even if they did or could philosophize, they would find that through the ages, philosophers "despite all their efforts . . . have been able to discover only a few contradictory notions." They have not even found new errors.

1. Tocqueville to Eugène Stöffels, July 24, 1836.

2. 2.1.5, 743. Citations are to volume, part, and chapter in AT's original. Page numbers are to Alexis de Tocqueville, *Democracy in America: Historical-Critical Edition of "De la démocratie en Amérique,"* ed. Eduardo Nolla, trans. James T. Schleifer, 4 vols. (Indianapolis: Liberty Fund, 2010), hereafter cited as *DA*.

3. See my essay, "Tocqueville's Alliance of Religion and Liberty," a companion study to this one [unpublished].

Those who try to rely on philosophy for the fixed ideas they need in their ordinary lives, Tocqueville says, do not find them but come to grief in "doubt." "Doubt takes possession of the highest portions of the intellect and half paralyses all the others."[4] Each person becomes accustomed to confused and changing opinions on matters of most interest to himself and people like him—for example, today, the question of abortion, which is so troubling to both sides and to those in the middle. We throw up our hands, feeling defeated, and in cowardly fashion refuse to think. Doubt "cannot fail to enervate souls" that will not think, thereby threatening the maintenance of liberty because enervated souls will not take the trouble to exercise liberty or defend it. Thus one of his memorable phrases: "I am led to think that if [a man] does not have faith, he must serve, and if he is free, he must believe."[5]

Here is a liberal rejecting liberal foundations in philosophy yet requiring them in religion. He seems to reject philosophy because it is not sufficiently or successfully dogmatic and to welcome religion because its dogmas support, or can support, human liberty. He turns to the practice of self-government in America—taking the antitheoretical way of today's antifoundationalism—yet claims to find in it the "philosophic method" that he avoids considering directly. He treats the American Constitution at length—what Abraham Lincoln called the "picture of silver"—but omits even to mention the more valuable "apple of gold," the Declaration of Independence, the philosophical document that in Lincoln's view makes sense of American politics, which he thought the Constitution framed and enshrined.[6] Tocqueville rejects a liberal foundation, such as Lincoln was so memorably to discover in the Declaration, yet also rejects the liberal pluralism of today that seems to be the sole alternative to it. He seems to leave a choice between ineffectual doubt endangering liberty and unguided, unreasoned dogma supporting it.

One should notice, though, that Tocqueville's statement against doubt blames it for preventing people from thinking, that is, from

4. *DA* 2.1.5, 744–45.
5. *DA* 2.1.5, 745.
6. Abraham Lincoln, "Fragment on the Constitution and Union," ca. January 1861; Proverbs 25:11.

thinking practically and usefully. Philosophical thinking leads to paralysis of practical thinking, in which overmatched would-be philosophers are led ultimately to passive acceptance of things as they are. Philosophy may begin from the questioning of authority, but when it appears that all the questioning leads to no answers, it stops and finds rest in the conclusion that nothing can be done. Faith, then, is not a substitute for reasoning simply but for philosophical reasoning; it is actually the basis for reasoning about one's closest interests.

In the chapter in *Democracy in America* that I have been discussing, a chapter on religion, he seems to criticize all philosophy, philosophy itself. But he particularly criticizes what one might call, but he does not, modern or liberal philosophy. He does use the word "foundation," however. In *Democracy in America,* he notes that Americans adopt the "philosophic method" of Descartes as their "foundation" because just by living in a democratic social state they already know what he writes without having read his works. They know that everything can be made clear by reason and that since no man's word can be trusted, no one's reason can be trusted but one's own. By questioning all authority, every man becomes his own authority. By this succinct interpretation, Descartes is made a philosopher of democracy, a point that has eluded many interpreters of Descartes![7] In *The Ancien Régime and the Revolution,* Tocqueville attacks the "men of letters," the eighteenth-century *philosophes* (led by Turgot), who used their own reason to substitute principles of reason and natural law for complicated, traditional customs; here he emphasizes reform rather than democracy as the main purpose of the new foundation. In his *Souvenirs* he opposes the simplistic theorists of socialism in the Revolution of 1848, who combine reform and democracy. In each of his three books, he selects for criticism, not any or all philosophers, but the foundational philosophers of liberalism, who clarify, simplify, and (less explicitly) democratize—and who, in all this, innovate.[8]

7. *DA* 2.1.1, 699–702.

8. See *DA* 2.1.1 for criticism of Descartes; Plato is praised for his philosophy in *DA* 2.2.15, 959 and criticized for his politics in *DA* 2.3.15, 1082. Machiavelli, the prince of innovators, is cited (inaccurately) in *DA* 2.3.26. In the *Souvenirs,* he denounces "absolute systems that make all the events of history depend on great first causes" and, not the liberals, but the socialists who aspire to found

Is faith the only resource against this modern, peculiarly ambitious philosophy? I want to argue that Tocqueville also has in mind a more modest philosophy, which to be modest must be modestly concealed.[9] But modesty in philosophy would do no good if it were not cautiously and prudently revealed to those who will recognize it and whom one wants to impress. Modesty has to be seen to be appreciated. I want to show that the very account of the nonphilosophical practice of Americans, which seems intended to provide an alternative to the works of the unbridled theorists of liberal foundation, actually contains a theory, or the elements of a theory, that readers of a philosophical bent could use for a foundation that will not ignore, but bridle, liberal foundationalism. The "showing" will consist in the interpretation of statements, phrases, words, implications, and suggestions, and it will necessarily, therefore, not have the character of a proof on the basis of which I could boast that no other interpretation is possible. I believe that Tocqueville himself wished to do no more than suggest an alternative foundation for his "new kind of liberal" to the one he thinks is doing damage to liberty, above all to political liberty. We know his statement that "a new political science is needed for a world entirely new."[10] We also know that he never provides that new political science in

---

"a social science, a philosophy, I would almost say a common religion" to teach to all mankind (2.1.2). The " men of letters" (*hommes de lettres*) of the eighteenth century, who theorized about politics, are criticized in Tocqueville, *The Ancien Régime and the French Revolution,* trans. A. Goldhammer (Cambridge: Cambridge University Press, 2011), 3.1 [Hereafter *OR*].

9. On philosophy in Tocqueville, see Eduardo Nolla, ed., *Liberty, Equality, Democracy* (New York: New York University Press, 1992), introduction; Peter A. Lawler, *The Restless Mind: Alexis de Tocqueville on the Origin and Perpetuation of Human Liberty* (Lanham, Md.: Rowman & Littlefield, 1993), chap. 5; Catherine Zuckert, "Political Sociology versus Speculative Philosophy," in *Interpreting Tocqueville's "Democracy in America,"* ed. Ken Masugi (Lanham, Md.: Rowman & Littlefield, 1991); Pierre Manent, *Tocqueville and the Nature of Democracy,* trans. John Waggoner (Lanham, Md.: Rowman & Littlefield, 1996), chap. 1; Sheldon S. Wolin, *Tocqueville between Two Worlds: The Making of a Political and Theoretical Life* (Princeton, N.J.: Princeton University Press, 2001), pt. 1.

10. *DA,* Introduction, 16.

any explicit form in *Democracy in America,* though one can find remarks about it there and elsewhere.[11]

I suggest that Tocqueville supplies it implicitly in that book, in a manner so as to be collected and ordered by the reader, who for his part must learn not to dismiss with tolerant condescension the apparent vagueness, imprecise terms, and seeming repetitions in the text. One must try to make sense of them, and not merely mutter to oneself that Tocqueville lacks rigor. One must not make excuses for Tocqueville under the presumption that he was not a deep thinker and perhaps even deserves praise for exposing and shaming the stultifying heaviness of deep thinkers. No, he deserves praise for deep thinking that conceals its depth with charming style and never-failing acuity of observation — and therefore accommodates the complacent democratic doubt, for example, that it is necessary to read philosophers such as Descartes in order to understand America or democracy. In fact, Tocqueville's quick summary of Descartes that I have mentioned,[12] seemingly superficial, reveals a deep understanding and criticism. The reader must reach out; he must be receptive to argument that insinuates its way instead of compelling him. I do not maintain that one will be compelled by my interpretation to make a philosopher out of Tocqueville. The test of falsifiability recommended by scientific positivism — can you prove the interpretation false? — cannot be applied, for a reader determined not to take a hint will never recognize one when it appears. This does not mean that the reader should abandon skepticism, rather the contrary; only by asking questions of Tocqueville's text can one see where it points.

Tocqueville's philosophical argument unfolds. Not being explicit or laid out to view, it is not inert. It moves. Its movement has stages, and the next stage frequently if not always corrects a previous stage; the whole becomes clear only at the end. Any formulation along the way is likely to be partial and provisional. I do not say that the whole is final,

11. See Harvey C. Mansfield and Delba Winthrop, "Tocqueville's New Political Science," in *The Cambridge Companion to Tocqueville,* ed. Cheryl B. Welch (New York: Cambridge University Press, 2006), 81–107.

12. *DA* 2.1.1, 699–702.

for Tocqueville as a liberal puts freedom first. His foundation shares with Aristotle the fundamental intention of defending politics, requiring one to explain politics in terms understandable to political actors but also to answer philosophical objections denying the importance of politics. But he is not Aristotle. His new political science contains and relies on an updated version of the old philosophy or metaphysics, a truncated version suitable to liberty in a democracy, not one culminating as Aristotle's or Plato's in an aristocracy of philosophers, the rule of the wise.

Because the argument proceeds by stages, I will give a preview of the whole of it now, a sketch of what I think Tocqueville means to establish. He begins from an obvious but inexplicit rejection of the liberal foundation of the state of nature. One cannot begin from a state of perfect freedom, because that is freedom from politics or government, and such a beginning could never establish the authority of self-government over the prior right, given in the foundational state of nature, to object to all government. The right to say no to government, based on the perfect freedom of the state of nature, will supersede and confound any necessarily derivative duty to establish and obey a government that necessarily limits one's perfect freedom. Perfect freedom, if it exists, will never be completely surrendered; it is always there, ready to be called on, in case of hardship or inconvenience as decided by the democratic citizen on his own. Democratic legitimacy will never be established by this sort of contract, for it will depend on a calculation subject to adjustment whenever it becomes necessary to pay for one's benefits.

Self-government, moreover, cannot be established by either fear or timidity or by any other passion that leaves men feeling impotent, isolated, and irresponsible. The liberal foundation contradicts itself by supposing that men can reach freedom through material motives, such as the fear for one's self-preservation or the passion for material well-being or for material enjoyments that Tocqueville considers repeatedly, implying that they are unfree. Yet liberty needs a foundation so as not to founder in doubt. So Tocqueville turns to a foundation in nature, perhaps in God as creator of nature, which comprises liberty together with restraints on liberty. In political liberty those restraints are freely made and accepted, so that the whole can be understood as for the sake of liberty. The noxious implication of the liberal foundation that liberty and restraint, or reason and authority, are at odds is avoided.

I do not say that Tocqueville believes he can prove that his philosophy is true and that materialist philosophy opposed to liberty is false—though he does believe that materialist philosophers contradict themselves. At the same time, I resist the conclusion that he considers his philosophy to be false but salutary. Perhaps he leaves this foundation rough and provisional, to be completed by someone with the taste and the learning for that sort of thing. The most general truths of political science would be identical to the truths and questions of philosophy, for Tocqueville's philosophy, if he has one, would surely be political philosophy. It would state the most general conditions under which self-government, or political liberty, is possible. These would be the notions, or truths, concerning which men have an "immense interest"—regarding God, the nature of human souls, and men's duties. These are the "very fixed ideas" that humans need, but these ideas need to be supported and connected.

Before we consider what these ideas might be, one may fairly ask what the evidence is for my view that a philosophy or metaphysics is hidden in the facts and analysis of *Democracy in America*. To begin with the reason why it is hidden, I say that in a democratic age, by Tocqueville's own account, philosophy will either not be listened to or will be appropriated for purposes hostile to political liberty, that is, by the materialist and pantheist philosophers common to that age. In defending political liberty, Tocqueville wants to preserve the perspective of political men—politicians and citizens—rather than allow it to be replaced by that of theorists or men of letters who know nothing of politics and do not conceal their distaste for it. To answer them on their apolitical level would concede too much to their contempt for politics.

Yet it is also apparent that to convey the facts of American democracy, Tocqueville uses heavy metaphysical language without embarrassment, particularly "the first cause," prominent in the early chapters of *Democracy in America,* and the "forms" that are said to be vital to democratic liberty throughout. These are the traditional terms from Plato and Aristotle by which nature is thought to be intelligible, as opposed to the chaos of sense impressions or atoms set forth by materialist philosophers. At the end of *Democracy in America,* in describing the new mild despotism democracy tends toward, Tocqueville says that despite the use of "free will" in elections, citizens will gradually lose it and thus gradually lose their humanity.[13] In none of these cases does Tocqueville identify his language as "metaphysical," but my argument will find a role for these terms beyond casual use. I believe he used them not haphazardly but mindfully, even though not expressly for the purpose of establishing philosophical or metaphysical truth. In the case of free will, he moves confidently from its use in politics to its use in defining a human being.

It is clear, too, from the first that Tocqueville is a strong opponent of materialism or fatalism; would he not want to indicate, if not develop, an alternative position to that harmful and mistaken view? Is it not also clear for him that the self-government he finds and describes in American politics depends on the free will, the self-government, of American souls? This is a question not merely moral but of the principles that sustain morality.[14] But the main evidence for a hidden philosophy in *Democracy in America* lies in the form of the work, the order of its parts and chapters that comes to light when its philosophical foundation is collected and composed. My argument will proceed through the text with a view to explaining the orderliness behind the seeming disorder that often perplexes readers and interpreters. I hope to show why he says what he says where he says it. My explanation is far from complete, but it opens the prospect of a complete explanation from a better interpreter.

It is true that Tocqueville in his letters expresses discontent with metaphysics, even contempt. In a well-known letter written from America to Charles Stöffels, he reproves him for living, as Tocqueville has done, in a "world of chimeras," as may often happen in the first stage of youth. From his own standpoint at the hoary age of twenty-six, he says: "I have always considered metaphysics and all the purely theoretical sciences that serve for nothing in the reality of life as a voluntary torment that man consents to inflict on himself."[15] But this reassurance to a friend not gifted in philosophy does not mean that Tocqueville

13. *DA* 2.4.6, 1251.
14. Cf. Aristotle, *Nicomachean Ethics*, 3:1.
15. Tocqueville to Charles Stöffels, October 22, 1831.

excused himself from such torment, especially if it should develop, as we saw above, that metaphysics is not so removed from the reality of life. Years later, in a letter to Francisque de Corcelle, he avows that he had never had much taste for studying metaphysics, perhaps because he had never given himself seriously to its study since he thought that good sense (*le bon sens*) would lead to the same goal.

Here he adds a remark on the influence of metaphysics, however, which may be contrasted to the attitude he shows in *Democracy in America*. He says that the centuries in which metaphysics was most cultivated were those in which men were drawn outside and above themselves, and that he has always been struck by the influence of such ideas on the condition of society, even on the mores of the crowd, from which they seem so remote. Condillac greatly contributed to driving into materialism (*pousser dans la matière*) many people who had never read him. Tocqueville's remark that in America the precepts of Descartes are of all places in the world "least studied and best followed"[16] implies as we have seen that they arose spontaneously out of the democratic social state without needing to be formulated by Descartes. But neither Condillac nor Descartes leads to the same goal as good sense.[17]

Descartes, with his "foundation," his "philosophic method," stands behind the democratic social state, revealing its principle before it was established in Europe, though not in America. Tocqueville emphasizes one feature of the method: to look to the result, not the means; "to see through the form to the foundation." Yet repeatedly in his book he emphasizes the value of forms (or formalities) in a democracy, and brings it out in his account of American government.[18] Is there not ambivalence or contradiction in the democratic social state, particularly in America, between the use of forms and "scorn" for them? Would not Tocqueville perform a useful, perhaps an indispensable, function by standing behind the democratic social state as an anti-Descartes, pointing out defects in his foundation not by writing a book of philosophy

16. *DA* 2.1.1, 699.

17. Letter of October 16, 1855, to Francisque de Corcelle.

18. See esp. *DA* 2.4.7, 1270; also 1.1.4, 96, 1.1.5, 114, 122–25, 135, 1.1.7, 181, 1.2.6, 376, 380, 1.2.8, 447, 1.2.9, 465, 498, 512, 1.2.10, 546, 588, 2.1.1, 699; 2.1.5, 750–52, 2.3.3, 1001, 2.3.14, 1076. Forms are not always praised but are sometimes subordinated to substance; see 512, 546, 1001, 1076.

or metaphysics but by showing how Americans refute Descartes (and themselves) in their practice of self-government? Americans might want to discover which of their practices is to be preferred—their scorn of forms (the can-do attitude) or their devotion to forms (the due process attitude).[19] They would decide on the basis of fact, not philosophical argument, that is, in accordance with the result, not with due process. But philosophy providing a foundation not contemptuous of forms would clarify the issue for readers who see this difficulty and wish to induce Americans to move in the right direction.

In the letter to Corcelle, Tocqueville uses two meanings of "metaphysics" to be found still today in nontechnical usage. One is for abstract reflection that goes beyond the facts, literally "beyond physics," in which case materialism or fatalism is still metaphysics, but democratic metaphysics. The other refers to what is spiritual in man, proper to aristocratic ages, presenting the case that having an immaterial soul is the only way to go beyond physics, the only metaphysics. Does he not suggest that the good sense of many people in democratic ages is pushed aside by bad metaphysics from democratic philosophers like Descartes and Condillac? If so, might not democratic good sense need the aid of good metaphysics to oppose the bad metaphysics, or antimetaphysics, that endangers it? Tocqueville's metaphysics, as suggested above, does not require the study of metaphysics but rather of the democratic social state. The very thing that inclines Americans to follow Descartes in judging for oneself leads them also to adopt beneficial political means of guiding their judgment.

One more point of introduction to Tocqueville's metaphysics: one should not confine the matter to the question of his personal Christian faith, as if this were his only concern unconnected to his thought.[20] For Tocqueville was a thinker. He may not have been able, or may not have wished, to demonstrate his metaphysics, but he left ample indica-

19. For an argument that both attitudes arise from an inherent difficulty in the foundation of liberalism, see Harvey C. Mansfield, *America's Constitutional Soul* (Baltimore, Md.: Johns Hopkins University Press, 1991), chaps. 1, 14.

20. See the letter to Sophie Swetchine, February 26, 1857, a personal confession regarding the doubt of "all the truths on which I built my beliefs and my actions," that is, not just the religious truths, that entered his soul as a youth.

tions of his intent. In another letter to Corcelle, he says that the most demanding and influential books are "not those in which the author has sought to tell [readers] dogmatically what is suitable to think, but those in which he has set their minds on the road leading to truths and has made them find these truths for themselves."[21] Let us now look for that road in *Democracy in America*. Precisely in the book where he affirms the need for dogma and fixed truths, he offers, not a foundation, but a road toward one.

The road begins in the capacious Introduction, where Tocqueville indicates the problem of his metaphysics, while giving his first formulation. Democracy, he says, is the democratic revolution, the establishing and continual progress of the equality of conditions. This is the "primary fact" setting the direction of events; it is also the "generative fact" generating other, more particular facts; and it is the "providential fact" revealing a design or trend, longer than one era or one generation or one founder could accomplish, hence the work of God. How should one judge this revolution? Either as accidental, hence as an event that might be checked or reversed; or as irresistible, as what seems continuous, the oldest and most permanent fact. The first case would imply that democracy is a choice; the second case would make democracy a brute fact imposed on men by nature or necessity. In sum, there is an unstated, though implied question of whether human beings have choice or must obey necessity. Tocqueville lets us see in his statement of the current world situation that neither extreme is correct. Democracy is irresistible, but we can choose what kind of democracy there shall be, with liberty or with slavery. We can *still* choose, he says: as the world becomes more democratic, the realm of choice is narrowed; "it escapes every day from human power."[22] Or, perhaps, there are democratic means to be considered of making democracy less democratic—a possibility of correcting (if not arresting) this movement. The fundamental situation we face does not make us either master or slave of our lives but leaves us free within the constraints, which seem ever-growing, of our democratic age. Apparently Providence does not impose democracy

21. Tocqueville to Francisque de Corcelle, September 17, 1853.
22. *DA,* Introduction, 12.

as a mysterious, chance necessity to be blindly accepted, not destiny or fate, but instead allows and requires democracy to be fashioned according to human purpose and understanding.

To call the coming of democracy providential raises the hope that what is imposed on us may be for our good. Immediately we learn that democracy is not a permanent but an old fact, seven hundred years old, dating from the twelfth century when the clergy opened its ranks to all, poor and rich. We note that democracy and religion begin in alliance, a theme, perhaps *the* theme, of *Democracy in America*.[23] Tocqueville gives a quick history of the rise of democracy, showing that democratic equality is too strong to stop, yet not so strong as to despair of directing it. Its imposition is, to repeat, not a mysterious dispensation of Providence understood as fate, but rather arises from a political cause that Tocqueville readily discerns. For the aristocracy preceding democracy destroyed itself. First, it was given to "great undertakings" by the kings and to "private wars" among the nobles, so that by its exhausting desire for glory it gradually lost out to the influence of money. Second, aristocracy was fatally divided between kings and nobles, and then within the nobility as well. The nobles occasionally appealed to the people for support against other nobles or royal authority, while the kings made a similar appeal against the authority of the nobles regularly and by settled policy. Apparently Providence works through politics, through human choice, but regularly, even predictably. But also, politics works underneath the overall cause, or asserted cause, of Providence that is not merely political but has a religious-metaphysical cast to distinguish it from blind historical necessity.

With this showing of political science at work, Tocqueville introduces the need now to "instruct democracy" with a new political science, in the famous phrase, "a new political science … for a world altogether new." This is the new world of democracy, now to be found in the new world discovered and made by European explorers and colonists. In this new world, the democratic liberty that men may choose requires

23. In his letter to Corcelle of September 17, 1853, Tocqueville says he is a man convinced that "the true greatness of man lies only in the accord of the liberal sentiment and the religious sentiment, working at the same time to animate and to restrain souls."

that they be instructed, which means that they *can* be instructed. Men are teachable. But the teaching Tocqueville proposes is the contrary of the program of the Enlightenment practiced by "men of letters," or *philosophes,* the "singular education" that he denounces in the famous chapter in his later work *The Ancien Régime and the Revolution* (1856). Their instruction ignored established practice, existing fact, and received opinion, replacing them with abstract, simple rules enforced from above by a "democratic despotism" advised by literary, theoretical instructors.[24] It was a "superficial education" contemptuous of "ancient wisdom." It was foundational liberalism, based on the foundation of a simplified human nature, or what might be called "formal liberalism," a system of formal rights and duties abstracted from actual practice.[25] It knew nothing of the "great science of government," which exists but is not laid out in a system by Tocqueville.

In *Democracy in America* also, Tocqueville never lays down the new political science explicitly, nor does he withhold it from view; readers have to follow its presentation by stages and gather its scattered parts. That this political science is new implies that Tocqueville is not satisfied with the existing political science that had proclaimed itself new—that of Machiavelli and Hobbes—as opposed to the old political science of the ancients. Tocqueville's political science does not *make* a new world but *adjusts* to the new world already made, the world of democracy. Neither revolutionary nor submissive, Tocqueville's political science will oppose the existing modern political science with its strange, paradoxical formula of expanding liberty by demonstrating that men are moved by material causes. But he does not openly oppose the existing political science. Instead, he says somewhat obliquely that the democratic revolution in Europe has taken place in the "material" of society without changing laws and mores so as to make it useful. Europe especially needs instruction in fashioning the material of democracy to bring it under human control, and for this it needs to be informed about America, where democratic laws and mores are at work. But perhaps America, too, needs instruction to become

24. Tocqueville, *OR* 3.1, 127–33; 3.3, 146.
25. Tocqueville, *Democracy in America,* trans. Harvey C. Mansfield and Delba Winthrop (Chicago: University of Chicago Press, 2000), xlviii.

conscious of what it does instinctively, so as to maintain, defend, and improve its instincts.

Now for the first time, Tocqueville contrasts democracy with aristocracy, a frequent occurrence in his book. Aristocracy proves to be a catch-all designation for every premodern regime, including ancient democracy. Aristocracy is in the past; it is not a live choice in the present. One cannot return to it, but we can recall it to mind to see better the character of our live choices. Tocqueville states that aristocratic privilege was based on the illusion of an immutable order of nature, justifying privilege for the nobles while assuring that serfs would obey without protest. But in democracy ranks are confused; there is no such obedience. There are no privileges, but also no legitimacy, no convincing, reasonable justification of rule to replace aristocratic illusion. With a view to seventeenth-century political science, one could repeat that the argument for a new foundation putting men in the state of nature is stronger than any argument for departing from it, because equality is easier to establish than the inequality required for any and all government. But Tocqueville refers only to the deformed matter of democratic society in Europe, not to the foundational argument about human nature of early liberalism.

In the ill-taught democracy of Europe, enlightened as to the justice but not to the practices of democracy, men live with "degraded souls." Their souls are degraded because the rulers exercise power they consider illegitimate, and the rest are in obedience to power they consider usurped. Degraded souls! These are not addressed in the political science of Hobbes and Locke, nor in its later, less formal, more practical version in Montesquieu and in *The Federalist*. Here is a manifest sign of metaphysical intent wrapped in political fact, for the legitimacy of democracy in the order of nature is a demand of the soul and not a material satisfaction of the self. Only beings with rational souls worry about the legitimacy or consistency of their beliefs. Only such beings can have souls, and only they can be degraded or ennobled. A self would not recognize that it is selfish. The unenlightened selfishness one sees in Europe now is a quality or consequence of democracy's lack of legitimacy.[26] With illusions of immutable nature, the old aristocracy

26. *DA,* Introduction, 22.

did not produce a true understanding but did succeed in legitimizing power and satisfying souls in a way that democracy has not.

One should note that the souls called degraded are democratic, distinct from aristocratic. Souls are political in character. This means that the souls are in parallel with regimes just as in the political science of Plato and Aristotle. Tocqueville does not agree with the idea of "culture" that took hold in the nineteenth century, according to which culture is independent of politics and perhaps above politics, as with Hegel. In volume 2 of *Democracy in America*, he shows how the thoughts and sentiments of humans are ruled by their politics, how disparate aspects of "civil society" that might seem remote from democracy, such as philosophy, literature, oratory, relations between masters and servants, and men and women, are given a democratic cast and made to contribute to a whole that is fundamentally and pervasively political.[27]

The degradation of souls is to be observed especially in the "intellectual miseries" that reflect or cause the moral disorder of democracy in Europe. Tocqueville could have alluded here to the two foundational features of modern political science—the state of nature (also immutable, also illusion?), followed by the social contract—which attempt to justify democratic authority, but his way, again, is to correct liberal theory with liberal practice rather than with an invasive new theory introduced as such to compete with existing theory. He will show how democratic liberty replaces aristocratic privilege, or how immutable nature can be seen to support democracy as well as, or rather than, aristocracy. He does not begin from nature like the liberal theorists, but he arrives at it through politics, through political fact, the primary, generative, not-so-permanent, accomplished or about-to-be-accomplished fact of democracy. He transforms this fact into a cause, as toward the end of the Introduction when he speaks of equality as the "generative cause." Turning from the situation in Europe, he will consider America, where democracy is an accomplished fact. He will consider both facts and ideas, but, confirming his antifoundational posture, he says he will submit ideas to the facts rather than adapt facts to ideas.

27. See Pierre Manent, "Tocqueville philosophe politique," in *Enquête sur la démocratie: Études de philosophie politique* (Paris: Gallimard, 2007), 381.

Still in the Introduction, Tocqueville saw in America "an image of democracy itself"—not just democracy, not just America, but democracy *in* America, making known what he saw there. He has "one mother thought" linking all parts of his work, but he does not say what it is. Those who "regard it closely" will find it "in the entire work."[28] At the end of the Introduction, he says he looks further than the six intellectual parties he discerns, but not differently, because he too is political. The six parties are three pairs of opposed parties: zealous Christians versus partisans of freedom against religion, noble men who vaunt their servility versus claimants for human rights who misunderstand them, and virtuous patriots who are reactionaries versus progressives who "strive to make man into matter." Tocqueville reviles the last party most, but he is nonpartisan because he neither serves nor combats a party. Yet he is also partisan, constituting the seventh party, because he is not an objective observer having the character of the modern political scientist, above it all and unconcerned.[29] He will derive "all the theoretical consequences" of his thought, the first of which appears in the question of the role of human intention.

The first two chapters of *Democracy in America* are on the problem of the "first cause" of America—a phrase we encounter for the first time, prepared by "generative cause" in the Introduction. The problem is: does the first cause include man, and if so, how? The possibility raised in the Introduction of freely choosing democratic liberty over democratic slavery depends on one's judgment of the cause of democracy, and judgment of the cause must allow for the power of human intention. Tocqueville wants to give human intention a role it does not have in standard liberal theory, in which man is driven by his passions and motivated by his interests.

"The Point of Departure" is the title of the second chapter but also the topic of the first, a beautiful description of the beautiful geography of America, above all the valley of the Mississippi in its center. This valley is "all in all, the most magnificent dwelling that God has

---

28. *DA*, Introduction, 31.

29. See Bryan Garsten, "Seeing 'Not Differently, but Further, than the Parties,'" in *The Arts of Rule,* ed. Sharon R. Krause and Mary Ann McGrail (Lanham, Md.: Lexington Books, 2009), 359–75.

ever prepared for the habitation of man," yet nonetheless it is a "vast wilderness." Who lives there? The Indians—poor, ignorant, equal, and free peoples—primitive, natural, or original man, uncivilized. Another, more civilized people preceded the Indians, some tombs of which remain: "Of all man's work, the most durable is that which best records his nothingness and misery." God creates a home for man, we see, but natural man does not necessarily become civilized, and civilized man returns to nothingness when he returns to nature. The Mississippi valley is the empty cradle of a great nation. Tocqueville's geography is teleological, showing that the earth is made for man, even for civilized man, but nature does not generate civilization or protect it from destruction. One cannot derive politics from nature even when nature is friendly to man, unlike the liberal state of nature, which is unfriendly. Geography is not the point of departure, for nature only gives potentiality and depends on human action for its realization. Yet to the extent that human action makes use of the Mississippi valley, it completes nature and can be considered part of nature. Again one must consider the contrast to the liberal state of nature, which does not display a home for man. On the contrary, it shows human action—the "war of all against all"—always in peril from nature, and consequently it justifies the conquest of nature by human civilization.[30]

The point of departure, then, is the Pilgrims who came to America. One sees in them the human, or rather the child in the cradle, the origins of the "national character," the political in America, "the first cause."[31] In America, as opposed to nations like France where these origins are obscure, they can be seen in "broad daylight" (*au grand jour*), one of Tocqueville's favorite phrases.[32] Providence has enabled observers of our time to discern "the first causes." Tocqueville switches to the

30. See the later discussion of the westward migration that creates "vast domains" in the wilderness, using "the immense prey that fortune offers" or "as if God had held it in reserve" (*DA* 1.2.9, 457–60).

31. "The first cause" occurs eight times in *DA*, five in the singular, of which three are *la cause première*, two *la première cause* (perhaps first in time if not in rank), and three times in the plural.

32. See Eduardo Nolla's comparison of Tocqueville with Rousseau, who thought all such origins obscure and wanted to bring clarity to politics solely through the social contract (*DA*, 48).

plural, perhaps because each nation has its own origin, or because every nation has for its cause both "the political and social state" and nature (for, as we see from the first chapter on geography, the fate of a nation does not depend solely on human action). The point of departure, whether cause or causes, explains every opinion, habit, law, and event "without difficulty." This second chapter, Tocqueville says, is "almost the key to the whole work," because, I suppose, it deals with the importance of human intention, and "almost," again because intent is limited in power.

The first cause of America was the civilized men who came there, not out of the dim past long ago, but recently and identifiably as "Pilgrims" on behalf of an idea rather than for money and adventure like the Spanish. Not only were they moved by an idea, "they wanted to assure the triumph of an *idea*."[33] Thus inspired by an idea rather than by incentives, they were the first cause of their own way of life, not determined by anything outside them but by God, their God, their ancestral God who provided an "atmosphere of antiquity" surrounding them. The circumstances of their origin, their departure from Holland, their landing in New England, though not ideas, were enshrined in their idea. Tocqueville remarks on the veneration of Plymouth Rock: "Does this not show very clearly that the power and greatness of man is entirely in his soul?"[34] The thought in this rhetorical question will not be found in standard liberalism.

The Pilgrims made themselves their own cause, finding God in antiquity and adopting Him to explain their mission in coming to America. In adopting a cause above themselves, they made themselves responsible for a divinity which as such they could not have chosen. In this sense of choice, expanded to include what one adopts and takes responsibility for, they "chose" the mission they adopted as theirs from God. In this sense, too, their human intention was not merely what humans can accomplish on their own but also comprises the whole—an ordered whole—in which human intention must operate. Just as a statesman takes responsibility for problems he did not cause, and thereby becomes their cause, so men, in what they intend, take responsibility for the

33. *DA* 1.1.2, 54.
34. *DA* 1.1.2, 57n8.

circumstances or the nature of things that permits their intention to be effective. Tocqueville implies a view of the whole as opposed to that of modern philosophy, according to which human choice and (the state of) nature are in conflict, and human choice must impose its will on recalcitrant nature.

The Pilgrims' piety, says Tocqueville, was almost as much political theory as religious doctrine, revealing a democracy hitherto unknown in the world, a society homogeneous in all its parts—illustrating again the alliance of religion and Enlightenment in the New World. The Pilgrims were innovators in freedom, exercising the rights of sovereignty, with a passion for regulation of mores and for public education. No doubt they went too far in their passion for regulation; the severity of their laws went beyond what laws can accomplish, and Tocqueville makes the same point against them that Nathaniel Hawthorne was to make in *The Scarlet Letter* (1850). Yet he has a much higher view of the "puritanical" than today's view of it as antidemocratic sexual prudery. For him, these zealous men were the cause of democracy in America.

The third chapter, on the "social state" (*état social*), returns to the first cause and introduces a modulation. The social state is a new term of Tocqueville's, part of his new political science. It is the product of a fact or of laws or of both united, fact being nature or chance—the given, and law being choice with regard to fact; in sum, the social state represents both choice and nonchoice. In this again, it differs from the liberal state of nature, which is nonchoice that leaves men in "perfect freedom." After speaking of resistance to Puritan laws at the end of chapter 2, suggesting the recalcitrance of human nature, Tocqueville must show how, despite human nature's resistance to human intention, man can be his own cause. The answer is that the social state in which he lives can be *considered* "the first cause" of most laws, customs, and ideas; the social state is both cause and result. Man cannot be considered his own point of departure entirely, only partly, and so the reader learns something new about how man can be the first cause. Tocqueville substitutes the social state for the Puritan idea; it appears that the first cause is no longer merely the point of departure.

The manner in which man becomes the cause of what he does not choose but what is imposed on him is discussed in the example of estate law given in the third chapter. Estate law as law is a choice, but its subject matter is inheritance when the owner dies, which is not by choice. In this case, law makes itself responsible for human mortality, a fact of human nature, as if death were not by nature but by legal command, so that the law can dispose of your estate to your heirs. A law of natural necessity is taken over by human legislation, made specific, and humanized so that it appears to be by human choice. In this way, man assumes the role of nature or Providence, becoming the cause of what appears at first to cause him. "Man is armed by [estate law] with an almost divine power over the future of his fellows."[35] Estate law is one way in which men attempt to prevent themselves from returning to nothingness when they die; they leave an inheritance. Inheritance in the large sense, not just landed estates, would be all the things, natural and human, that human beings inherit, all that they are given. Tocqueville speaks specifically of the change in American estate law about the time of the American Revolution that abolished aristocratic entailed estates with primogeniture brought over from England and established democratic choice and equality. Aristocratic inheritance is often founded on the illusion of selfish individuals who believe they will achieve a sort of immortality by securing their estate for their future families; democratic inheritance is closer to the truth of human nature, which is more selfish and more concerned with present comforts than aristocrats wish for. By modifying inheritance, Americans made themselves the first cause of inheritance, accepting nature and willing it, but in such a way as to exercise men's freedom within nature and to establish their chosen kind of sovereignty over nature.

The next chapter is on the sovereignty of the people, the subject that Tocqueville has been discussing all along. Democracy in chapter 3 is the democratic revolution creating a social state with political consequences that can either be democratic slavery or democratic liberty. Now we see, in a further development, that in America, where democracy is most advanced, it installs the sovereignty of the people, which means the people as first cause. He says that the people are somehow sovereign in all regimes, but they are almost buried out of sight; in democracy they are sovereign in broad daylight. This means that only in democracy can you see the people as sovereign, adopt what you see,

35. *DA* 1.1.3, 79.

and *intend* it as your guiding principle. You can intend the principle that dominates you—in which case, in your manful acceptance, together with your own addition or specification of what sort of democracy, representing your freedom and choice, it no longer dominates you. Democracy is the single choice that through the sovereignty of the people makes possible the best choice and the most choice. The best choice is for equality that "incites men to want all to be strong and esteemed," as opposed to depraved taste for equality that brings the weak to want to bring the strong down to their level, and that therefore "prefers equality in servitude to inequality in freedom."[36] Democratic servitude is less democratic than democratic liberty, but democratic liberty requires that the people be visibly sovereign and not just implicitly so, as in the democratic social state. Indeed, the fact that the *social* state has a political name—democratic—indicates that it is not enough by itself to establish democracy.[37] The social state is not after all the first cause in the full sense of the deliberately chosen sovereignty of the people, but it seems designed to set a choice before his readers between the correct and the incorrect democracy. The first cause fully would be making the correct choice.

Shortly afterward, Tocqueville says: "I said previously that from the origin, the principle of the sovereignty of the people had been the generative principle of most of the English colonies in America."[38] But previously he had stressed that the principles of New England had "penetrated the entire confederation," and that in New England, the Puritan idea, blended with "the most absolute democratic and republican theories," was that the Puritans came to America "to pray to God in freedom," and that, quoting Cotton Mather, they were by their liberty all inferior, under the authority of God.[39] The people was sovereign but under the sovereignty of God; so in the previous statement Tocqueville is praising the Americans for combining the spirit of liberty with the somewhat contrary spirit of religion. At that time, too, Americans were still under the sovereignty, however mild, of England. It was when the

36. *DA* 1.3.1, 89.
37. Manent, *Nature of Democracy,* 2–5.
38. *DA* 1.1.4, 92.
39. *DA* 1.1.2, 53–54, 68–69.

American Revolution broke out that the "dogma" of the sovereignty of the people took hold and became the law of laws. Tocqueville goes back and forth from "dogma" to "principle" in this brief chapter. He mentions the broadening of the suffrage but omits to mention the disestablishment of religion going on at this time by which the theocratic character of the Point of Departure was reduced or eliminated. But at the end of the fourth chapter he says: "The people reign over the American political world as does God over the universe. They are the cause and end of all things; everything comes out of them and everything is absorbed into them."

This strange statement surely exaggerates the power of the people, for if God reigns over the universe, and the universe includes the people and the American political world, then He reigns over both of these too. The people are like God but replace God, so that the principle of the whole—all things—is human, not divine. The principle of the whole, one must add, is human by virtue of human exaggeration. The American Revolution marked a change from the Point of Departure, making its first cause more visible, or visible as God is not. The Puritan use of the ancestral disappears. Religion in the form of theocracy is the cradle of liberty, but liberty grows up and dispenses with its cradle. For all Tocqueville says in support of the alliance between religion and liberty in the United States, the people have no authority above themselves. They may believe in God, which he later shows to be good, but the separation between church and state, which he also heartily approves, prevents God's authority from interfering with man's. The sovereignty of the people is based on the sovereignty of man, on the idea of choice. This is the Puritan idea made actual, material, and consistent with itself in the principle, or the dogma, of the sovereignty of the people. Tocqueville calls it both principle and dogma because a principle, when sovereign, becomes a dogma, and because this dogma restates and replaces the religious dogma of theocracy. Religion is now established not as theocracy but as the choice of a free, sovereign people.

The ambivalence between principle and dogma relates to the fact that the principle of choice can only be established with a particular choice, the American Point of Departure. After making a choice, one no longer has a choice, at least not the same choice as before. One's present choice is partly determined by the choice previously made. Choice is subject to fact, the choice of democracy to the fact of the democratic revolution, but that revolution as it develops becomes more visible and reveals itself as the principle of the sovereignty of the people as the people grasp for themselves the idea given to them by kings and, perhaps, though Tocqueville does not care to say so, by philosophers.[40] Any principle given by philosophers becomes dogma when it is held by the people, all the more true when the principle is the sovereignty of the people. As dogma, the principle is open to abuse, and because the principle gives the people a choice, they may make the wrong choice.

Tocqueville calls the social state the first cause, but he does not apply the term to the sovereignty of the people, which is the democratic social state having become aware of itself and capable of moving itself consciously in the exercise of democracy. In the sovereignty of the people, the first cause is the second cause too, because it is the first cause no longer invisible but actual and visible in daily life. Thus, the first cause is not more fundamental than the actual politics of democracy, as would be the liberal state of nature, which always stands behind liberal politics, calling citizens away from politics to their rights as individuals, a standard that judges politics by a condition that is prepolitical. Tocqueville's social state is already democratic (or aristocratic) in name and character before it becomes active and visible in the actual working of democratic government.

In the rest of *Democracy in America*, Tocqueville works out the character and the problems of the sovereignty of the people. In a brief essay, I can only indicate some of these, and in any case, needless to say, I do not have a complete understanding. I do suggest that the order of

---

40. In the eighteenth century, the French nobility lost its power over opinion and allowed it to be usurped by literary men whose "general theories," once accepted, were inevitably "transformed into political passions and into actions" (*OR* 3.1, 130). This disaster is less likely in America because—as Tocqueville does not fail to point out—the American people are more experienced in politics than the French, which means more practiced in the sort of details that reveal the weaknesses of theories. Still, to point out this resource against the danger, actually greater in democracy with its penchant for general ideas than in aristocracy, might be the work of a philosopher who does not share this penchant (*DA* 2.1.4, 738–39).

topics in the book can be explained by following out the course of Tocqueville's metaphysical argument. The order of topics thus becomes evidence for the existence of a metaphysical argument.

The sovereignty of the people being America's first cause, how does that sovereignty become effective? The answer is through forms of government, a new consideration we encounter for the first time in chapter 5. Forms are official, public, vested with authority; they are made visible through formalities, which proclaim to everyone that you are dealing with a form. Forms are government in broad daylight, visible, open, public. (These forms are completed by informal institutions, as we shall see, in part 2 of volume 1.) The form of government overall consists of various forms in an order. Tocqueville studies the form of American government from the bottom up, starting from the township, preceding the state government though authorized by it. The township is a communal effort that forms itself spontaneously, naturally, unplanned; it is not deliberate though not unconscious. Though township is found in all regimes, township freedom is fragile because it is exposed to invasion from those of higher authority who want to impose expert uniformity and efficiency on inferior jurisdictions usually held by amateurs. Yet, for Tocqueville, township is the home of freedom in America.

In the principle/dogma of the sovereignty of the people "each individual is...considered to be as enlightened, as virtuous, as strong as any other of his fellows."[41] Why then does he obey? He obeys because it is useful to him, not because he is inferior. Nonetheless, the offices in a township—the "selectmen" whom Tocqueville names in English—do create formal inequalities. The first cause of popular sovereignty works through forms that permit exceptions to the dogma of equality for the sake of accomplishing some job together. Freedom becomes actual when it leaves the private sphere, in which an individual is isolated and weak, and becomes public by performing a task, such as laying a road, that individuals need but cannot accomplish by themselves. Freedom is only actual when free men are strong, and they are strong only when they are together, which requires organization in a form of government with some elementary hierarchy. In Europe, freedom and order are

41. *DA* 1.1.5, 108.

thought to be opposed to each other, but the use of forms allows Americans to be both free and orderly, more free because they are orderly, more orderly because they are free. Freedom for Tocqueville is not prepolitical as it is for liberal theorists such as Hobbes and Locke. What he later calls "associations" appear here in their archetype, the township.

America is not a township, of course, and township government is only the beginning of popular sovereignty, the beginning from which we learn that freedom is political. Tocqueville goes on to describe the state governments in America, with emphasis on the wide use of elections and the particular reliance on judges. Elections distribute the sovereignty of the people, preventing it from being concentrated in the central administration. Judges moderate the sovereignty of the people, expressing it because they have the last word, but limiting it because they keep the sovereign people within the Constitution. In America, judges are above ordinary law because they are below constitutional law.[42] Tocqueville concludes part 1 of the first volume with an analysis of the American Constitution. In a famous passage, he praises the making of the Constitution before praising the result: "What is new in the history of societies is to see a great people," warned by its legislators, turn its regard to the problem, sound the depth of the ill, contain itself for two entire years to discover the remedy at leisure, and submit to it voluntarily "without its costing humanity one tear or drop of blood."[43] The praise goes first to the American people, not to the founders, whom he calls "the finest minds and the noblest characters that had ever appeared in the New World." Tocqueville later praises the Federalists as an aristocratic party Americans were lucky to enjoy,[44] but here he has the people as the cause, using its "legislators" wisely for their own good, and even "submitting" (*soumettre*) to them. In contrast to the township, the Constitution was a "work of art" based on a complex mixing of two opposite theories of association. One was that the Union should be a league of independent states; the other that it should unite all inhabitants into one people. This is the difference between a whole with heterogeneous parts that are also wholes and

42. *DA* 1.1.6, 170.
43. *DA* 1.1.8, 189.
44. *DA* 1.2.2, 283.

a whole consisting of homogeneous units. Tocqueville first says that the Constitution "reconciled by force two theoretically irreconcilable systems," then decides it is a beautiful creation, "free and happy like a small nation, glorious and strong like a great one."[45]

At the end of part 1, one can sense that Tocqueville's brow begins to furrow as he regards the beautiful picture of American government, from bottom to top, that he has displayed. The Constitution, based on a complicated theory, asks perhaps too much knowledge and discernment in those it must rule. With its fragmented sovereignty, it relies on the chance that America is sufficiently distant from Europe not to become the prey of one of its great military monarchies.[46] As his description proceeds, chance as opposed to choice plays an increasing role—for example, in his charming analysis of a presidential election. He compares it to a storm that makes a river overflow its banks, which then, "as soon as fortune has pronounced," returns peacefully to its bed. Here is a steep descent from the Point of Departure inspired by a grand idea chosen by a brave people.[47] As nature makes room for chance, so human choice allows for the routine of mediocrity in democratic elections, which debases, yet also maintains, the principle of government through election. At the same time, however, while speaking of the framers of the Constitution, "the American legislators," he brings up "the legislator," a man "who plots his course"; he can direct his vessel but he cannot "change its structure, create winds, or prevent the ocean from rising under his feet."[48] On the last page of part 1, he mentions himself, saying what he appreciates, envies, and refuses to believe about America's good luck.[49] If *Democracy in America* has for its purpose "to instruct democracy," Tocqueville is the instructor, blessing America's choices and managing the chance that attends them.

45. *DA* 1.1.8, 197, 263–69.

46. *DA* 1.1.8, 264, 276.

47. A later reference to the Puritan Point of Departure can be found among the "accidental or providential causes" that maintain a democratic republic in America. What was the choice of the "first Puritan" was favorable chance for his posterity (*DA* 1.2.9, 455).

48. *DA* 1.1.8, 264.

49. *DA* 1.1.8, 276.

The American people exercises its sovereignty through forms, whether low and simple or high and complex, but it also asserts itself against them informally. Human freedom has an arbitrary aspect, a willfulness arising from the human material of irrational passion that wants to assert its importance regardless of what is rational or good for it. Tocqueville is not so optimistic as Hegel, and he does not agree that reason has sufficient power or cunning to use passion for its own ends. Thus, following the discussion of forms in part 1 of the first volume, part 2 is devoted to the informal power of the people. The principle of the sovereignty of the people must account for the abuse of power that brings on slavery as well as its healthy exercise in orderly forms.

In the title of chapter 1, Tocqueville announces that one can say *strictly* that the people govern in the United States, which proves to mean that although the form of government is representative, the people encounter no lasting obstacles to their opinions, prejudices, interests, and even to their passions. So much for the efficacy of the representative principle, dear to Benjamin Constant and François Guizot, which James Madison in *Federalist* No. 10 made the touchstone of modern republicanism as opposed to the failed democracies of ancient times! Public opinion, which first appears in the discussion of the presidency in part 1,[50] comes to the fore in part 2 as the informal expression of the sovereignty of the people, so potent and so far from the ability of representatives to "refine and enlarge,"[51] that it brings Tocqueville to say that he does not know any country with less independence of mind and freedom of discussion than America.[52]

Institutions of the people's informal power in America are parties, great and small, the press, and political associations. From these, Tocqueville moves to a discussion in chapter 5 of how democratic

50. *DA,* 207.

51. Madison, *Federalist* No. 10. Madison had his own reason for distrusting the form of representative government, for he thought that the form of republicanism, which establishes majority rule, made majority faction, the main danger to republics, difficult for republicans to discern and oppose. Nonetheless, with a view to the advantage of "extending the sphere," he rested his case for the Constitution—"wholly popular" yet "exclusively representative"—on the efficacy of representation.

52. *DA* 1.2.7, 417.

choices are affected by unhealthy democratic instincts,[53] and next, to the "real advantages" of democracy to American society, the informal fact that rights are tied to interests, "the only fixed point in the human heart,"[54] and then, in a crescendo, to the problem of majority tyranny. Part 2 ends with the very long chapter on the three races, the only chapter with its own table of contents, which are said to be "American without being democratic." It proves to be the story of majority tyranny by the white race against the red and the black—political tyranny in addition to the tyranny over thought already denounced. America, in fact, chose the wrong sort of sovereignty of the people. Tocqueville uses the occasion to deliver a lesson on the relation between pride and liberty, the reds representing ignorant pride, free but refusing civilization, and the blacks representing obedience to civilization but not allowed to live free. Liberty requires the pride of the reds together with the submission to civilization of the blacks. The first volume ends with an open choice between "two great peoples," the Russians[55] and the Anglo-Americans, to be decided, seemingly, by "a secret design of Providence." The design is not so mysterious as not to be discernible by Tocqueville, however. He says that the Russians stand for the sovereignty of man over man; the Americans (the Anglo prefix is dropped), the sovereignty of man over nature. The lesson seems to be that the form of popular sovereignty, or the forms of democratic self-government, are unable to control the matter of human nature and nature in order to produce a responsible choice.

The diremption Tocqueville proposes between the American, who struggles with nature, and the Russian, who grapples with men, cannot stand as it is. Somehow the sovereignty of man over man (Russia) must be in accord with the sovereignty of man over nature (America), and vice versa, for man is within nature as well as above it. This is perhaps the simplest statement of the need for metaphysics: that man is both subject to nature ("physics") and capable of mastering it, or at least of

53. *DA* 1.2.5.

54. *DA* 1.2.6, 391.

55. The Russians under the Czar are a democratic people because they are equal to one another as his subjects. Equality is possible without liberty, Tocqueville reminds us.

understanding it (hence beyond physics). Man within nature is a slave, in the first instance to the Czar of Russia; but if he is within nature, he only conveys man's servitude to those over whom he is "sovereign" and does not cause it. He has to do what he forces others to do, that is, obey nature's necessities, and he is as much a slave as his "subjects." When democratic theorists find men to be subject to vast, impersonal forces, as we shall see they do, they justify the despotism of one over all other men (the immense being of centralized government, Tocqueville will say in volume 2) as opposed to the liberty of self-government, which depends on a special status for mankind within nature. If man has this status, he could justly take pride in it; his pride would not be based on the illusion of ancestors who were gods or had relations with the gods, like the pride of the red Indians. What would justify human pride? Tocqueville gives the same answer as Aristotle—the intellect of man. It is therefore no accident that the first topic of volume 2 is the democratic intellect. Somehow democracy must come to terms with the intellect, the faculty that elevates man above the rest of nature, thus giving him rights and liberty by contrast to the rest of nature, but that also elevates one class of men above other men, thus seeming to justify aristocracy.

I will now indicate still more briefly what I think happens in volume 2 of *Democracy in America*. Volume 2, Tocqueville says, concerns civil society, as volume 1 was on laws and political mores. "The two parts [volumes] complete one another and form a single work." I will take this statement as his answer by anticipation to interpreters today who speak of "two *Democracies*," as if the two volumes of the book were separate and not merely different but contradictory.

In my view, "the two parts" of the book do complete one another as Tocqueville says, and they do so not by being identical; rather, the second volume answers the problem set in the first volume. Volume 2 is on the end or ends of democracy in America, the sort of civil society produced by democracy. In order to resolve the misfit between form and matter at the end of volume 1, Tocqueville finds it necessary to align the form with the end, which is liberty and human greatness together. Instead of a choice between America and Russia that will be made according to the secret design of Providence, in volume 2 we have democracy seen in the light of the contrast between itself and aristocracy, almost two distinct humanities, and we have God understood as intellect, with man left "powerful and free" notwithstanding the impositions of Providence.[56]

In the preface to volume 2, Tocqueville declares that he is not an adversary of democracy, but he does not say he is a friend. Since the democratic revolution is irresistible, he can stress the dangers in democracy without appearing to be an adversary, and he can also address its friends, particularly its unwise friends. Part 1 of volume 2 is a sustained attack on the friends of democracy, who maintain that democracy is irresistible in a different way from Tocqueville, so as to rob men of choice, of the possibility of voluntary intellectual movement toward the goal, the end of democratic liberty. These are the materialists: Descartes (yes, Descartes) at the beginning, then the pantheists[57] and the "democratic historians."[58] The title of part 1 is "Influence of Democracy on Intellectual Movement in the United States," an early use of the phrase "intellectual movement," not in the plural as it would be used today. Tocqueville does not accord influence to the intellectuals but rather to "democracy," on the intellectuals—as we see in his very amusing description of Americans as Cartesians without having read Descartes.

To use the intellect is to use one's own mind, hence to doubt authority. Yet motion toward an end requires stifling doubt and accepting authority, Tocqueville shows in the first two chapters of part 1, here clarifying the confusion he had left earlier between dogma and principle. Intellectual movement rests on the dignity of man; it requires that man govern and control himself and his environment, but in democracy even the philosopher, or especially he, tends to deny that this is possible. Modern science wants to manipulate nature, but modern philosophy ("pantheism") shows that the manipulators are manipulated; reason is not in control, and everything is determined by blind fatality.

Thus in a democracy, as in any society, intellectual authority is needed to provide a "salutary servitude" under which freedom can be practiced. Its "principal source" in democratic peoples is the majority, which in the United States "takes charge of furnishing individuals with

56. *DA* 2.4.8, 1282–85.
57. *DA* 2.1.7.
58. *DA* 2.1.2.

a host of ready-made opinions," maintaining an "intellectual empire," becoming "a sort of religion" with the majority as its prophet.[59] Democracy likes "general ideas" that bring a number of analogous things under the same form so that one can think about them more conveniently. In that description, one can hardly help noticing the parallel, not mentioned, between the generalizing of democratic majorities and the mathematical character of modern philosophy. Tocqueville says that God is superior to the human mind in being able to consider general similarities and individual differences at the same time. Instead of trying to set forth explicitly the philosophical truth that would consider both similarities and differences in imitation of God, thus reconciling the facile generalizing of democracy with the overemphasis of aristocracy on differences, he says that only God, rather than human philosophy, rises above the partiality of the two outlooks. With this remark, he indicates the direction human philosophy should take, but he implies it will never reach the goal. To overcome the partiality of aristocrats for human differences, hence for the difference between free men and slaves, he says that "it was necessary that Jesus Christ come to earth to make it understood that all members of the human species are naturally similar and equal."[60] This much-quoted remark gives credit to Christianity for making known a natural truth that could not be established on its own or by humans.

Perhaps, then, nature, or the aspect of nature most needed by humans—such as the natural similarity between the free man and the slave[61]—is best understood by humans through religion, and religion is best understood as revealing the intellect, rather than the will, of God. If it was necessary that religion should establish democracy, it will be necessary that religion moderate democracy and direct it to freedom. The philosophy that Tocqueville intimates must be carried on through the religion that he specifies; his muted philosophy can do this because the goal of religion has become the understanding of the

59. *DA* 2.1.2, 719–24.
60. *DA* 2.1.3, 733.
61. Tocqueville says that the "vast geniuses" of Rome and Greece "did their utmost to prove that slavery was in nature and that it would always exist" (*DA* 2.1.3, 732–33). He does not say they were wrong, however, though he gives that impression. One might note that slavery could always exist without being natural.

whole. Philosophy differs only in seeking understanding for its own sake, whereas religion wants to be useful to mankind. We have now reached the chapter[62] that served as our introduction on the need humans have for "very fixed ideas." Tocqueville had discussed religion in volume 1 as a political institution together with mores, explaining its psychology and showing how it "extends its empire over intelligence";[63] now, in volume 2, he shows how it *constitutes* the "necessary truths" of intelligence. The chapter heading says that "religion knows how to make use of democratic instincts,"[64] making democracy an instrument of religion, whereas in volume 1, religion had been the means of maintaining democracy. But at the same time, he suggests that religion may be an instrument of philosophy—by which philosophy makes itself effectual against the sort of philosophy that simply exaggerates democratic instincts. The lesson with which Tocqueville ended the preceding chapter is not that democracy needs a new philosophy but that it needs democratic institutions that force each citizen to be occupied with government, and thus "moderate the excessive taste for general theories in political matters that equality suggests."[65] Nonetheless, he shows a new philosophy (or "political science") where to go, what to do, and what to stay away from.

Philosophy must reject democratic pantheism, the view seen in German philosophy and French literature that attempts to make a general idea of the whole, making diverse things into mere parts or pieces of a single "immense being."[66] Pantheism does away with the personhood of God and denies the distinction between God and nature, His creation. Hence pantheism would be hostile to the worship of God, to the external forms of religion that "fix the human mind in the contemplation of abstract truths." Religion helps to correct the philosophic method of the Americans, which as we have seen, scorns forms because they seem to be obstacles to the direct perception of truth.[67] Forms make the invisible God visible but also cover Him up and prevent Him from being seen directly. Democratic peoples tend to deny everything

62. *DA* 2.1.5.
63. *DA* 1.2.9, 474.
64. *DA* 2.1.5.
65. *DA* 2.1.4, 740.
66. *DA* 2.1.7, 758.
67. *DA* 2.1.5, 750.

supernatural, thereby exaggerating the power of human reason, power facilitated by the manipulation of "general ideas." Religion limits the power of human reason by maintaining the distinction between God and humans through worship of God in external forms or ceremonies. Given the impotence of philosophy to move beyond doubt, philosophy needs to support religion, perhaps to present itself in the external form of religion.

Equality suggests the idea of the indefinite perfectibility of man, man being perfectible as opposed to other animals. Progress therefore presupposes that pantheism is wrong not to make this distinction and to deny the dignity of man.[68] Perfectibility would be human motion toward the perfect, an end democrats prefer because it is not above man, not divine. But the difficulty is that perfectibility is indefinite; it keeps going and has no view of the perfect, no place to stop; it is perfectibility without the perfect. The last section of chapters in part 1[69] is on speech. We see that democrats are tempted to boast in their speech, particularly in their "parliamentary eloquence."[70] The American democratic representative is a person of no independent standing, unlike his aristocratic fellow, and is perpetually stung by the need to acquire and show his importance, and derivatively, that of his constituents ("the people of my district," as they say today). Democratic man wants to be honored, and he has a desire unknown to himself to live in an aristocracy where he would receive his due. This desire is in contradiction with pantheism and democratic history, which subject democratic peoples to vast, impersonal forces that hold man to be powerless and insignificant. Intellectuals in a democracy must learn to appreciate the aristocratic truth that the individual is important, for the sovereignty of the people is not established if each individual in the people is a slave to vast, democratic forces, the forces expressed in general ideas.

Part 2 of volume 2 is on the sentiments Americans feel because of their theories, especially "individualism," and the ways they combat it, particularly the art and science of association. Much has been written about individualism, a term not invented by Tocqueville but one he

68. *DA* 2.1.8–9.
69. *DA* 2.1.13–21.
70. *DA* 3.1.21.

first defined. I would stress that it is not a passion, but a calm and considered sentiment, as he says, in which each individual tries to isolate himself from the mass in the belief that he can take his entire destiny in his own hands, becoming an "entire whole" (*tout entier*). It is perhaps an attempt to rescue his sense of importance, but it is perverse because it renders him impotent. Americans combat individualism through the art and science of association, of which much could be said. I note that he says first that the *science* of association is the mother science, and then that, "as I said above," the *art* of association is the mother science that all study and apply.[71] Association is an art because human construction is required; it is a science because something is there to be known, namely, what willing beings, human beings, are and how they behave. Both together are political science, as Tocqueville calls it, or political metaphysics, as I will call it. "Political associations can therefore be considered great schools, free of charge, where all citizens come to learn the general theory of associations."[72] Citizens learn by doing, and the "general theory of associations" (or metaphysics) comes out of politics rather than being imposed on it by a general theorist.

There follows a section of chapters on materialism and the soul[73] in which is found Tocqueville's beautiful analysis of the love of immortality in human nature, the restiveness of American souls, and the need and desire for religion. Democratic work is discussed in chapters 17 to 20, in which Tocqueville says that it is the task of philosophers and those who govern to seek to move back the object of human actions and to give democratic peoples the habit of acting with a view to the future. This is the salutary way to "banish chance"—not by the conquest of nature but by showing that long-range enterprises by human beings are possible if one learns to resist the thousand daily petty urges that distract them (think television).[74]

Mores are the subject of part 3 of volume 2. They had been treated in volume 1,[75] where Tocqueville said that laws are more important than

71. *DA* 2.2.5, 7, 902, 914.
72. *DA* 2.2.7, 914.
73. *DA* 2.2.10–16.
74. *DA* 2.2.17, 967.
75. *DA* 1.2.9, 494.

circumstances, and mores more important than laws. Mores develop gradually out of laws, however, a product of law over time, and so do not seem to be legislated, arising as they do "naturally" and freely. They are human legislation combined with what cannot be legislated, an informal expression of popular sovereignty. Here mores are treated with a view to nature to answer the question, thematic in part 3, of whether democracy is in accord with nature. In Plato's *Republic,* the rule of the wise is said to be in accordance with nature: what does democracy do with this and other kinds of human inequality? In the first seven chapters, Tocqueville discourses on democratic compassion, democratic politeness, and the master-servant relationship in democracy. He stresses the notion of "fellow," "someone like oneself" or "one's similar" (*semblable*), considering whether equality is natural or conventional: is democratic equality conveyed spontaneously by the recognition of a fellow human being, or does one have to have a conventional disposition to recognize another person not quite as equal but as similar? The notion of *semblable* helps explain a point often raised against Tocqueville, which is why the democratic revolution toward ever-greater equality can be held to be a fact when manifest inequalities still remain—the reply being that we democrats consider ourselves more equal and do our best to equalize our inequalities. The inequalities we recognize, for example, in intelligence and wealth, are there by virtue of majority consent of those equalized as similar.

Then comes the notable section of five chapters on the American woman, Tocqueville's lovely utopian description, or hopeful picture, of women who never complain but willingly accept the bonds of matrimony after enjoying the half-freedom of girlhood, in which they had "pure mores rather than a chaste mind."[76] Tocqueville had to treat the alleged inequality of women to men and to show how democracy might handle it. His American women uphold mores, using reason alone without resort to authority, and they have a kind of honor that serves as an alternative to the mediocrity and vanity of democratic males. Sadly, but not surprisingly, women today prefer to adopt the mediocrity and vanity of democratic males, rejecting Tocqueville's manly boasting on their behalf.

76. *DA* 2.3.9, 1043.

After the virtue of women comes a section on honor in democracy,[77] essentially an aristocratic sentiment but an attribute of human nature that must find a place in democracy. Tocqueville takes care to attack modern moralists who complain of pride: "I would willingly trade several of our small virtues for this vice."[78] Pride, for him, is not so much a moral virtue as due reward for the accomplishments of political liberty, but whether moral or political, its metaphysical consequence is not just elevation of one human over another but of the human, as capable of deeds worthy of pride, over the nonhuman. Pride is incompatible with pantheism and materialism. Honor is connected to revolution, as being the motive for which one might lead a great revolution, which might be a great revolution "in intellect" with "new religious, philosophical, political and moral principles." Such a revolution "all at once" is unlikely in a democracy; much more likely is a change "in discovering new consequences rather than seeking new principles."[79] As opposed to impersonal "intellectual movement" in part 1 of this volume, in which the name of Descartes is presented as "the intellectual method of the Americans," we now have the possibility that intellectual movement comes through intellectual revolutions made by a single powerful man. Could he be a philosopher, as, for example, Descartes? But Tocqueville cites only the example of Luther, the author of new religious principles. As usual, he presents philosophy in the shadow of religion.

Then comes a paragraph of one long sentence (not infrequent in Tocqueville's style): "I believe that rarely, in a democratic society, will a man come to imagine, at a single stroke, a system of ideas very removed from the one that his contemporaries have adopted; and if such an innovator appeared, I imagine that he would at first have great difficulty making himself heard and still more making himself believed."[80]

Is it too much to suppose that Tocqueville may have himself in mind here? Great intellectual revolutions such as Luther's are produced less by "the force of reasoning" than by "the authority of a name," and Luther would have had greater difficulty with his if he had lived in a

77. *DA* 2.3.13–20.
78. *DA* 2.3.19, 1126.
79. *DA* 2.3.21, 1144.
80. *DA* 4.3.21, 1145.

democratic century, when men distrust the general idea of the intellectual superiority of one man—even in the form of the word of God, one might add. Certainly Tocqueville seeks new consequences rather than new principles, or indeed draws his principles from consequences, his understanding of liberty from the practice of political liberty in America. He uses the force of reasoning and avoids relying on the authority of his, or anyone's, name. But there is more to come.

The discussion of revolution leads to a section on democratic armies that considers how democracy will treat the warrior and the captain or prince. In chapter 26, Machiavelli's name appears, just this once in Tocqueville's book.[81] His mention is prepared, one might say, by a previous reference he makes to "princes in our time" who instead of merely allying with the people should have done something more: "it would have been more honest and more sure to teach each of their subjects the art of being self-sufficient."[82] Machiavelli is quoted, or misquoted, by Tocqueville together with the name of Napoleon, who invented the mode of conquest by capturing the great capitals of the world. What one might make of this hint I leave to another occasion with the remark that Tocqueville must have had high thoughts for himself. It is not altogether surprising that despite three statements in the book that human inequalities in intelligence have been established by God,[83] he never finds space to discuss that ruling inequality in the part of *Democracy in America* where it would best fit.

Yet, whatever his own pride may have been, Tocqueville makes his proud submission to democracy in part 4 of volume 2. He says he is

81. On the significance of the number 26 in Machiavelli, see Leo Strauss, *Thoughts on Machiavelli* (Glencoe, Ill.: Free Press, 1958), 48–49. For another instance of this sort of use of Machiavelli soon after Tocqueville's, see William H. Prescott, *History of the Conquest of Mexico* (1843), pt. 4, chap. 3.

82. *DA* 2.3.20, 1132. See Tocqueville's remarks on Machiavelli in his letters to Louis Kergorlay, August 5, 1836, and to Pierre-Paul Royer-Collard, August 25, 1856. In the first, he says to Kergorlay that in reading Machiavelli, ideas came to him "that I want to share with you, following our old method of philosophizing ceaselessly between us." In the second, he offers advice to Machiavelli on how he might better have achieved his end by showing his readers how to "wrap their vices in feigned virtues." Tocqueville, who himself teaches princes, here teaches the teacher of princes.

83. *DA* 1.1.3, 2.2.13, 946.

not God and cannot see what God sees, but he is not incapable of taking an impartial view of democracy and aristocracy and submitting to the former one, which God has chosen to install. Humans do not have a choice between those two regimes, which make almost two distinct humanities, nor can they adopt the principle of mixing them, the mixed regime being a chimera. But they can adopt and keep hidden the various aristocratic features of American democracy: the jury, its lawyers, its religion, associations, the notion of rights, pride, and honor. These things can be democratic if one considers democracy to be not only a form of government, and thus asking "is this democratic?" but also an end to which they are a means. Democracy is not fundamentally pluralistic, as we believe; it's all democratic.[84] Democracy (like aristocracy) is driven to maintain that it has the full truth, so that democracy makes a democratic society just as Aristotle said of the regime. But democracy can contain these aristocratic features not so called that improve democracy and keep it free and great despite its overweening passion for equality.

The mild despotism Tocqueville fears is quite compatible with the sovereignty of the people. When they vote, "citizens emerge for a moment from dependency to indicate their master, and return to it."[85] He does not succeed, and does not want to succeed, in making human choice altogether in accord with human nature and nature, for such a metaphysics would destroy liberty and human greatness. We humans have to be capable of systematic error, even fated to that, if we are to live in accordance with nature's unspoken promises.

In the last part, Tocqueville addresses "the true friends of freedom and human greatness."[86] Greatness is his substitute for the good life of the classical philosophers and the life of comfortable self-preservation of the liberal philosophers. It is more compatible with freedom than either. Anyone who seriously undertakes the good life must question the use that most men, including those we commonly think great, make

84. A contrary view that Tocqueville's democracy enshrines "openness" can be found in Steven Bilakovics, *Democracy without Politics* (Cambridge, Mass.: Harvard University Press, 2012), 12–13.

85. *DA* 2.4.6, 1255.

86. *DA*, 1272.

of their freedom. Pascal was perhaps beyond greatness; he had an "ardent, haughty, and disinterested love of the true" that is distinct from profit and glory.[87] Yet his "extraordinary efforts" resemble greatness in power and rarity, and Tocqueville does not make a point of excluding them from greatness. In contrast, to limit oneself to comfort and security risks trading one's freedom for these lesser goods. Greatness is rare, and so inherently aristocratic, but democratic peoples are capable of great actions, as when Americans conceived their Constitution. They are also endowed by their religion with the greatness of the human spirit afforded by belief in the immortality of the soul. Throughout *Democracy in America,* the main enemy of freedom is materialism, both in its theory, which teaches impotence and passivity, and in practice, as it deflects citizens from politics into soft enjoyments. The possibility of greatness refutes materialist theory and inspires the practice of self-government. Freedom and human greatness belong together, and Tocqueville's philosophy gives substance and support to the friends of them both.

87. *DA* 2.1.10, 78–82.

9

An Undertow of Race Prejudice in the Current of Democratic Transformation: Tocqueville on the "Three Races" of North America

BARBARA ALLEN

In *Democracy in America,* Alexis de Tocqueville portrayed European history as a complex set of transformations producing a "providential" democratic revolution. "Democracy," defined as the condition of social equality, swept away the aristocracies of the Western world and established a new basis for society in the New World. The gradual, progressive, irresistible development of equality emerges as the main current of Tocqueville's analysis of the dramatic *political* changes wrought by the revolutions of the late eighteenth century. These political revolutions, he contended, made manifest profound *intellectual* transformations affecting *all* social relations: political and economic, civic and intimate.

Equality of conditions reflected a mental stance as much as a social circumstance. The new ideation included a belief in the equal moral status of all human beings and concepts of equity, fairness, and justice that demanded rule of law, due process of law, and equality under law. Birth no longer provided the main channel to power. Intelligence became a social force, and knowledge a currency of public affairs. Commerce, industry, invention, and, most generally and powerfully, money aided the course of equality, which Tocqueville concluded was a universal, lasting, inescapable force.[1]

1. Alexis de Tocqueville, *Democracy in America: Historical-Critical Edition of "De la démocratie en Amérique,"* ed. Eduardo Nolla, trans. James T. Schleifer,

[242]

In neither New World nor Old were the effects of this progressive force uniformly positive. Tocqueville identified a profoundly paradoxical trend in social relations whenever equality gained at the expense of political liberty. He warned of a democratic tendency toward mediocrity, conformity, and heedless assent to mass opinion. His analysis of the myopic individualism and excessive materialism that would plague democracies and dim the light of liberty was summed into a single ominous phrase: democratic despotism. From the time of Tocqueville's birth in 1805, throughout his career as an analyst and as an actor in politics, France indeed faced the specter of despotic regimes. As the place where the equality of social conditions had "reached the most complete and most peaceful development," America suggested a case study that might foretell what could be hoped and feared from similar circumstances in France. Like the Americans, France would "sooner or later...arrive...at a nearly complete equality of conditions." America was not a model for France, but "in the two countries the generating cause of laws and mores is the same": equality of social conditions. Among Tocqueville's analytical tasks was distinguishing what was "democratic" from the peculiarities of "America."[2]

In America, Tocqueville discovered a countercurrent colliding with the powerful force of the democratic revolution. A strong undertow of race prejudice threatened to destroy the American Union while taking down the captives of an economy and society based on race slavery and Indians whose "removal" was essential to the Anglo-Americans' westward expansion. American race ideology poses several puzzles for Tocqueville's main narrative of increasing equality of social condition, in which aspects of birth status emerge as exceptionally resistant to the force of the democratic revolution. Is the equality of social condition less compelling and less universal after all? Are the institutional and ideational remnants of race slavery uniquely "American" and not "democratic"? Similarly, are colonial enterprises, which in the New World included strategies such as Indian removal, set apart from democratic impulses?

------

4 vols. (Indianapolis: Liberty Fund, 2010), 7–12. This edition is hereafter cited as *DA*.

2. *DA*, 28.

A Point of Departure: Democracy, Nationalism, and the Habits of Liberty

It is necessary to take stock of oneself, to struggle against the current in order to perceive that these institutions which are so simple and so logical would not suit a great nation that needs a strong internal government and fixed foreign policy; that it is not durable by nature; that it requires, within the people that confers it on itself, a long habit of liberty and of a body of *true* enlightenment which can be acquired only rarely and in the long run. And after all that is said, one comes back again to thinking that it is nonetheless a good thing and that it is regrettable that the moral and physical constitution of man prohibits him from obtaining it everywhere and forever.[3]

Tocqueville wrote these observations to his friend, Louis de Kergorlay, on June 29, 1831, shortly before he and Gustave de Beaumont set out for the Michigan frontier of American settlement. His thoughts reflect his more general concerns with a people's "point of departure," which included their mores, or "habits of heart and mind," and the specificities of place and time that, in the case of their physical environment, shaped their experience and reckoned their status in international arenas of geopolitics. The democratic social condition affected such particular facts, institutions, and intellectual qualities, but the response of each people to the force of equality varied according to the "national character" such a point of departure had formed.

In *Democracy in America,* Tocqueville turned first to the New England point of departure: its covenant-based federal theology and the federated unions constituted among numerous colonial governments, which the covenantal mental stance produced.[4] The covenanted groups shared the same language, moral outlook, and purpose for coming to the New World; as Tocqueville put it, "[T]hey tore themselves from the comforts of their homeland to obey a purely intellectual need. By

3. Tocqueville to Louis de Kergorlay, June 29, 1831, in Tocqueville, *Selected Letters on Politics and Society,* ed. Roger Boesche, trans. James Toupin and Roger Boesche (Berkeley: University of California Press, 1985), 58.

4. Barbara Allen, *Tocqueville, Covenant, and the Democratic Revolution: Harmonizing Earth with Heaven* (Lanham, Md.: Lexington Books, 2005), 31–65.

exposing themselves to the inevitable hardships of exile, they wanted to assure the triumph of *an idea.*[5] Their methods of dealing with contesting ideas and their general orientation to a voluntaristic society, Tocqueville claimed, had filtered through the institutions of the entire American Union.

In his letter to Kergorlay, he described "the ease with which [this people] does without government." Here was a democratic people that exhibited an "extreme respect for the law; alone and without public force, it commands in an irresistible way... [because] they make it themselves and can change it." Admirable, too, was the resulting ethic of self-control, self-organization, and self-government.

> Every man here considers himself interested in public security and in the exercise of laws. Instead of counting on the police, he counts only on himself. It follows, in short, that without ever appearing, public force is everywhere. It is...incredible...how this people keeps itself in order by the sole sentiment that it has no safeguard against itself except within itself.[6]

After an additional five months of travel throughout the eastern coast, French Canada, and Michigan on the western frontier, Tocqueville expanded the range of American voluntarism to include associations of all kinds. Not only did this people seem to provide for itself the most basic requirement of government (security through law, order, and enforcement), but nearly every collective choice and activity appeared to be accomplished through voluntary associations. When Tocqueville ultimately published these observations in *Democracy in America,* he used them to *define* the true meaning of the democratic "dogma," the sovereignty of the people: it was the conviction, principle, and actuality that society "acts by itself on itself."[7] This conception of governance set a high bar for the political capacities of citizen-sovereigns and demanded a novel network of institutional arrangements to engage officials of government in the public entrepreneurship characterizing this kind

5. *DA,* 54. Italics in original.
6. Tocqueville to Louis de Kergorlay, June 29, 1831, in Tocqueville, *Selected Letters,* 57.
7. *DA,* 91, 96.

of self-government. Not every people could exhibit such a national character or maintain its institutions.

Two important themes emerge in Tocqueville's 1831 letter to Kergorlay: (1) the importance of gaining political experience that enlightens, if a people were to meet the necessary condition of gaining the *habit* of liberty; and (2) if we suppose a "great" nation required an authoritative "government" in order to take its proper place in international affairs, the difficulty of maintaining the highly institutional foundations conducive to political enlightenment. The requirements of self-governance, Tocqueville suggested, would inevitably be buffeted by the strong currents of international relations. The former theme is expressed throughout *Democracy in America*. In his later observations of the French mission to Algeria, Tocqueville confronted the ideational primacy of the nation-state and the effects of this ideal on his generation's aspirations to spread enlightenment on the crest of the democratic revolution.[8]

THREATS TO LIBERTY AND THE CAPACITIES OF CITIZENS

Tocqueville emphasized the importance of individual capacities for democratic self-government. These capacities, he suggested, were in many ways circumscribed by the conditions of a people's social order, conceived as its stage of "civilization." A well-ordered society characterized by the condition of equality demanded a capacity for exercising liberty, properly understood as a conjunction of right and obligation. In the daily realities of communal life, legal constructions of "individual" and individual rights acknowledged the mutual integrity and interdependence of individuals and their associations. To conceptualize the "individual," even in the abstract, as an entity wholly removed from social concourse was to encourage hubris and a new malady, *"l'individualisme."*

8. Melvin Richter, "Tocqueville on Algeria," *Review of Politics* 25 (July 1963): 362–98; Jennifer Pitts, "Empire and Democracy: Tocqueville and the Algeria Question," *Journal of Political Philosophy* 8, no. 3 (2000): 295–318; Jennifer Pitts, introduction to *Writings on Empire and Slavery*, by Alexis de Tocqueville, ed. and trans. Jennifer Pitts (Baltimore: Johns Hopkins University Press, 2001, ix–xxxviii; Cheryl Welch, "Colonial Violence and the Rhetoric of Evasion: Tocqueville on Algeria," *Political Theory* 31, no. 2 (April 2003): 235–64.

More than selfishness, which he defined as an exaggerated love of self, individualism was a "considered and peaceable sentiment that disposes each citizen to isolate himself from the mass of his fellows and to withdraw to the side with his family and his friends; so that after thus creating a small society for his own use, he willingly abandons the large society to itself."[9] This perversion of self-interest would ultimately bring about a despotic, tutelary power, a "second providence," the genesis and terminus of individual and social existence.[10]

Equality could be an accessory of despotism or a condition enabling the rich associational life of a self-governing society. The social mobility that equality promoted severed the artificial bonds of aristocracy and increased the strength of natural sentiments of kinship. But the democratic age also weakened traditional and intergenerational dependencies; family ties and bonds of friendship could enlarge the sphere of sentiments and interests or induce insularity and isolation. A mild (yet potentially severe) despotism of an increasingly totalizing state was the destiny facing societies that were governed by the self-justifying rationale of individualism. Institutions alone would not counter the effects of individualism; the effectiveness of institutional constraints and incentives depended upon a people's habits of heart and mind.[11] It is in this context of evaluating "civilization" in terms of self-governing capacities that Tocqueville speaks of "national character," and the shorthand terminology of "race."

Within the broad structure of history, particularities of culture, the specific responses of individuals, as well as "accident" and happenstance brought short-term variations in the democratic social condition and influenced the trajectory of long-term historical development. Antecedent "facts," unique to a given polity, brought variation in responses to the democratic revolution. The range of individual or collective choice was circumscribed by the *mentalité* of an age; still, within that "fatal

---

9. *DA*, 882.

10. Tocqueville described "*le régné de l'égoïsme*" in a letter to Charles Stoffels, April 21, 1830, as quoted in Aurelian Craiutu, "Tocqueville and the Political Thought of the French Doctrinaires (Guizot, Royer-Collard, Rémusat)," *History of Political Thought* 20 (Autumn 1999): 476.

11. *DA*, 466.

circle," the individual was powerful and free.[12] To view the situation otherwise was to abandon analysis to determinism, conceiving individuals and peoples as victims of "I do not know what insurmountable and unintelligent force that arises from previous events, the race, the soil, or the climate."[13] "Race," thought of as a genetic inheritance, was such an "unintelligent force"; race, for Tocqueville, signified the cultural inheritance, which, combined with history, political geography, and environment, reflected "circumstances" (*les circonstances*), which influenced laws and mores.[14]

The circumstances of the English settlers, Tocqueville noted on several occasions, had reached a level of "civilization" that in many respects uniquely enabled their self-governing capacities. Whole communities had immigrated to New England, bringing a complete set of institutions that reflected their national character and temperament as well as the particular beliefs inspiring their covenanted communities. Whatever was particular to their religious ideas and motivations or the institutional and intellectual adaptations necessitated by their colonial experiences, their national character was "English."[15] As Puritans they were strivers; as the English they drew on a long history of rule of law, individual right, and communal obligation. Their arts and letters and even their religion were oriented toward political philosophy. Their notions of progress—gained from their covenant orientation and their English political culture—constantly brought them beyond their circle of intimates into the world, a possession, they believed, bestowed by grace for their continued cultivation. Tocqueville raised doubts about the worldview

12. *DA*, 1285.

13. *DA*, 1284.

14. *DA*, 466–67. See also James Schleifer, *The Making of Tocqueville's "Democracy in America,"* 2nd ed. (Indianapolis: Liberty Fund, 2000), 78–79; Tocqueville denounced race determinism in letters to Arthur Gobineau. See *Oeuvres complètes*, vol. 9, *Correspondance d'Alexis de Tocqueville et d'Arthur de Gobineau*, ed. M. Degros (Paris: Gallimard, 1959), 203; *Alexis de Tocqueville on Democracy, Revolution and Society: Selected Writings*, ed. John Stone and Stephen Mennell (Chicago: University of Chicago Press, 1980), 320–22.

15. *DA*, 72–73.

of other European cultures and their consequent capacities for self-government.[16]

Reflecting upon American Indian civilizations and circumstances, Tocqueville explained that firsthand observation alone showed "their race is in no way inferior to ours." Their social state had circumscribed their experiences, drawing "around the mind of the Indians a narrow circle, but in this circle, they show themselves the most intelligent of men."[17] The "natural genius" of such peoples as the Cherokee did not stem the colonial invasion, however. The English colonists enjoyed "intellectual preponderance," if not actual superiority, and means to exercise greater physical force. It was the latter, not the former, that secured their polities. Tocqueville suggested a path of transculturation between colonists and colonized by which Indian communities could have learned enough of English ways, particularly English political and legal culture, to preserve their communities as colonial settlements pushed westward. Indeed, historians of seventeenth-century colonial developments document the eastern tribes' use of just such resources.

16. For example, Tocqueville questioned whether members of the "German race" would adopt the Anglo-American mores in support of a voluntaristic society. German communities in western Pennsylvania, Tocqueville maintained, formed insular enclaves. Although their communities were clearly self-determining and, in that sense, self-governing, institutional arrangements were based on a conception of liberty and authority that he viewed as custodial. Individual enterprise, he suspected, would be stifled by a resulting servile approach to authority. Here, and in other cases, he suggested that a self-determining community might not express a passion for individual liberty and self-governance, but could, instead, exercise a form of collective liberty resulting in insularity, parochialism, and intolerance. See Barbara Allen, "Racial Equality and Social Equality: Understanding Tocqueville's Democratic Revolution and the American Civil Rights Movement, 1954–1970," in *Conversations with Tocqueville: The Global Democratic Revolution in the Twenty-first Century*, ed. Aurelian Craiutu and Sheldon Gellar (Lanham, Md.: Lexington Books, 2009), 85–115; Françoise Mélonio, *Tocqueville and the French*, trans. Beth G. Raps (Charlottesville: University Press of Virginia 1998), 91–93; Tocqueville, *The Old Regime and the Revolution: Notes on the French Revolution and Napoleon*, trans. Alan S. Kahan, 2 vols. (Chicago: University of Chicago Press, 1998), 2:247–50, 279–82; Tocqueville to Gustave de Beaumont, May 18, 1849, in Tocqueville, *Selected Letters*, 230–32.

17. *DA*, 535*nt*.

Unfortunately, knowledge of the law did not ensure lawful treatment or protect lawful order on the frontier where the law of retribution taught the mores of vigilante violence.[18]

Slavery presented an obvious counterprinciple to equality and liberty. Tocqueville described the political economy of slavery as counterproductive, arguing that a culture of false aristocracy and racial antipathy maintained the philosophy on which the practice depended. In the case of race slavery, "race" ultimately represented more than a cultural inheritance. The status of slaves and freed persons did not arise from genetically inherited capacities, Tocqueville argued; each generation inherited the social stigma of slavery along with the physical feature of skin pigmentation. Tocqueville suggests that in a different circumstance, one in which the ignominy of status was not marked by physical characteristics, the emancipated slaves' capacities for self-government could have emerged.[19] Although Puritan strivers had in many cases extended themselves beyond the close circle of intimates, the English race, Tocqueville asserted, was the most likely of all European races "to preserve the purity of its blood and has the least mingled with the native races." Added to the "powerful reasons drawn from national character [and] from temperament" had been the historical happenstance of immigration as whole communities.[20] Prejudices, which had been put into law, prevented such social integration between English and African.

Stepping back from the particularities of English mores and Anglo-American circumstances, Tocqueville described universal tendencies that helped preserve racial divisions. The drive to rectify inequalities depended on the capacity to see inequalities. Inequalities within the same class of persons are more easily seen and appear more egregious than inequalities among individuals of different classes.[21]

18. *DA*, 535; James Axtell, *The Invasion Within: The Contest of Cultures in Colonial North America* (New York: Oxford University Press, 1985); Yashuhide Kawashima, *Puritan Justice and the Indian: White Man's Law in Massachusetts, 1630–1763* (Middleton, Conn.: Wesleyan University Press, 1986).

19. *DA*, 576–77.

20. *DA*, 547*n*a.

21. *DA*, 571–72.

When differences in status were associated not merely with social class but with physical differences, how could such blindness be more absolute?

If they were noted at all, "racial" distinctions alone would justify disparities in treatment. These observations modify one of Tocqueville's broad themes: the potential for social relations in a democratic age to soften the divisions among peoples.

In a democratic age, Tocqueville expected the "extreme mobility of men" and their drive to improve their material well-being to enable not only in commercial but also in cultural exchange. The "inhabitants of different countries mingle together, see and hear each other, and borrow from each other."[22] In what he viewed as a natural evolution of shared ideas and interests, "not only the members of the same nation . . . become similar; nations themselves assimilate." The resulting global scene could be imagined as a "vast democracy" where each "citizen is a people" and the "figure of the human species" could be seen in its own light.[23] Before the essence of the human being could emerge for all to see, however, Tocqueville's observations of racial difference indicate that peoples must find sufficient similarities to listen, hear, and borrow from each other.

THE NECESSITIES OF NATIONALISM: IMPERIALISM,
SLAVERY, AND THE GLOBAL COMMUNITY
OF THE DEMOCRATIC REVOLUTION

Tocqueville witnessed the American continental expansion, forecast the annexation of Texas, and learned from his American correspondents of American designs on California, Cuba, and Spanish colonies in the Pacific.[24] Although he shared the misgivings about American imperialism voiced by his American friends, his journey to the Amer-

---

22. *DA*, 837.

23. *DA*, 838.

24. Tocqueville to Theodore Sedgwick, Paris, December 4, 1852, and Jared Sparks to Tocqueville, Cambridge, June 13, 1853, in *Tocqueville on America after 1840: Letters and Other Writings*, ed. and trans. Aurelian Craiutu and Jeremy Jennings (New York: Cambridge University Press, 2009), 135–36 and 144–45, respectively.

ican frontier left him smitten with the pioneering spirit. Soon after his return to France, believing that he might be able to see ideas put into practice by taking part in a colonial founding, Tocqueville considered buying land in Algeria and undertaking his own pioneering adventure.[25] His early speculations on his country's Algerian policy reflect this vision. He described the Kabyles living in the Atlas Mountains as an independent, entrepreneurial people whose minds would be open to alliances with French trading partners. In the second of two letters he published on Algeria as part of his bid for election to the Chamber of Deputies, he concluded a lengthy discussion of the future of Arab-French relations with even greater optimism, suggesting that there was no "incompatibility of temper between the Arabs and us." The "races intermix without trouble," the French daily understand the Algerians better, and Algerian youth were learning French and adopting French mores.[26] After visiting Algeria twice and becoming the primary figure in France's foreign policy in the region, Tocqueville articulated a different rationale for colonization. International relations and the prestige of the nation motivated his thinking: if France abandoned its colony in Africa, a rival European nation would quickly step in.[27]

The preponderance of Tocqueville's writing on international relations and French imperialism reveals a primary assumption with broad implications for domestic and international relations that guided his policy positions. He believed that increasing equality of social conditions—the "democratic revolution"—was, at least in Europe, an unstoppable force that must be regulated to favor political liberty over the vices potential in the condition of social equality. Enlightened European nations had an obligation to steer the new age toward the virtues of political freedom. Among other implications, that imperative required that a balance be maintained among the great world

25. Tocqueville, *Writings on Empire and Slavery,* xii.

26. Tocqueville, "Second Letter on Algeria, 22 August 1837," in *Writings on Empire and Slavery,* 26.

27. André Jardin, *Tocqueville (1805–1859): A Biography,* trans. Lydia Davis and Robert Hemenway (London: Peter Halban, 1988), 309–314; David Clinton, *Tocqueville, Lieber, and Bagehot: Liberalism Confronts the World* (New York: Palgrave Macmillan, 2003), 17–43.

powers—France, Britain, Austria, Prussia, and Russia—most immediately in dividing the spoils of a fragmenting Ottoman Empire.[28]

Instabilities in domestic affairs also influenced Tocqueville's perspective on French foreign policy. He forecast increasing passions for material equality expressed personally in envy and jealousy, and publicly in a totalizing government's welfare policy. In his view, the dangers he had theorized for bourgeois society were indeed emerging in workers' strikes, as a harbinger of *socialism*, the extreme opposite of *individualism* on a spectrum of threats to liberty. He described "great projects of imperialism" as an outlet for discontentment. His proposals for ending slavery in the French Antilles also reflect fears that materialist doctrines would gain ground with French workers, especially in light of rising prices for colonial sugar and other changes in the international political economy expected to follow abolition and emancipation.[29]

Tocqueville's writings on Algeria and his proposals for abolition and emancipation in the Antilles, some of which were written as he drafted *Democracy*, illuminate the international dimension of his views on race and race relations in America. In 1841, Tocqueville wrote "Essay on Algeria," an analytical account of his travels in Algeria to be shared only with confidants. He began the "Essay," which was not published until 1962, with the same sentiment that would start later published reports: "*Algeria must be colonized.*"[30] Once this doctrine had been accepted, the only path was to provide "good government" to pacify colonizer and colonized, and enable "a very notable diminution in our army." He held few hopes for such policies, and he found himself advancing measures to fund the Algerian military mission while also pleading for a policy that would not surround, push aside, or crush "Algerian inhabitants." He predicted that policies set to "smother" the Algerians (a term that

28. Jardin, *Tocqueville (1805–1859)*, 309–314.

29. Tocqueville, "Report on Abolition," in *Tocqueville and Beaumont on Social Reform*, trans. and ed. Seymour Drescher (New York: Harper & Row, 1968), 111–13, 115, 135, 166; *Ouevres complètes*, vol. 3, pt. 1, *Écrits et discours politiques*, ed. André Jardin (Paris: Gallimard, 1962), 53–54, 57, 78, 105; Allen, *Tocqueville, Covenant, and the Democratic Revolution*, 233–39.

30. Tocqueville, "Essay on Algeria, October 1841," in *Writings on Empire and Slavery*, 59; Tocqueville, "Second Report on Algeria, 1847," in *Writings on Empire and Slavery*, 174. See also Richter, "Tocqueville on Algeria," 362–98.

was not merely metaphorical) would bring a race war to "a walled arena, where the two peoples would have to fight without mercy, and where one of the two would have to die.[31] Very little in Tocqueville's recommendations for administrative reform actually portended an alternative to this dénouement. We find, instead, social segregation, with little hope that administrative and judicial reforms would lead toward political integration, or indication that this remained a goal. As we now also know, the peoples of Algeria and France were not delivered from this destiny.

As a practical matter of foreign policy, Tocqueville connected democratization and imperialism in a manner that complements his observations of the imperial urge and national pride in *Democracy*. His proposals for the abolition of slavery and emancipation of slaves in the Antilles likewise reflect the effects of the democratic social condition and necessities of international political economy. In this case, sugar production and sugar prices lay at the core of the imperial imperative. Emancipation could cripple colonial and domestic economies tied to colonial sugar. For France, a new colonial labor regime and the increase in sugar prices it might bring could exacerbate the problems associated with an increasingly agitated labor force in metropolitan France. Tocqueville, who authored the policy recommendations of two legislative commissions on abolition, found example in British policies designed to limit such effects of emancipation on its domestic economy. He rejected aspects of the British model that seemed to replicate a master-slave relationship with wage laborers. Liberty, in this case, demanded extensive government intervention to change the dynamics of these heinous labor practices.[32] Ultimately, the sugar economy dictated the new relationship among master, laborer, and government, with Tocqueville writing to support policies of emancipation that forbade the property ownership and self-employment of former slaves.

In a series of newspaper articles, Tocqueville insisted that the incentives produced by these laws could instill moral values and change the

31. Tocqueville, "First Report on Algeria, 1847," in *Writings on Empire and Slavery*, 146.

32. Tocqueville, "Report on Abolition," in *Tocqueville and Beaumont on Social Reform*, trans. and ed. Seymour Drescher (New York: Harper & Row, 1968), 123–25.

harmful habits that slavery had instilled. He expected the former slaves to respond to opportunities in ways that "resemble other men perfectly": to be law abiding under a just regime, self-sufficient under a system of fair labor practices, and desirous of education, property rights, and civil order.[33] Logic predicted that property ownership would only increase the attractiveness of self-employment, encouraging individual industry, perhaps, but certainly destroying the colonial economy. No philosophy or economic need could justify slavery, but, Tocqueville maintained, France should not destroy slavery only to ruin white colonials who would then abandon their former slaves to the abject poverty of a collapsing economy. France, he said, "intends not only to bestow liberty on the enslaved, but to constitute civilized, industrious, and peaceable societies."[34] Such a society was intimately associated with the uninterrupted production of colonial sugar and other aspects of trade and security in the ongoing race between England and France for maritime dominance.

The imperatives motivating colonization and the labor relations of abolition had nothing to do with race, Tocqueville insisted. Interactions with French plantation owners had brought the former slave in the Antilles to a level of self-sufficiency that threatened the present circumstance of political economy; Algerian Arabs had refused French institutions, necessitating territorial conquest and war waged not against government but "on people."[35] Tocqueville described the effects of these imperatives at length in the American case. His expectation was that the restive character of the Americans would sweep them toward the Pacific in a wave that would "push aside or trample underfoot," like so many obstacles, the original inhabitants of the territory.

A THEORY OF CIVILIZATION APPLIED TO THE
THREE RACES OF NORTH AMERICA

Tocqueville's analysis of the "three races" occupying North America not only calls upon the concept of origins, circumstances, and social learning, but also his construction of the "Indian," the "slave," and the

33. Tocqueville, "On the Emancipation of Slaves," in *Writings on Empire and Slavery*, 214–15.
34. Tocqueville, "Report on Abolition," 15.
35. Tocqueville, "Essay on Algeria," 70.

"master" as ideal types. Typological generalization, while illuminating differences in sharp relief, may also hide analytical gradations in role and response. By adopting role typology as one of his methodological tools, Tocqueville underestimated the potential of the human being to transcend imperialism and slavery, and the relevance of federal bonds in doing so.[36]

Slavery, Tocqueville correctly predicted, would bring unending racial discord and, if the Union were to survive, an increasingly powerful Federal government. He accurately foresaw that political maneuvers aimed at containing the crisis created by race slavery would speak primarily to the shared interests of whites, North and South. But he underestimated the existence and significance of cultural, political, and economic institutions that freed blacks developed in the midst of segregated America.[37] Tocqueville also accurately described the dispossession, dislocation, removal, relocation, and reconstitution of American Indian tribes as administrative units under Federal supervision. He, however, predicted the complete annihilation of these peoples down to the last individual and did not imagine the modern resurgence of American Indian communities with claims to a semisovereign legal status. He saw the start of American imperial adventures and forecast the ascendance of American military might and cultural influence. The culture he envisioned was monochromatic, however, and he had difficulty imagining a multicultural or multiethnic continental republic.

Democracy and the Imperial Urge: The Westward Expansion of Anglo-Americans and American Indian Removal

A little more than two months into their American journey, Tocqueville and his traveling companion, Gustave de Beaumont, ventured through the Michigan territory to Saginaw and the frontier of Anglo-American westward expansion. Their aim was to "travel across the farthest limits of European civilization" and "visit a few of those

36. Allen, *Tocqueville, Covenant, and the Democratic Revolution*, 234–39.
37. Allen, "Racial Equality," 89–91.

Indian tribes that have preferred to flee into the most untamed wilderness than to yield to what whites call the delights of the life of society." At first it seemed, however, that everywhere they went, Tocqueville and Beaumont encountered the same disappointing news about these peoples: "ten years ago they were here; there, five years ago; there, two years ago." As they crossed the valleys and rivers the Indians had named, they could find only places of historical interest like the site of the tribal council creating the Iroquois confederation more than a century before.

This people, Tocqueville recorded, the "first and the legitimate master of the American continent[,] melts away daily like snow in the rays of the sun and disappears before your eyes from the surface of the earth."[38] When finally they encountered Indians near Buffalo, New York, the sight was deeply unsettling. Instead of their hopes for dignified personages, muscular bodies sculpted by hunting and war-making, and exotic beauty, they found emaciated beggars, whose visages seemed "ignoble and nasty." They exhibited "the vices that they got from us... mingled [with] something of the barbaric and uncivilized that made them a hundred times still more repulsive."[39] Writing retrospectively of these first impressions, however, Tocqueville remarked that to judge Native American peoples by this unfortunate remnant would be a mistake.

As Tocqueville and Beaumont journeyed westward, they at first took as the normative expression of "the Indian" the demeanor of their two silent, stoic, solitary young guides. They soon resolved that the fate of the Iroquois near Buffalo—a life shortened by poverty, alcohol, and idleness amid the economic boom of newly settled towns—portended what lay ahead for encounters between Anglo-Americans and Indians. Although it was far too early to speak of "urban" poverty, villages that overnight grew into cities, encroaching on forests and waterways, signaled the dislocation and dispossession that was to come.

As shocking as the condition of the Indians in western New York was the speed with which the settlers felled the forests, drained swamps, and built the roads and bridges of their new colonies. That these settlers

38. *DA*, 1303–4.
39. *DA*, 1306.

were Americans rather than Europeans, emigrants rather than immigrants, was also a surprise. More amazing still, Tocqueville noted, was
the settler's perception of events: an "unbelievable destruction" that
for the American was not a result of choice but part of the "immutable
order of nature."[40] Were these sentiments "American" or "democratic"?
Was the "democratic revolution" inevitably entangled with the territorial conquests of an imperial age? Tocqueville's observations of the
Michigan wilderness raised myriad questions drawn from these riddles,
most of which he wove into his analysis of the agitation and anxieties
of the democratic age.

THE DEMOCRATIC SOUL AND THE COLONIZING PROJECT

Introducing the chapter on the "three races," Tocqueville told his
reader that although he had spoken about "Indians and Negroes" and
the spirit and laws of the "Anglo-American confederation," these topics had not entered into his subject: "they are American not democratic." As Eduardo Nolla points out, Tocqueville repeatedly substituted
the term "Anglo-American" for "European" in his description of the
encroachment upon Indian lands. Americans, it would seem, were the
agents of destruction; "democracy" could presumably take another
course. Yet Tocqueville also discovered in the United States an agitated,
highly mobile, anxious population driven inexorably into the "wilderness," and these anxieties and motivations he ultimately attributed to
the democratic social condition.

The democratic social condition never provided perfect equality—
of opportunity or results. If there were not always materially "better"
states, there were surely different states of being—and difference alone
could motivate the next great effort. Democratic mores lent an infla-
tionary character to a growing list of contesting desires; the democratic soul oscillated between a desire for ease and for fame, for leisure
and for striving, and no amount of success dimmed the hope for even
more—more material pleasures and more "equality." Equality, which
encouraged vast hopes and portended a great destiny for each individual, also limited the likelihood that one of the vast number eying the
same prize could rise above the crowd and achieve such ambitions. The

40. *DA*, 1304.

inevitable disappointments that followed brought a "singular melancholy," which, Tocqueville noted, might account for the rising rate of suicide in France and, in America, insanity.[41] Tocqueville made copious notes to himself about his analysis of this "restless curiosity," "restlessness of spirit," and "care-ridden" existence. He considered deleting the chapter, which had been difficult to compose.[42] A deleted section recalled the following experience from his Michigan travels.

Tocqueville tells of stopping at the home of a rich American plantation owner, while in the company of several Indians. He was taken into a "well-lighted, carefully heated room" where the planter and his neighbors, all of whom "were more or less drunk," spoke in somber tones about public affairs and economic worries. By contrast, the Indians, who sat outdoors around a fire with nothing but ragged blankets to protect them from the steady drizzle, conversed happily: "the noisy bursts of their joy at each instant penetrated to gravity of our banquet."[43] The frontier society of the Anglo-Americans reflected the temperament of a people harried by modern life, which Tocqueville contrasted with "small populations that have been as if forgotten amid the universal tumult." The latter could be found with increasing rarity left "unchanged when everything around them moved."[44] The contrast between the care-ridden frontiersmen and the carefree conviviality of the Indian campfire is only one side of Tocqueville's narrative. Particular to Tocqueville's "Indian" is also a distinct lack of community owing to the prideful independence of "les sauvages de l'Amérique du Nord."[45]

Placed at the extreme limits of liberty, the social condition of the Indian condemns him to inexpressible miseries culminating in extinction. His pride inhibits assimilation, Tocqueville claimed, while the political economy of colonization at once demands and makes impossible his entry into "civilization." To explain the Indians' plight, Tocqueville started with a conventional portrayal of the "savage

41. *DA*, 946–47.
42. *DA*, 942*n*a.
43. *DA*, 943*n*b.
44. *DA*, 942.
45. *DA*, 518–20.

populations" as a part of the natural world taken under by the force of the institutions, technologies, and societies of settled peoples. His ultimate analysis, however, offers several remarkable insights about the problems of adaptation and transculturation.

CIVILIZATION IN THE WILDERNESS

Tocqueville introduced *le sauvage* as one who is "left to himself as soon as he can act." He knows neither the authority of the family nor that of a community; the concept of law is meaningless and he cannot distinguish subjection from voluntary obedience.[46] This characterization did not fit the ideal that Tocqueville had carried to the United States. What had happened to the constitutional form of the Great Iroquois Confederacy or to the politically sophisticated Narragansett and Mohican?[47]

Tocqueville described Indian societies able to meet their subsistence needs before colonization increased both their desires and their needs inordinately. Staples, particularly furs, became a medium of exchange in trade "to satisfy the frivolous passions of Europeans";[48] forests hunted to depletion were felled for colonial settlement, and famine hounded their remnant societies from forest to plains. While imbalanced trade relations, colonial land use, and later Anglo-American migration progressively destroyed the capacities of hunting societies to sustain forest resources, the legislated removal of the Indians led to the dramatic exodus that Tocqueville observed.[49]

From the American case, Tocqueville drew a more general trajectory of colonization: dispossession, first occurring by degrees, according to the "greediness of the colonist," joins "the tyranny of the government." In America, state legislatures expelled the Indians, seized their lands, and resisted meager congressional efforts to contest these "tyrannical

---

46. *DA*, 519.

47. Allen, *Tocqueville, Covenant, and the Democratic Revolution*, 231–33, 253–58; Francis Jennings, *The Invasion of America: Indians, Colonialism, and the Cant of Conquest* (Chapel Hill: University of North Carolina Press, 1975), 265–81; Alden T. Vaughan, *The New England Frontier: Puritans and Indians, 1620–1675* (Boston: Little, Brown, 1965), 155–61; James Axtell, *Invasion Within*, 286, 307–10, 318–20.

48. *DA*, 523.

49. *DA*, 523–26.

measures." Ultimately, Congress cleared the way for expansion, resolving "to let a few savage tribes . . . perish in order not to put the American Union in danger."[50] The federal form (if congressional thinking truly differed from the expansionist vision) could not moderate democratic impulses. Law finished what "European tyranny" had started; their societies decimated, isolated Indians wandered the countryside.[51]

This narrative suggests that more than the Indians' supposed "habits of the wandering life," American migration to the Pacific, spurred by the democratic social condition, extinguished indigenous life. Tocqueville offers several additional hypotheses, leading him to conclude that Europeans had the power to destroy, but they lacked the will to assimilate the Indian into European civilization, as well as the power to compel him to assimilate.

Why not assimilate? At several points Tocqueville reduces the answer to a single term: pride. Pride in a culture that had already perished, a culture romanticized but largely forgotten by Europeans; the pride of resistance, and a perversely prideful self-image mirrored in a desire for natural liberty—these are among Tocqueville's suppositions. As supporting evidence of a prideful character, Tocqueville cited numerous military officers, legislators, jurists, and other notables whom he had interviewed or whose accounts he had read. Yet this answer failed to satisfy him.

He also suggests that a subjugated group cannot easily compete— or indeed cooperate—with its vanquishers as it attempts to join their society. Agriculture, an art that Tocqueville associated with superior civilizations, was unknown to the Indian, he claimed. Knowledge of such practice would do little for the vanquished, however: they would be

---

50. *DA,* 541–42.

51. Tocqueville applied this characterization to colonial treatment of Indian populations in North America and described as "monstrous crimes" the treatment of these communities in Central and South America. Such crimes, Tocqueville commented in irony, failed "in exterminating the Indian race" or "preventing it from sharing" in the rights of a colonial regime. By contrast, "the Americans of the United States have achieved this double result with a marvelous ease, calmly, legally, philanthropically, without shedding blood, without violating a single one of the great principles of morality in the eyes of the world. You cannot destroy men while better respecting the laws of humanity." See *DA,* 519, 547.

forever catching up to European innovators and thus unable to establish their own markets as efficiently as their European competitors — even within Indian communities, he observed.[52] Although he also saw examples of transculturation and assimilation — in French Canada, where marriage had joined colonist and colonized — Tocqueville portrayed these cases as exceptions.[53] Another hypothesis brought these several threads together: the intractable race prejudice of the Anglo-Americans. On his journey to the Michigan territory, he witnessed Anglo-Americans' profound prejudice against the dispossessed Indians hovering at the edges of their towns and cities. Following one incident, he believed he could read their thoughts: "What [matter] is the life of an Indian?"[54] In the case of this colonized people, the democratic tide had perhaps met in race prejudice an insurmountable barrier.[55] Efforts to join the Americans' community were futile; the possibilities for transculturation went unrealized; prejudice eclipsed understanding; law became an instrument of conquest.

Tocqueville was resigned to the fate of the American Indians. Statements deleted from the text ask: "Why of these three races, is one born to perish, the other to rule, and the last to serve?" "Why this unequal

52. *DA*, 532–37.

53. *DA*, 539*n*19. Tocqueville also expressed ambivalence toward his countrymen's capacities as colonists and noted that their settlements, many of which included cultural as well as commercial exchange with Indians, were often easily overtaken by the more entrepreneurial Anglo-Americans. See Tocqueville, "Some Ideas about What Prevents the French from Having Good Colonies," in *Writings on Empire and Slavery*, 1–4, and *DA*, 1307.

54. Tocqueville, *Democracy in America/De la démocratie en Amérique*, 1307.

55. Historians of Indian relations with French and English colonists underscore the opportunities for transculturation that Indians seized in order to survive European conquest. Opportunities for exchange declined with each decade, however, with war and the threat of war as well as the inadequacy of law and treaty enforcement among new waves of migration on the frontier. Violence, particularly lawful violence, provided the necessary and sufficient conditions to decimate the Indian communities, as Tocqueville described. Kawashima, *Puritan Justice*, 225–39; Axtell, *Invasion Within*, 4, 286, and chap. 13; Jean O'Brien, *Dispossession by Degrees: Indian Land and Identity in Natick, Massachusetts, 1650–1790* (Cambridge: Cambridge University Press, 1997), 91; Axtell, *Invasion Within*, 4–5, 332–34.

sharing of the good things of this world? Who can say?"[56] To these existential questions Tocqueville offered a rational analysis of choices resulting in the flight of Indians into the woods in search of prey for their next meal. The tableau is strikingly individualistic; indeed, during his travels, he generally saw only dispossessed individuals, not Indian communities. Assimilation to neither European civilization nor the mores of the democratic social condition protected Indian communities. Ironically, the same individualism that propelled Americans westward is the essence of the Indian's tragic fate. Tocqueville's discussion of Anglo-American restiveness and its link to the democratic mental stance draws on hypothesized relations between high expectations for opportunity and gratification under equality and the anxieties flowing from the reality of competition and limitation. What is "democratic," what constitutes the "good colonist" of a democratic age, and what is uniquely "American," all coalesce in the narrative of the imperial enterprise and the American Indian.

Democracy and Slavery

After returning from the Michigan territory to Buffalo, New York, in late August, and visiting French Canada, Tocqueville and Beaumont returned to their studies of the penitentiary system and ways of life in New England, New York City, and Philadelphia. In mid-November, they embarked on their excursion to the southern states. It was a harrowing journey punctuated by stagecoach breakdowns, frozen rivers, and shipwreck, as well as a life-threatening bout with the influenza. They arrived in New Orleans on New Year's Day and started their return trip only forty-eight hours later. Their twelve-day return covered Alabama, Georgia, South Carolina, North Carolina, and Virginia, on their way to meet President Andrew Jackson in Washington, D.C.

Their grueling excursion not only offered an opportunity to read *The Federalist* and Justice James Kent's *Commentaries on the U.S. Constitution* but also the chance to talk with several leading American figures, including former Texas governor and future Republic of Texas

---

56. *DA*, 516*nc*, 517*nd*.

president Sam Houston and former ambassador to Mexico Joel Roberts Poinsett.[57] To these discourses, Tocqueville added conversations with plantation owners and interviews with several well-informed northerners: President John Quincy Adams, attorney Timothy Walker, and historian and later Harvard president Jared Sparks. These figures had a great deal to tell Tocqueville about federalism, interposition and nullification, republican government, American expansionism, and slavery. From Timothy Walker, a recent Harvard graduate who would later distinguish himself as an Ohio jurist, Tocqueville learned of the "prodigious" difference between Ohio and Kentucky, which Walker said could only have been caused by slavery. Slavery, Walker pointed out, dishonored labor and esteemed idleness; Ohio grew and prospered, while Kentucky remained a backwater.[58] Tocqueville quoted extensively from these conversations in *Democracy*.[59]

Adams agreed that slavery had changed the entire culture of the South into a false aristocracy in which "whites form a class of their own" with "every white man ... an equally privileged being whose destiny it is to make the Negroes work without working himself."[60] As a result, no undertaking that failed to include subservient labor could succeed in the South; in their idleness the southern white devoted himself to "bodily exercises, to hunting, and races.... They are more touchy on 'points of honor' than anywhere else." Tocqueville incorporated this description with the observations of Henry Clay on inheritance laws, which kept southern plantations intact.[61] The result, Tocqueville said, was "each family was represented by a rich man who did not feel the need any more than he had the taste for work; the members of his family that the law had excluded from the common inheritance lived

57. George Wilson Pierson, *Tocqueville in America* (Baltimore: Johns Hopkins University Press, 1996), 543–678.

58. Tocqueville, "Pocket Notebook Number 3, 21st–25th Second Conversation with Mr. Walker: *Important*, December 1831," *Journey to America*, trans. George Lawrence, ed. J. P. Mayer (New York: Doubleday Anchor, 1971), 91.

59. *DA*, 557–58.

60. Tocqueville, "Non-alphabetic Notebooks Number 2 and 3, Boston, 1 October 1831," *Journey to America*, 48–50.

61. Tocqueville, "Non-alphabetic Notebooks Number 2 and 3, 18 September 1831," *Journey to America*, 36.

around him in the same manner, as so many parasitic plants." The southern culture could produce poor men, but not workers; "poverty there seemed preferable to industry," because work meant slavery. Anything to be done must be done by slave labor, because no white would dishonor himself by showing that he *needed* to earn a living.[62]

In *Democracy*, Tocqueville emphasized the economic consequences of degraded labor, reduced productivity, and the creation of a dependent class—of masters—who relied on an insecure resource in the midst of a more productive wage-based national economy. Along with citing harmful economic effects, Tocqueville also underscored slavery's psychological consequences. He linked the literally dehumanizing conception of a property right in a human being to the incapacitation of any would-be emancipated citizen. Sam Houston explained the loss of political capacities that came with slavery. The Negro, he told Tocqueville, was a slave before he was born; "his first notion of existence [was to] understand he was the property of another." As such, he was of no use to himself; care for his own future is no concern of his.[63] Tocqueville carried Houston's insight into his own analysis.

Violence created the slave. In the trauma of capture, sale, transport, and auction, "the Negro," Tocqueville said, "lost even the memory of his country; he no longer hears the language spoken by his fathers; he has renounced their religion and forgotten their mores. . . . The Negro has no family, he cannot see in a woman anything other than the temporary companion of his pleasures and, at birth, his sons are his equals."[64] Tocqueville described the slave as "useless to himself." It was the master in whose interest it was to "watch over [the slave's] days." Emancipation brought the *burden* of liberty, because "in the course of his existence, he has learned to submit to everything, except reason," a voice he cannot recognize. He would be "besieged" by needs he had never known and, lacking reason, could not master. As a result, "servitude brutalizes him and liberty destroys him."[65] The capacities of citizenship would evade most emancipated individuals. The typology of roles and relationships

62. *DA*, 563.
63. Tocqueville, "Notebook E," *Journey to America*, 254.
64. *DA*, 517.
65. *DA*, 518.

of "slave" and "master" suggested a postabolition culture marked by continuing segregation based in race ideology. Neither abolition nor emancipation would reform the mores learned, North and South, in a constitutional regime of southern slavocracy.

With its systematic dehumanization, American race slavery was particularly vicious, and its consequences would be particularly long lasting. Tocqueville described the consequence of such victimization as passivity and accurately portrayed the many laws aimed at destroying the slave's humanity and cultural identification, including prohibitions on slave marriage, education, and use of the languages or religions of Africa. He expected such aspects of human relationships to become subjects of control after abolition. "The non-material and transitory fact of slavery is combined in the most fatal way with the material and permanent fact of the difference of race." The mark of race slavery, skin color, forever branded persons of African descent.[66] The perception that any person so identified had been reduced from human capacity to an object lacking a sense of self and the rational faculties that motivated self-preservation, self-esteem, self-control, self-interest, and, above all, self-government pervaded the minds of Americans with whom he spoke. The hypothesis is overshadowed by another dimension of the analysis: the continuing violence supported by opinion when law no longer raised a barrier.

From interviews conducted in Philadelphia, Boston, and New York, Tocqueville learned that where slavery had been abolished and equal rights conferred, prejudice prevented their exercise. Terrorist intimidation awaited former slaves who came forward to vote.[67] In Kent's *Commentaries*, Tocqueville likewise read of continuing segregation and constraints on marriage and voting rights in the northern states.[68] He was told, "Laws have no force...where public opinion does not support them." Facing "strong prejudices against Negroes... the magistrates feel that they have not the strength to enforce laws."[69]

66. *DA*, 551–52.
67. Tocqueville, "Pocket Notebook Number 3, Philadelphia, 15 October 1831" and "Alphabetic Notebook B, N/Negroes," *Journey to America*, 156 and 232–33.
68. Tocqueville, "Notebook E," *Journey to America*, 267, 279.
69. Tocqueville, "Pocket Notebook 3, 25th October 1831," *Journey to America*, 156.

He reported in *Democracy* that the free black could seek relief from oppression through the courts, "but he finds only whites among their judges." Although the free black may legally serve as a juror, prejudice prevents it. Segregated schools and other public institutions, segregated civil associations and public places, and the stigmatization of intimate relations preserved the barriers between the races. The slave had been taught that he was inferior to the whites and, Tocqueville said, the freedman believed it. Rather than making his own way, he "bows to the tastes of his oppressors," imitating them and aspiring "to mingle with them." Such hopes exceed merely assimilating, Tocqueville conjectured, for they sprang from a desire to repudiate the stigma that shames him, his color and his race—an absolute repudiation of himself.[70]

Tocqueville concluded that however the grip of slavery was eased, a culture of prejudice would consume American civil society for generations, with lasting destructive political, social, and economic effects. His interviews with Americans provided the propositions that Tocqueville placed within his framework linking experience, culture, and character to reach this conclusion. His American interlocutors apparently did not alert him to facts that, while not wholly changing his analysis of race prejudice and its effects, might have illuminated an alternative scenario for freed persons of African descent.

Tocqueville did not see the strong networks among African American–created institutions in New York, Boston, and Philadelphia. He could not imagine the growth of African American financial, business, educational, religious, and civic organizations that, during the hundred years of constitutionally supported racial segregation, paralleled "white" institutions, North and South. Although he remarked, "[I]t can be interesting to visit," he never made the trip to Wilberforce, Canada, to learn about a "Colony that the *colored men* are establishing."[71] Whatever he might have seen there, something of the possibilities for African American institutional development might have occurred to him from his acquaintance with the American Missionary Society

70. *DA*, 519, 551, 554.

71. Tocqueville, *Democracy in America/De la démocratie en Amérique*, editor's note "d." Allen, "Racial Equality and Social Equality," 96–105.

project of colonizing a new country on the west coast of Africa, Liberia, with freed African Americans.[72]

The fate of the slave was relevant to *Democracy* primarily as it affected the fate of America. Tocqueville was more quizzical than analytical about how the art of being free could have been learned in the prison of slavery. If he had turned his attention to that topic, he would have found far greater capacities for self-government among freed blacks than his presuppositions allowed. The task of considering how Frederick Douglass or Booker T. Washington arose from slavery to become moral and intellectual leaders of a biracial civil rights movement is left to his readers, as is the effort of understanding how African Americans in the South could establish one of the few banks to survive the 1893 depression among numerous other institutions, societies, and missions. Tocqueville's typological method described the state of many black sharecroppers in the rural South following the Civil War and well into the twentieth century. His analysis did not explain the institutional and social evolution that, after a century, brought new constitutional and social opportunities to end legal segregation and make advances in political and social integration in many cases through the same processes that he described as a democratic revolution.[73]

The "Third" Race and the Dangers to American Federalism

The vast majority of Tocqueville's analysis of America and democracy is devoted either to the "third race" of Anglo-Americans proper, or, more generally, to the effects of the democratic social condition on the (white) people of the "Christian nations." Tocqueville described the third race in America as preeminent, but there were "two branches"

72. *DA*, 576–77. The two hundred thousand freed American slaves transported by the society introduced institutions to Liberia that included "a representative system, Negro jurors, Negro priests, . . . churches and newspapers."

73. Allen, *Tocqueville, Covenant, and the Democratic Revolution*, 246–52, 258; Allen, "Racial Equality," 94–107; Barbara Allen, "Martin Luther King's Civil Disobedience and the American Covenant Tradition," *Publius: Journal of Federalism* 30, no. 4 (2000): 71–113.

of the "great Anglo-American family," the northern and the southern, which "have grown up without being completely merged," and their futures diverged.[74] Tocqueville indicated that for northern whites, the union of racial brotherhood brought the dilemma of maintaining the southern way of life or dealing with the escalating issue of racial discord that disunion would bring. For southern whites, the consequences of secession were more immediate and, perhaps, more dire. Whites, North and South, had a shared interest in maintaining their supremacy, in Tocqueville's analysis. Southern whites had an interest in enlisting northern whites in any cause requiring protection against African Americans. Northern whites had numerous reasons to preserve peace to their south. Whether that goal was to be accomplished through abolition and emancipation or not (and, if so, the form abolition and emancipation would take) remained to be seen.

Tocqueville expected Southerners to recognize the inefficiency and harm slavery brought to the master, while also seeing that it would be nearly impossible to destroy the system without risking their lives.[75] Any moral censure about maintaining slavery, he said, should not be placed on the present generation of slaveholders, which was trapped by this dilemma. Fault the generations who centuries earlier had introduced this bane in the New World and the political economy of the states, which would shape choices more than moral arguments. Ultimately, Tocqueville surmised, "[s]lavery is being destroyed in the United States not in the interests of the Negroes, but in that of the whites."[76] Whatever policies followed from abolition and emancipation would likewise be made in the interests of whites, North and South.

Common interests did not prevent Civil War, however. Whatever they shared, differences in the mores of whites, North and South, meant that their Union ultimately could be maintained only by force of arms. In the final sections of the chapter on the "Three Races of North America," Tocqueville turned again to questions of national character and interests, to show that differences in mores may eclipse apparent similarities of interests—in this case, where interest included maintaining

74. *DA*, 51.
75. *DA*, 579–82.
76. *DA*, 555.

the security of the federal bond as well as economic prosperity and material well-being.

The consequences of slavery for the Union were immediately obvious; the continuing results for American federalism and democracy more generally, perhaps less so. A third branch of the Anglo-American family was also gaining strength; they were the adventurers "plung[ing] into the West . . . impatient of any kind of yoke, greedy for wealth, often cast out by the states where they were born." They took little cognizance of the rule of law or the dictates of civilized mores; they were "inferior in all ways to the Americans who inhabit the old limits of the Union." Although they demonstrated little experience with governance or capacity for self-control, they were very influential in politics.[77] They would become the actors in a proxy war between North and South as pro- and antislavery surged into Kansas, hoping to tip the majority vote of the territory in favor of one of these options.

Tocqueville's American friends kept him apprised of the vigilante battles known as "Bleeding Kansas," which were set in motion under the Kansas-Nebraska Act (1854). A policy known as "popular sovereignty" that would purportedly let the "people" of the territory decide by majority rule whether the new state would be slave or free motivated self-interested pro- and antislavery politicos to bring migrants supporting their faction en masse to Kansas for the vote deciding the proposed state's status. Tocqueville consistently distinguished "democracy" as majority rule, "which can do great evils while perceiving good," from republican government, composed of deliberative bodies, each comprising representatives of many diverse majorities. In the United States, the latter, plus the mores of voluntarism, revealed the true meaning of "popular sovereignty," the "slow and tranquil action of society on itself."[78] In Kansas, the intimidation, violence, and tyranny brought by a self-proclaimed majority fit anything but this description. Although Tocqueville voiced opposition to "extreme" abolitionists, who, he believed, agitated with little thought of the consequences, he called the efforts of proslavery forces to spread the "abominable institution

77. *DA*, 603.
78. *DA*, 630.

...dreadful and unpardonable."[79] Tocqueville identified the cause of such terrible public policy as the poor judgment of leaders who pandered to the worst instincts of democracy.[80] In facing the crisis of the disunion, Americans were also facing a critical juncture in their practice of "democracy."

In his introduction to the 1862 translation of *Democracy,* the American editor, Francis Bowen, underscored the distinctions that Tocqueville made between "democracy" and "federalism" in the United States, which, Bowen contended, the Civil War made more germane than ever to American self-understanding. Readers who wondered whether the federal union could survive—whether, indeed, a federal republic could extend across a vast continent—would find in *Democracy* an exceptional understanding of the distinctive features and vulnerabilities of the Union.[81] Bowen focused on Tocqueville's evaluation of the 1789 U.S. Constitution as a compact among states. In fact, Tocqueville had little to say about the alternative, Unionist ideal of a "great national covenant" joining the states and the people of the states.[82] Tocqueville and his American friends likewise did not discuss the junior senator from Illinois, Abraham Lincoln, who in speeches as early as 1854, and later debates with Senator Steven A. Douglas, enunciated this view. Perhaps Tocqueville drew his constitutional interpretation from his firsthand observation of the "Tariff Question" debates and the legal constructions of "interposition and nullification" articulated most persuasively

79. Tocqueville to Edward Vernon Child, April 2, 1857, in *Tocqueville on America,* 224.

80. Tocqueville to Charles Sumner, March 28, 1858, in *Tocqueville on America,* 285–87. Tocqueville, who had stock in American railroads, also wrote to Sumner of his concern for the railroads in the wake of Bleeding Kansas (Tocqueville to Charles Sumner, November 14, 1857, in *Tocqueville on America,* 265–67).

81. Tocqueville, *Democracy in America,* trans. Henry Reeve, as revised by Francis Bowen (Cambridge, Mass.: Sever and Francis, 1862), 1:iv.

82. Vermont antislavery Republican Charles Rich characterized the relationship thus, see *Acts of Congress,* 16th Cong., 2nd sess., 1395. See also language of House member Timothy Fuller of Massachusetts; see Sean Wilentz, "Jeffersonian Democracy and the Origins of Political Antislavery in the United States: The Missouri Crisis Revisited," *Journal of the Historical Society* 4, no. 3 (Fall 2004): 375–401, 395; *Acts of Congress,* 15th Cong., 2nd sess., 1180.

by South Carolina senator John C. Calhoun. His conclusion reflects Calhoun's understanding; in Tocqueville's view, "The confederation has been formed by the free will of the states; the latter by uniting did not lose their nationality and did not merge into one and the same people." Secession is constitutional.[83]

The tariff debates also revealed the potential for rival interests between North and South, emerging from the uneven pace of regional development and the possibility that differences in mores rather than the difference—or coincidence—in interests could determine loyalties and policies. The southern export economy depended on northern shipping, and maintaining the Union should have been each region's greatest interest. Northern industrialists were destroying the basis of this mutually advantageous relationship with tariffs to their benefit and to the detriment of the South. Regional economies could be explained as a result of diverse natural resources and infrastructure—harbors, canals, roadways, and industry—but Tocqueville maintained that the true difference was a work ethic destroyed by slavery in the South and propelled by freedom in the North. Slavery, he concluded, did not attack the Union directly through diverse interests, but indirectly through diverse mores.[84] Contesting understandings of the federal bond and regional interests alike figured less prominently than differences in mores and regional character to the future of the American democracy, in Tocqueville's final analysis.

Beyond the impending confrontation between North and South, the rapid growth of the Anglo-American population and its diffusion across the continent tested the federalist and republican principles. Expansion, as we have seen, resulted from the enterprising, adventurous American national character of the Anglo-Americans and, in the final sections of Tocqueville's *Democracy,* more clearly as a consequence of the democratic revolution itself. The tumult of democratic society, the concern with well-being that democracy encourages, along with a belief in unending progress and the anxiety and restiveness such

83. *DA,* 267–68, 592, 609–12, 267–68; Allen, *Tocqueville, Covenant, and the Democratic Revolution,* 142–48.
84. *DA,* 603.

beliefs bring, all of these habits of heart and mind plus their institutional results pushed emigration to the Pacific, the tundra, and the Rio Grande.[85]

American expansionism augured several possible futures; the main republican idea—that reason provided to every person sufficient capacity for self-direction—would prevent an aristocracy from reasserting the institutions of a ruling class in the United States. Whether the Americans would restrict their political rights or "confiscate" them "for the profit of one man" was less certain.[86] Their tremendous, often unfounded or misplaced fear of federal powers in some instances mitigated the very protections they needed, Tocqueville observed. The Americans easily forgot the necessity of a federal government, acting in its sphere, to articulate the promise of republican principles to each individual.[87]

Democracy and Liberty

In his final word on the "third race," Tocqueville presented a preview of the currents leading to a new reigning class, the "aristocracy of manufacturers," and a new form of servitude, "democratic despotism," if the Americans find their projects hampered by their republican institutions and grow impatient of a society working slowly and tranquilly upon itself. The Anglo-Americans were poised to become a commercial giant. The U.S. merchant fleet filled harbors around the globe; the spirit of innovation and enterprise drove its captains to withstand the greatest hardships and take the greatest risks to reap the greatest profits by outflanking every competitor in the maritime maelstrom. "For the American all of life happens like a game of chance, a time of revolution, a day of battle."[88] But that did not mean commercial interests would leave to chance the security of their markets.

85. *DA,* 607–9.
86. *DA,* 633–37.
87. *DA,* 615–16.
88. *DA,* 643.

Commercial greatness demanded military power. The structure of international relations motivated the United States to seize power in a competition that required increasing means merely to maintain a balance among the maritime nations. The American position was, Tocqueville said, analogous to that of France: "It is powerful, without being dominant; it is liberal because it cannot oppress."[89] Tocqueville expected that situation to change, however; American commercial success would lead the United States to become the "premiere maritime power of the globe." France would be relegated to playing the spoiler by joining weaker powers to balance U.S. domination and maintain the liberty of the seas.[90]

In the final two decades of Tocqueville's life, he took part in the efforts of his country to maintain this balance through, among other means, colonization, militarization, and imperialism. He corresponded with Americans who witnessed their country following the same path, despite and in some respects because of its civil discord. As American Indians and other occupied peoples engaged in the self-governing efforts of resistance or accepted the necessity of transculturation that likewise promoted the spirit of self-determination, the great maritime powers laid down the institutions that generated another century of violent domination and resistance. The citizenship capacities developing in communities that were set aside by segregation, as in the case of African American and Anglo-American relations in the United States, went unnoticed. Where highly centralized administrative systems were teaching the lessons of autocracy, as Tocqueville predicted of the French colonial legacy in North Africa, these ways and their likely outcome for future generations also submitted to immediate necessity. The questions that Tocqueville raised about the course of the democratic revolution remain with us today. Are "we" to realize that "they" are "like 'us' in every way"? Tocqueville remarked that the features of an enlightened, enterprising people included the ability of individuals to solve problems, a capacity that developed through the experience of providing for oneself the diverse necessities of life. "[T]he same man

89. *DA,* 647.
90. *DA,* 648.

plows his field, builds his house, fashions his tools, makes his shoes, and weaves by hand the crude fabric that has to cover him."[91] The description begs us to consider what the basis of enlightenment may include as necessary foundations for self-government. The analysis also begs us to ask where this sort of intellectual diversity is found today.

91. *DA,* 642.

10

Tocqueville's Reflections
on a Democratic Paradox

JEAN-LOUIS BENOÎT

The final chapter of the 1835 volume of *Democracy in America* has a rather special status in that, as Tocqueville points out to his readers, it is an *addendum*, different from the rest of the book.[1] The need for it had apparently not been initially obvious, because the last drafts and proofs that he gave to his friends and relatives to read and comment on[2] finished at the end of chapter 9, vol. 2, part 2, which concluded, "My goal has been to show, by the example of America, that laws and above all mores could allow a democratic people to remain free."[3]

Then, in sharp contrast to what he had written previously, Tocqueville provides the reader with a final chapter that constitutes practically a new part on its own, qualitatively—by its themes—and quantitatively, because it represents a quarter of the book. His warning to the reader at the opening of chapter 10, vol. 2, part 2, is also striking.

> The principal task that I had set for myself has now been fulfilled.
> ... I could stop here, but the reader would perhaps find that I have not satisfied his expectation.

---

1. Alexis de Tocqueville, *Democracy in America: Historical-Critical Edition of "De la démocratie en Amérique,"* ed. Eduardo Nolla, trans. James T. Schleifer, 4 vols. (Indianapolis: Liberty Fund, 2010). This edition is hereafter cited as *DA*.

2. *DA*, 5ne. Tocqueville's manuscript was read over in particular by his father, Hervé de Tocqueville; his two brothers, Hippolyte and Édouard; by Louis de Kergorlay, his cousin and friend; and by Gustave de Beaumont, who commented on a number of passages and suggested many modifications, the most numerous coming from Hervé (a hundred or so remarks) and Édouard (fifty or so).

3. *DA*, 512–13.

You encounter in America something more than an immense and complete democracy....

In the course of this work, my subject often led me to speak about Indians and Negroes, but I have never had the time to stop to show what position these two races occupy in the midst of the democratic people that I was busy portraying....

These topics touch on my subject, but do not enter in it; they are American without being democratic, and above all I wanted to portray democracy. So I had to put them aside at first; but I must return to them as I finish.[4]

These last comments might be considered ambiguous because race-based slavery, the African Americans' present and future situation, and the fate of the Native Americans—spoliation, deportation, extermination, and genocide—constitute a genuine paradox within a democracy.

For Tocqueville, the American republic and its democracies represented an entirely new social state.[5] These regimes were quite unlike those of Athens or Rome:[6] "I would very much like people to stop citing to us, in relation to everything, the example of the democratic republics of Greece and Italy,"[7] nor did they have anything in common with the Italian republics of the Renaissance. As he emphasizes in the introduction to *Democracy*, Tocqueville believes that the *continuum* of history, like a *providential* movement, has inevitably led to the rise of modern democracy. It was born from the spirit of the Enlightenment, so close to the hearts of French philosophers and to the Founding Fathers of the United States, such as Thomas Jefferson.

The principles of the Enlightenment were for Tocqueville a

---

4. *DA*, 515–16.

5. The consideration of the notion of the "democratic social state" is fundamental to the understanding of Tocquevillian analysis; see http://classiques.uqac .ca/contemporains/benoit_jean_louis/tocqueville_et_la_presse/tocqueville _et_la_presse_texte.html. (Jean-Louis Benoît, web page Les Classiques des science sociales, collection "Les sciences sociales contemporaines," Université du Québec à Chicoutimi.)

6. *DA*, 490–91.

7. *DA*, 1142*n*n.

secularized version of the universal values at the origins of Christianity, as he asserts to Arthur de Gobineau, whose essay, *The Inequality of the Human Races,* he condemned vigorously.[8] Tocqueville views only one human race. "Man, according to Buffon and Flourens, is thus a single species and human strains are produced by three secondary and external causes: climate, food and way of life."[9] Tocqueville thus considered man's equality as a cardinal principle, the foundation of all modern democracies.[10]

This cardinal principle is incompatible with slavery and the genocide of the Native Americans; thus, the existence of both of these things in America can be considered a veritable democratic paradox, an antinomy. The problem posed by this paradox is, in essence, both democratic and American, for it is indeed American democracy called into question: "There are many ironies in this theoretical exclusion of the problems that would pose the deepest moral challenge to American democracy and, one might argue, to any modern democratic society. Some of these ironies were apparent to Tocqueville himself, who did not avert his gaze from the lived contradiction of an 'egalitarian' and 'free' people that practiced racial despotism and genocide but rather gave this contradiction a penetrating look before moving on to his chosen concerns," as Cheryl Welch rightly observes.[11]

What explains the sudden change in direction in Tocqueville's analysis of American democracy? Why this last-minute addition?

On their return from the United States, Gustave de Beaumont and Tocqueville agreed that the latter would compile a work on the institutions in America, while the former would deal with American mores in

8. See Jean-Louis Benoît, *Tocqueville Moraliste* (Paris: Champion, 2004), 88–89, 112–22.

9. Tocqueville, *Oeuvres complètes,* vol. 9, *Correspondance avec Gobineau* (Paris: Gallimard, 1959), 197. This letter from Tocqueville to Gobineau, dated May 15, 1852, precedes by a year the controversy over *L'inégalité des races.* Flourens was Cuvier's assistant at the Collège de France.

10. Equality is mentioned in the second paragraph of the United States Declaration of Independence: "all men are created equal..." and in the French Declaration of the Rights of Man and of the Citizen, the first article of which stipulates: "Men are born and remain free and equal in rights."

11. Cheryl B. Welch, *de Tocqueville* (New York: Oxford University Press), 61.

a novel. The two works were written at the same time and intended for publication more or less simultaneously, each referring to the other. Since Beaumont's novel, *Marie, or Slavery in the United States,* addressed the problems of race and racism, of slavery, and of the poverty and ultimate extinction of the Native Americans, Tocqueville had at first decided against discussing these questions. At the end of the introduction to *Democracy,* he wrote in a note: "At the time I published the first edition of this work, M. Gustave de Beaumont, my travelling companion in America, was still working on his book entitled *Marie, or Slavery in the United States,* which has since appeared."[12]

The very existence of chapter 10, vol. 2, part 2, in *Democracy in America* is thus problematic because the questions dealt with are rather those of mores, society, and politics than of actual institutions. What is the reason behind this new approach that can only have been decided on by agreement between the two friends?

On the 15th August of that year,[13] his manuscript under his arm, Tocqueville arrived at the château de Gallarande, in the Sarthe, invited by Madame Eugénie de Sarcé, sister of Gustave de Beaumont. He remained with the Beaumonts until the middle of September....

Did Beaumont persuade Tocqueville to treat a question that, in the beginning, belonged to *Marie?* Does Toqueville's decision have something to do with the racial problems that broke out on the East Coast of the United States during the summer of 1834? Did Tocqueville review and correct this chapter while with the Beaumont family at the end of the summer? The manuscript . . . attests to a rapid composition.[14]

The most likely explanation is that chapter 10, vol. 2, part 2, was based on information gathered by Tocqueville and added to the

12. *DA,* 29. For his part, Beaumont wrote in the foreword to his novel, *Marie, or Slavery in the United States*: "At the very moment my book will be published, another will appear which will throw the brightest of lights on the democratic institutions of the United States. I am talking about the work of M. Alexis de Tocqueville entitled: *Democracy in America.*" Edition online in http://classiques. uqac.ca/classiques/beaumont_gustave_de/marie_ou_esclavage_aux_EU/ marie.html, 12.

13. 1834.

14. *DA,* 515*n*a.

original text at the last moment, at Gallarande, by mutual agreement, because of the riots that broke out in New York on July 9, 1834, and that Beaumont also included in his book, in chapter 13, "L'Émeute!" (The Riot!).

The historical and political circumstances at that time made this addition obligatory for Tocqueville, who wanted to provide the French political class with a seminal work on the institutions of the United States. Without undermining the scientific value of his work, he could not ignore two major political, moral, and societal issues that posed and would continue to pose problems for American democracy.[15]

A Reversal of Perspective on the Fate of the Native Americans

The last chapter of *Democracy* is all the more remarkable for the fact that, on the Native American question, it reverses the judgments Tocqueville had made about their condition and their destiny in the book's opening chapter. In chapter 1, vol. 1, part 1, Tocqueville, having presented the virtues of the Native Americans, situates himself within a historical perspective, admitting that, though the Native Americans were the first occupiers of the country, they were not really its owners. He had come round to the point of view that, in accordance with the laws of historical development and the beliefs held by the Americans, the Native Americans had up to then merely held temporary usufruct of the land. The same Providence that had placed them there just to occupy the space in a non-Promethean way had also determined their necessary and inevitable disappearance—a strange Providence that sacrificed natural rights and left the first occupants at the mercy of the law of the jungle.

15. In spite of the inclusion of this final chapter to the 1835 *Democracy*, on February 2, 1835, *La Gazette de France* accused Tocqueville of having praised "a land of three-colored humanity in which the red men who are its natives are being exterminated by the white usurpers; where black men are sold willy-nilly in public." *La Gazette de France*, 2 février 1835, quoted by Françoise Mélonio, *Tocqueville et les Français* (Paris: Aubier, 1993), 58.

Although the vast country just described was inhabited by numerous tribes of natives, you could justly say that, at the time of discovery, it was still only a wilderness. The Indians occupied, but did not possess it. Man appropriates the soil by agriculture, and the first inhabitants of North America lived by the hunt. Their implacable prejudices, their untamed passions, their vices and perhaps even more their wild virtues delivered them to an inevitable destruction. ... Providence, while placing them in the midst of the riches of the New World, seemed to have given them only a short usufruct; in a way these people were there only waiting.[16]

"The prison system was only a pretext: I used it as a passport which would allow me to go everywhere in the United States," wrote Tocqueville to his cousin Camille d'Orglandes in November 1834.[17] He had several other reasons for going on this voyage, among the first of which was the need to keep away from France's new regime. He also had a strong desire to see American democracy operating *in situ*, following the traditional interest of the Tocqueville and Beaumont families in the political life of the United States, the country in general and in its inhabitants, including the Native Americans who had haunted the imagination of French readers since the voyages of Jacques Cartier and the evangelizing of the Jesuits. Their heads were full of the texts of James Fennimore Cooper and François-René de Châteaubriand, and upon viewing actual rather than literary Native Americans, their disappointment was total.[18]

The spectacle of the Native Americans deeply shocked the two travelers, and they were moved by the plight of those who were for them the embodiment of the noble savage. What a strange contrast between their native virtues and their present poverty, in the context of that

16. *DA*, 43–44.

17. Tocqueville, *Lettres choisies:* Quarto/Gallimard (Paris, 2003), 311.

18. *DA*, 1304; Eduardo Nolla notes that "it was at Oneida Castle that the travelers had seen Indians for the first time. Some among them had run after their coach asking for alms. 'We met the last among them on our route,' writes Tocqueville to his mother about the Indians; 'they ask for alms and are as inoffensive as their fathers were formidable'" (*DA*, vol. 4, Appendix 2, "A Fortnight in the Wilderness," 1304*n*b).

great, primeval nature, described by Tocqueville like a romantic painting by Jean-Baptiste-Camille Corot or Eugène Delacroix: "A kind of
methodical order presided over the separation of land and waterways,
mountains and valleys. A simple and majestic arrangement is revealed
even in the midst of the confusion of objects and among the extreme
variety of scenes."[19] Tocqueville's early vision of the American wilderness cast it as a new Genesis, peopled by savages who had not yet lost
their primitive innocence and gentleness nor their ferocity and pride;
full of the virtues of nobility, courage, selflessness, and perfectly suited
to the natural life and to death.

> The Indians, at the same time that they are all ignorant and poor,
> are all equal and free....
> In peace, mild and hospitable, in war, merciless even beyond the
> known limits of human ferocity, the Indian risked death by starva-
> tion in order to aid a stranger who knocked at night on the door of
> his hut and, with his own hands, tore apart the quivering limbs of
> his prisoner.... The Indian knew how to live without needs, how to
> suffer without complaint, and how to die singing.[20]

Tocqueville traced a Rousseauian history to the Native Americans'
encounters with Europeans: the Native Americans were naturally good,
originally showing generosity and hospitality to the Europeans, and
Tocqueville was assured by the Canadians with whom he spoke that
they had had no experience of theft before coming into contact with
modern "civilized" society that had corrupted them: "I think they are
much better when they have no contact with us, and certainly hap-
pier,"[21] a Bois-Brûlé[22] said to him. Yet by the time Tocqueville and
Beaumont arrived in America, these noble savages had been slaughtered; only a few thousand remained in the thirteen original colonies;
all the others had disappeared, driven from their lands, eliminated.
As they journeyed on through the country, the two Frenchmen began

19. *DA,* 33.
20. *DA,* 41–42.
21. Tocqueville, *Oeuvres complètes,* vol. 5, *Voyages en Sicile et aux États-Unis*
(Paris: Gallimard, 1957), vol. 1, pt. 3, 74; George Wilson Pierson, *Tocqueville in
America* (Baltimore: Johns Hopkins University Press, 1996), 303.
22. The son of a Canadian and an Indian woman.

to realize they were witnessing a process of mass extermination that would continue to its final, inevitable conclusion.

Like many other observers and analysts, Tocqueville drew a distinction between the relationships with the Native Americans of the French on the one hand and the English on the other.

Most of the judgments favorable to the Native Americans to which he refers seem to Tocqueville to be by settlers of French stock,[23] French or French Canadian, underlining the friendly feeling among the Native Americans, the Canadians, and the French. Furthermore, the manuscript drafts reveal that in chapter 10, vol. 2, part 2, of *Democracy in America,* he replaces the term *Europeans* with *Anglo-Americans.*[24]

True to the teachings of Montesquieu in *The Spirit of the Laws,* Tocqueville believes that a spirit of nations truly exists and, regarding the question of the future of the Native and African Americans, he considers that what is happening in the United States is the result of the political and ideological choices of these emigrants, mostly of English stock. Tocqueville's position approaches the point of view articulated several years later by Francis Parkman: "Spanish civilization crushed the Indian; English civilization scorned and neglected him; French civilization embraced and cherished him."[25] He recalls that the governor of Canada informed Louis XIV of the ambivalent attitude of the French, held back by their parochial mentality while at the same time able to share the life of the savages.

> Two great nations of Europe peopled this portion of the American continent: the French and the English.
>
> The first did not take long to enter into unions with the young native women. . . . Instead of giving the barbarians the taste and

23. See Tocqueville, *Oeuvres complètes,* vol. 5, *Voyages en Sicile et aux États-Unis* (Paris: Gallimard, 1957), pt. 1, 212. "The English and the French mix so little that the latter only call themselves *Canadian,* the others continuing to call themselves English."

24. *DA,* 526*n*n.

25. As all general observations, this is only partly true. It does not take into account the acts of cruelty and barbarity of French settlers on certain Native American tribes, such as the extermination of the Natchez, referred to by Beaumont in *Marie:* "The French in Louisiana entirely destroyed the great nation of the Natchez." *Marie, or Slavery in the United States* (Paris: C. Gosselin, 1835), 2:358.

habits of civilized life, it was they who often became passionately attached to savage life....

The Englishman, in contrast...wanted to establish no contact with the savages that be defuse, and carefully avoided mingling his blood with that of the barbarians.[26]

And Tocqueville adds: "'If we pay attention,' say Messrs. Clark and Cass in their report to Congress,... 'to the influence acquired and exercised by the French on the Indians, influence whose visible traces you still see today after two generations have passed, you will be led to conclude that the French used their power with honor and impartiality.'"

THE LAST FEUDAL LORDS

After their stay in Canada and the Great Lakes had put the travelers in direct contact with the Native Americans and had made it possible to speak with them through interpreters, the Frenchmen's awareness of their fate had sharpened.[27] The Native Americans were no longer complete strangers to Tocqueville, and he began to consider them less as abstract noble savages and more as a people possessing—and trying to keep, at risk of their very survival—their own virtues and values, disdaining work and material objects while prizing freedom, combat, and war, and having an acute and deep-rooted sense of honor. They were, in their own way, the last feudal lords and true aristocrats.

There is no Indian so miserable who, in his bark hut, does not maintain a proud idea of his individual value; he considers the cares of industry as degrading occupations.... He still believes himself superior to us. Hunting and war seem to him the only cares worthy of a man. So the Indian, deep within the misery of his woods, nurtures the same ideas, the same opinions as the noble of the Middle Ages in his fortress, and to resemble him fully he only needs to become a conqueror....

26. *DA*, 534*n*s. E. Nolla: "Note on a small sheet of paper separate from the manuscript, but which, according to Tocqueville's indications, should have been placed here...."

27. Tocqueville, *Oeuvres complètes*, vol. 5, *Voyages en Sicile et aux États-Unis* (Paris: Gallimard, 1957), pt. 1, 174–75; Pierson, *Tocqueville in America*, 296–97.

I cannot prevent myself from thinking that the same cause has produced, in the two hemispheres, the same results, and that amid the apparent diversity of human affairs, it is not impossible to find a small number of generative facts from which all the others derive. So in all that we call Teutonic institutions, I am tempted to see only the habits of barbarians, and the opinions of savages in what we call feudal ideas.[28]

This is a fundamental point. When writing his work, Tocqueville was directly addressing those for whom *Democracy in America* was originally intended: his kin, his caste, the legitimists. He wanted to convince the political elite that the rise of democracy in the legally constituted states of Western Europe was ineluctable.

The aristocracy was to the French society of 1835 what the Native Americans were to the historical and economic development of the United States, that is, a relic of the past, destined to disappear. When he writes of "the political institutions of our fathers, the Teutons," he is alluding to the tradition that began with Henri de Boulainvilliers and was taken up by thinkers from Montesquieu to Guizot, and to which he himself referred.[29] According to this, feudalism and the resulting aristocracy could be traced back to the invasions by the Germanic tribes who imposed their rule on the Gallo-Romans—the Hegelian dialectic of the master and the slave, at the end of which the slave becomes the master's master, and an illustration of the historical process that led to the French Revolution.

Boulainvilliers's theory had inspired the ideology that the reaction of the nobility had accelerated the revolutionary process. As early as 1788, Abbé Sieyès had written in *Qu'est-ce que le Tiers état?*:

Why should not [the Third Estate] send back to the forests of Franconia, all these families who wildly claim to be descended from the race of the conquerors and to have inherited their rights?

The nation, thus purged, could console itself, I think, for being reduced to believing itself composed just of the descendants of the Gauls and the Romans. In truth, if one is intent on distinguishing

28. *DA,* 531–32.
29. *DA,* 532*nr.*

one birth from another, could we not show our poor fellow citizens that to descend from the Gauls and the Romans is at least equal in value to descending from the Sicambers, the Welches and the other savages that came out of the woods and ponds of old Germany?[30]

Tocqueville considered Sieyès's speech to be true in substance, even if too harsh in form.[31]

Like his relative Châteaubriand,[32] Tocqueville believed he was witnessing a disappearing world, the end of the old aristocracy as such, in its relationship with the Old World. His message was thus first and foremost destined for these aristocrats, calling on them to adapt to the nascent democratic world in order to transfer to it their own values, one of the most important of which would be the unquenchable appetite for liberty.

Tamara Teale has observed that Tocqueville's empathy for the Native Americans, a race doomed to die out, reveals a deep sympathy, a fellow-feeling, with the Native American nations who shared a common fate with the French aristocracy: "Tocqueville compared the Native person to the feudal noble in his castle refusing to take part in the new 'social state' until 'driven to it at times by necessity.' In the paradox of the twin birth of liberty and genocide, we can see Tocqueville's 'appropriation of his inheritance,' as a type of vanishing aristocrat, and his mapping of it onto the situation of American Indians."[33]

The Question of Interracial Mixing

In the course of their American trip, Tocqueville and Beaumont became aware of the importance of interbreeding in human societies.

---

30. Emmanuel Joseph Sièyes, *Qu'est-ce que le Tiers état?* n. p., 1789, pp. 10–11. This text is at the BNF, Bibliotheque Nationale de France, and can be consulted on the Internet.

31. Tocqueville, *Oeuvres complètes*, vol. 2, *L'ancien régime et la révolution* (Paris: Gallimard, 1953), pt. 1, 140–41.

32. Châteaubriand's eldest brother had married Aline-Thérèse de Rosambo, Malesherbes's granddaughter and the eldest sister of Alexis's mother.

33. Tamara M. Teale, "Tocqueville and American Indian Legal Studies, the Paradox of Liberty and Destruction," *Tocqueville Review* 17, no. 2 (1996): 57–65.

They discovered the interracial mixing between Native Americans and whites in Canada and in the Great Lakes region and that of African Americans and whites in Louisiana, which was unique to that state and impossible elsewhere. They became convinced that the problem of slavery was insoluble in the United States in the short term, because it concerned a single race, making abolition legally possible in theory but impossible in practice, because prejudice against the African Americans ran counter to any attempt toward abolition. The problem could only be solved if the two populations agreed to live side by side, on an equal footing, to mingle—something that was impossible there at the time, and there was no way of knowing if it ever would be.[34]

Several times, Tocqueville evokes a particularly surprising encounter with some people of mixed race, one of his first, when he was going to Saginaw Bay with Beaumont.

As I prepared to climb in, the supposed Indian advanced toward me, put two fingers on my shoulder and said to me with a Norman accent that made me start: "Don't go too fast, there are times here when people drown." My horse would have spoken to me, and I would not, I believe, have been more surprised.... The Canadian pushed the skiff with the paddle, all the while singing in a low voice an old French tune, of whose verse I grasped only the first two lines:
Between Paris and Saint Denis
There was a girl....[35]

In Saginaw, there was a further encounter with a Native American woman and her son: "The Frenchman was her husband and he had already given her several children. An extraordinary race, a mixture of savage and civilized man...."[36]

A few days later, they discovered, in Sault Saint Marie, a singular village in which three peoples were mixed, French, Native American, and mixed race, as Beaumont wrote to his brother, Achille:

34. Beaumont's book, *Marie, or Slavery in the United States*, is, in part, a novel on race mixing.

35. *DA*, 1344.

36. Tocqueville, *Oeuvres complètes*, vol. 5, *Voyages en Sicile et aux États-Unis* (Paris: Gallimard, 1957), pt. 1, 171.

The sixth of August early in the morning we entered the village which bears the name of Sault Ste. Marie [where] everybody...speaks French. There are as many Native Americans as Canadians there. Each day the two populations mingle further. This half-European, half-Indian population is not disagreeable....The Canadians call *métiches* (métis) those who come of this double origin. I have seen some young métiches girls who seemed to me of noteworthy beauty.[37]

Tocqueville, too, stresses several times the happy result of interracial mixing, as regards both beauty and intelligence, and several of the people they spoke to thought that interbreeding with whites made, or could have made, it possible for the Native Americans to survive and be successfully assimilated.[38] Tocqueville and Beaumont, however, were quickly convinced that interbreeding could no longer be a path to salvation for the Native Americans whose fate was sealed once they met Anglo-American civilization, both because some tribes refused to adapt and because those who tried to adapt were deemed all the more undesirable by the colonists who wanted to claim the entirety of the continent, all the way to the Pacific.

The Clash of Civilizations and the Spirit of Nations

From his American experience, Tocqueville put forward a law[39] of the development and cohabitation of societies that places a less

37. Gustave de Beaumont, *Lettres d'Amérique* (Paris: PUF, Publications de la Sorbonne, 1973), 122–23. In New Orleans, too, Tocqueville and Beaumont also admired the beauty of the young women whose mixed blood condemned them to prostitution, the reason for which the heroine of Beaumont's novel, *Marie,* had to leave New Orleans.

38. Pierson, *Tocqueville in America,* 652.

39. In using the term "law" here, I follow Raymond Boudon's analysis, which demonstrates with clarity how Tocqueville employs a multiplicity of interactive mechanisms among social factors as well as historical events (see Boudon, *Tocqueville aujourd'hui* [Paris: Odile Jacob, 2005], esp. chap. 4, 83–130). Sociologists and political analysts speak of "laws," while historians present theories of the development of the historical process. In the introduction to *Democracy in America,* Tocqueville writes, "[R]ecognize that the gradual and progressive development of equality is at once the past and the future of their history." While he

advanced one in jeopardy when confronted with a more modern one. The meeting between two very unequally developed civilizations is fundamentally different according to whether the one victorious by force is more or less advanced. Historically, in the latter case, the invaders integrate the country, assimilate the civilization surrounding them, and learn from those they have conquered. He chooses as his example, for reasons previously mentioned, the invasion of the Roman Empire by the Teutons, basing his arguments again on Boulainvilliers's theory, so revered by the French aristocracy.

> If you cast an attentive eye on history, you discover that in general barbaric peoples have risen little by themselves, and by their own efforts, toward civilization....
>
> The barbarians end by introducing the civilized man into their palaces, and the civilized man in turn opens his schools to them. But when the one who possesses physical force enjoys intellectual preponderance at the same time, it is rare for the vanquished to become civilized; he withdraws or is destroyed.[40]

As a follower of Montesquieu, Tocqueville highlighted the law of development derived from his American experience and reminded his reader of three situations in which the French had come into contact with the English in North America and had been dominated by them. In the first case, the French had had no alternative but to leave the city of Vincennes on the Wabash; in the second, they submitted—and continued to submit—to English political control in Canada; in the third, they were subject to the economic domination by the English in Louisiana.[41]

---

does not use the word "law," he conveys the same inevitability, noting also that "this discovery alone would give this development the sacred character of the will of God. To want to stop democracy would then seem to be struggling against God himself, and it would only remain for nations to accommodate themselves to the social state that Providence imposes on them" (*DA*, 14). Similarly, Tocqueville's explicit references to Montesquieu's theory of climates employ neither the word "theory" nor the word "law," the latter being reserved in Tocqueville's writings for the legislative arena. Tocqueville's terminological usage is deliberate, for considerations of elegance and style.

40. *DA,* 535.
41. *DA,* 539–40*n*19.

In the name of the universal values of human rights, Christianity, and democracy, the more developed and powerful civilization had a duty to introduce a modus vivendi, providing certain safeguards to allow the original, less advanced civilization to survive. Tocqueville recalls that George Washington addressed these words to Congress: "We are more enlightened and more powerful than the Indian nations; it is to our honor to treat them with kindness and even with generosity." But he adds, "This noble and virtuous policy has not been followed."[42]

It is clear from the acts of Congress and from the texts of various reports to Congress that the politicians were fully aware of what should have been done to safeguard the Native American population: to make treaties with the tribes that would guarantee to them a significant part of their ancestral lands and to respect these treaties, rather than restricting the tribes to more and more limited areas. Treaties, properly made and properly enforced, should have recognized Native American property rights, enabling them to survive and accommodate their traditional lifestyle and civilization to those of the Anglo-Americans, but "the misfortune of Indians [was] to come into contact with the most civilized, and I would add, the most grasping people in the world."[43]

The Judgment of History: A Testimony
Denouncing the Fate of the Cherokees

As their American expedition progressed, Tocqueville and Beaumont became convinced that the Native American case had already been settled and that the genocide would go ahead. They decided to record this for posterity; the one as a novelist, the other as a lawyer. Therefore, Tocqueville's final chapter to the 1835 *Democracy* serves almost as a legal brief, in which he presents evidence in defense of the Native American nations against the states of the Union and the Union itself. This explains the unusual nature of this part of *Democracy*: it is

42. *DA,* 541.
43. *DA,* 536–37.

the only part in which the notes—extracts from reports, legal texts, quantitative data—are longer than the text itself.[44]

By July 1834, Tocqueville and Beaumont had built up detailed knowledge of the Native American question from their meetings and discussions with the most varied of people: the Native Americans, the Bois-Brûlés, the pioneers. They had also gathered evidence and commentaries from important people like Joel Roberts Poinsett and John Spencer, and even more significantly, from John Tanner and Sam Houston, who had lived for years with the tribes. In addition, they read a large number of official reports on the Native American question dating back two centuries, "with their uncanny—sometimes it almost seemed their providential—knack of finding the most important men who were doing, or would accomplish, the most in the America of their generation,"[45] from Houston to Davy Crockett and Tanner, from John Quincy Adams to Andrew Jackson.

From all this evidence, Tocqueville devised an overall theory, a *pensée mère*. He was convinced that with the Indian Removal Act, it was possible to have a complete overview of the Native American question that was both synchronic—certain as he was that the same fate would befall all the tribes—and diachronic—because he now had the "reason," in the strongest and almost mathematical meaning of the word, for what had happened to the Native Americans from the arrival of the first settlers in Virginia, to the treaties of 1790, of what had been happening since the beginning of the Jackson presidency, and what would be its inevitable result.

He believed that the ultimate destiny of the Native American tribes was preordained, hence the subheading: *"Present state and probable future of the Indian tribes living in the territory of the Union...."*[46] Their fate was already sealed, as in the tragedy: "And there you are. Now the spring

44. In *DA*, 1835, all Tocqueville's notes, both footnotes and appendices, make up 5 percent of the text (7,935 words out of 158,023), in chapter 10, 13.5 percent (8,117 out of 59,945), and in the subsection on the Native Americans, 67 percent (3,800 words out of 5,669)!

45. Pierson, *Tocqueville in America*, 609.

46. *DA*, 515.

is stretched. The story will unfold on its own.... There is no hope left.
...There is nothing left that can be done."[47]

Most of the people to whom Tocqueville spoke thought the Native
Americans had to die out: "I believe they are a race that will perish
sooner than try to become civilized,... success in that would be impossible without the aid of the half-breed. Aside from that, I think the
civilized man has the right to take from the savage the land which the
latter does not know how to use."[48]

If the Native American tribes incapable of becoming civilized or
refusing to do so were therefore condemned to vanish, this was even
more true for those who chose the path of civilization. They would have
to be dragged from the land which belonged to them, where they had
tried to settle and to farm, as had the Cherokees with the remarkable
intelligence and courage referred to by Houston when he compared
the qualities of the various tribes.

> Foremost of all are the Cherokees. The Cherokees live entirely from
> farming the land. They are the only Indian nation to have a written
> language.
>   After the Cherokees come the Creeks. The Creeks live both from
> hunting and farming. They have a positive penal code and a form
> of government.
>   Afterwards I place the Chickasaws and the Choctaws.[49]

For the majority of citizens, the situation was simple: some had to
die because they refused to become civilized, and others because they
were even more in the way since they had chosen to become civilized.
Tocqueville described the American's thought process:

> They have to die.... I shall do nothing against them; I shall only
> furnish to them everything that will haste their loss. After a time, I
> shall have their lands and I shall be innocent of their death.
>   Satisfied of his reasoning, the American goes to the temple where

47. Jean Anouilh, *Antigone* (Paris: La Table Ronde, 1947), 54–55.

48. Tocqueville, *Oeuvres complètes*, vol. 5, *Voyages en Sicile et aux États-Unis*
(Paris: Gallimard, 1957), pt. 1, 149; Pierson, *Tocqueville in America*, 652.

49. Tocqueville, *Oeuvres complètes*, vol. 5, *Voyages en Sicile et aux États-Unis*
(Paris: Gallimard, 1957), pt. 1, 265.

he hears a minister of the gospel repeat to him that men are brothers and that the Eternal Being, who has made them all on the same model, has given all duty to succor each other.[50]

To underline the size of the problem, Tocqueville refers to the official figures and to compliance with the treaties signed by the federal authorities in 1790. The tribes that occupied the thirteen original colonies had been slaughtered; they numbered, according to the official figures of the 20th Congress, no more than 6,273 individuals, dying of starvation, reduced to begging—the very ones Tocqueville and Beaumont had met in Oneida.[51]

Regarding the Native American population still existing in the territory of the United States, he quotes three other official figures: in 1830 there remained 75,000 Native Americans from the four great nations—the Choctaws, Chickasaws, Creeks, and Cherokees, 313,000 in the "lands occupied and claimed by the Anglo-American Union."[52] A note indicates that it was the remaining members of the four nations, the most easily assimilated tribes, whose deportation had already been decided on by the Jackson government: "See the instructions of the Secretary of war...dated 30 May 1830. There are 75,000 Indians to transport."[53] To force the tribes to accept this "voluntary" deportation, the American regime had used the most underhanded methods, as Tocqueville wrote to his mother, in a letter full of compassion, irony, and anger.[54]

COMPLIANCE WITH TREATIES AND FALSE PROMISES

Houston, who had lived among the Creeks, assured Tocqueville, who was still in a state of shock over the appalling spectacle of the

---

50. Tocqueville, *Oeuvres complètes*, vol. 5, *Voyages en Sicile et aux États-Unis* (Paris: Gallimard, 1957), pt. 1, 225; Pierson, *Tocqueville in America*, 596; *DA*, 1308.

51. *DA*, 523*n*2. It is remarkable that Jackson's first political act on this question was the eviction of the four most civilized tribes, because they undermined the official and ideological policy line. They had to be the first to go.

52. *DA*, 533.

53. *DA*, 542*n*x.

54. Tocqueville, *Oeuvres complètes*, tom. 14, *Correspondance familiale* (Paris: Gallimard, 1998), 159–60; Pierson, *Tocqueville in America*, 596–98.

embarkation of the Choctaws in Memphis a week earlier (on Christmas Day, 1831), that the relocation of the Native American tribes to the west of the Mississippi was a good opportunity for them, for possession of lands in Arkansas had been guaranteed to them. According to Houston, "The United States have sworn, by the most solemn oaths, never to sell the lands contained within these limits, and never to allow the white race to work itself in by any means." He added: "10,000 Indians are already to be found in the territory. I think that with time there will be 50,000 of them. The region is healthy and the land extremely fertile."[55]

Did Houston really believe what he was saying? Beaumont and Tocqueville thought the truth lay elsewhere, and they did not include Houston's testimony in their respective works. Indeed, in three notes to *Democracy,* Tocqueville recalled that these same promises had already been solemnly made to the Creeks and the Cherokees, in 1790 and 1791. Now, in 1829, "The central government, while promising these unfortunate people a permanent refuge in the West, is not unaware that it is not able to guarantee it to them."[56]

False promises willfully corrupt oaths. Tocqueville and Beaumont appeared to share the view of Tanner, who had lived for many years with the Native Americans and who was convinced that the process could only end in their extinction. He said to Beaumont:

You, who sympathize with their misfortunes, . . . hurry to know them! for soon they will have disappeared from the earth. The forests of Arkansas are *given forever* to them! These are, it is true, the terms of the treaty! But what a mockery! The lands that they occupied in Georgia had also been given to them, thirty years ago, *forever!* The Indian who goes closely along with them is only following his means of existence, but by constantly advancing toward the west, he will meet the Pacific Ocean.—This will be the end of his journey and of his life. How many years will pass before his ruin? You could not say.[57]

55. Pierson, *Tocqueville in America,* 614–15.
56. *DA,* 544.
57. *DA,* 537–38.

Having assembled all the elements of the evidentiary file, the only task remaining to Tocqueville was a closing argument. He chose to let those who were condemned to disappear speak for themselves, recounting the moving testimony of the Cherokees before Congress:

> By the will of our Father in Heaven, the Governor of the whole world, . . . the red man of America has become small, and the white man great and renowned. . . . The Northern tribes, who were once so numerous and powerful, are now nearly extinct. . . .
>
> Shall we, who are remnants, share the same fate?[58]
>
> The land on which we stand we have received as an inheritance from our fathers, who possessed it from time immemorial, as a gift from our common Father in Heaven.[59]

He then denounced the illegal acts depriving them of their lands and added: "Such is the language of the Indians; what they say is true; what they foresee seems inevitable to me."[60]

In 1830 the Congress of the United States passed the Indian Removal Act. President Andrew Jackson quickly signed the bill into law. The Cherokees attempted to fight removal legally by challenging the removal laws in the Supreme Court and by establishing an independent Cherokee Nation. In 1832, the U.S. Supreme Court ruled in favor of the Cherokee, and Chief Justice John Marshall ruled that the Cherokee Nation was sovereign, making the removal laws invalid. The Cherokee would have to agree to removal in a treaty, and the treaty would then have to be ratified by the Senate.

Despite the Supreme Court's verdict, President Jackson refused to make treaties with the Indian nations, declaring, "John Marshall has made his law, now let him enforce it."

"This world is, it must be admitted, a sad and ridiculous theater,"[61] writes Tocqueville with the irony of despair at the end of this chapter, and he concludes:

58. In French: "Nous faut-il aussi mourir?"
59. *DA,* 545.
60. *DA,* 546.
61. *DA,* 547.

The conduct of the Americans of the United States toward the natives radiates in contrast, the purest love of forms of legality. . . . The Americans of the United States have achieved this double result with a marvelous ease, calmly, legally, philanthropically, without shedding blood, without violating a single one of the great principles of morality in the eyes of the world. You cannot destroy men while respecting the laws of humanity.[62]

What a terrible injustice also when Mr. [John] Bell canceled with one stroke of his pen the property rights of the Native Americans to the land that was theirs, "[dismissing] arguments based on natural law and reason,"[63] and thus violating the human rights to which those virtuous lawyers claimed to be so attached. Tocqueville and Beaumont were fully aware of the crime against humanity that was being perpetrated. The publication of Beaumont's book and the inclusion in Tocqueville's of chapter 10, vol. 2, part 2, corresponded to their need to testify to this and to denounce the double violation of natural law and of individual and collective rights as a denial of democracy within the greatest modern democracy. It had become vital for Tocqueville to establish that he had not missed the existence of this dual democratic antinomy.

AMERICAN LESSONS BROUGHT TO FRANCE: ALGERIA

Between 1837 and 1848, Tocqueville was one of the main contributors to France's debate on Algerian colonization. Whenever he gave his opinion, in all his newspaper articles, notes, and reports, whenever he spoke in Parliament, he treats the question of the cohabitation of the indigenous people with the colonizers in reference to his experience in America. This lay always in the background, even when as an example of what not to do: "Let us not repeat, in the middle of the 19th century, the story of the American conquest. Let us avoid imitating bloody acts that have been condemned by the judgment of the human race."[64]

This recommendation, which comes from the end of his 1847 report on Algeria, was at the heart of his concerns from when he first took

62. *DA*, 546–47.
63. *DA*, 547.
64. Tocqueville, *Oeuvres complètes*, vol. 3, *Ecrits et discours politiques* (Paris: Gallimard, 1962), pt. 1, 329–30.

a stance, in 1837, right to the end. The comparison to the American treatment of the Native American tribes was all the more justified by the fact that among those in favor of settling the country were those who believed the native peoples should be got rid of, to make way for the settlers, explicitly placing the Algerian case in the same category as that of the Native Americans and stating that "the extinction of this race [would be] a harmony."[65]

In his two 1837 *Lettres sur l'Algérie*, Tocqueville explored the idea that France should have followed the Greek model and set up trading posts as well as two strategic positions on the coast, in Algiers and Mers El Kebir: "Colonizing some places on the coast and controlling the interior like the Turks is the only practical plan."[66] He thought that it was possible for the Europeans and Arabs to interbreed, as the Native Americans and Canadians had done, permitting "these two peoples of different civilizations to merge into one" and in the long run, "fusion [would come] on its own." The strength of his hopes is reflected in his choice of verbs, *amalgamate:* "There is no reason to believe that in time the two races could not amalgamate. God does not prevent this; only the faults of men could be an obstacle."

However, after his first journey to Algeria in 1841, he changed his mind, coming to believe that religious antagonisms excluded any possibility of an interracial society: "The first objection could only be made by people who have never been to Africa. . . . The fusion between these two populations is a dream one can have only if one has never been there."[67] He then explores the idea of using force to establish "total domination," which would allow "partial colonization."[68] Basing his views again conversely on his American experience, he states, for exam-

---

65. Tocqueville, *Oeuvres complètes,* vol. 3, *Ecrits et discours politiques* (Paris: Gallimard, 1962), pt. 1, 294.

66. Tocqueville, *Oeuvres complètes,* vol. 3, *Ecrits et discours politiques* (Paris: Gallimard, 1962), pt. 1, 173. "Notes prises avant le voyage d'Algérie et dans le courant 1840."

67. Tocqueville, *Oeuvres complètes,* Gallimard, *Écrits et discours politiques, Travail sur l'Algérie* (octobre 1841), tom. 3, vol. 1 (Paris, 1962), 275.

68. Tocqueville, *Oeuvres complètes,* Gallimard, *Écrits et discours politiques, Travail sur l'Algérie (octobre 1841),* tom. 3, vol. 1 (Paris, 1962), 218. On the Algerian question, see Jean-Louis Benoît, *Comprendre Tocqueville* (Paris: Armand Colin, 2004),

ple, that an attempt should not be made to extend the colony to the area of Bône because, "to succeed in colonizing a certain area, not merely violent but manifestly unjust methods would have to be used. Several tribes would have to be dispossessed and transported elsewhere, where they would most likely have been less well-off."[69] He also suggests that the situation in the colony had deteriorated because the politicians had given a free hand to the military, something "that has never been wise, nor human, nor even reasonable in a civilized century."[70]

After 1846, Tocqueville clashed head-on with Governor-General Thomas Bugeaud because he did not agree that the state of war should be permanent. Regarding settlement and the territorial question, Tocqueville put forward a policy of land occupation in his 1847 *Report* that would allow the establishment of a colony with sufficient agricultural land to sustain it, while also guaranteeing ownership of a significant and adequate area of land for the native population to live decently.

He believed the south of the country should remain in the hands of the indigenous peoples because the population there were "our tributaries and not our subjects." Kabylia had absolutely to remain in the hands and under the control of the Kabylian people, for Tocqueville considered them a distinct people, possessed of noble characteristics and with whom he thought it would be possible to trade. Moreover, the Kabylians were proud and had become rebellious when invaded because they had a "natural hatred of strangers." He noted, "As for the Kabylians, it is clear that there is no question of conquering or colonizing their country: their mountains are presently impassable to our armies and their inhabitants' inhospitable temperament allows no security to the isolated European who wants to go there peaceably and to create a refuge. The Kabylian territory is closed to us, but Kabylian's soul is open and, it is not impossible for us to penetrate there."[71]

123–44; Benoît, *Tocqueville un destin paradoxal* (Paris: Bayard, 2005), 191–95, 264–79.

69. Tocqueville, *Oeuvres complètes,* Gallimard, *Écrits et discours politiques, Travail sur l'Algérie (octobre 1841),* tom. 3, vol. 1 (Paris, 1962), 242.

70. Tocqueville, *Oeuvres complètes,* Gallimard, *Écrits et discours politiques, Examen du livre intitulé Actes du Gouvernement,* tom. 3, vol. 1 (Paris, 1962), 196.

71. Tocqueville, *Oeuvres complètes,* Gallimard, *Écrits et discours politiques, Deuxième lettre sur l'Algérie, 23 juin 1837,* tom. 3, vol. 1 (Paris, 1962), 146. (The first

Tocqueville would never shift from this position and would categorically condemn Thomas Robert Bugeaud's military operations in Kabylia in 1847 as the stupid actions of an ambitious *matamore*, to whom he makes this premonitory remark: "What are we going to do in Kabylia?... We will defeat the Kabyles but how will we govern them after defeating them."[72]

In Mitidja, the situation of the ownership of the lands by the settlers would have to be regularized, following a legitimate procedure. Regarding the rest of the Tell Atlas region, the useful part of Algeria, Tocqueville thought this was the main area suitable for new colonization; thus, lands should be acquired, either by having recourse to the "rights of war" or by buying the land from the indigenous population. However, he specified that the sale of land to settlers by the locals would have to be forbidden in order to avoid fraudulent transactions and despoliation, although his encounters with the Native Americans in the United States reminded him that such practices provided no guarantees. He added:

> By conquering Algeria, we did not claim, like the Barbarians who invaded the Roman Empire, to take possession of the lands of those we had defeated.... The city was handed over to us and, in return, we ensured that the religious and property rights of all its inhabitants were upheld.... Does it follow that we cannot take possession of the lands necessary for European colonization? Doubtless it does not.
> ... It is important for our own security as much as for our honor, to show true respect for indigenous property, and to thoroughly convince our Muslim subjects that we do not intend to take from them without any compensation any part of their heritage, or, what would be even worse, obtain it through deceitful and derisory transactions in which violence was concealed under the form of purchase and fear under the appearance of sale.[73]

---

and second letters on Algeria are works by themselves; Tocqueville published them in *La Presse de Seine et Oise,* June 23 for the first and August 22 for the second. These letters are also published separately; see the website UQAC, where I published the first one.)

72. Tocqueville, *Oeuvres complètes,* Gallimard, *Écrits et discours politiques, Rapports sur l'Algérie,* tom. 3, vol. 1 (Paris, 1962), 360.

73. Tocqueville, *Oeuvres complètes,* Gallimard, *Écrits et discours politiques, Rapports sur l'Algérie, 1847,* tom. 3, vol. 1 (Paris, 1962), 326–27.

Tocqueville continued to think and hope that by rubbing shoulders with each other, the two populations could find a common interest in working and trading together.

It would not be very sensible to believe that we will succeed in forging links with the indigenous people through common ideas and customs, but we can hope to do so through common interest....

The European needs the Arab to make his land profitable; the Arab needs the European to obtain a good wage. In this way mutual interest brings together in the same field, and inevitably unites in the same thought, two men whose upbringing and origins placed so far from each other.[74]

The 1846–47 texts on Algeria can be considered as Tocqueville's political legacy on this subject. He emphasized how many serious mistakes and blunders were made when colonization began. Not only had the army proved to be unsuited to the job, but the administrative authorities in Algeria also had all the faults of the French Civil Service, but to a higher degree: "In Algiers, the most oppressive and pernicious power is that of the civil authorities."[75]

With regard to the colonization of Algeria, Tocqueville believed that France was at a crossroads. Its choice was either to change its methods completely, including its relationships with the indigenous people, or be condemned to serious failure in the long run, leading ultimately to the disappearance of one of the two populations, Algerian or European.

The future of our domination in Africa depends on our manner of treating the indigenous population.... If we act in a way that shows that in our eyes the former inhabitants of Algeria are just an obstacle to be brushed aside or trodden underfoot; if we enfold their population, not to raise them up in our arms to lead them towards well-being and light, but to smother and oppress them, the question

74. Tocqueville, *Oeuvres complètes*, Gallimard, *Écrits et discours politiques, Rapports sur l'Algérie, 1847*, tom. 3, vol. 1 (Paris, 1962), 329.

75. Tocqueville, *Oeuvres complètes*, Gallimard, *Écrits et discours politiques, Travail sur l'Algérie (octobre 1841)*, tom. 3, vol. 1 (Paris, 1962), 261.

will arise of the life and death of the two races. Algeria will become sooner or later, you will see, an enclosed battlefield, a walled arena, where the two peoples will have to fight without mercy and where one or other will have to die. May God save us, Gentlemen, from such a destiny![76]

This situation was comparable to what was happening and what was likely to happen in the southern states of the United States, and it is to that situation he referred at the end of his 1847 report.

"In America I Saw More Than America"

In the same way if the same thoughts in a different arrangement do not form a different discourse, no more do the same words in their different arrangement form different thoughts! (Pascal, Pensées *L. 696)*

"I have thought some of the things I made known to you just now for nearly ten years already," wrote Tocqueville to Camille d'Orglandes,[77] in November 1834, explaining thus that even before his American journey, he had had his basic idea with its conceptual framework of democracy's inevitable rise and its challenges. The essence of Tocqueville's discoveries and innovation was in his new and original way of looking at and presenting the ideas of the time. As regards political science, political philosophy, and the issues of the day, all he said or wrote had already been said or written by others. However, Tocqueville's genius, his originality, lay in his skill of knowing what questions to ask and of whom, and what conclusions to draw from their answers. Similarly, throughout *Democracy*, his particular ideas may have already been expressed elsewhere, but the way Tocqueville summarizes and arranges them is completely his own.

The journey also caused Tocqueville to reflect on many issues, and thereafter his American experience would figure constantly in his major reports on economic, social, and political questions. It would

76. Tocqueville, *Oeuvres complètes*, Gallimard, *Écrits et discours politiques, Rapports sur l'Algérie, 1847*, tom. 3, vol. 1 (Paris, 1962), 329.

77. See above, note 17.

play a vital part in his campaign for the abolition of slavery, in his efforts to establish and pass a law on the reform of the French penitentiary system, and in his contributions to the drawing up of the 1848 constitution.

The final chapter of the 1835 *Democracy in America,* Tocqueville's "legal file" on the Native American genocide, is particularly enlightening on three levels. First, it reminds us of the Tocquevillian system of values and of the ethics of his politics. Second, it is very informative on Tocqueville's methods, and third, it shows clearly how wrong it is to speak of Tocqueville's prophetic insight.

For Tocqueville, political thinking and behavior must be based on an ethical conception of politics, which is why he was critical of Machiavelli. He was profoundly attached to the values of the Enlightenment in which he saw a secularized version of original Christian values, his admiration of which he emphasized to Gobineau while stressing his complete agnosticism.[78] He sees himself as following immediately from Montaigne, for whom: "Every man bears within himself the entire human condition"[79] and for whom there exists only one human race, rich in its diversity. It is in the name of universal values and human rights that he denounces the genocide of the indigenous populations.

His position on the genocide of the Native Americans and the enslavement of African Americans gives us an insight into Tocquevillian methods and what is wrongly called his "prophetism." He established a rational process of anticipation, putting down in detail all the available information, referring to the laws of historical development, and by taking into account the forces present and the parameters at stake, he was already able to determine how far progress had advanced. He was certain then that the Native American genocide was neither an accident nor a reversible process, but that it would proceed to its inevitable conclusion. In contrast, as far as the African Americans and the abolition of slavery were concerned, the number of unknown and unpredictable parameters were such that it was impossible, in 1834–35, to move beyond the stage of pure conjecture, while, concerning the prospects for the French colonization of Algeria, if it was not possible

78. Benoît, *Tocqueville moraliste,* 282–83.
79. Montaigne, *Essais,* vol. 3.

to know how long the process would take, it was at least possible to determine the two possible outcomes.

In this way, therefore, the journey and the use made of it plays a crucial role in the formation of Tocqueville's methods and the procedures he instituted in the new political science that underlay all his political analysis and actions.

11

Out of Africa: Tocqueville's Imperial Voyages

CHERYL B. WELCH

As a member of the *Chambre des députés français* (Chamber of Deputies) during the July Monarchy, Tocqueville often reminded his fellow
deputies that seeing new worlds prevents intellectual self-delusion and
corrects political judgment. In *Democracy in America,* as well as in his parliamentary speeches and pamphlets, he drew heavily on the legitimacy
conferred by "eye-witnessing."[1] Indeed, the authority of the firsthand,
filtered through an acute intelligence and expressed with deceptively
classical simplicity, became Tocqueville's writerly signature. There has
been much controversy, however, about the extent to which Tocqueville
saw America primarily through European lenses, and about whether he
actually learned anything of importance there. It is one of the virtues
of the Nolla critical edition of the *Democracy,* now made available to
English readers, to show that viewing the United States firsthand—its
culture, society, politics, and predicaments—was decisive for the formation of his view of democracy as well as for his self-presentation as
a truth-telling traveler.[2]

1. Reflecting on the process of translating the critical edition of *Democracy
in America,* James Schleifer notes the recurring images of being "struck" by an
idea or event and of witnessing something "new" and important in America. See
"Tocqueville's *Democracy in America* Reconsidered," in *The Cambridge Companion
to Tocqueville,* ed. Cheryl B. Welch (Cambridge: Cambridge University Press,
2006), 131–32.

2. Gary Wills has perhaps taken the most extreme position on how little
Tocqueville allegedly learned in America. See "Did Tocqueville 'Get' America?"
New York Review of Books 51 (April 29, 2004; available online, but without original
page numbers). Many other scholars, however, have debated the question. The

"Seeing Africa" was to play an analogous role in Tocqueville's writing and political rhetoric. In his first letter on Algeria, written to bolster his parliamentary candidacy, Tocqueville notes that he has not been to Africa, though he is not so foolish as to boast of it.[3] After he had visited Algeria, he did not fail to exploit this privileged access in his speeches and reports ("if the Chamber will permit me to speak only of my own personal experience... I am profoundly convinced of the opposite").[4] In this essay, I ask how we should evaluate Tocqueville's encounter with Africa within the context of his larger voyage into the territory of modern democracy. What were his justifications for the imperialist move into Africa? What lessons did he (and should we) draw out of this theoretical voyage?

Into Africa: Tocqueville's Imperial Voice

Compared to other nineteenth-century European imperial ventures, the French conquest of North Africa was relatively long, violent, and destructive. After displacing the Turks in 1830, France was

---

notes, variations, and outlines now made available to English readers in the Liberty Fund translation of the Nolla edition help us to see how much Tocqueville's observations in America shaped his basic organizing ideas and the extent to which he "got" America, even when he decided not to include what he had seen in the published text. As he notes in a first version of his introduction, "I have not said everything that I saw, but I have said everything that I believed at the same time true and useful [v. profitable] to make known." Alexis de Tocqueville, *Democracy in America: Historical-Critical Edition of "De la démocratie en Amérique,"* ed. Eduardo Nolla, trans. James T. Schleifer, 4 vols. (Indianapolis: Liberty Fund, 2010), 4nc. This edition is hereafter cited as *DA*.

3. "First Letter on Algeria (23 June 1837)," in Tocqueville, *Writings on Empire and Slavery,* ed. and trans. Jennifer Pitts (Baltimore: Johns Hopkins University Press, 2001), 5. Tocqueville refers here to Amedée Desjobert, the indefatigable critic of the conquest and colonization of Algeria, who had noted in the preface to his *La question d'Alger* (Paris: Dufart Libraire, 1837) that it was better to seek out the best research and the testimony of experts than to rely on vague and incomplete impressions of an isolated personal visit (vi–vii).

4. "Intervention in the Debate over the Appropriation of Special Funding (1846)," in Tocqueville, *Writings on Empire and Slavery,* 121.

at first unsure about how to consolidate her position. This indecision changed, however, with the emergence of significant resistance under Abd-el-Kader, a charismatic young religious and political leader who united Arab forces in the mid-1830s. Eventually the French decided to establish military dominance over the entire territory, a decision leading to a costly war that ended only in 1847. The struggle for control over Arab territory—the term of art began to be "pacification"—was entwined with an ambitious but "anarchical" policy of European colonization.[5]

For many years, the war in North Africa appeared to be a matter of one step forward, two steps back. In 1840, however, Governor-General Thomas Bugeaud formalized the goal of total conquest and systematized the war's sporadically brutal tactics. Under his command, mobile columns of French troops deliberately ravaged all territory not under French control in order to prevent Arabs from sowing, harvesting, and grazing.[6] The aim of these successful *razzia* was to instill terror and destroy tribal cohesion by taking war to the civilian population in Arab villages. The predictable result was disease, famine, and eventual Arab disaffection from the war effort.[7] Beyond the use of *razzia,* Bugeaud defended controversial episodes of mass killings of civilians by French

5. See Charles-André Julien, *Histoire de l'Algérie contemporaine: La conquête et les débuts de la colonisation (1827–1871)* (Paris: Presses Universitaires de France, 1964), 107–63.

6. Steeped in the Greek and Roman classics, French military men frequently invoked the Roman conquest of North Africa in discussing the conduct of the war. Bugeaud noted that he was reviving the tactics of Metellus (mobile striking columns and *razzia*) that were tailored to the North African enemy. On the preoccupation with Rome, see Patricia M. E. Lorcin, "Rome and France in Africa: Recovering Colonial Algeria's Latin Past," *French Historical Studies* 25 (2002): 299–300.

7. In 1843 a French captain wrote in letters home: "Grass no longer grows where the French army has set foot; . . . We scour the country, we kill, we burn, we carve up, we chop down, all for the best in this best of all worlds." Lucien-François de Montagnac to Célestine de Montagnac, May 2, 1843, *Lettres d'un soldat: Neuf années de campagnes en Afrique* (Paris: E. Plon Nourrit, 1885), 308. By 1848 it is estimated that over a tenth of the Arab population had been killed and the economy was in ruins. Raphael Danziger, *Abd al-Qadir and the Algerians: Resistance to the French and Internal Consolidation* (New York: Holmes & Meier, 1977), xi.

officers as salutary episodes of terror that would hasten the end of the war.[8]

In the seventeen years until conquest was attained, there was a high degree of self-consciousness among members of the French political class about the aims and conduct of this colonial war. In pamphlets and in the Chamber of Deputies, they debated the potential value of any North African possession, the wisdom of colonization, the organization of the settler colony, the rationality of apparently ever-expanding military operations, the morality of French conduct of the war, the frightening "barbarism" of the enemy, and the nature of military/civilian relations in a democratic regime. Tocqueville was a keen participant in these debates.

TOCQUEVILLE AND "*LA GRANDE AFFAIRE D'AFRIQUE*"

Shortly after the dispatch of French troops to blockade (and eventually to seize) Algiers, Tocqueville discussed this expedition in letters to his brother Édouard. Like most of the French political class, he believed that the alleged trigger—the need to avenge a slight to the French envoy—was merely a cynical ploy by Charles X to shore up the government's popularity before parliamentary elections.[9] More important for his subsequent defense of French policy in Africa, however, Tocqueville was struck by the tendency of this incident to mute petty partisanship. There was, he noted, "truly a national spirit in the way in which this question has reunited

8. General Bugeaud called the military policies alleged to be necessary in Algeria (including infamous "enfumades," or the smoking of populations in caves) a different kind of legality, "brutal but logical." Quoted in Jean-Pierre Bois, *Bugeaud* (Paris: Fayard, 1999), 379. On this scorched-earth warfare, see also Julien, *Histoire de l'Algérie contemporaine*, 177–78.

9. "Le ministère n'a pas fait coïncider sans dessein l'affaire d'Alger avec les nouvelles élections," Tocqueville wrote to his brother Édouard and sister-in-law Alexandrine, March 24, 1830. Tocqueville, *Oeuvres complètes,* vol. 14, *Correspondance familiale,* ed. J. P. Mayer, André Jardin, and Françoise Mélonio (Paris: Gallimard, 1951–), 60. The projected war, Tocqueville notes in a subsequent letter, is only "un coup de tambour, comme tu sais, pour tourner toutes les têtes." Tocqueville to Édouard and Alexandrine, April 6, 1830, in *Oeuvres complètes,* 14:64.

opinions."[10] Although his trip to America and the writing of the two volumes of *Democracy* absorbed much of his energy during the next decade, Tocqueville continued to follow events in Africa closely, even thinking briefly of settling there.[11]

In 1837, Tocqueville launched his first election campaign by writing two "Letters on Algeria" that acknowledged many mistakes in the French conduct of the war but nevertheless looked forward to a revitalization of North Africa, to "two peoples of different civilizations [managing] to refound themselves as a single whole."[12] He painted an optimistic portrait in which the French would hold North Africa with the willing consent and support of the indigenous populations. A year later, he began to read the Koran, hoping to find points of affinity between Muslim and Christian doctrine that would ease such a joint venture.[13] Tocqueville traveled to Algeria for the first time in May 1841 as part of an official parliamentary group, and on his return he wrote a substantial "Travail sur l'Algérie," concluding grimly that his former hope to fuse the two populations had been a chimera.[14] Now his focus was on the need to quell resistance as quickly as possible, on the morally dubious measures that were necessary for such a victory (a war in which "we burn harvests, ... empty silos, and finally ... seize unarmed men, women and children"), on the relationship between domination and colonization, and on the pressing challenges involved in implanting a successful European colony.[15]

10. Tocqueville to Édouard and Alexandrine, April 6, 1830, in *Oeuvres complètes*, 14:65; cf. Tocqueville to Édouard and Alexandrine, March 24, 1830, in *Oeuvres complètes*, 4:60.

11. André Jardin, *Tocqueville: A Biography*, trans. Lydia Davis with Robert Hemenway (London: Peter Halban, 1988), 319–20.

12. Pitts, "Second Letter on Algeria (22 August 1837)," in Tocqueville, *Writings on Empire and Slavery*, 24.

13. "Notes on the Koran (March 1838)," in Tocqueville, *Writings on Empire and Slavery*, 27–35. Eventually Tocqueville became convinced that the religion of Mohammed was an impenetrable barrier to assimilation.

14. "Essay on Algeria (October 1841)," in Tocqueville, *Writings on Empire and Slavery*, 111. This work remained unpublished until it was included in volume 3 of the *Oeuvres complètes* in 1962. Soon after it was written, Tocqueville passed it on to Beaumont, who at that time was planning a book on Algeria.

15. "Essay on Algeria," 70, 123, 127. Tocqueville's belief that France could not abandon Algeria without dishonor never wavered; see his claim in the "First

It is clear from these writings that Tocqueville was a steadfast proponent of French emigration to Africa to create a settler society, and that by 1837 he was convinced of the need to control a substantial part of the territory (in contrast to limited or restrained occupation) in order to secure a zone of colonization. Both were contested policies among the center left groups in the Chamber with which he was loosely aligned. For the most part, he supported the Ministry on Algerian policy, even though he remained a sharp critic of its implementation. He supported Bugeaud's scorched-earth policies as necessary to break the hold of Abd-al-Kader on the tribes and had by 1840 completely given up on any "quick, brilliant, honorable" end to the war.[16]

In a characteristic reach for a comparative perspective, Tocqueville began in the early 1840s to envision writing several articles on "the causes that produced and that sustain the astonishing greatness of the English in India." This subject was central, he wrote in a letter to François Buloz, since "the crux of all great European affairs lies in Asia. This is particularly so for us now that we have the colony of Algeria."[17] The implicit contrast between successful Britain and struggling France, bogged down in a battle to pacify North Africa and regularize her rule, is clear in the organization of his reading notes on India and in the draft of the first part of this projected work.[18]

Tocqueville gave his only major speech on Algeria in June 1846,

---

Report on Algeria (1847)," in Tocqueville, *Writings on Empire and Slavery,* 167–68: "Our preponderance in Europe, the order of our finances, the lives of part of our citizenry, and our national honor are engaged here in the most compelling manner."

16. Tocqueville to Léon Faucher, July 5, 1840, unpublished (from Françoise Mélonio, to be published in a forthcoming volume of the *Oeuvres complètes*). I do not believe that Christian Bégin's portrait of Tocqueville as a reluctant colonizer and halfhearted supporter of the war, pushed into this position by French public opinion, can be sustained. See the largely exculpatory account in Bégin's "Tocqueville et l'Algérie," *La Revue Tocqueville/The Tocqueville Review* 30, no. 2 (2009): 179–203.

17. Tocqueville to F. Buloz, October 2, 1840, unpublished (from F. Mélonio).

18. Apparently he abandoned the work, he said much later, because "he would have had to go there in order to understand well what I wanted to talk about." Tocqueville to Lord Hatherton, November 27, 1857, in Tocqueville, *Selected Letters on Politics and Society,* ed. Roger Boesche, trans. James Toupin and Roger Boesche (Berkeley: University of California Press, 1985), 359. For

followed by a second three-month trip to Africa. As victory finally appeared imminent, and driven by the desire to "see and judge African affairs for myself," he toured Algeria from October to December 1846.[19] His study of the country during this trip, as well as the perspective on *arcana imperii* he had gained by his study of India, are reflected in the two long parliamentary reports that he wrote in 1847 as the *rapporteur* of a legislative committee on the organization of the peace and the future of the colony.

In what ways are Tocqueville's journeys into Africa analogous to those earlier trips to America, England, and Ireland that provided much of the raw material for *Democracy in America?* In 1841, until illness forced his return from Algeria to France, Tocqueville kept a diary in which he recorded long passages from his interlocutors' conversations, and his own vivid first impressions.

> First appearance of the town: I have never seen anything like it. Prodigious mix of races and costumes, Arab, Kabyle, Moor, Negro, Mahonais, French. Each of these races, tossed together in a space much too tight to contain them, speaks its language, wears its attire, displays different mores. This whole world moves about with an activity that seems feverish. The entire lower town seems in a state of destruction and reconstruction. On all sides, one sees nothing but recent ruins, buildings going up; one hears nothing but the noise of the hammer. It is Cincinnati transported onto the soil of Africa.[20]

He also reported in a series of letters to friends and family. As in his earlier voyages, we find him grilling his informants, always returning to the central questions that preoccupy him, and trying out formulations

---

original French, see Tocqueville, *Oeuvres complètes,* ed. Gustave de Beaumont (Paris: Michel Lévy-frères, 1864–66), 6:423.

19. Tocqueville to Francisque de Corcelle, October 11, 1846, in *Oeuvres complètes,* 15:218.

20. "Notes on the Voyage to Algeria in 1841," in Tocqueville, *Writings on Empire and Slavery,* 36. Much of the evidence for Tocqueville's activities on this trip comes from a journalist's account. See Auguste Bussière, "Le Maréchal Bugeaud et la colonisation de l'Algérie, souvenirs et récits de la vie coloniale en Algérie," in Tocqueville, *Œuvres,* Bibliothèque de la Pléiade (Paris: Gallimard, 1991–), 1:907–53.

of ideas that later appear in his manuscripts and published works. He is at once observer, thinker, and potential pedagogue. What he says at the beginning of *Democracy in America* (in a passage suppressed in the published edition) will be quite true of his Algerian texts as well: "[T]he work that you are about to read is not a travelogue."[21] But when he visited Boston, London, or Dublin, Tocqueville was primarily a private citizen and a passionately curious intellectual, on the lookout for ways to refine and elaborate his general *idées mères* about the effects of the democratic revolution and its impact in different societies. In Africa he was not merely a citizen but a representative of France, not just an intellectual but an official partly responsible for solving an immediate political problem. His informants, found disproportionately among French civil and military officials, rather than among colonists or *indigènes*, supply a narrower type of knowledge.

America and England appear in Tocqueville's texts as teeming laboratories for studying modern political culture and for identifying the possible interactions among ideas, institutions, and political action. They offer a fertile mix of familiarity and distance: close enough to be brought into the same comparative frame, far enough away to induce analytical clarity through a productive sense of wonder. Africa, in contrast, seems less an open territory over which his thought roams freely than a restricted field of interrogation or, as Jennifer Pitts has put it, "a laboratory for ideas of governance."[22] It is not that he is unwilling to face uncomfortable facts—he details the failings of France with sometimes brutal clarity—but the range of his imaginative sympathy is reduced. Tocqueville does not forget that Africa is there to be mastered even more than understood.

As Tocqueville's writings on empire have become more available in translation, and as both Anglophone and Francophone political theorists have begun to grapple with the transnational aspects of liberal democratic theory, scholars have increasingly puzzled over the dissonance between Tocqueville's imperial and liberal voices. One fault

21. *DA*, 3.

22. Jennifer Pitts, "Liberalism, Democracy and Empire: Tocqueville on Algeria," in *Reading Tocqueville: From Oracle to Actor*, ed. Raf Geenens and Annelien De Dijn (London: Palgrave Macmillan, 2007), 18.

line in these debates centers on the question of whether the apparent tension between Tocqueville's defense of French imperialism and his liberalism is illusory or real. Tzvetan Todorov and Stéphane Dion, for example, construe Tocqueville as a proponent of realpolitik who believed that the claims of justice stopped at national borders. By projecting the liberal rights of individuals onto sovereign national entities acting in an anarchic international state of nature, Tocqueville could put French national interests first without inconsistency. Thus, there is no real paradox to be explained.[23] Tocqueville, however, was never a liberal social contract theorist in the classical sense. Moreover, he always maintained that national majorities are not morally free to do whatever they choose either within or beyond their borders. Thus, this interpretation rather implausibly ignores a wealth of textual evidence. In contrast, beginning with Melvin Richter's classic article "Tocqueville on Algeria," more careful readers have perceived a real interpretive conundrum in Tocqueville's inconsistent universalism. What Roger Boesche has recently called the "dark side of Tocqueville," his apparent readiness to ignore the insights of his own liberalism, has called for explanation and contextualization.[24] How did he square his commitment to liberty with his embrace of permanent colonial domination?

23. "Introduction: Tocqueville et la doctrine coloniale," in Tocqueville, *De la colonie en Algérie,* ed. Tzvetan Todorov (Paris: Editions complexe, 1988), 24–27; Stéphane Dion, "Durham et Tocqueville sur la colonisation libérale," *Revue d'études canadiennes/Review of Canadian Studies* 25, no. 1 (Spring 1990): 60–77.

24. See Roger Boesche, "The Dark Side of Tocqueville: On War and Empire," *Review of Politics* 67 (2005): 737–52. Melvin Richter initiated the discussion of Tocqueville's imperialism in "Tocqueville on Algeria," *Review of Politics* 25 (July 1963): 362–99. In the growing literature that addresses this tension, see especially the works of Jennifer Pitts, "Empire and Democracy: Tocqueville and the Algeria Question," *Journal of Political Philosophy* 8, no. 3 (2000): 295–318; her introduction to Tocqueville, *Writings on Empire and Slavery,* ix–xxxviii; *A Turn to Empire: The Rise of Imperial Liberalism in Britain and France* (Princeton: Princeton University Press, 2005), 189–239; "Liberalism, Democracy and Empire: Tocqueville on Algeria," *Reading Tocqueville,* 12–30; and "Republicanism, Liberalism, and Empire in Postrevolutionary France," in *Empire and Modern Political Thought,* ed. Sankar Muthu (Cambridge: Cambridge University Press, 2012). See also Michael Hereth, *Alexis de Tocqueville: Threats to Freedom in Democracy,* trans. George Bogardus (Durham, N.C.: Duke University Press, 1986), 145–65;

ARGUMENTS FOR EMPIRE

Tocqueville does not directly address the normative issues of whether and when the aggression of one nation against another can be considered just. On the contrary, he assumes that conquest is a fact of political life, in both aristocratic and democratic times. This assumption does not mean, however, that one cannot distinguish morally better and worse types of domination. In his various discussions of the Spanish conquistadores, the Anglo-American encounters with indigenous peoples, and the English in Ireland, the following distinctions emerge. The conquered may be assimilated and treated humanely (good) or shunned and exploited (bad), or driven away, even exterminated (very bad).[25] One may also condemn deliberate bad faith and warfare that is more barbarous than necessity requires. These moral judgments sporadically surface in his writings on Algeria and India, but for the most part he ruthlessly disregards them, defending the brutal war against the Arabs and the invasive colonization project as vital for France.[26]

Scholars have identified three kinds of arguments in Tocqueville's texts justifying the conquest of Asian or African territories by European powers: the requirement of a great power to maintain international standing by projecting "grandeur," the beneficial effects on domestic

---

Richard Boyd, "Tocqueville's Algeria," *Society* (September/October 2001): 65–70; Cheryl B. Welch, "Colonial Violence and the Rhetoric of Evasion: Tocqueville on Algeria," *Political Theory* 31, no. 2 (April 2003): 247–57, and "Tocqueville on Fraternity and Fratricide," *The Cambridge Companion to Tocqueville*, 303–36; Margaret Kohn, "Empire's Law: Alexis de Tocqueville on Colonialism and the State of Exception," *Canadian Journal of Political Science* 42, no. 2 (June 2008): 255–78. In French the literature is more sparse, but see Jardin, *Tocqueville: A Biography*, 316–42; Françoise Mélonio, "Nations et nationalismes," *La Revue Tocqueville/ The Tocqueville Review* 19, no. 1 (1997): 61–75; Seloua Luste Boulbina, "Présentation," *Tocqueville sur l'Algérie* (Paris: Flammarion, 2003), 7–41; Jean-Louis Benoît, *Tocqueville: Un destin paradoxal* (Paris: Bayard, 2005), 264–79; and Bégin, "Tocqueville et l'Algérie."

25. In his later writings on Algeria, he settles uneasily on a different projected scenario, in which conquerors treat the conquered humanely without assimilation. See the section *Les anciens habitants de l'Algérie*, below, for my discussion of the tensions in this view.

26. I have explored some of these mechanisms of assuaging moral qualms in "Colonial Violence."

politics and nation-building, and a duty to civilize the uncivilized (the infamous *mission civilisatrice*). The first two, closely linked in his mind, are quite evident in Tocqueville's discussions of the French in North Africa and the English in India. The third, however, is a trickier business. In context, Tocqueville appears the most tepid of civilizers. Given his rich sociological appreciation of the persistence of *moeurs,* and his dread of imposing uniformity on plurality, this hesitance to embrace a civilizing mission is not surprising.

International Imperatives

From his first speech in the Chamber (expressing outrage and even threatening war because of the pointed exclusion of France from the settlement of the Eastern question) it was clear that Tocqueville believed that the primary goal of French foreign policy must be to reclaim her rightful position in Europe. The debacle of the revolutionary and imperial years had damaged France's standing among the great civilized nations. To play this role again, she needed to project her power on a par with the other great nations, especially England.[27] Success in Algeria was key to this parity. The great project of launching a civilized colony in Africa would help France reclaim her role as an equal arbiter of Europe's destiny.[28] Indeed, if France abandoned North Africa, then another civilized power would move into the vacuum and would reap any potential advantages in power and prestige. By the late 1830s, Tocqueville is convinced that retreat would be ruinous. To withdraw from Africa would disgrace France and weaken her beyond repair in Europe, which would regard this action as "yielding to her own impotence and succumbing to her own

27. See Seymour Drescher for the clearest articulation of Tocqueville and Beaumont's strategy of offering an independent alternative to what they characterized during the 1840s as Guizot's spineless pandering to England. *Tocqueville and England* (Cambridge, Mass.: Harvard University Press, 1964), 152–69.

28. Beaumont had explicitly argued in a parliamentary report on the organization of civil law in the colony, "Algeria is comparatively as great an enterprise for France as India is for England," Ministère de la Guerre. Commission de colonisation de l'Algérie. *Rapport fait au nom de la seconde sous-commission, par M. Gustave de Beaumont, le 20 juin 1842. Organisation civile, administrative, municipale et judiciaire* (Paris: Imprimerie royale, 1843), 40.

lack of courage."[29] As Hugh Brogan has noted, this was the logic of Pericles: "[Y]ou now hold your empire down by force; it may have been wrong to take it; it is certainly dangerous to let it go."[30] The argument for French grandeur, however, was not merely a matter of national hubris. Tocqueville believed that France had an obligation to assume the responsibilities of a great power, to set civilized norms, to arbitrate disputes, and to counteract the influence of other powers. Reestablishing the preeminence of France would indirectly promote the interests of Europe and the stability of the international system.[31] To abandon this duty was shameful.

Domestic Drama

A second reason for persisting in Algeria was the impact of the French colonizing venture on domestic French politics, in particular the provision of a dramatic common focus and the diffusion of class rancor. Drawn into an imaginative vision that transcended petty self-interest, all citizens could find in this expansion into a new world a patriotic renewal of faith in *la grande nation*. Tocqueville, of course, believed that this capacity to subordinate personal interest to the good of the whole was the sine qua non of a free people. He was struck again and again by the ability of the English to sustain such cross-class cooperation, and he saw a common pride in their Indian "possession" as an important ingredient in this mix.[32] Unlike some on the Left, Tocqueville doubted that France could successfully expand toward the Rhine, a foreign policy course that would cause Europe to close ranks

---

29. "Essay on Algeria," 59. Cf. the social economist Eugène Buret, who argued that if France abandoned the conquest she would—like Spain earlier—leave only "humiliating traces of her own powerlessness" in Africa. *Question d'Afrique* (Paris: Ledoyen, 1842), 35.

30. Hugh Brogan, *Alexis de Tocqueville: A Life* (New Haven, Conn.: Yale University Press, 2006), 399.

31. See the discussion by David Clinton, *Tocqueville, Lieber, and Bagehot: Liberalism Confronts the World* (London: Palgrave, 2003), 24–43.

32. The domination of India, Tocqueville argues, brings a "sentiment of greatness and power" to the whole people, and he notes that a conquest should be judged by other criteria than financial and commercial value. "L'Inde," *Oeuvres complètes*, 3:478.

against her. But the conquest and colonization of Algeria offered a glorious outlet. André Jardin has commented that Tocqueville saw the African venture as a way to unite the political class (*le pays légal*) with the rest of the country (*le pays réel*).[33] Projecting French power into the world indirectly built domestic bridges.

A Civilizing Mission?

A third potential argument justifying French domination over the Arabs and Kabyles of North Africa, and European rule over "barbarous" countries in general, is the right and duty of the advanced to rule the backward in order to civilize them. All careful readers of Tocqueville have noted that he thoroughly rejected racial arguments for the inferiority of a people, but it is just as clear that he accepted cultural and historical ones. He believed that peoples become enlightened at different rates, that enlightenment entails economic and social development, that development brings power, and that the power of civilized nations seduces the less civilized. These beliefs underlie Tocqueville's discussion of relations among European nations no less than his understanding of Europe's colonial diaspora.[34] In these assumptions, Tocqueville reflected a widely accepted theory that all peoples pass through the stages of hunting/gathering, herding, and agriculture before arriving at civilization. Adopting contemporary usage, Tocqueville often referred to hunter-gatherers as savage, while conflating pastoral and agricultural stages as barbaric or imperfectly civilized.

Tocqueville had no doubt that civilization definitively transformed the pattern of confrontation and conflict among nations by privileging the European powers.[35] But this belief in European superiority

33. Introduction to *Oeuvres complètes* (Pléiade), 1:xxxiv.

34. On the different levels of civilization among Europeans, see *DA*, 539–40*n*19. Tocqueville, for example, speculates that Swiss federalism is difficult because of the differing levels of civilization of the cantons. See *DA*, 590–91*n*t, and "Voyage en Suisse (1836)," *Oeuvres complètes* (Pléiade), 1:631.

35. See Tocqueville's letter to Henry Reeve, April 12, 1840, in *Oeuvres complètes*, 6:58. See also a much later letter to Gobineau, November 13, 1855, *Oeuvres complètes*, 9:243: "[The Europeans] will be in another hundred years the transformers of the globe that they inhabit and the masters of their species. Nothing is more clearly announced in advance by Providence. If they are often, I admit it,

does not mean that he appealed to civilization as a defense of empire in anything like the strong manner used by English liberals or many of his French contemporaries. If a "civilizing mission" calls for the deliberate conversion of indigenous peoples to European civilization through education, missionary efforts, or state policy, with the aim of eventually transforming native law, custom, and religious practice, then in Tocqueville the call was faint.

In exploring the question of the ways in which Tocqueville saw the right and duty to civilize connected to European colonial rule, we first must take heed of a key distinction that runs through everything Tocqueville has to say about expansion into new worlds: the difference between domination (ruling a defeated population) and colonization (displacing or replacing a part or the whole of that population).[36] There can be domination without significant colonization (for example, the case of Ottoman Algeria or British India); colonization without domination (if the territory is "empty," or if the indigenous population dies out or is exterminated, as sometimes happened in North America or the Caribbean); or a combination of domination and colonization (the French in Algeria). Tocqueville's civilizing rhetoric must be understood in relation to these different sorts of imperial expansion.

Invasion and domination of one people by another is an old story. It is what the Turks did in Algeria, and Tocqueville sometimes uses the phrase "to rule in the manner of the Turks" as a shorthand for dominating another country successfully with the tacit consent of the conquered, a consent inferred by the lack of overt resistance. Indeed, he does not always use the phrase "in the manner of the Turks" in a pejorative way. It sometimes just means the shrewd and prudent administration of a foreign country (in one's own interest to be sure) by judiciously dividing and conquering, and by conciliating key members of the defeated elites. But sometimes he does seem to condemn rule "in

---

great knaves, they are at any rate knaves to whom God has given force and power, and whom He has manifestly put for a time at the head of the human race."

36. "There are two ways to conquer a country: the first is to subordinate the inhabitants and govern them directly or indirectly. That is the English system in India. The second is to replace the former inhabitants with the conquering race. This is what Europeans have almost always done." "Essay on Algeria," 61.

the manner of the Turks." Though they were not ineffective as conquerors, the Turks were too greedy and rapacious, a result of their own
barbarism. For example, they collected taxes from Arab and Berber
indigènes to swell the coffers of the *dey,* without using those taxes to
defray the expenses of governing the conquered territory, to maintain
roads, or to dispense impartial justice.

The British, Tocqueville notes, ruled India in the manner of the
Turks—albeit as kinder, gentler Turks—and it is just this achievement
that he initially admires. In his projected work on India, Tocqueville
intended to capture the attention of his readers by first puncturing the
myth of the supposedly great British feat in conquering the subconti-
nent. On the contrary, he argues, the conquest was completely understandable given the distraction of the French with revolution and war,
the acquiescent nature of the major Indian religions, the indifference
and self-sufficiency of Indian communes, the lack of Indian national
feeling due to the caste system, the petty squabbling of Indian princes,
and the familiarity of the Indians with rule by foreigners of another
religion. Indeed, "the English were swept into domination of India by
a current stronger than themselves."[37] What needs to be explained is
something quite different: the ability of the British to organize the conquest and to govern India, despite many initial injustices and scandals,
despite policies that impoverished the population, and despite such
potentially disastrous mistakes as importing the complicated forms of
British justice. The eventual establishment of regular and moderate
government, of civilian control that was superior to the military but
not itself above the law, of rule over a large, diverse empire that forsook
the imposition of uniformity or centralization, and of functional coor-
dination between the East India Company and the British state—these
are the feats worthy of study.

Tocqueville is quite clear that these achievements fall far short
of bringing civilization to India. Despite pious and self-justifying
rhetoric—they claim to do everything out of principle, or for the "good
of the indigenous people," or for the benefit of the very princes they are
attempting to conquer—the British actually rule as milder and more
skillful Turks. While they do use taxes raised from their subjects to

37. "L'Inde," *Oeuvres complètes,* 3:458.

defray the expenses of governing, they do nothing to revive the country, for example, by building public works. "So far the English have ruled over India for themselves and not for her."[38] Moreover, according to Tocqueville, while Indian social structures were slowly beginning to weaken, the Indians gave no sign of wishing to adopt European civilization or religion. He writes in a marginal note that India cannot be civilized while she retains her religion, and a religion "of this kind" is so tightly mixed with the social state, morals, and laws that it is impossible to destroy, maintaining its hold even after people have ceased to believe in it. To civilize one must break into this "vicious circle," a daunting and dangerous business.

Despite the British failure to bring either economic development or cultural change to India, Tocqueville holds up their ability to dominate the continent successfully as instructive for France. Having achieved her conquest of North Africa, France must not shrink from the little acts of violence necessary to consolidate it. In 1846, Tocqueville wrote a long revealing letter to General Lamoricière outlining the following possible "*violences de détail*" the French might adopt in Algeria to consolidate their rule.[39]

1. Turn the masses against the elites. A tried-and-true method of consolidating a new regime, this strategy probably would not work in Algeria, because elites had a religious hold on the people, and because the indigenous populations had not yet reached a social state that would make them susceptible to it. Tocqueville adds that such an appeal to the masses is, in any case, always dangerous.
2. Give some families individual property in exchange for their tacit support of French seizure or "purchase" of tribal lands.
3. Link the interests of some indigenous elites to the French by giving them property and power confiscated from unfriendly tribes. These elites will then become "usurpers like us," and will deflect hatred of the French onto themselves.

38. "L'Inde," *Oeuvres complètes*, 505; 480.
39. Tocqueville to Louis de Lamoricière, April 5, 1846, in *Lettres choisies: Souvenirs (1814–1859)*, ed. Françoise Mélonio and Laurence Guellec (Paris: Gallimard, 2003), 561–67.

Though apparently callous, such measures, Tocqueville insists, correspond to the practice of all conquerors. He concludes:

> In places where no revolution occurred in ownership or in the social state, a revolution did nevertheless take place in the basis of political power. The locus of power shifted. The ambition of some was used to counter the hostility of others. *This was the fundamental method of the English in India.* Can nothing similar be done in Africa? If I'm not mistaken, political power was constituted in Algeria as it has always been in nations that are at once aristocratic and half-civilized: the government associated itself with part of the population in order to govern the rest. With the aid of certain privileged tribes, it acted on the remainder of the population. *This was the method of the Turks.* I believe that in this respect they were imitated by Abd-el-Kader, who probably did no more than transfer the privilege from one set of hands to another. Why don't we do the same thing? [emphasis added][40]

Tocqueville assumes that for a very long time France will rule over the Arab *indigènes* in North Africa as "better" Turks.[41] I take up a more detailed discussion of his view of the fate of the *indigènes* below.

The demands of civilized conquest—that is, acting as better Turks—appear in Tocqueville's writings to be more arduous than awe inspiring. France was struggling, he admitted in 1841, even to do as well as the "barbarous" Turks or the Arabs, whose actions could sometimes be construed as more civilized than those of the French.[42] Much less keen

40. *Lettres choisies: Souvenirs,* 563 (passage translated by Arthur Goldhammer).

41. In a letter to Corcelles, September 26, 1840, Tocqueville acknowledges that the goal is to achieve domination analogous to the Turks: "cette domination à des conditions analogues à celle des Turcs est très praticable et qu'elle aurait lieu si, ce qui est possible, nous arrivons enfin à détruire Abd-el-Kader." *Oeuvres complètes,* 15:151. See also "Essay on Algeria," 62, 65.

42. It is painful to Tocqueville that the French bungled the initial conquest and never really recovered from their mistakes. They dismissed anyone who knew how to administer the *indigènes*; they unsettled property rights; they antagonized the Arabs and threw them into the arms of new nationalist leaders. Rather than exploit the undisputed technical, administrative, and moral strengths of French civilization, the French squandered those advantages, thus necessitating a brutal war. "I returned from Africa with the distressing notion that we are now fighting

on the domination of Algeria than on the founding of a new society, Tocqueville supported the conquest only because he believed it necessary for the safety and growth of a French/European colony. "Colonization is not an accessory to the thing that we are doing in Africa, it is the thing itself."[43] In a country like Algeria, with a restive warlike population and without truly settled agriculture or well-formulated notions of individual property, domination *tout court*, according to Tocqueville, would be precarious and unproductive. But colonization—founding a new society where freedom could flourish—engaged his deepest instincts.

Colonization complicates the debate over whether Tocqueville believed in a civilizing mission, for some of his soaring rhetoric about the march of European civilization refers to the displacement rather than the development of populations. The valley of Metidja, he wrote from Algeria in a letter to Jean Denis Lanjuinais, appeared to be populated only by a few Arabs thrusting and parrying with knives. As such, it presented "a spectacle at once admirable and saddening. In the hands of a civilized people this immense valley would be one of the most beautiful countries on earth."[44] Tocqueville found the sheer spectacle of a dynamic European people transforming the desert into a developed commercial society to be a beautiful vision; a way for the French to make a striking move into the democratic future.

Out of Africa: Lessons for Democratic Founders

UNE FLORISSANTE NATION

The ideal of "a flourishing nation" in North Africa filled with roads, modern communications, capitalist agriculture, and energetic and self-interested colonists inspired in Tocqueville an awe surprisingly

---

far more barbarously than the Arabs themselves. For the present, it is on their side that one meets with civilization" ("Essay on Algeria," 70). Cf. "First Report on Algeria," 141, and a letter of Tocqueville to his father, May 23, 1841, in *Oeuvres complètes*, 14:218–19.

43. "Notes diverses sur la colonisation de l'Algérie," in *Oeuvres complètes*, 3:289. Cf. "Essay on Algeria," 65.

44. Tocqueville to Lanjuinais, May 16, 1841, unpublished (from F. Mélonio).

free from ambivalence.[45] Though always guarded in his writings on free trade in the context of economic policy in France, Tocqueville enthusiastically endorses "libre-échange" and its effects in his colonial writings. Indeed, he hunts down all the economic errors committed in the European colony by misguided reformers who advocate collectivist schemes of colonization (whether military, socialist, monastic, or statist), and by military or civil officials who interfere in the economic affairs of the colony or arbitrarily suspend the rule of law.[46] Unlike the English, who do not subsidize their emigrants, but merely assure them a new territory where property and contracts are safe from force and fraud, the French, according to Tocqueville, export their administrative penchant to micromanage everything, but they fail to create a governmental structure with clear lines of responsibility. Indeed, the French have created a bureaucratic nightmare worse than anything found in France itself.[47]

In his second "Letter on Algeria," Tocqueville had argued that the alleged decline of the religious motive and the rise of material interest among indigenous peoples were among the most hopeful signs for their joining the French in a new civilization.[48] In the 1840s, when he had abandoned his earlier belief in these signs, he champions the cause of the economic colonists against the military, who manifest an imbecilic irritation with the colonists' desire to make money.[49] From a limited military point of view, Tocqueville admired French warriors in Africa, but he also believed that they "take on distorted proportions in the public imagination" and that their influence in the colony should be restricted.[50] It is not the exploits of citizen soldiers like Cincinnatus

45. The phrase appears in a letter to Léon Faucher, July 15, 1841, unpublished (from F. Mélonio).

46. "Essay on Algeria," 90–93. For a discussion of the political economy implicit in his colonial writings, see Christian Bégin, "Tocqueville et l'économie politique," *La Revue Tocqueville/The Tocqueville Review* 29, no. 1 (2008): 202–5.

47. "First Report on Algeria," 148–49.

48. "Second Letter on Algeria," 25.

49. "Notes on Algeria," 57; see also "Essay on Algeria," 101.

50. "Essay on Algeria," 78; "Second Report on Algeria," 153–54.

that capture his imagination, but rather the "heroic" creation of a commercial "Cincinnati transported onto the soil of Africa."[51]

Tocqueville focuses above all on establishing a viable agricultural colony, commercially profitable and based on the "allure of gain and comfort."[52] He is absorbed in the need to attract independent capital, circulate credit, speed up the workings of the profit motive, and open up French markets to the colonists. "[W]hen [the colonist] is not exposing his own resources or counting on himself alone, he rarely displays that ardor, tenacity, and intelligence that make capital productive." The objective is not to benefit economic interests in France (in the short term, those interests may even suffer) but to create a vital economic and civic society peopled by colonists with "ardor, tenacity, and intelligence" who make both capital productive and (eventually) local civic life possible. Tocqueville's hope is that the state can create the conditions for this new society: civil and economic freedoms that will reinforce each other to create an invigorated character, "free, passionate and energetic."[53] Against much evidence and against all odds, he hoped that a new colonial venture—less like the old French empire in Canada and Louisiana and more like the vigorous English colonies in America—might create an inspiring monument to the glory of the French.[54]

Some characterizations of Tocqueville's analysis of the sources of vitality in American democracy overstate the extent to which he thought civic energy flowed from public to private life, rather than in the other direction.[55] In Tocqueville's America, we should remember,

51. "Notes on Algeria," 36.
52. "Essay on Algeria," 92.
53. "Essay on Algeria," 92. What was necessary was a rational governing infrastructure, and Tocqueville was willing to envision a very firm metropolitan hand in its creation. "You do not perceive any powerful, central conception guiding it toward a common end and keeping each of the parts that compose it within their natural limits" ("First Report on Algeria," 157).
54. "J'ai vu sous mes yeux les manières dont se peuplait l'Amérique du Nord. Quel grand exemple!" Tocqueville to Lamoricière, April 5, 1846, in *Lettres choisies,* 566–67.
55. For example, see Sheldon Wolin, *Tocqueville between Two Worlds: The Making of a Political and Theoretical Life* (Princeton, N.J.: Princeton University Press, 2001):

the qualities of independence and self-reliance needed for success in commerce tend to carry over into political life.[56] Good business requires steadiness, practical shrewdness, farsightedness, the ability to calculate risk, and a determination to beat the odds. So too does free politics. The trick is to create a structure in which these spillovers are productive, in which positive economic energies are harnessed to the public good. This vision is not bound geographically or conceptually to America. Tocqueville's writings on Algeria (composed during the period of his greatest private criticism of the mediocrity, place hunting, and individualism of the French middle classes) remind us of the extent to which he saw economic and political liberalism as both mutually reinforcing and in tension. When Tocqueville writes from the perspective of Algeria, where legal irregularities and military violence were the norm, the vision of a settled society that protected property and contracts takes on a positive allure. In 1841, for example, he contrasts what an ordinary citizen could expect in France—above all, guaranteed property rights, settled civil law, independent magistrates, and some influence on events—with the horror of their absence in the Algerian colony. How, he despaired, could France attract rational economic immigrants to such a "miserably anarchic" place?[57]

Tocqueville's embrace of economic civil society in Africa is all the more surprising in that the self-governing aspects of such a democratic society are muted. While he hopes that civil and political freedoms will eventually flourish in Algeria—indeed, without collective interests and actions there will be no "society"—he condones short-term restrictions on the press, a system of advisory councils that are appointed rather than elected, and tight control over all relations with the *indigènes:* "the electoral system, freedom of the press, the jury. These institutions are not necessary for the infancy of societies."[58] Tempering his enthusiasm for the potential future of the settler colony was the sober recognition

---

"[P]olitics vitalized the whole society, transmitting its energies to civil society rather than reflecting the impulses coursing through civil society" (208, cf. 258).

56. *DA*, 642, 1138.

57. "Essay on Algeria," 93, 98–105.

58. "Essay on Algeria," 111–12. See also Tocqueville's letter to Jules Dufaure from Algeria, November 6, 1846, which complains of the "profound anarchy" that characterizes the civil organization of the colony. *Lettres choisies,* 568.

that it was being formed amid a sea of Arab enmity and was populated by flawed immigrants whose passions could not be allowed free rein. The metropole had to police the fragile borders between two peoples, isolate the Europeans from the simmering resentment and hatred of the *indigènes,* and protect the natives from the aggression and intolerance of the settlers.

LES ANCIENS HABITANTS DE L'ALGÉRIE

In his "First Report on Algeria," written on the eve of victory, Tocqueville speaks about the obligation of the French to govern the "old inhabitants of Algeria" with decency, that is, to provide "a power that guides them, not only toward our interest, but in theirs... that works ardently for the continual development of their imperfect society ... that does not restrict itself to exploiting them."[59] But, Tocqueville admits, these sentiments are aspirations: statements of what ought to be "the permanent tendency and the general spirit of our government."[60] When he turns to concrete details of French policy, even in this public report attempting to reassure its readers that France will of course act with humanity and justice, the true difficulty of maintaining a balance between "our interest" and "theirs" emerges.

A Public Agenda for Algeria

The problem of acquiring territory for European settlement—not just any territory, but "the most fertile, best-irrigated, best-prepared lands"—was perhaps the most difficult policy issue facing the French.[61] Stubbornly attached to the American analogy, Tocqueville argues that Algeria was sparsely settled by peoples who, if not true nomads, were still "mobile" and had not developed settled agriculture. Thus there was room for French settlement.[62] Although he warns against "deceitful

59. "First Report on Algeria," 142.
60. "First Report on Algeria," 145.
61. "First Report on Algeria," 139.
62. Tocqueville introduces this theme in the "Second Letter on Algeria," 24, and continues to reformulate it throughout his writings on Algeria. He also pursues the analogy between Amerindians and Arabs in his correspondence with Francis Lieber, even as Lieber tries to disabuse him of it. See Tocqueville to Lieber, July 22, 1846, in *Œuvres complètes,* 7:109–12.

or derisory transactions" (the clear reference here is to the Americans' duplicitous treatment of the Indians), against confiscation without indemnity, and against expulsion from the land, he still thinks it is possible to gain access to land "either in concessions of rights, or in an exchange of lands."[63] He is referring here to the practice that he had mentioned in his letter to Lamoricière, that is, inviting Arabs to cede lands to the French state that they did not "need," in exchange for recognition of their individual or collective ownership of lands it allowed them to keep. Known as "cantonnement" (delimitation), such a policy was in fact pursued by the French and was deeply resented by the Arabs as unjust. In practice, it rapidly did turn into a policy of "refoulement" (expulsion from territory), helping to reopen an era of insurrection in 1859, the year of Tocqueville's death.[64]

A second issue was how to make the goal of "working ardently for their development" more than empty rhetoric in a society structured around inequality. At the very least, Tocqueville thought the French needed to address the damage they had done to Arab society. He recommends a modest rebuilding of the Muslim educational and charitable institutions, but he warns against going too far in that direction.[65]

63. "First Report on Algeria," 143. In the unpublished "Essay on Algeria," Tocqueville had admitted that it would never be possible to gain the land around Algiers without "violence" and that the army and initial civilian rule had left property relations in such a mess that the state might have to use forced expropriation of contested territories (often held by land speculators) once and for all to fix titles (87–88).

64. See Charles-Robert Ageron, *Modern Algeria: A History from 1830 to the Present,* trans. and ed. Michael Brett (London: Hurst & Company, 1990), 34–37. Even André Jardin, quite tolerant of the imperialist Tocqueville, notes that "the theory of *cantonnement* under which they [the tribes] were compensated with absolute title to part of the lands [they were forced to forfeit] would seem rather illusory" ("Second Report on Algeria," 255n4). The future held many acts of despoliation that would be presented as progress. Tocqueville warned against some of them—such as allowing Muslim lands to be thrown onto the free market. By 1919 the Muslims had lost 18.5 million acres, and 98 percent of lands in the Tell (the most favorable agricultural region) had been expropriated. See Benjamin Stora, *Algeria, 1830–2000: A Short History,* trans. Jane Marie Todd (Ithaca, N.Y.: Cornell University Press), 6–8.

65. Apparently Tocqueville wished to be even more severe about the excessive generosity of the French toward the Arabs, especially with regard to military

Next the French must abstain from interfering in Muslim religious institutions or civil law, which would dishonor the peace they had made with the *indigènes*. Tocqueville foresaw the creation of a permanently segregated society, and was opposed even to admitting young Arabs to French schools, because it would be "as dangerous as it would be useless to seek to suggest to them our mores, our ideas, our customs."[66] Indigenous society, then, should be pushed only in the "direction proper to it." By this phrase, Tocqueville seems to mean that any voluntary movement toward European notions of individual property and labor should be encouraged and that Arabs should be able to sell their labor to Europeans. "The European needs the Arab to make his lands valuable; the Arab needs the European to obtain a high salary."[67] It is hard to see how this "community of interests" (a sort of internal guest worker policy) could be expected to reconcile the Arabs to the French presence, especially because it was combined with exclusion from the political community. Tocqueville is quite clear that the Arabs were to be governed from above, that is, would be granted no civil guarantees beyond the provisions of Muslim civil law and no political rights. He thought it would be suicidal for the French to forget that the Arabs' warlike nature and legitimate grievances made them a formidable potential military threat; the Arab *indigènes* must be ruled by what amounted to a law of exception and subject to summary imprisonment or exile.[68]

The Kabyles (Berbers) posed a different problem. Settled agricultural peoples ensconced in mountain areas and fervently attached to the soil, they could be brought within the French orbit by a hands-off policy. One certainly shouldn't try to civilize them. In a dig at philanthropic civilizers, he noted that if you traveled to a Kabyle village to "speak about morality, civilization, fine arts, political economy, or

---

favors bestowed on Algerians, but he was dissuaded by other members of the commission. See "First Report on Algeria," 255*n*22.

66. "First Report on Algeria," 142. See also Jardin, *Tocqueville: A Biography*, 335.

67. "First Report on Algeria," 145.

68. Cf. Beaumont's *Rapports*, 2–7, which makes it clear that, politically, Arab rights would be the same as those of foreigners; that is, he explicitly placed the *indigènes* under an unaccountable political regime that ruled by decree rather than law.

philosophy,... they would assuredly cut off your head."[69] The Kabyles were not a threat to French colonization, as long as their lands
weren't confiscated or directly attacked. Tocqueville always vehemently
opposed expeditions into Berber territories, which he thought foolish
and unnecessary. If not attacked, the Kabyles would be peaceful trade
partners and would accept living in the dominant orbit of the French
as they had accepted the hegemony of the Turks.

Private Doubts

The dreaded example of American crimes against the Amerindians—
expulsion and extermination—was frequently invoked in French
debates about relations with the North African *indigènes*. In both public
and private, Tocqueville strenuously denied that he or the French government had any such intentions, and there is no reason to doubt his
sincerity. Nevertheless, Tocqueville thought that a very likely effect of
prolonged contact between the "civilized" French and the "barbarous"
Arabs would be to demoralize and dispirit the latter through no one's
explicit intention.[70] In his *Essay on Algeria,* never intended for publication in its unrevised state, he notes that those who have been to Algeria
"know that this state of things seems to become more so every day, and
that nothing can be done against it. The Arab element is becoming
more and more isolated, and little by little, it is dissolving. The Muslim
population always seems to be shrinking, while the Christian population is always growing."[71] Tocqueville's version of "lifting [the Arabs] in
our arms toward well-being and enlightenment," then, seems restricted
to allowing them to live in well-policed proximity to European commercial civilization, a contact from which he hoped rather vaguely that they
would eventually profit, but which he believed was much more likely to
produce demoralization and democratic decline.

69. "First Letter on Algeria," 7.
70. "First Report on Algeria," 144.
71. "Essay on Algeria," 111. In fact, the Muslim population continued to
decline during Tocqueville's lifetime. In 1830 there were probably around 3
million inhabitants; in 1851 the native population numbered not more than
2,324,000. In 1866 it was estimated at 2,652,000, but in the late 1860s it declined
again after a series of natural disasters (locusts, animal epidemics, and drought).
See Ageron, *Modern Algeria,* 4, 31, 44*n.*

In 1846, Tocqueville had a telling public and private interchange with his friend and usual political ally Francisque de Corcelle. A strong supporter of the conquest, Corcelle had turned a blind eye to the morally troubling slash-and-burn policies that brought success because he—like Tocqueville—had come to the conclusion that only by such policies would France ever defeat the Arabs. Corcelle, however, became alarmed at rhetoric in the colonial press that called for the extermination of the Arabs. In a long speech in the Chamber, he argued that having achieved military victory, the French now faced the urgent question of the treatment of the *indigènes*. Indeed, he was a more active civilizer than was Tocqueville, holding out modest hopes for conciliation and conversion of the Arabs by extending French law (which Tocqueville opposed) and by attracting Arab "colonists" to new villages (a process known as internal colonization). Increasingly religious, Corcelle also was more hopeful of eventual Christianization. He was even willing to consider supporting military colonization— Tocqueville's bête noire—precisely because he had become convinced that the army might be necessary in the countryside to protect the *indigènes* from settler violence.

In public, Tocqueville replied to Corcelle by misrepresenting his speech as a utopian hope to hold Algeria with the willing support of the Arabs. (Corcelle interjected, "I said nothing of the kind!")[72] In private, he acknowledged to Corcelle that the moral issue of what to do with the *indigènes* was very important, but establishing and protecting the European colony had to be the priority. In addressing Corcelle's fears that extermination would be the result of French policies, Tocqueville asserts that to push for the disappearance of the Arabs is cruel, absurd, and impractical. He adds, however: "[B]ut what should be done so that the two races enter into contact with one another? I confess with chagrin that here my mind is troubled and hesitates."[73] Even more frank in a letter to Laromicière, he says that his own experience and his study of history have shown that when conquerors are both more civilized and stronger, they do not assimilate the conquered but destroy or expel them. He ardently hopes the French will do better, but he has little

72. "Intervention in the Debate," 118.
73. Tocqueville to Corcelle, December 1846, in *Oeuvres complètes*, 15:224.

expectation of it.[74] The decline or disappearance of the Arabs in Algeria, like the Indians in America, then, is not something to be wished for, but it is something that may be overdetermined. Tocqueville's conscience troubles him at the thought because he realizes that this decline of the Arabs would conveniently remove their threat to the colony and solve a thorny problem for the French. Because such a wish is criminal, it must be resolutely repressed.

Final Thoughts: The Sepoy Rebellion

Although Tocqueville says almost nothing about Algeria after 1849, he does revisit the question of European imperialism in a series of letters about the Sepoy Rebellion in 1857 and 1858. Estranged from his own imperial government and just home from a triumphant trip to England after the publication of *L'ancien régime et la révolution*, Tocqueville was as well disposed to his "second homeland" as he ever would be.[75] His letters to English correspondents strike a uniformly sympathetic note of the following sort: your problems are our problems; my thoughts are with you in your hour of need, as should be those of all right-thinking Europeans! During the rebellion, he commiserates that English withdrawal from India would "be disastrous for the future of civilization and the progress of humanity."[76] After the British have regained control, he calls the British triumph a "victory for Christianity and civilization."[77] But why exactly would British defeat have been a disaster, and what sort of victory had been won? I do not believe that Tocqueville thought that the calamity averted was the loss of British tutelage in India, or that the victory gained was the eventual Christianization and civilization of the Indian peoples. Rather, a withdrawal from India would have been a great blow to English prestige and would have put in doubt the possibility of "civilized" imperial rule in general.[78] Civilized and humanitarian nations should be able to rule

74. Tocqueville to Laromicière, in *Lettres choisies*, 565–66.

75. Drescher, *Tocqueville and England*, 188–92.

76. Tocqueville to Henry Reeve, August 2, 1857, in *Oeuvres complètes*, 6:230

77. Tocqueville to Lord Hatherton, November 27, 1857, in *Oeuvres complètes* (Beaumont), 6:422.

78. See Tocqueville to Lady Thereza Lewis, October 18, 1857, in *Oeuvres complètes* (Beaumont), 6:411–12.

backward peoples more successfully and humanely than did semibarbarous conquerors like the Turks. Though, like all conquerors, they have to depend to some degree on force and fraud, they can also bring to bear technical superiority, administrative regularity and fairness, and the moral suasion exerted by a higher level of civilization. To abandon India would be to undermine the European claim to a superior technical and moral civilization (a claim in which Tocqueville believes passionately and proudly) and to bring shame on civilization by exhibiting cowardice in times that call for steady resolve. Abandoning India would also, of course, produce collateral damage: discrediting the sole liberal state among the European great powers and destabilizing international relations, as well as endangering French rule in Africa.

This whole episode, however, also causes Tocqueville to rethink his previous judgment that English rule in India constituted a successful model of rule as "better Turks." He now looks at English policy for mistakes rather than for positive lessons. Their very mildness allowed nationalism to grow and to swell into rebellion. At the same time, they antagonized native elites through their haughty exclusivity. In fact, the English no longer look all that superior to the French. Moreover, Tocqueville now appears to be more sensitive to the problem of indigenous elites who are treated as foreigners in their own land. After reading Henry Reeve's long piece about India in the *Edinburgh Review* of January 1858, an essay that proposes the introduction of a large English population into India, Tocqueville protests that such colonization would be a grave mistake that could only worsen England's particular problems.[79] He does not retract his support for colonization in Africa but does betray a heightened awareness of the connection between a European presence and native resentment, noting that the Arabs and Kabyles in Algeria resented colonists much more than soldiers.[80] Moreover, thickly populated and agricultural, India was not a candidate for colonization or for the founding of a new society. The physical and moral issues of acquiring territory for settlement—difficult but not

79. Tocqueville to Henry Reeve, January 30, 1858, in *Selected Letters*, 362–64. *Oeuvres complètes* (Beaumont), 6:426–30.

80. Tocqueville to Lord Hatherton, March 6, 1858, in *Oeuvres complètes* (Beaumont), 6:434.

impossible in societies like North America and North Africa, according to Tocqueville—would be insoluble in India. Thus, the English had no choice but to make a success of domination without colonization.

After the rebellion, Tocqueville assumes that successful domination (holding India with the tacit consent of indigenous elites) would require some basic reforms. He is forced to confront the issue that was implicit but muted in his earlier work on India: what did civilized England owe to her Indian subjects? While he repeats his judgment that the British have trumpeted a civilizing mission, but in a hundred years have done nothing to better the condition of their subjects, he is no longer content to pass over this hypocrisy with a few ironical comments. He now draws out the obvious inference. The English should have done better, and now must do better, or risk the loss of their empire. In a letter to Lord Hatherton, he notes, "[M]ore could have been expected of them" than to have ruled like better Turks.[81]

What is the "more" that the British should have done? Their task was "not only to dominate India, but to civilize it. These two things, indeed, are closely connected."[82] Tocqueville seems to be calling here for a form of domination that will gradually provide Indians access to economic opportunity. At the very least, the exploitative East India Company, which deliberately ruined native industries and put its own commercial interests above the well-being of Indian subjects, should be replaced by direct rule under the eye of Parliament and the public. He writes to Jean-Jacques Ampère that the rebellion shows that England must not only reconquer India but govern in a new way.[83] Tocqueville's correspondence with Reeve suggests that the new direction in British rule should focus on building an infrastructure of public works (roads, canals, and bridges) that will allow the country to become more self-sustaining and prosperous, with Indians eventually sharing in this development. Or, as he says to Lord Hatherton, "[A]s the [British] government tends more and more to apply the general principles that

81. Tocqueville to Lord Hatherton, November 27, 1857, in *Selected Letters*, 360. *Oeuvres complètes* (Beaumont), 6:423.

82. Tocqueville to Lord Hatherton, November 27, 1857, in *Selected Letters*, 360. *Oeuvres complètes* (Beaumont), 6:424.

83. Tocqueville to J. J. Ampère, August 9, 1857, in *Oeuvres complètes* (Beaumont), 6:404.

make Europe rich and enlightened, it will little by little make the Indians feel the advantages of our civilization and will bring them closer to it."[84] There is still, then, little taste for robust civilizing in the sense of transforming, educating, and moralizing a "backward" people.

Placing Tocqueville in the political landscape he inhabited allows us to understand why he succumbed to the temptation to ignore the claims of "imperfectly civilized" peoples to a free way of life. To have acknowledged such claims, he thought, would have led inevitably to the humiliation of France, the weakening of the system of civilized states, and the loss of an opportunity to strengthen France's democratic political culture by engaging its citizens in a transcendent common purpose. He hoped that French dominance of the Arabs would be no worse than that of their own leaders or previous conquerors, and might eventually even improve their lot—if they survived the experiment. He resolutely repressed moral unease about violence—large and small—as a political burden that a statesman must bear. How accurate and insightful were Tocqueville's judgments about European imperial and colonial aims and policies? Like Tocqueville himself, who dissected and criticized the ideas and policies of French ancien régime and revolutionary statesmen from the perspective of the political culture they inadvertently created, we must in part judge him from the point of view of the postcolonial world we have inherited. From that perspective, we must acknowledge that despite his sometimes shrewd and far-seeing insights, his vision was blinkered and his choices often wrong.

Tocqueville saw quite clearly that European imperialists had by their own failures created reactive violence and stimulated the growth of new nationalist ideologies. But he never thought these animosities could be lessened by any form of shared governance; rather, he believed that Europeans must rule in the manner of better Turks in order to contain these enmities and let them dissipate slowly in the mists of time. Although he resisted the impulse of French philanthropists to see the conquered peoples as clay to be shaped, he saw them largely as a threat to be managed and controlled, a threat that would naturally

---

84. Tocqueville to Lord Hatherton, March 6, 1858, in *Oeuvres complètes* (Beaumont), 6:434.

recede as Arab populations dwindled. Seduced by the American example, Tocqueville mistakenly believed that time was on the side of the French in Algeria. But the situation of two peoples inhabiting a common space without equity and parity unraveled along the seams that Tocqueville's own sensitivity to the dynamics of political struggle over status and honor would lead us to expect. His policy choices contributed to this ominous result, helping to set France on the course that he feared. Algeria did indeed become "a closed field, a walled arena, where the two peoples would have to fight without mercy, and where one of the two would have to die."[85] Tocqueville was warning against the moral disaster of expelling or destroying the Arabs, but ironically it was French Algeria that died. The imperial voyage ended with the French being driven out of Africa in a traumatic period of decolonization that ended as it had begun: in debates over torture and atrocity. If Tocqueville was no more blind to this future calamity than most of his contemporaries, those with a deep affinity for Tocquevillian analysis have done him the honor of arguing that "more could have been expected of him."

85. "First Report on Algeria," 146.

Part Two

Tocquevillian Voyages

12

Tocqueville's Voyage of Discovery from Sicily to America

FILIPPO SABETTI

The Liberty Fund bilingual edition of *Democracy in America,* with its extensive selection of early outlines, drafts, manuscript variants, correspondence, and other materials, provides unprecedented insight into the power of observation and method of inquiry Tocqueville displayed in his American voyage and how much he engaged in a conversation with himself and with others. With these unique features, the edition ensures that *Democracy in America* will continue to instruct, inspire, and foster interest in the "new political science"[1] that Tocqueville sought to create for a society of free men and women.

Numerous and diverse ingredients went into the launching of the new political science. The bilingual edition draws attention to the educational formation Tocqueville received at home, the stimulation from old and new literary sources, and the insights he derived from his own observations.[2] One important ingredient is Tocqueville's largely

Conferees of the Liberty Fund Colloquium "Tocqueville's Voyage I," Chicago, Ill., January 8–11, 2009, contributed ideas and suggestions to earlier drafts of this chapter. Barbara Allen, Aurelian Craiutu, Jeremy Jennings, and James T. Schleifer shared with me their knowledge of French history and thought. Christine Henderson played an essential role in the evolution of this work, help which I wish to gratefully remember.

1. Alexis de Tocqueville, *Democracy in America: Historical-Critical Edition of "De la démocratie en Amérique,"* ed. Eduardo Nolla, trans. James T. Schleifer, 4 vols. (Indianapolis: Liberty Fund, 2010), 16. This edition is hereafter cited as *DA.*

2. See also Alan Kahan, *Alexis de Tocqueville* (New York: Continuum, 2010), 5–6, 28–34; James T. Schleifer, *The Making of Tocqueville's "Democracy in America,"* 2nd ed. (Indianapolis: Liberty Fund, 1999).

forgotten 1827 notes on Sicily. There we can see how he manifested a passion to understand public affairs in a comparative perspective. In the American journey, we see how he amplified and extended that passion to a passion for liberty and self-government. Thus his voyage of discovery from Sicily to America was as much the discovery of new realities and relating them to his own country as it was the maturation of a mode of analysis that has given his work enduring quality.

In what follows, I first try to show why the 1827 Sicilian notes may be viewed as the start of Tocqueville's intellectual journey. I then set out to present the chief elements in his mode of analysis that transformed his power of observation into a political science appropriate to the new world of democracy, and I go on to discuss the reception and importance of that political science beyond France and the United States, and especially in Italy. In the final section, I discuss contemporary attempts to translate Tocqueville's pioneering mode of analysis into a public philosophy of modern civilization.

Point of Departure

Tocqueville was twenty-two years old when, in the company of his brother Édouard, he traveled to Sicily in 1827. His recorded reflections amounted to about 350 pages. Gustave de Beaumont, who edited the first publication of Tocqueville's writings, wrote that the manuscript allowed him "to study the course of Tocqueville's thinking, his tentative advances, his mistakes, his backtrackings, and the roundabout ways which he returned to his path."[3] Unfortunately, only about 30 pages remain of the original manuscript. Perhaps because of their brevity, the extracts have not received the attention they deserve. Their last English-language edition, titled "Extracts from the Tour of Sicily," edited by Beaumont, was published in 1862.[4]

3. Quoted in André Jardin, *Tocqueville: A Biography*, trans. Lydia Davis (Baltimore, Md.: Johns Hopkins University Press, 1988), 71.

4. "Extracts from the Tour in Sicily," in *Memoir, Letters, and Remains of Alexis de Tocqueville*, ed. Gustave de Beaumont (Boston: Ticknor and Fields, 1862), 105–30. The original French edition is in Alexis de Tocqueville, *Oeuvres complètes, Voyages en Sicile et aux États-Unis*, ed. J. P. Mayer (Paris: Gallimard, 1957), vol. 5, 37–54.

Since the Enlightenment, travel to Italy had become an essential rite of passage for young aristocrats and inquiring minds in Europe. Tocqueville had been an avid reader of accounts like the *Letters from Italy* by Charles de Brosses.[5] Such accounts often mixed love for the country and its landscape, fulsome praise for the presumed restorative climate, and wonder at the classical ruins of its rich history. These homages to Italy's past were often accompanied with contempt for the people, scorn for their religion and customs, and commiseration over their political and economic conditions.

Tocqueville was lured to Sicily as "the home of the divinities of Grecian mythology" and "the land of gods and heroes."[6] Another reason for the voyage may have been that Sicily shared a common Norman past with Britain that caused the two islands to be often viewed, by knowledgeable observers[7] and Sicilian noblemen, as "sister islands." There is something to this view.

Prior to the abolition of feudalism in 1812, and up until the Congress of Vienna in 1815 decreed otherwise, Sicily retained institutions of government, such as parliament, dating back to the twelfth century. Whereas the Neapolitan parliament, tamed to servility and silence, had fallen into desuetude by 1642, the Sicilian parliament, though weakened in its organization and powers by successive vice-regal administrations, stubbornly clung to its last vestiges of authority in matters of taxation and to its claim of representing the Sicilian nation before the monarch. As late as 1814, the Sicilian aristocracy, somewhat like its British counterpart, still exercised some of the functions inherent in the prerogatives of rule.

The extension of centralized government and administration by the Neapolitan government in 1816 meant not only the end of both that parliamentary tradition and the Sicilian nation and its flag but also a wholesale

---

5. May Gita, "Tocqueville and the Enlightenment Legacy," in *Reconsidering Tocqueville's Democracy in America,* ed. A. S. Eisenstadt (New Brunswick, N.J.: Rutgers University Press, 1988), 38–39.

6. Tocqueville, "Tour in Sicily," 120.

7. See, for example, Charles H. Haskins, "England and Sicily in the Twelfth Century," *English Historical Review* XXVI (no. 103, July 1911): 433–47, and (no. 104, October 1911): 641–65. For a wide-ranging overview, see Charles H. Haskins, *The Normans in European History* (London: Constable, 1916).

remodeling of the structure of basic social institutions. Tocqueville may have had these events in mind when, in the words of Beaumont, witnessing "the misery inflicted on the people by a detestable government," he was "led to reflect upon the primary conditions on which depends the decay or the prosperity of nations. His first intention was to describe only the external aspects of the country; but soon he paints the institutions and manners, and ideas take the place of descriptions."[8]

Beaumont identified the Sicilian notes as Tocqueville's "first literary performance."[9] One scholar suggests that they are one of Tocqueville's earliest statements concerning his reactions "to the movement of his soul."[10] Another biographer cites Beaumont to the effect that the true personality of Tocqueville emerged in the account of his Sicilian travels.[11] The notes point for the first time to features in Tocqueville's mode of analysis that emerge in full force and are uniquely conveyed in the bilingual edition of *Democracy in America:* his mental habits; skills of observation and conceptual apparatus; passion for comparison as the heart of clear thought and action in understanding human affairs, and composing what one has seen and understood with concision and force; as well as a way of sharing with the reader a commentary on his own thoughts and writings.[12]

Multiple Discoveries

In the journey to Sicily, Tocqueville discovered, or perhaps recorded for the first time, that every journey is also a journey into the self. He

8. Tocqueville, "Tour in Sicily," 14.

9. Tocqueville, "Tour in Sicily," 105.

10. Edward Gargan, *De Tocqueville* (New York: Hillary House, 1965), 12.

11. Jardin, *Tocqueville*, 71.

12. See also Roger Boesche, *The Strange Liberalism of Alexis de Tocqueville* (Ithaca, N.Y.: Cornell University Press, 2006); Seymour Drescher, "Tocqueville's Comparative Perspective," in *The Cambridge Companion to Tocqueville*, ed. Cheryl B. Welch (New York: Cambridge University Press, 2006), 21–48; Joseph Epstein, *Alexis de Tocqueville: Democracy's Guide* (New York: HarperCollins, 2006), 4, 41; Saguiv A. Hadari, *Theory and Practice: Tocqueville's New Science of Politics* (Stanford: Stanford University Press, 1989); James T. Schleifer, "Tocqueville as Historian," in Eisenstadt, *Reconsidering Tocqueville's Democracy in America*, 121–38.

found the time to reflect on many things he had not noticed at home, including what was required for a life of productive scholarship. This led him to the realization that one "cannot command the mind to work as you do a laborer to dig or delve. There must be a cause, a motive to set it in action"—namely, something or someone to urge and to excite you, some motivation, obligation, or sense of purpose that comes only by involvement in the world, including the "hurry of public life." This reflection hints at the commitment and passion he revealed later, in the introduction to *Democracy*, to understand the "irresistible" democratic revolution.[13]

Time itself was not a great help, Tocqueville observed. Too much free time "crushes you by its slow progress; a long perspective of similar hours and days discourages you." Nor was isolation, like that of men in prison, conducive to work. "*Ennui,* that overpowering kind of *ennui* which is not produced by idleness alone, but by the influence of a painful position, benumbs the faculties, makes the heart sink, extinguishes the imagination, and at last one dies, like a miser starved in the midst of his riches."[14] The travel to England in 1833, when he was still struggling with the preparation of the first volume of *Democracy*, may have also been a way to overcome ennui and recover imagination.

His journey to Sicily also formed other features of his mode of analysis. There Tocqueville discovered his attachment to France and the importance of understanding one's own society in a comparative perspective. He converted his observation of a poor fisherman's family greeting one another on arriving home into broader generalizations. He put matters this way: "[T]ill now I had never understood the misery of exile and the reality of those instincts which, however far one may be from one's country, draw one towards it in spite of obstacles and dangers." Commenting on these feelings, he acknowledged that the longing for France "was so vehement, as to be far beyond any wish that I had ever formed for anything, and I know not what sacrifice I would not have made to find myself instantly on her shores."[15]

In the notes, Tocqueville reflected on the fact that the human mind becomes clearer through comparison: "[T]he happiness of

13. Tocqueville, "Tour in Sicily," 122.
14. Tocqueville, "Tour in Sicily," 123.
15. Tocqueville, "Tour in Sicily," 121–22.

living in one's country, like other happiness, is not felt while it is possessed."[16] Often many things that in one's own country look insipid take on an entirely different meaning when viewed from afar. In a similar way, the time he spent in America was—we now know from the texts, notes, and correspondence that went into the making of *Democracy in America*[17]—also the time when his understanding of and love for France increased.

We can see in the Sicilian notes other features of Tocqueville's inquisitive mind that informed the way he framed his American inquiry. In the notes, he based the discussion of human behavior on a given society and not on some abstract conception of human nature, while emphasizing the importance of general ideas for making sense of what he found. Recurring themes in *Democracy*—the physical conditions, the powerful force of nature, and the fragility of human civilization—can be first observed in the Sicilian notes. Tocqueville had scarcely set sail for Sicily when he encountered a violent storm at sea, making him "remember the religion we were born in" and review his past life.[18] In the essay "A Fortnight in the Wilderness," first written in 1831, Tocqueville recalled visiting the site in Sicily where the city of Imera had been built, noting that "never in our path had we encountered a more magnificent witness to the instability of things human and to the miseries of our nature."[19]

The notes and marginalia in the Liberty Fund edition of *Democracy* also confirm and reinforce what many careful readers of the work have pointed out—Tocqueville's conscious effort to be descriptive, analytical, and philosophical all at once.[20] This method of proceeding, in the form of paired comparison, is already evident in the notes on Sicily. Two illustrations suffice.

---

16. Tocqueville, "Tour in Sicily," 122. See also Tocqueville to his father, Hervé de Tocqueville, 1831, cited in Epstein, *Alexis de Tocqueville,* 41.

17. See also Eduardo Nolla's introduction to *DA,* lxiv–lxvi.

18. Tocqueville, "Tour in Sicily," 108–9.

19. *DA,* 1354.

20. Roger Boesche, *Tocqueville's Road Map: Methodology, Liberalism, Revolution and Despotism* (Lanham, Md.: Lexington Books, 2006), 2–26; Seymour Drescher, *Tocqueville and England* (Cambridge, Mass.: Harvard University Press, 1964), 26; Epstein, *Alexis De Tocqueville,* 58; Jardin, *Tocqueville,* 67.

Tocqueville observed, and sought to explain, the prosperity and productivity of the farms at the base of Mount Etna. He first reviewed, for himself and future readers, the standard explanations that readily come to mind: the importance of the rich soil and the proximity to the markets provided by the cities of Messina and Catania. There was something to these explanations, he said, but concluded that they were not the whole story. A more convincing reason—which, he admitted, he had been reluctant to accept at first for it was something that many sensible people in France regarded as an evil to avoid—was the division of land in small plots owned by the peasants.[21] Satisfied with having found a convincing explanation to the local situation, he then used it to draw more general deductions.[22]

First, an extreme division of land may be hurtful to agriculture in some countries but not in others. Second, there are different ways to enhance the well-being of people: that is, the institutions that work well in one country cannot automatically be expected to do the same in other countries. Third, there were at the time no absolute principles of political and economic governance equally applicable to England and Sicily.[23]

These observations led Tocqueville to suggest the need to be open to the possibility that diverse social, economic, and political practices can be equally conducive to the well-being of society. He acknowledged that institutions as rules of the game do matter; they make a difference in the way people order and give meaning to their lives. Then, he immediately added that there is not one single way to organize collective undertakings to promote human welfare.

Toward the end of the notes, Tocqueville used an imaginary discussion between a Sicilian and a Neapolitan to present contradictory

21. For an extended discussion of this issue, see Philip T. Hoffman, *Growth in a Traditional Society: The French Countryside, 1450–1815* (Princeton: Princeton University Press, 1996), esp. 3–80.

22. Tocqueville, "Tour in Sicily," 115–16.

23. Tocqueville, "Tour in Sicily," 116. Tocqueville did not, and could not have been expected to, elaborate on regional geographic and demographic differentiation. For this, see Stephan R. Epstein, *An Island for Itself: Economic Development and Social Change in Late Medieval Sicily* (Cambridge: Cambridge University Press, 1992), esp. 25–74.

assessments of political authority in Sicily.[24] The Sicilian complained that Bourbon rule from Naples was bringing ruin and misery to his island. The Neapolitan answered that complaint by voicing what in postunification Italy became the predominant explanation of governmental weakness and failure in Sicily.

> Are you not your own worst oppressors? Granted that tyranny exists in Sicily, but where has it held in its grasps such base instruments? Is it Neapolitans who occupy your public offices? No, one encounters only Sicilians. It is Sicilians—Sicilians alone—who bear the yoke of Naples; who bless their burden as long as they are in turn permitted to impose it upon the unfortunate Sicily. It is Sicilians who sit in your tribunals and make of justice a public auction. If we wanted to corrupt you, you certainly have more than met our expectations.[25]

Tocqueville's presentation may have a deeper texture than is generally realized.

Simply because islanders occupied public offices in Sicily, it did not necessarily follow that institutional weakness and failure were related to basic faults in Sicilian character. By drawing upon the distinction between individuals engaged in constitutional choice and individuals pursuing their relative advantage within governmental structures, it was possible to provide a better understanding of what strategic opportunities are afforded by different types of decision-making arrangements—from constitutional contracts to property rights. With this in mind, the Neapolitan's questions confronted institutional and not personality problems.

> What were the terms and conditions under which Sicilians acted in public offices, following the advent of centralized government and administration from Naples in 1816? Could they be held accountable for their authoritative actions and by whom? At the same time, the conditions of sole proprietorship over large tracts of land especially

24. I first used this imaginary conversation to introduce the challenge of making sense of Sicilian history in my *Political Authority in a Sicilian Village* (New Brunswick, N.J.: Rutgers University Press, 1984), 3–4.

25. Tocqueville, "Tour in Sicily," 126. I have translated the passage in a slightly different way from Tocqueville, *Oeuvres complètes*, 5:52–53.

in Western Sicily meant that landowners or landlords could also be powerful "governors" in practical control of the daily lives and living conditions of the masses of peasants and rural workers. What were the legal prerogatives of Sicilians as citizens and workers and could they be sustained? To what extent were Sicilians in public offices required to impose the yoke of Naples on other Sicilians? Were islanders allowed to solve their own problems?

Tocqueville's comparison between Naples and Sicily through the imaginary conversation between a Neapolitan and a Sicilian can be taken to suggest how people can be expected to behave when they are locked in a many-person analogue to the prisoner's dilemma of modern game theory. It may seem anachronistic to attribute to Tocqueville the language of constitutional political economy that has come to be recognized as the James Buchanan public choice tradition. But it is clear that he knew something about it when he referred to Thomas Hobbes; Eduardo Nolla reminds us that Tocqueville wondered "what is a gathering of rational and intelligent beings bound together only by force?"[26] It is, therefore, possible to conjecture that Tocqueville also knew of Hobbes's suggestion (taken up by modern public choice analysts) about how to assess when institutional arrangements do not work as they should: "[T]he fault is not men, as they are the *matter;* but as they are the *makers* and orderers of [commonwealths]."[27]

The imaginary discussion offers the possibility to understand the logic of mutually destructive relations and the strategic opportunities afforded to individuals by the different types of decision-making arrangements that emerged in Sicily following the wholesale institutional reforms between 1812 and 1816. It is interesting that Tocqueville did not resort to a similar mode of analysis in his depiction of master-slave relations or the plight of native people in America. But in *Democracy,* he did note that democracy modified servant-servant relationships and that the sentiments of democratic people bring them to favor concentration of power and even a particular type of despotism.[28] In the

26. *DA*, editor's introduction, cxxxiii*n*172.

27. Thomas Hobbes, *Leviathan*, ed. Michael Oakeshott (New York: Collier Books, 1962), 237.

28. *DA*, 1007–19, 1245–77.

Recollections, he went on to reflect on the collective-action dilemma of the French political class when he observed that "in France there is only one thing that we cannot make: a free government; and only one that we cannot destroy: centralization."[29]

We know now[30] the impact that François Guizot's lectures on civilization had on the formation of Tocqueville's mode of analysis. But the notes on Sicily reveal key elements that shaped Tocqueville's formidable apparatus of research,[31] which allowed him to launch a political science appropriate to the new world of democracy.

A Political Science for a New World

The notes and correspondence of the Liberty Fund edition of *Democracy in America* reveal how Tocqueville confronted this puzzle: "[T]hat is where civilized men had to try to build society on new foundations. Applying, for the first time, theories until then unknown or considered inapplicable, civilized men were going to present a spectacle for which past history had not prepared the world."[32] Thus, the attempt to study the United States was not "to satisfy a curiosity"—a chief feature of much of the travel literature about America that had flourished in Europe—but rather to present "an image of democracy itself, its tendencies, its character, its prejudice, its passions; [he] wanted to know democracy, if only to know at least what we must hope or fear from it."[33] The opening lines of the Liberty Fund edition reveal clearly and, for the first time, what Tocqueville intended.

29. Tocqueville, *Recollections,* ed. J. P. Mayer, trans. George Lawrence (Garden City, N.Y.: Anchor Books, 1971), xviii.

30. Thanks to Aurelian Craiutu, *Liberalism under Siege: The Political Thought of the French Doctrinaires* (Lanham, Md.: Lexington Books, 2003), 92.

31. This point is powerfully brought out by Jeremy Jennings in his review of the Liberty Fund edition of *Democracy in America,* "Origins of Democracy," *Times Literary Supplement,* October 8, 2010, 10–11.

32. *DA,* 44.

33. *DA,* 28.

The work that you are about to read is not a travelogue, the reader can rest easy. I do not want him to be concerned with me. You will also not find in this book a complete summary of all the institutions of the United States but I flatter myself that, in it, the public will find some new documentation and, from it, will gain useful knowledge about a subject that is more important for us than the fate of America and less worthy of holding our attention.[34]

In a first version of the drafts, almost as if to anticipate criticisms that he had not covered everything, he made the following point:

I have not said everything that I saw, but I have said everything that I believed at the same time true and useful (profitable) to make known, and without wanting to write a treatise on America, I thought only to help my fellow citizens resolve a question that must interest us deeply.... I see around me facts without number, but I notice one of them that dominates all the others: it is old; it is stronger than laws, more powerful than men; it seems to be a direct product of the divine will; it is the gradual development of democracy in the Christian world.[35]

"Equality of conditions" was the "primary fact" that governed and gave direction to the advance of democracy.

Tocqueville was writing at the time when the nascent social science did not provide much help. In taking hold of the subject matter, he made a skillful use of "general ideas"[36] to launch "a new political science...needed for a world entirely new."[37] This allowed him to do several things: to go beyond the "apparent disorder prevailing on the surface," to "examine the background of things,"[38] and to achieve and communicate understanding of the democratic revolution through the use of paired comparison. To be sure, he was not the first analyst to use that mode of analysis. What made his method of paired comparison

34. *DA*, 3.
35. *DA*, 3–4.
36. *DA*, 728–29.
37. *DA*, 16.
38. *DA*, 152.

exceptional for his, and our, own time was its animating spirit: he combined a passion to understand public affairs with a passion for liberty and, concurrently, a deep concern that a misguided spirit of equality and republicanism in both American democracy and Western civilization posed a potential threat to individual liberty and self-government.

The framework of analysis that Tocqueville constructed for himself included multiple dimensions:

- Large processes (aristocracy versus democracy; long-term developments toward social equality; the democratic revolution and democratic despotism; democracy versus civilization).
- Country comparisons (America versus France; America versus England; Anglo-America versus New France Quebec and Latin America).
- Different levels and foci of analysis (federalism versus centralized government and administration; political centralization versus decentralized administration; local liberties in unitary and federal systems; state government in federal systems versus provincial administration in systems of centralized government and administration; prospects for institutional reform and learning in federal versus unitary systems; contrast between American and European republicanism).
- Microlevel analysis focusing on what motivates individuals to act and what shapes law and ethics, public opinion, including democratic despotism, in different political regimes (showing a fusion of concepts and ideas later dichotomized as republican and liberal discourse involving human virtues and self-interest; priority of both individualism and collective life; individualism versus egoism; love of country and fraternity; democratic and aristocratic sentiments; sources of pride in self-government and moderation in religion).
- The art of association and the accompanying associational topography (permanent associations; political associations; civic associations; and private associations; without losing sight of the question of whether or not particular kinds of constitutional and institutional arrangements make a

difference in promoting or hindering self-government and civic spirit).

- The most fundamental "pairs in tension" may be the volumes of *Democracy* themselves: the first two volumes (1835) focus on the liberty and the institutions of self-government; volumes three and four (1840) focus on the soft despotism that Tocqueville saw as democracy's drift, something that in his own time was already happening in France. Just as the French needed to appreciate how the Americans had developed quite a different system of republican institutions that offered the prospects of maintaining liberty under conditions of social and economic equality, so the Americans could look to France to understand the vulnerability of democracy to the administrative state and soft democratic despotism.

This way of proceeding allowed Tocqueville, in the first two volumes, to dig below the "appearance of disorder, which reigns on the surface" of American society,[39] and contrast the government that administers the affairs of each locality with one where the citizens do it for themselves. In comparing the two, he concluded that "the collective strength of the citizens will always be more powerful for producing social well-being than the authority of the government."[40] The American case demonstrated how it is possible for self-interest to work for the common good, and address issues of interpersonal relationship or the practice of civic virtues.[41] Whereas freedom and order were understood in Europe to be in conflict with one another, the American experience suggested that they could be put together to work for the common weal. He went on to observe that, excepting the United States,

> there is no country in the world where men make as many efforts to create social well-being. I know of no people who have managed to establish schools so numerous and so effective; churches more appropriate to the religious needs of the inhabitants; town roads better maintained. So in the United States, do not look for uniformity

39. *DA*, 152.
40. *DA*, 153.
41. *DA*, 918–29.

and permanence of views, minute attention to details, perfection in administrative procedures. What is found there is the image of strength, a little wild, it is true, but full of power of life, accompanied by accidents, but also by activities and efforts.[42]

The American form of government founded on the principle of sovereignty of the people provided Tocqueville with an approach to politics that led him to question the entrenched view of the European state and to place in sharp relief the importance of federalism: "There are almost as many independent officials as there are offices. Administrative power finds itself scattered among a multitude of hands."[43] Unlike the Europeans, Americans had successfully found a way to address the issue of power, not by decreasing it, but, rather, by dividing it. In an often-cited passage, Tocqueville forcefully drew out the distinction, with clear comparative and evaluative dimensions.

> What most strikes the European who travels across the United States is the absence of what among us we call government or administration. In America, you see written laws; you see their daily execution; everything is in motion around you, and the motor is nowhere to be seen. The hand that runs the social machine escapes at every moment.
>
> But just as all peoples, in order to express their thoughts, are obliged to resort to certain grammatical forms that constitute human languages, all societies, in order to continue to exist, are compelled to submit to a certain amount of authority; without it, they fall into anarchy. This authority can be distributed in different ways; but it must always be found somewhere.[44]

The notes and marginalia of the chapter from which this long quotation is drawn, chapter 5 of volume 1 of the Liberty Fund edition, powerfully evidence how much Tocqueville relied on conversations with himself and others to arrive at the "necessity of studying what happens in the individual states before speaking about the government of the Union." These unique features of the Liberty Fund edition put to

42. *DA,* 156–57.
43. *DA,* 133.
44. *DA,* 116.

rest the view that somehow the conversations Tocqueville had with his father and others in the preparation of *Democracy* were "perfunctory" and not substantive.[45]

In the last two volumes of *Democracy,* Tocqueville extends his mode of analysis to note why systems of centralized government and administration are not unique to particular European nations but, rather, are very much part of the habits of democracy. Centralization is a universal tendency, "the natural government." By contrast, "individual independence and local liberties will ever be the product of arts"[46] that can easily be brushed aside as people become intolerant of differences and acquire a misguided spirit of equality and republicanism. This is so, Tocqueville, warned, because

> [m]en who live in democratic centuries do not easily understand the utility of forms: they feel an instinctive contempt for them.... Forms excite their scorn and often their hatred. Since they usually aspire only to easy and present enjoyments, they throw themselves impetuously toward the object of their desires; the least delays lead them to despair.[47]

Tocqueville further explained,

> This disadvantage that men of democracies find in forms is, however, what makes the latter so useful to liberty, their principal merit being to serve as a barrier between the strong and the weak, those who govern and the governed, to slow the first and to give the second the time for them to figure things out. Forms are more necessary as the sovereign power is more active and more powerful and as individuals become more indolent and more feeble.[48]

From the Liberty Fund edition, we equally learn that Tocqueville relegated to "rubish" two related observations: first, that he had had a good conversation with his friend and cousin Louis de Kergorlay about an

45. Arthur Kaledin, *Tocqueville and His America: A Darker Horizon* (New Haven, Conn.: Yale University Press, 2011), 46.

46. *DA,* 1206.

47. *DA,* 1270.

48. *DA,* 1271.

early draft of the chapter; and second, a statement clarifying to himself that "forms are not liberty, but they are its body."[49]

The political science that Tocqueville constructed for himself allowed him to anticipate the possibility that egalitarian envy might lead to centralization of authority in the American federal system as well.[50] Hence, he saw the need for the new political science to ask how liberty and institutions of self-government could be maintained to promote a society of free men and women. In his view, the threat to freedom posed by the natural tendencies of democracy toward despotism could be held in check in several ways: through the practice of interest well understood and tempered by religion; through recourse to "a science of association" to take advantage of the "utility of forms"; and through the design of self-governing institutions so as to maintain freedom under conditions of equality. This way the vulnerability of democracies might be held in check.[51]

Comparativists and methodologists alike remind us that paired comparison has its pitfalls. It does not follow, for example, that the observed variables will cover all the possible causes of particular outcomes. There may be other factors at work missed by the researcher. The fact remains that no method of analysis, no matter how good it may be, points to exactly what the researcher should study, or guarantees that it will be used properly, with both internal and external validity.

Against this backdrop, it is no surprise that even some sympathetic readers have drawn attention to facts that possibly Tocqueville overlooked.[52] The criticism seems overdrawn—when we consider that

49. *DA*, 1270, 1271*n*s.

50. *DA*, 1020–30. Modern expressions of this concern can be found, among others, in Vincent Ostrom, *The Meaning of Democracy and the Vulnerability of Democracies: A Response to Tocqueville's Challenge* (Ann Arbor: University of Michigan Press, 1997), and Paul A. Rahe, *Soft Despotism, Democracy's Drift: Montesquieu, Rousseau, Tocqueville and the Modern Prospect* (New Haven, Conn.: Yale University Press, 2009).

51. As noted in the previous note, above, this is also the major concern of Vincent Ostrom's *The Meaning of Democracy and the Vulnerability of Democracies.*

52. See, among others, Hugh Brogan, *Alexis de Tocqueville* (New Haven, Conn.: Yale University Press, 2006), 277–78; Joseph Epstein, *Alexis de Tocqueville,* 44; Fraçoise Mélonio, *Tocqueville and the French* (Charlottesville: University of Virginia Press, 1998), 77, 147; Garry Wills, "Did Tocqueville 'Get' America?" *New*

researchers today have not yet found ways to insure reliability in the practice of empirical research—and misguided, as noted earlier, when ranged against what Tocqueville wrote in the first version of the drafts, that he did not say everything he had found but only those facts that shed light on his main concern. Indeed, one of the unique features of the bilingual edition of *Democracy* is that it brings to light the truly massive scholarship and care behind the work. For this reason, it is hard not to marvel at the manner in which Tocqueville used paired comparison as an analytical leverage to make several discoveries, to emphasize what was distinctive and universal about the political dynamics in the United States, and to gain institutional leverage for predicting differences in intrasystemic behavior. The method of analysis that Tocqueville constructed for himself allowed him to generate findings about the American Republic that ran radically counter to the Jacobin way of understanding republicanism, and to give a hand to, and go beyond, the growing liberal traditions in France and the rest of Europe of his time. In taking hold of the American political experiment, Tocqueville showed a way "to study the future of the world."[53]

Beyond France and the United States

Tocqueville's *Democracy* was worthy of serious consideration outside France and the United States because it offered a comparative context for understanding that "the organization and the establishment of democracy among Christians [was] the great political problem" in nineteenth-century Europe.[54] Self-rule required new ways of thinking

---

York Review of Books, April 29, 2004, 52–56. But cf. Aurelian Craiutu, "What Kind of Social Scientist Was Tocqueville?" Department of Political Science, Indiana University, paper 2008; Schleifer, "Tocqueville as Historian," 158–60; and Alan B. Spitzer, "Tocqueville's Modern Nationalism," *Society for the Study of French History* 19, no. 1 (2005): 48–66.

53. Catherine Zuckert, "The Role of Religion in Preserving American Liberty: Tocqueville's Analysis 150 Years Later," in *Liberty, Equality, Liberty,* ed. Eduardo Nolla (New York: New York University Press, 1992), 21.

54. *DA,* 504. Tocqueville's concern was widespread. See, for example, Craiutu, *Liberalism under Siege;* Filippo Sabetti, *Civilization and Self-Government: The*

about political order as well as new ways of governance, a radical reordering of political ideas and practices that could not be achieved in a short time. Critical issues were emerging that could be ignored only at great peril: Where could people turn for the likely sources of such ideas? What conditions were necessary for new habits of heart and mind—"the proud freedom that makes self-government possible"[55]—to flourish and be sustained over time? What mechanisms and processes were conducive to positive changes in social, political, and economic relations, creating an open space where ordinary people would have their share in shaping society?[56]

Tocqueville's study was attractive because it offered answers to these questions not couched in the form of a philosophical treatise or a manifesto but, rather, in the form of an empirical investigation of how Americans had come to terms with what it means to be free and self-governing. The American republican experience extended the meaning of liberalism beyond representative government to the idea of a self-governing society that included both ancient and modern meanings of liberty. The Americans practiced what Benjamin Constant theorized.[57] The American political experiment equally overturned the established European idea of the state as the only way to establish and maintain political order. It offered radically new implications for understanding the meaning of democracy in civil society beyond particular forms of government, for building the commensurate institutional structures, and, equally important, for conceptualizing a new mode of analysis appropriate for a democratic age. A science of the state, government, or legislation could not encompass what is required for the development of self-governing units and federal arrangements. Instead, a science of association was called for as the appropriate theoretical

Political Thought of Carlo Cattaneo (Lanham, Md.: Lexington Books, 2010), 12–15; Nadia Urbinati, "Mazzini and the Making of the Republican Ideology," *Journal of Modern Italian Studies* 17, no. 2 (2012): 183–204.

55. Harvey Mansfield and Delba Winthrop, "Tocqueville's New Political Science," in Welch, *Cambridge Companion to Tocqueville,* 90.

56. I elaborated these questions at some length in my *Civilization and Self-Government,* chap. 1.

57. Benjamin Constant, *Principles of Politics Applicable to All Government,* trans. Dennis O'Keefe (Indianapolis: Liberty Fund, 2003), esp. book 16.

foundation for the multiconstitutional world of a self-governing society. Tocqueville's science of politics also drew attention to the importance of long-term development in equality of conditions to suggest "what sort of despotism democratic nations have to fear," though most Europeans in the nineteenth century were more preoccupied with what mechanisms and processes generated and sustained the practice of liberty and self-government, the themes of the first two volumes of *Democracy*.

What could Europeans learn from America? Leaving aside Georg Wilhelm Friedrich Hegel's point[58] around 1830—that Europeans did not have much, if anything, to learn from the American political experience—Tocqueville suggested that American republican experience could teach Europeans several things:

1. that human beings are not forever destined to depend for their political constitutions on accident and force and can indeed exercise reflection and choice in creating systems of government;

2. that popular sovereignty could be generated through acts of associations of citizens themselves and not conferred from above or heredity;

3. that such choices draw upon certain conceptions articulated as principles that are, in turn, used to specify structures or forms so that when acted upon, these conceptions and structures have effects that bear significantly upon the safety and happiness of a people, and upon other fundamental values important to their lives (indeed, the governance of daily life is the necessary starting point for understanding the capabilities that a system of governance needs to supply in order to sustain a self-governing society);

4. that it is possible to have local autonomy, and to fashion self-governing units, without reference to unitary conceptions of rule or to central authority;

58. Hegel suggested this in response to a question from a student, following a lecture he gave in Berlin. See G. W. F. Hegel, "The Natural Context or the Geographical Basis of World History," in his *Lectures on the Philosophy of World History*, ed. D. Forbes, trans. H. B. Nisbet (New York: Cambridge University Press, 1975), 170.

5. that rulers can also be ruled through a system of overlapping jurisdiction, checks and balances, juridical defense, and individual sovereignty;

6. that possibilities other than central government monopoly exist for solving public-sector problems;

7. that the property qualification was not a measure of capacity but a measure of one's stake in, and commitment to, the public good (e.g., understood as the public sphere and as a set of all things shared in common);

8. that commerce and industry were not just means for generating wealth but also ways of substituting self-governance in human affairs for conquest;

9. that, contrary to prevailing fears in Europe, equality of conditions was not incompatible with the practice of freedom and civic virtues, communities as nurseries of a certain form of patriotism, self-restraint, and good life, and the maintenance of liberal practices like representative institutions, rule of law, individual liberties, local autonomy, private property, and even religion; and

10. that popular sovereignty can serve to advance the common good and to sustain productive economic orders, just as public economy involving a rich mix of private and public enterprises can serve to advance the common good of humanity, to sustain nonunitary patterns of human interaction, and to help combine equality and freedom.

For all these reasons, Tocqueville's *Democracy* came to occupy an important place in accounts of how to reorder and align political ideas and practices in advancing the prospects of liberty and institutions of self-government among the people of Europe.

There is considerable literature available on the reception of Tocqueville by successive generations of English intellectuals in their attempts to build a science of politics in the nineteenth century.[59] We know that the informed public in Germany (and northern Europe)

---

59. Stefan Collini, Donald Winch, and John Burrow, *That Noble Science of Politics: A Study in Nineteenth-Century Intellectual History* (Cambridge: Cambridge University Press, 1983). See also Harold Laski, "Alexis de Tocqueville and

was introduced to Tocqueville's thought thanks in part to the work of Francis Lieber and others.[60] Wilhelm Dilthey, in his *Collected Works* published in 1927, referred to Tocqueville as "undoubtedly the most illustrious of all political analysts since Aristotle and Machiavelli," but placed him below Leopold von Ranke among the thinkers of his time.[61] There seems to have been no writer in Germany to undertake a sustained analysis of Tocqueville's work after World War II.[62] By contrast, and unlike the case of both France and the United States where interest in Tocqueville has been intermittent,[63] the author of *Democracy* has been the focus of uninterrupted attention in Italy since volume 1 was first published in 1835.

Tocqueville was widely read among leaders of all political currents before and after Italian unification. Before 1860, Italian patriots showed more interest in the first volume, on the institutions and properties of popular sovereignty, to gain a renewed appreciation of the Italian republican tradition that could be used to counter the Jacobin and Napoleonic designs of centralized government, to argue against the forced creation of a unitary system of government and administration, and to suggest the possibility of a multiform, polycentric political

---

Democracy," in *The Social and Political Ideas of Some Representative Thinkers of the Victorian Age*, ed. F. J. C. Hernshaw (London: George Harrap, 1933).

60. Teddy Brunius, *Alexis de Tocqueville: The Sociological Aesthetician* (Uppsala, Sweden: Acta Universitatis Upsaliensis, 1960); Francis Lieber, *On Civil Liberty and Self-Government* (Philadelphia: J. B. Lippincott, 1901).

61. Quoted in J. P. Mayer, *Alexis de Tocqueville: A Biographical Study in Political Science* (New York: Harper, 1960), xiii. There is, surprisingly, little or no trace of Tocqueville in much of the Austrian School of economics, though Tocqueville's reference to "the new servitude" inspired Hayek to title his 1944 book *The Road to Serfdom*.

62. Michael Hereth, *Alexis de Tocqueville: Threats to Freedom and Democracy* (Durham, N.C.: Duke University Press, 1986); Stefan-Ludwig Hofmann, "Democracy and Associations in the Long Nineteenth Century: Toward a Transnational Perspective," *Journal of Modern History* 75 (June 2003): 269–99.

63. Françoise Mélonio, "Tocqueville and the French," in Welch, *Cambridge Companion to Tocqueville*, 337–58; Matthew Mancini, *Alexis de Tocqueville and American Intellectuals: From His Time to Ours* (Lanham, Md.: Rowman & Littlefield, 2006).

order.[64] After unification, the expansion of the franchise and the change of government from the Right to the Left in the 1870s led concerned Italians to read Tocqueville for what his work could teach on the vulnerabilities of representative institutions to democratic despotism.

Because most Italian intellectuals and politicians read French, *Democracy* was not translated into Italian until the 1880s, when it appeared along with the Italian edition of Thomas Erskine May's *Democracy in Europe: A History* as the inaugural volumes of a new political science series.[65] The Hegelian Fascist philosopher Giovanni Gentile also promoted a new translation of *Democracy* in the early 1930s so as to teach Italians what they should avoid. The translation had the opposite effect, for concerned citizens could now openly read and discuss Tocqueville as a way of looking to a future without Fascism.[66]

In the post-1945 period, interest in Tocqueville's political science in Italy continued on three fronts. The first involved a largely philosophical stream of works exploring the meaning of democracy and the connection among the volumes of *Democracy*. The second, which has continued to this day, is an emphasis on what is alive and dead in

64. Antonio Rosmini (1797–1855), nobleman, priest, founder of two religious orders, and a leading liberal Catholic philosopher in the first half of the nineteenth century, incorporated Tocqueville's ideas at length in his two-volume treatise on political philosophy that was and is available in English as well. See his *The Philosophy of Politics* (Durham, UK: Rosmini House, 1994). Perhaps the more prominent early reader of Tocqueville in Italy was the future prime minister of Piedmont, Camillo Benso di Cavour. He had come to know Tocqueville in Paris and London (at Nassau Senior's house in 1835). Cavour admired *Democracy in America* for, in his own words, it "throws more light than any other on the political questions of the future." Cavour, cited in Jardin, *Tocqueville,* 228; Hugh Brogan, *Alexis de Tocqueville,* 300–301. See also Adrian Lyttelton, "Sismondi, the Republic and Liberty: Between Italy and the England, the City and the Nation," *Journal of Modern Italian Studies* 17, no. 2 (2012): 168–82; Filippo Sabetti, *The Search for Good Government: Understanding the Paradox of Italian Democracy* (Montreal: McGill-Queen's University Press, 2000), chaps. 2 and 3.

65. Attilio Brunialti, *Le scienze politiche nello stato moderno: La democrazia* (Turin: Unione Tipografico-Editrice, 1884).

66. Tocqueville, *Alexis de Tocqueville: La democrazia in America,* ed. Giorgio Candeloro (Bologna: Cappelli Editore, 1933). This edition was reprinted after the war and published by Rizzoli Editore. This edition is still available.

Tocqueville's thought. The third stream consists of new translations of Tocqueville's main and less-known works, and several collections of his writings and letters, each with exhaustive and multilingual bibliographies.[67]

The analyst who most closely shared Tocqueville's method of work and his admiration for the American political experiment was Carlo Cattaneo (1801–69), a radical figure in the republican (federalist) current of the Risorgimento. Cattaneo looked to federal, nonunitary principles of organization as a way of reconciling liberty with authority, equality with liberty, and national unification and independence with local autonomy. Cattaneo's interest in American republican federalism developed independently of Tocqueville, as each analyst applied himself as a public intellectual to the analysis of practical problems in the world. In 1833, just around the time when Tocqueville was still composing the first volume of *Democracy*, Cattaneo used the Nullification Controversy between South Carolina and President Andrew Jackson to reflect on the American political experiment.[68] It is no accident that we find him approvingly citing the first volume of Tocqueville's work— on the issue of how self-interest can, under appropriate institutional arrangements, be made to work for the common good—two years after *Democracy* was published in France.

Like Tocqueville, Cattaneo was a master of paired comparison and combined, also in a pioneering way, a passion for liberty with a passion to understand human affairs. They were both preoccupied with the problem of how to combine equality and freedom through institutions of self-government. They both aspired to map a territory now divided into many specialized subdisciplines. They agreed that there were critical differences in the republicanism of the "sister republics"

67. Some of the best works include Vittorio de Caprariis, *Profilo di Tocqueville* (Naples: Edizioni Scientifiche Italiane, 1962); Nicola Matteucci, ed., *Scritti politici di Alexis de Tocqueville* (Turin: Unione Tipografico-Editrice Torinese, 1977); Roberto Pertici, "Tocqueville in Italia: Le origini di una tradizione di studi," *Ricerche di Storia Politica* VIII, no. 3 (2005): 327–46.

68. Cattaneo, "Notizie sulla questione delle tariffe daziarie negli Stati Uniti d'America desunte da documenti ufficiali (1833)," in his *Scritti economici,* ed. Alberto Bertolino (Florence: Le Monnier, 1965), 1:11–55.

of the United States and France, and both looked to the American political experience for what it could teach Europeans. Attempting to do for Italy what Tocqueville had tried to do for France, Cattaneo can justifiably be regarded as Italy's Tocqueville.[69]

Cattaneo was convinced that neither economic progress, nor armed revolt, nor nationalism would automatically lead to liberation and freedom. He sought to move people to recast what they knew and to act on that knowledge so as to achieve two objectives at once: to become free of foreign rule and illiberal regimes without falling back on the entrenched view of the European state, and to contribute their share to "the common enterprise of humanity."[70] By 1849, following the collapse of the 1848 revolts throughout Europe, he predicted that there would not be peace in Europe until there was a United States of Europe. That Tocqueville and Cattaneo, independent of one another, shared these common concerns constitutes a powerful reminder about the extent to which certain ideas, perspectives, and aspirations cut across accidents of birth, speech communities, and national boundaries. Both Tocqueville and Cattaneo worked on a public science that, in spite of all the interest, never developed in the nineteenth century but may now be developing in the form of Tocquevillian analytics, or a discipline of civics and science of citizenship.

A Public Science for the Future

The richness of Tocqueville's analysis accounts for its high theoretical profile in addressing various aspects of the democratic revolution after World War II. Since the 1950s, American pluralists assimilated and deployed Tocqueville's reflections on civil society to suggest explanations of a wide range of social ills besetting American society.[71] Succes-

---

69. I have dealt at some length with the similarities between the two in my *Civilization and Self-Government*.

70. Carlo Cattaneo, quoted in Sabetti, *Civilization and Self-Government*, 4.

71. For example, see Dana Villa, "Tocqueville and Civil Society," in Welch, *Cambridge Companion to Tocqueville*, 216–44.

sive generations of social scientists have woven, or invoked, Tocqueville into their conceptual schemes and research projects beyond the United States, often distorting his mode of analysis and neglecting its animating spirit.[72]

Yet other scholars have attempted to carry out contemporary research in a spirit closer to Tocqueville's own. Vincent Ostrom, for example, has drawn upon Tocqueville in assessing the potential for citizens as constitutional artisans to develop a science of association and to become "citizen-sovereigns,"[73] and has coined the term "Tocquevillian analytics" to describe how it is possible to translate Tocqueville's normative and empirical mode of analysis into a public science for the future.

This public science refers to an eclectic but cohesive interdisciplinary methodology for studying governance systems in comparative perspective (especially monocentric versus polycentric systems), the relationship between individual liberty and institutions of self-government and the movement of societies from aristocratic to democratic orders. In this formulation, Tocquevillian analytics is used to explore the prospect of self-government and what conditions are needed for individual and joint self-government to flourish. The emphasis on the individual and his or her liberty goes beyond methodological individualism. Self-interest well understood is viewed as a way of coming to terms with interdependent relationships.

The following components are regarded as its core elements:[74]

72. For an elaboration of this assessment, see Carlos Forment, *Democracy in Latin America, 1760–1900* (Chicago: University of Chicago Press, 2003), 8–9, 15–36; Robert T. Gannett, "Bowling Nine Pins in Tocqueville's Township," *American Political Science Review* 97 (February 2003): 1–16; Pierre Manent, *Modern Liberty and Its Discontents* (Lanham, Md.: Rowman & Littlefield, 1990), 65–77; and Sabetti, *Search for Good Government*, chaps. 7 and 8, on Edward C. Banfield and Robert D. Putnam, respectively.

73. Vincent Ostrom, "Citizen-Sovereigns: The Source of Contestability, the Rule of Law and the Conduct of Public Entrepreneurship," *PS: Political Science & Politics*, no. 1 (January 2006): 13–17.

74. Aurelian Craiutu and Sheldon Gellar, eds., *Conversations with Tocqueville: The Global Democratic Revolution in the Twenty-First Century* (Lanham, Md.: Lexington Books, 2009); and Sheldon Gellar, *Democracy in Senegal: Tocquevillian Analytics in Africa* (New York: Palgrave-Macmillan, 2005).

Contextual Components

1. The impact of the physical environment in shaping political, economic, and social structures and relationships.
2. The importance of history in shaping national character and institutions.
3. The importance of laws, especially property rights and inheritance laws, in shaping political, economic, and social structures.

Sociocultural Components

1. The degree of social equality in society and the extent to which there is movement toward greater equality.
2. The importance of mores, customs, and values (cultures) in shaping political institutions and political behavior.
3. The central role of religion and religious institutions in shaping political attitudes, institutions, and relationships.
4. The crucial role of language as an instrument for promoting mutual understanding and group identity.

Political Components

1. The importance of popular sovereignty and constitutional choice in the design of political institutions.
2. The identification of the concentration of power in centralized governments and bureaucracies as restricting freedom and initiative and leading to despotism and dependency.
3. The importance of local liberties and the constitution of self-governing communities as vital to democracy.
4. The crucial role of political and civil liberties, especially freedom of association and of the press as bulwarks against tyranny.
5. An empirical approach to the study of societies that rejects the application of abstract political theory and philosophies.

Ostrom and his colleagues have also endeavored to overcome what might be seen as shortcomings in Tocqueville's formulations, particularly Tocqueville's lack of attention to issues of constitutional choice; how civil society can be connected to the operations of government;

Filippo Sabetti   [363]

and how the concept of public economy might be used to overcome the conceptualization of the public and private sectors as mutually exclusive. This last point is crucial for rescuing the concept of public from the false notion that the "public" means the state (à la John Dewey) or is a single unit, and for focusing attention on the importance of public spirit and entrepreneurship required for a self-governing society.[75] Patterns of order or organized relationships among individuals, organizations, and communities can take on different configurations depending on contexts and knowledge.[76]

The sustained appreciation of Tocqueville's voyage of discovery promoted by the work of Ostrom and his associates has also led to a "new voyage" to Sicily, by refocusing the way we have viewed Sicilian development and Italian political thought. By framing research around the question of whether or not the structures of basic social institutions in Sicilian history were organized in such a way as to advance the pursuit of joint opportunities and human welfare or were an essential course of human adversity and misery, it has been possible to extend and amplify Tocqueville's exploration. What has emerged from this "new voyage" to Sicily is that people, in some basic sense, build their own social and political realities and opportunities, and that what officialdom may do in the formal regime is only part of the story. If some concepts or institutions do not work, or work against them, people will create—as it happened in Sicily—their own adaptations, which may develop into extreme forms of illegal problem solving if officialdom continues to think it can govern while people are actually going their own way.[77] Tocquevillian analytics has also led to discovery and appreciation of

75. Cattaneo's contributions to the development of a public science of self-government have also been discovered by the Tocquevillian analytics. See, for example, my "Constitutional Artisanship and Institutional Diversity: Elinor Ostrom, Vincent Ostrom and the Workshop," *Good Society* 20, no. 1 (2011): 73–83; "Carlo Cattaneo come Tocqueville?" *Confronti* 10, no. 1–2 (2011): 65–88.

76. For a book-length study of these developments, see Paul Dragos Aligica and Peter J. Boettke, *Challenging Institutional Analysis and Development: The Bloomington School* (New York: Routledge, 2009).

77. See Filippo Sabetti, *Village Politics and the Mafia* (Montreal: McGill-Queen's University Press, 2002), and "Stationary Bandits: Lessons from the Practice of Research from Sicily," *Sociologica* 2 (2011): 1–22.

the contributions made by Cattaneo in the development of a public science of self-government.

There is something to George Wilson Pierson's point that, after more than a century of comments on Alexis de Tocqueville, it is hard for any paper to be altogether original or inclusive.[78] But the new Liberty Fund edition of *Democracy* suggests that it is not the whole truth. With its formidable apparatus of notes, commentaries, and drafts, the new edition places us in a position to understand Tocqueville as much as he understood himself and to appreciate anew the revolutionary significance of his attempt to launch a new political science for the new world of democracy. We now know he was not a lonely voice then. There were others in neighboring countries who addressed similar concerns. But Tocqueville remains a foremost master of a public science of liberty, self-government, and comparative analysis. This science is struggling to emerge today,[79] and in this sense, Tocqueville's voyage of discovery continues, for social scientists and concerned citizens willing to carry his journey forward.

78. George W. Pierson, *Tocqueville and Beaumont in America* (Baltimore: Johns Hopkins University Press, 1996), 756*n*.

79. In addition to the works on Tocquevillian analytics cited earlier, see also Karol E. Soltan, "A Civic Science," *Good Society* 20, no. 1 (2011): 102–18.

13

Tocqueville, Argentina, and the Search for a Point of Departure

ENRIQUE AGUILAR

*Democratic government, which is based upon such a simple and
natural idea, always supposes the existence of a very civilized and
learned society.*
—Alexis de Tocqueville, *Democracy in America*

For someone born in the south of the American continent, the reading
of *Democracy in America,* and in particular that of the chapter called "Of
the Principal Causes That Tend to Maintain the Democratic Republic in the United States," which is part of its first volume, may still be
disheartening, although more than a century and a half has gone by
since its publication.[1]

Certainly, South America is not the same it was in 1835/1840, and
the United States has also changed quite a lot. Technological developments have spread all over the world and have also contributed to the
social and economic welfare of populations. Indeed, we have accumulated experience, much of which has been costly in terms of human
lives, but we have also progressed in many other aspects. In any case,
my reference to Argentina will not be made in terms of progress and
decline, but rather in terms of underlying conditions.

I am writing from a country once regarded as "the great disappointment of the twentieth century" (an opinion which has been attributed to
Raymond Aron), with just over 40 million people concentrated mostly

---

1. Alexis de Tocqueville, *Democracy in America: Historical-Critical Edition of "De
la démocratie en Amérique,"* ed. Eduardo Nolla, trans. James T. Schleifer, 4 vols.
(Indianapolis: Liberty Fund, 2010). This edition is hereafter cited as *DA*.

in the city of Buenos Aires and the so-called Conurbano Bonaerense—
which comprises the districts surrounding the capital city—and in just
a few other cities such as Rosario and Córdoba. A country that expected
to become a melting pot of races and that, according to the preamble
of its constitution (1853), opened its doors to all the people who wished
to live on its vast ground.

Undoubtedly, immigrants from neighboring and distant countries
looking for better living conditions still continue to arrive. However,
hundreds of professionals, technicians, scholars, and blue-collar workers driven by the search for a future that they consider to be unattain-
able in Argentina have left the country in recent decades. In addition,
we are pressed by time, especially because of the high rates of social
exclusion and the famine faced by the millions of people (7.5 percent
of the population, according to official estimations, and more than 20
percent according to private figures) who are below the poverty line.
Well acquainted with lost opportunities, we seem not to have learned
from our mistakes and to have always been forced to start from scratch.
As Argentine philosopher and essayist Santiago Kovadloff recently
wrote, "[P]roclivity to repeating the same mistakes exerts among us
[the Argentines] a fascination without detriment."[2]

Nevertheless, I would not say that Argentina has to face a foundational period (a pompous phrase at a time when modesty, not only in
manners, but also in speech, should act as a guiding principle for our
conduct) but that our priority is to give an initial step, to establish a
"point of departure," an expression borrowed from Tocquevillian theory and that is present in the title of one of the most important Argentinean political books, Juan Bautista Alberdi's *Bases y puntos de partida
para la organización política de la República Argentina* (Bases and points
of departure for the political organization of the Argentine Republic),
written in 1852, almost at a sitting during the author's Chilean exile,
when he learned about the fall of the dictator Juan Manual de Rosas.
Indeed, in the present Argentina, deciphering this concept is not only

2. Santiago Kovadloff, "El laberinto político," in *La Nación* (Buenos Aires),
December 26, 2011. For this paper, I have personally translated into English all
the quotations that were originally written in Spanish or in French.

a way to imagine a possible solution but also the easiest manner to measure the real size of the problem.

We know that, in line with Montesquieu (one of his most influential sources), Tocqueville believed that the politics of a country, with its virtues and vices, cannot be explained only on the basis of an internal logic, but in relation to the society that necessarily conditions such politics. That is to say, that society and its mores, understood in a sense that includes "the whole moral and intellectual state of a people,"[3] is reflected in politics and in the institutional design in a way not comparable to that which can be seen in the opposite direction. In a September 1853 letter to his friend Francisque de Corcelle, Tocqueville wrote: "[P]olitical societies are not what laws make of them, but what feelings, beliefs, ideas, habits of the heart and the spirit *prepare them in advance to become,* what nature and education have made of them."[4] In the same light, in *Democracy in America* we can read: "Laws are always shaky as long as they do not rely on mores; mores form the only resistant and enduring power among a people,"[5] which is an idea that has been metaphorically expressed in a previous page, where the author compares the legislator to "a man who plots his route in the middle of the sea. He too can navigate the ship that carries him, but he cannot change its structure, raise the wind, or prevent the ocean from heaving under his feet."[6] There is a phrase by Montesquieu (which, like the ones above mentioned, probably has its roots in Horace's statement: *Leges sine moribus vanae*) that may summarize this argument in a unique manner: "The customs of an enslaved people are a part of their servitude; those of a free people are a part of their liberty."[7] Therefore, we may infer, in principle, that given certain social and customary or historical

---

3. *DA,* 467.

4. Tocqueville, *Lettres choisies: Souvenirs, 1814–1859,* édition établie sous la direction de François Mélonio et Laurence Guellec (Paris: Gallimard, 2003), 1081 (my emphasis).

5. *DA,* 447.

6. *DA,* 265.

7. Montesquieu, *Del espíritu de las leyes* (Madrid: Tecnos, 2007), 350. In the final pages of this paper I will briefly go back to this topic and to the way in which, both for Montesquieu and for Tocqueville, the relation between mores and politics can also work in an inverse direction.

conditions, only some political options would be attainable, which is a viewpoint also shared by some of Tocqueville's elder contemporaries, such as François Guizot, and which may be illustrated by an eloquent paragraph from his *Essays on the History of France* (1823).

> It is by the study of political institutions that most writers...have sought to understand the state of a society, the degree or type of its civilization. It would have been wiser to study first the society itself in order to understand its political institutions. Before becoming a cause, political institutions are an effect; a society produces them before being modified by them. Thus, instead of looking to the system or forms of government in order to understand the state of the people, it is the state of the people that must be examined first in order to know what must have been, what could have been its government....
>
> Society, its composition, the manner of life of individuals according to their social position, the relations of the different classes, the condition [*l'état*] of persons especially—that is the first question which demands attention from...the inquirer who seeks to understand how a people are governed.[8]

Despite his later political differences with Guizot, it would not be wrong to conclude that Tocqueville would have basically agreed with this argument. Indeed, this is a very important issue in the first volume of *Democracy in America*, whose chapter 9 of part 2 is dedicated to it. As it has already been pointed out, in this chapter, titled (as mentioned above) "Of the Principal Causes That Tend to Maintain the Democratic Republic in the United States," Tocqueville "addresses a classic problem of political science: the stabilization and preservation of a political order."[9]

---

8. Quoted in Larry Siedentop, "Two Liberal Traditions," in *The Idea of Freedom: Essays in Honour of Isaiah Berlin,* ed. Alan Ryan (Oxford: Oxford University Press, 1979), 158. I have included this quotation and, with some changes, some other paragraphs of this paper, in my book *Alexis de Tocqueville: Una lectura introductoria* (Buenos Aires: Sudamericana, 2008). I am grateful to Editorial Sudamericana for having allowed me to incorporate them in this paper.

9. Donald J. Maletz, "Tocqueville on Mores and the Preservation of Republics," *American Journal of Political Science* 49, no. 1 (January 2005): 1. Stable URL: http://www.jstor.org/stable/3647709.

He first refers to some "accidental" or "providential" causes ("independent of the will of men" and also called "secondary"), which are factors that facilitate such persistence. The first one would be geographical isolation, a circumstance that makes northern America safe from invasions or conquests and, consequently, from the risk of having the military state elevated over the civil one; the second one would be the absence of a large capital city that concentrates all the political and economic activities of the nation, thus subjecting the provinces to it; the third one and "most effective of all" would be "the good fortune of birth," that original fact or circumstance that, from the very beginning, enabled Americans to import equality of conditions, habits, ideas, and mores, all of which were apt, according to Tocqueville, "to make the republic flourish"; and last but not least, would be the "unlimited continent," vacant and desert, where the original settlers established, an "immense prize" that fortune offered to the Americans.[10]

Next, Tocqueville summarizes three aspects of American political life related to the goodness of laws and institutions, which are in accordance with the American social state and physical position and which he has deeply analyzed in previous chapters: (1) the federal form that has been adopted, which "allows the Union to enjoy the power of a large republic and the security of a small one"; (2) the local autonomy and the town institutions, which Tocqueville considers real schools of political participation and which "give the people at the same time the taste for liberty and the art of being free"; and (3) an independent judicial power, which becomes a guardian of the Constitution and serves to "correct the errors of democracy."[11] Finally, Tocqueville dedicates the main part of this chapter to the influence of mores, giving to this word a meaning that not only includes the "habits of the heart" but mental habits as well, that is, the "different notions that men possess," the "diverse opinions that are current among them" and "the ensemble of ideas from which the habits of the mind are formed."[12] Above all, it is in the field of mores where the author stresses the importance of religious beliefs as an essential element for the health of democracies,

10. *DA*, 452–65.
11. *DA*, 465.
12. *DA*, 446.

though he limits his analysis to their social and political implications, as a means to regulate mores and mind, instilling "habits of restraint" and moral boundaries, independent of their intrinsic truth and of the concerns about eternity these beliefs could awaken.[13]

Accordingly, it is precisely mores that explains, much better than any other reason, the maintenance of the democratic republic. Somehow, they are the result of the mixture of the enlightenment, habits and practical experience of the Americans, that is to say, the result of education (which "regulates mores") rather than the result of instruction (which "enlightens the mind"). In fact, Tocqueville believes that teaching people how to read and write is not what makes them become citizens. This is so because for him "True enlightenment arises principally from experience," as it happened with the Americans, who little by little got accustomed to the practice of self-government and who learned about laws "participating in legislation."[14] The reason for this is that, in the United States, education, whose very purpose is, in Donald Maletz's words, "knowledge about and support for democracy," contributes to stimulate public life, while in Europe, its principal purpose is to prepare people for the private sphere. Hence, in Tocqueville's view there is a cultural conditioning that limits, from the start, the possibility of sowing the seed of pluralistic and participatory democracy on other soils.[15]

Actually, when brooding on why democratic institutions have flourished only in the United States, and not in South America, Tocqueville does not deem the reference to the circumstances related to origin to be valid: neither the geographical isolation of the American Union, nor the fact that Anglo-Americans had brought equality of conditions to

13. *DA*, 472, 955.

14. *DA*, 494.

15. While interpreting Tocqueville, Maletz clearly explains that "education for a democratic and practical enlightenment comprises two elements. First is cultivation of experiential familiarity with the operations of democratic society and government, their formalities and procedures. The second, equally necessary, is absorption of democratic mores through the experience of collaboration with others in public activities. The mind and the mores are formed together, for in both cases, what is to be learned is how society deliberates, decides, and acts" (Maletz, "Tocqueville on Mores," 11).

this continent, nor the fertile and limitless fields, nor any other material factor. He thinks so because nature has also isolated the Spaniards in South America, not preventing them, because of it, from maintaining armies and from waging domestic or external wars. Besides, the soil in the South was as much, or even more fertile, and on top, the South American colonies had also been settled by equals, or by men who would eventually become equals once settled. Thus, it is not on such circumstances related to origin, especially the physical causes, where the secret about the difference between the United States and South America lies, but on the laws and mores.[16] Nevertheless, Tocqueville thinks that laws are less influential than mores within this range of "predominant" causes. This explains why Mexico, which has adopted the same laws that rule the Anglo-Americans, has not been able to get accustomed to democratic government, and why within the American Union the newly born western states, which exhibited "the inexperience and the unruly habits of emerging peoples," had proceeded haphazardly and not orderly, like those of the East, where democracy had permeated habits, opinions, customs, and beliefs. Therefore, he concludes that mores are the very reason, the real comparative advantage, which explains why only some societies prove to be capable of supporting a democratic regime, keeping it from degenerating into authoritarian forms. As he writes: "I am persuaded that the most fortunate situation and the best laws cannot maintain a constitution in spite of mores, while the latter still turn to good account the most unfavorable positions and the worst laws. The importance of mores is a common truth to which study and experience constantly lead. It seems to me that I find it placed in my mind like a central point; I see it at the end of all my ideas."[17]

What could this extraordinary traveler have written about politics in Argentina and its connection with mores and the prevalent behavior of our society? According to a very simplistic analysis, a chronic dissociation between the corruption of the political system and the health of society may be observed in this country. In my opinion, this analysis

16. *DA*, 495ff.
17. *DA*, 499ff.

(which was aired through the expression "Out with them all!" in the aftermath of the December 2001 crisis) somehow evokes the Spanish Regenerationist Movement of the late nineteenth century and, particularly, the distinction that the politician and historian Joaquin Costa (1846–1911) made between the "two Spains": the official Spain of the ruling class (composed of oligarchs and "caciques"); and a "rising" or, as he also called it, a "new" Spain, which he found "contemporary with humanity," as proposed in his report about *Oligarquía y caciquismo como la forma actual de gobierno en España* (Oligarchy and caciquism as the present form of government in Spain), published in 1902.[18] However, as regards Argentina, it seems that the very many failures that occurred during the last decades should induce us to dig deeper into the temperament, customs, and values of our society, which underlie political order and laws, and which, perhaps, have prepared the latter "in advance" to become. In other words, it does not seem to be mistaken to believe that Argentina's disorder is primarily cultural and does not exclusively have to do with the *abuses* of rulers, but rather with the *uses* of a society in which it is possible to discover the same defects that are strongly disliked in governors.

By the way, the concepts of *uses* and *abuses* were already employed by the Spanish philosopher José Ortega y Gasset to disagree with a central point in Joaquín Costa's thesis, despite his praises of the author who had oriented his own thoughts and hopes on the Europeanization of Spain for many years. In fact, as he said in his conference "Vieja y nueva política" (Old and new politics), as from 1914, the opposition between "the two Spains" did not have to do with the antagonism between the alleged healthy part of the nation and the corrupt ruling classes, but with the opposition between the "official Spain" and the "vital Spain," in view of the fact that such classes had governed wrongly, not only owing to their own "sins" or political mistakes but also because the Spain that was being governed was as ill as them. From Parliament to newspapers, from rural schools to universities, the "official Spain"—with its abuses and its uses—looked, in Ortega's view, like the "huge skeleton of an evaporated and vanished body." Given

---

18. Joaquín Costa, *Oligarquía y caciquismo, Colectivismo agrario y otros escritos* (Madrid: Alianza Editorial, 1969), 38.

this reality, a cultural transformation was needed so as to make that budding Spain—"perhaps not very strong, but vital," though somewhat hindered by the other one—come true.[19]

Coming back to Argentina, I think that it is much easier for us to identify in politics and in the vices and abuses of politicians the explanations of our decline, instead of considering them a mirror in which our current habits or certain collective features reflect. Nevertheless, I am inclined to believe, as Enrique Valiente Noailles says, that there is a sort of bilateral though implicit agreement, an invisible consent that ties the private and public vices, which cannot be undone by blaming only one of the parties and absolving the other one.[20] Does it mean that everything depends on culture? I would not go that far. Nobody denies, broadly speaking, the influence of political and economic settings, and mostly in this case, the responsibility of the Argentinean ruling class that, with few exceptions and ignoring the role of political representation, has not ever taken the population into account. On the contrary, they have frequently manipulated the laws and the institutions for their own corporative benefits, thus feeding, through their unscrupulous behavior, the spread of irregularity, the flow of bad examples, so that what is wrong has become widely accepted.

Needless to say, we have the right to demand probity from our representatives despite our shortcomings as citizens (which, after all, lies at the basis of representative government). In this manner, it is not unreasonable to think that the presumption of aptitude and "wisdom to discern the true interest of the country" (to quote Madison's words in *Federalist* No. 10) applies primarily to those who voluntarily propose themselves to elective positions. Just as Juan José Sebrelli expressed in his *Crítica de las ideas políticas argentinas* (Critique of Argentine political ideas), "The degree of responsibility is proportional to power and the capacity for decision. Guilt, in the long run, is always individual."[21] In other words, saying that we are all responsible for what is happening to

19. José Ortega y Gasset, "Vieja y nueva política," in *Obras Completas* (Madrid: Taurus, 2004), 1:713–15.

20. Enrique Valiente Noailles, *La metamorfosis argentina* (Buenos Aires: Perfil, 1998).

21. Juan José Sebrelli, *Crítica de las ideas políticas argentinas* (Buenos Aires: Sudamericana, 2003), 10.

us is the same as saying that no one is, or that there is no need to blame anyone, which makes guilt just fade away. However, if we go deeper into the reasons for our sufferings and failures, the fact that politicians have governed so badly for so many years does not appear to be the result of chance or even fatality.

The Argentine sociologist Ernesto Aldo Isuani has studied this issue in a working paper called "Anomia social y anemia estatal" (Social anomie and state anemia), in which he argues that the phenomenon of transgression in Argentina has profound cultural roots that even turn what is legal into illegitimate. In short, the author considers that the massive character of our transgressions (whose demonstration par excellence is bribe), and the widespread impunity, which involves the public sector as much as the civil society, cannot only be explained by the existence of a state that is so much hypertrophied that it is not capable of executing the most basic public policies, such as justice, defense, education, and health. Instead, he believes this phenomenon may be primarily explained by the Argentinean society, in which, except for some local solidarities (advocacy groups, NGOs, etc.), mutual mistrust and incredulity increase together with factionalism and social conflict. For instance, and apart from bribery, Isuani mentions the permanent violation of the traffic rules (which daily produces a high rate of accidents), tax evasion, frequent infringement of alimentary regulations, and the neglecting or damaging of public places. The author comes to the conclusion that Argentineans suffer from severe *anomy*, a term that has been defined by Émile Durkheim, with the meaning absence of standards and values that regulate the relationship among the different parts of a society, resulting in lack of cooperation and unsocial behaviors.[22]

In the following paragraphs, let me go into details about these and some other facts that may also be considered significant when analyzing our reality from a Tocquevillian perspective. In the first place, as regards the state, it is evident that Argentina is experiencing the consequences that had been foreseen by Tocqueville with extraordinary sagacity in the chapter about "What Kind of Despotism Democratic

22. See Ernesto Aldo Isuani, *Anomia social y anemia estatal* (Buenos Aires: FLACSO, 1996).

Nations Have to Fear," which might be considered to be a continuation of the description, made in the previous chapter, about the increasing state interventionism in Europe at that time. In short, Tocqueville considered that, principally in France, the central power had become "more inquisitorial" than anywhere else, exerting a sort of "intellectual centralization," and had also become the unique administrator of charity. Likewise, he was struck by the excessive number of state officials who formed "a nation within each nation" and by the way the government controlled public and private wealth, as well as invaded, from the executive, the judicial power. More particularly, the development of industry was a sphere where government regulation and supervision had clearly grown. Taking into account that the progress of industry entailed the building of roads, ports, and "other works of semi-public nature," there was a tendency for the state to "undertake alone" their execution, thus becoming "the greatest industrialist," "the leader or rather the master of all the others." Civic associations, which could eventually resist such interference, were also under its control. In this fashion, nations that had once escaped from the authority of nobles and kings, and who had broken down many barriers on behalf of liberty and independence, daily sacrificed them to the public administration, bowing "more and more, without resistance, to the slightest will of a clerk."[23]

No matter whether the pages on the kind of despotism democratic nations have to fear are a premonition or a description of his contemporary reality, or even of the centralized administration created by Napoleon, "whose formidable unity... left no refuge for liberty,"[24] what we know is that Tocqueville was undoubtedly aware of the feelings he

23. See, in general, the complete chapter "That Among the European Nations of Today the Sovereign Power Increases Although Sovereigns Are Less Stable" (*DA*, 1221–44).

24. See Tocqueville's inaugural address, on the occasion of his being appointed member of the French Academy on April 21, 1842, in Tocqueville, *Discursos y escritos políticos*, ed. Antonio Hermosa Andujar (Madrid: Centro de Estudios Políticos y Constitucionales, 2005), 89–93. See also Melvin Richter, "Tocqueville, Napoleon, and Bonapartism," in *Reconsidering Tocqueville's "Democracy in America,"* ed. Abraham S. Eisenstadt (New Brunswick, N.J.: Rutgers University Press, 1988).

had had while writing the first volume of *Democracy in America,* about the chances Western nations had of suffering a modern version of the "tyranny of the Caesars,"[25] embodied in the person of only one man or in the will of the majority. However, "five years of new meditations" and a more detailed observation of those times had made the object of his fears change toward a kind of despotism without precedent and whose novel characteristic lay on the fact that it was "more extensive and milder," and would "degrade men without tormenting them."[26] As a matter of fact, the words "despotism" and "tyranny" did not satisfy the author when he had to name this form of consensual oppression that threatens democratic peoples. "The thing is new, so I must try to define it, since I cannot name it." As a result, thanks to its "immense and tutelary power," and after having molded each individual "as it pleases," the state reaches out to embrace society as a whole with "a network of small, complicated, minute, and uniform rules, which the most original minds and the most vigorous souls cannot break through to go beyond the crowd."[27] There is no need to go on quoting these very well-known paragraphs to grasp that the reality of many countries, either past or present, is reflected in them. With regard to Argentina, it might be said that the state has also managed to spread a mesh of regulations that "hinders," "represses," "enervates," and "stupefies" the population, finally reducing it "to being nothing more than a flock of timid and industrious animals, of which the government is the shepherd."[28] Particularly, state intervention over economy is expressed in price control; uncontrollable growth of the public spending and debt; a huge and authoritarian bureaucracy that can only be supported with increasing taxes; a central bank usually submitted to political vicissitudes; the nationalization of the foreign trade; the strengthening of a so-called capitalism for friends, which offers the best opportunities for business, based on obscure agreements, only to relatives of those in power, comrades or dominant companies that have an open affinity for the government and who operate in fields such as public works,

25. *DA,* 511.
26. *DA,* 1248.
27. *DA,* 1245–61.
28. *DA,* 1252.

the power industry, or the progovernment press; illegal enrichment of some government officials; intentional distortion of the consumer price index so as to conceal high inflation, and so on.

This is just a brief, a very concise description of what is going on. It would take very many pages to complete it, and it may even include funny references about the way in which this immense machinery is present in the lives of all Argentineans, although there are some who do not realize that this kind of serfdom has been voluntarily accepted by their votes. Actually, they are victims and passive subjects of an authority who truly represents them, although it progressively places obstacles in their path, thus making them lose their will and their confidence in their own capacities, that is, the very sense of individual responsibility. In the end, it might be said, quoting Bill Emmott when referring to the collapse of Enron in December 2001, that "every element of liberal capitalist democracy" has been damaged in Argentina, not temporarily, due to an affair of an energy-trading company, but much more permanently, because of the many mistakes that we have been making, from both the political and the economic points of view, and the way we have been manipulating our institutions. This means that we have lost faith in the "honesty of management," the "accounting and auditing standards," the "transparency and reliability of capital markets," the "application of the rule of law," and above all, in "government as the disinterested arbiter of the whole system."[29]

Apart from this, but still concerning the state, it should be said that Argentina does not have a tradition of civil service, that is, a professional and depoliticized public administration that is not submitted to the electoral outcomes or party influence, and with officers chosen after a rigorous selection process based only on merit. Furthermore, it does not seem unwise to think that, if this road were chosen, the risk of corruption would tend to diminish as well as the venal practices that are deeply rooted in our political culture. By the way, I believe the speech delivered by Tocqueville at the National Assembly on January 18, 1842, is very clear about the matter, specifically in the fragment where he alludes to those public offices that had actually turned out to

---

29. Bill Emmott, *20:21 Vision: Twentieth-Century Lessons for the Twenty-First Century* (New York: Farrar, Straus and Giroux, 2003), 205.

be "the permanent object of all the ambitions in the country" because anyone, no matter what his background was, felt capable of becoming a civil servant, believing that favor or fate would be enough to swiftly climb from the bottom to the top of the ladder.[30] It might be said that in Argentina there are many such people, though they are not ready to climb, because they expect to enter directly into a top position, because of the fact that they have the necessary influential contacts.

Returning to Tocqueville's mild despotism, it is worth mentioning that the image that immediately precedes that famous description is that of a fragmented society, where men seemed to be and act as strangers to each other, spinning around "restlessly, in order to gain small and vulgar pleasures with which they fill their souls," which indirectly favored the expanding of the state.[31] In other words, it could be said that the submission to which we are exposed under an interventionist state could be considered the obverse or, indistinctly, the reverse of another phenomenon that Tocqueville will call, with a negative connotation, *individualism,* an expression coined in France by the Saint-Simonian circle and that probably inspired Tocqueville because of the lack of concern for public affairs he noticed in the French bourgeoisie and in a country in which every man seemed to consider politics "as something which is alien, whose care does not affect him, concentrated—as he is—on the contemplation of his individual and personal interest."[32] In a letter to Pierre-Paul Royer-Collard, dated June 23, 1838, Tocqueville had complained about the selfishness of the local people in a revealing manner: "It refers to a soft, pleasant and tenacious love for his particular interests, which little by little absorb all the other feelings of the heart and exhaust almost all the sources of enthusiasm. To this selfishness they add a certain number of private virtues and domestic qualities which, in all, shape respectable men and poor citizens."[33] "I have never seen a country in which the first symptom of public life,

30. Tocqueville, "El deseo de cargos públicos," in *Discursos y escritos políticos,* 73–77.

31. *DA,* 1249.

32. *DA,* 70.

33. Tocqueville, *Lettres choisies,* 416. See, about the importance of this letter within the French social and political context of that time, Seymour Drescher, "Tocqueville's Two *Démocraties," Journal of the History of Ideas* 25, no. 2 (April–June,

which is the frequent contact among men, is so scarce," he will write to the same recipient two years later.[34] Likewise, in the first volume of *Democracy in America,* he had referred to those societies in which, once the source of public virtues is exhausted, it is no longer possible to say that there are citizens, but just mere inhabitants, which in Tocqueville's words would mean, to invert his famous formula, a wrong application of interest, that is to say, an interest not "well," but on the contrary, wrongly understood. Let us see what he eloquently wrote:

> There are such nations in Europe where the inhabitant considers himself a sort of settler, indifferent to the destiny of the place where he lives. The greatest changes occur in his country without his participation.... [H]e thinks that all these things are of no concern to him whatsoever, and that they belong to a powerful stranger called the government. As for him, he enjoys these benefits like a usufructuary, without a sense of ownership and without ideas of any improvement whatsoever. This disinterestedness in himself goes so far that if his own security or that of his children is finally compromised, instead of working himself to remove the danger, he crosses his arms to wait until the entire nation comes to his aid. Moreover, this man, even though he has so completely sacrificed his own free will, likes to obey no more than anyone else. He submits, it is true, to the will of a clerk; but, like a defeated enemy, he likes to defy the law as soon as power withdraws. Consequently, you see him oscillate constantly between servitude and license.[35]

Five years later, in the second volume of *Democracy in America,* Tocqueville would go back to that topic in the chapter called "On Individualism in Democratic Countries," in which he differentiated this form from pure egoism. On the one hand, egoism "is a passionate and exaggerated love of oneself, which leads man to view everything only in terms of himself alone and to prefer himself to everything." On the other hand, individualism "is a peaceful sentiment that disposes each

---

1964): 206–7. In a letter to Odilon Barrot dated September 16, 1842, Tocqueville even called individualism "*la maladie du siècle*" (Tocqueville, *Lettres choisies,* 505).

34. Tocqueville, *Lettres choisies,* 461.

35. *DA,* 157.

citizen to isolate himself from the mass of his fellows and to withdraw to the side with his family and his friends." "Egoism is born out of blind instinct; individualism proceeds from an erroneous judgment rather than from a depraved sentiment. It has its source in failings of the mind as much as in vices of the heart."[36] As far as politics is concerned, this "erroneous judgment," the individualism that Americans combat by the doctrine of "interest well understood,"[37] has its consequence in apathy, that is to say, political indifference, which fosters, in turn, the emergence of a centralized and paternalist power. For Tocqueville, this was the "greatest danger" that banged on the doors of democracy: "*general apathy*, fruit of individualism," a hazard even bigger and "the same and single cause" of other evils to be feared, such as anarchy or despotism and that, due to the same reasons, it was urgent to combat, without delay.[38]

It is a matter of opinion if it is the state's interference or the society's withdrawal that comes first. In any case, once the process has started moving, it might be said that it works in a rotary way, and a vicious circle is formed. The more the state grows, the more society tends to become indifferent to public affairs. The more society becomes indifferent, the bigger the chances are for the state to fill, because of its intrinsic voracity, the empty space that citizens or civil associations used to fill themselves. This is, in my view, an aspect of the social and political picture that could be painted about Argentina and that I consider quite illustrative when highlighting mores as one of the main causes

36. *DA*, 882.

37. Actually, it looks as if Tocqueville puts forward the argument of the interest well understood as a formula to call French citizenship to participate in public affairs and "to combine their own well-being with that of their fellow citizens," rather than to describe the real behavior of American people, who "show with satisfaction how enlightened love of themselves leads them constantly to help each other and disposes them willingly to sacrifice for the good of the State a portion of their time and their wealth." In fact, he thinks that "they often do not do themselves justice," taking into account that sometimes "citizens give themselves to the disinterested and unconsidered impulses that are natural to man." Americans, Tocqueville concludes, "hardly ever admit that they yield to movements of this type; they prefer to honor their philosophy rather than themselves" (*DA*, 918–25).

38. *DA*, 1294.

for our failures. Indeed, it is worth mentioning that individualism can be run across not only on the individual level but also on the collective level as well, which Tocqueville defined as "collective individualism," when in *The Old Regime and the Revolution* he referred to the groups completely disconnected from each other that the French society was made up of before the Revolution and that had prepared the spirit of French people for the isolation described in *Democracy in America*.[39] Definitively, it is true that, in the latest years, we were eyewitnesses of many protests and demonstrations by thousands of people claiming in the streets, applauding a political speech, celebrating the results of a polling day or even paying their last respects to a former president. But, at the same time, it is quite evident that obedience to the laws and Constitution, concern for what is public, meditated and responsible vote, and respect for the opinion of others—especially when it is different from ours—seem to be values that have fled away and that have retreated when facing the advance of a democratic experience that is far from embodying what the theory prescribes and where it is easy to sense, together with the lack of ideals that may transcend or move us, the disbelief in politicians and party machineries owing to the presumption that all political decisions come from a system that is incapable of being modified.[40]

However, there are other interpretations. For instance, the Argentine political scientist Isidoro Cheresky points out that the citizen's indifference could be better understood as the disappearance of lasting affiliations or permanent political identities, which is reflected on the electoral behavior inasmuch as parties are incapable of keeping a floating voter, who is learning to deliberate before he votes, under control. Besides, the state of opinion measured by the polls becomes, for this author, another effective way in which the population expresses itself at present, nonetheless more important than the presence of demonstrators in streets and routes, the signature collection campaigns, and

39. See Tocqueville, *El antiguo régimen y la revolución*, trans. Dolores Sánchez de Aleu (Madrid: Alianza Editorial, 1982), 1:124.

40. To enlarge, I recommend, among other readings, Carlos Strasser, *La vida en la sociedad contemporánea: Una mirada política* (Buenos Aires: Fondo de Cultura Económica, 2003).

so on, all of which could be considered symptoms indicating an active citizenry that speaks for itself (and consequently, it is not indifferent), although it is obviously divorced from classical representation.[41]

Yet, as Cheresky himself admits, the expansion of civil life to those spheres does not bring about a renaissance or the predominance of democratic virtue (as understood by Montesquieu, it might be evoked, in the manner of "the love of the laws and of our country"),[42] which leads him to suggest the thinking of other forms of participation, including the calling for referendums and popular consultations, the promotion of the revocability or the shortening of the legislative terms of office, meant as measures to link representation with self-government.[43] As far as I am concerned, I would add that we still keep the faculty of rewarding or, otherwise, punishing through our vote, which goes beyond considering politics a mere formal obligation, and that we also have the chance to practice some type of neighborhood citizenship and find refuge in volunteering, the nongovernmental organizations and other sectorial networks that are not supposed to be political entities but appropriate spheres, in any case, to favor solidarity and public engagement and to prevent us from egoism, a vice which, as Tocqueville knew, "parches the seed of all virtues," even the public ones, once individualism, in the long run, is absorbed into it.[44]

There are many positive aspects Tocqueville observed in the American democracy, which are not present in Argentina. One we can mention is the importance he gave to local government (the towns), which

41. Isidoro Cheresky, *Ciudadanía, sociedad civil y participación ciudadana* (Buenos Aires: Miño y Dávila, 2006).

42. Montesquieu, *Del espíritu de las leyes*, 45.

43. Even though I am not a specialist in this field, I believe that these are topics to be deeply studied, especially due to the metamorphosis which, according to Manin's well-known thesis, representation has suffered on its way from parliamentary democracy, which later became party democracy, to today's *audience democracy* (*démocratie du public*), in which, unlike what happens with party democracy, everlasting loyalties tend to disappear and the personalities of the candidates prevail in the limelight, and media performance becomes decisive to induce the vote. See Bernard Manin, "Metamorfosis de la representación," in *¿Qué queda de la representación política?* Fernando G. Calderón and Mario R. dos Santos, coordinators (Caracas: Nueva Sociedad, 1992).

44. *DA*, 882.

"*scatter* power...in order to interest more people in public life," thus becoming the most adequate premise to exercise an active citizenship. He regarded town powers as true schools of public participation, where the inhabitant "gathers clear and practical ideas about the nature of his duties as well as the extent of his rights." At the same time, he regarded them as channels to put political liberty into practice: the place where "native land has marked and characteristic features," where the "strength of free peoples" resides, and where "independence and power," which always captivate men, can be found together.[45] Second, we can also mention his pages on associations with their unlimited purposes, which indirectly acted as fences to control the advancement of central power (such as the secondary bodies in aristocratic nations) and even as a necessary guarantee against abuses, a real "dike against any sort of tyranny."[46] Besides, we should remember the way administrative decentralization really attracted Tocqueville's attention; the significance he attached to an independent judicial power and to judicial review; the advantages he saw in the federal system, "a work of art" based on "legal fictions" and on a "division of sovereignty";[47] and finally his considerations against a concentrated press, which prevents the expression of dissident voices, and on the independence of the so-called Fourth Estate as a means to guarantee the freedom of the citizens, because it "lays bare the secret motivating forces of politics and compels public men, one by one, to appear before the court of opinion."[48]

Most of these elements, whose real, tangible presence Tocqueville had highlighted in his portrayal of the United States, do not seem to go beyond being a rhetorical fact in Argentina, just discourse on politicians' and rulers' lips. The local government is not a place in which citizen participation is truly encouraged. Among us, associative bonds and the virtues that lead to this end are still scarce, although they have lately increased. Though constitutionally speaking our federal regime is a mixture that combines "the liberties of every province and

45. *DA*, 99–114.
46. *DA*, 307.
47. *DA*, 264–65.
48. *DA*, 295–98.

the prerogatives of the whole Nation,"[49] it actually gives huge power to the federal state, at the expense of the provinces. Moreover, the judiciary is far from being considered independent: the judicial review is an almost unapplied constitutional regulation, some judges seem to work as mere agents of the executive branch, and besides, in the last decades there has been practically no government that has not tried to fill vacancies to their advantage, thus tipping the scales to definitely favor the ruling party. In addition, the press is also rather far from being truly free, and those newspapers which are not progovernment are daily subjected to intimidation exerted on behalf of the government. On top, an evil that enormously affects the performance of our democratic regime is the consolidation of *hyperpresidentialism,* which means that power is being totally focused in the executive, whereas the Congress partly delegates its legislative responsibilities, thus reducing such regime only to an electoral event, no matter what the conditions under which it is exercised are. In other words, we can affirm that the supremacy of the Constitution, the division of powers, and the rule of law only have a merely formal existence, although in practice the autocrat's wishes are satisfied, without letting any formula of democratic accountability interfere between his/her decision and his/her passive recipients. It is clear that we still have a long way ahead to become a democratic republic, according to the model presented by Tocqueville, and taking into account the distance separating our Constitution and laws and the everyday practices of both the government and the society, which leads us to say, paraphrasing him, that we have "the letter of the law" without "the spirit that gives it life."[50]

In his *Bases,* Alberdi wrote: "The problem of the possible government in the America which used to be Spanish has only one sensible solution, which consists of raising our peoples to the level of form of government that necessity has imposed on us; giving them the aptitude they lack to be republican; making them worthy of the republic we have proclaimed, but which we can neither practice today nor give up; improving the government through the improvement of those

49. Juan Bautista Alberdi, *Bases,* ed. Jorge M. Mayer (Buenos Aires: Sudamericana, 1969), 290.

50. *DA,* 266.

being governed; improving society to obtain the improvement of power, which is its expression and direct result."[51] Regardless of the many theoretical developments that have taken place since then, and of the lessons we may have learned from the world and from our own history, unfortunately, this diagnosis is still valid and I do not see any other way out except for encouraging education and the civilizing action that is involved in an opening into the world, an attitude we have been stubbornly rejecting for many for a long time.

From what has been said up to now, it could be possible to infer that social causality is a one-way avenue that necessarily conditions politics and institutional designs to the existence of set practices (beliefs, behaviors, etc.) in line with such designs. However, a more correct interpretation should make us think that there is a reciprocal influence between the social and the political system, between mores and laws. Such influence has also been defined by Sheldon Wolin, in relation to Tocqueville's reasoning, as an interactive way of thinking, which connects "a distinctive type of politics and the social relations and cultural values and practices that transmitted definition and character to politics." As Wolin adds, Tocqueville believed that "[p]olitics was not simply the 'expression' of societal beliefs and practices but was as much constitutive of society as it was reflective of it."[52] This seems to be right, taking into account the degree of creativity that Tocqueville attaches to laws and politics (as Montesquieu did in his time when stating that in England the laws of this free nation had contributed to forming the mores) and his confidence in the possibility that some changes in mores could take place, so as to invert the given order of the United States.[53]

In fact, he confessed his conviction about the possibility democratic institutions may have of surviving outside the United States, if they were "introduced prudently into society, which would mix little by little with

51. Alberdi, *Bases*, 229.

52. Sheldon S. Wolin, *Tocqueville between Two Worlds: The Making of a Political and Theoretical Life* (Princeton: Princeton University Press, 2001), 8.

53. See Montesquieu, *Del espíritu de las leyes*, bk. 19, chap. 27. See also Donald J. Maletz, "Tocqueville on Mores," who explains how Montesquieu first examines the constitution of England (11, 6) to show later (19, 27), the effects this constitution had on the English character. "... The laws or the constitution in this case precede the manners" (p. 5).

the habits and would gradually merge with the very opinions of the people."[54] On that ground, European peoples had to face the challenge of regenerating public life by reforming, with favorable laws, those traditions that were hostile to freedom, and of illustrating public opinion in this regard.[55] After all, American lawmakers had to combat some natural defects of democracy and the weaknesses of human nature by confining the ambitions of citizens within the limits of towns, by means of the municipal laws; they also had to respond to theoretical ignorance with practical experience, and to counter "the hotheadedness of their desires" with "their habits of affairs."[56] Certainly, using America as an example that could provide lessons from which other peoples might profit did not necessarily mean for Tocqueville to draw the same "political consequences"[57] from a similar social estate, nor that other nations must imitate its means and remedies to link democracy with freedom. In other words, American laws were not the only imaginable democratic laws. In the introduction to *Democracy in America*, Tocqueville wrote (once again in line with Montesquieu): "I am among those who believe that there is hardly ever absolute good in laws,"[58] because he was aware of the influence exerted by nature and the historical background of each country on its political constitution, and thus he would regard it as "a great misfortune for humankind if liberty, in all places, had to occur with the same features."[59] Let me quote this other paragraph from *Democracy in America*.

> It does not depend on the laws to revive beliefs that are fading; but it does depend on the laws to interest men in the destinies of their country. It depends on the laws to awaken and to direct that vague patriotic instinct that never leaves the human heart, and, by linking it to thoughts, passions, daily habits, to make it into a thoughtful and lasting sentiment. And do not say that it is too late to try; nations do

54. *DA*, 502.

55. See André Jardin, *Alexis de Tocqueville, 1805–1859* (México: Fondo de Cultura Económica, 1988), 143, 169.

56. *DA*, 503.

57. *DA*, 27.

58. *DA*, 28.

59. *DA*, 513.

not grow old in the same way that men do. Each generation born within the nation is like a new people who comes to offer itself to the hand of the law-maker.[60]

At least, such was Tocqueville's hope for France: he wished that through progressive reforms, meant to improve education and incentivize the civic spirit and participation of the electorate, democratization could be carried out in a peaceful manner and without undermining liberty. Maybe this summarizes, after all, the underlying political intention of the pages of *Democracy in America*. In a note written in October 1831, during his stay in America, he said: "In America free morals (mœurs) have made free political institutions; in France it is for free political institutions to mould morals."[61] How can this be achieved? On the one hand, by instilling in all the citizens "the ideas and sentiments that first prepare them for liberty and then allowing them the practice of those ideas and sentiments";[62] on the other hand, by giving "political life to each portion of the territory, in order to infinitely multiply for citizens the occasions to act together, and to make the citizens feel, every day, that they depend on each other."[63] Administrative centralization, general apathy and tyranny of the majority—or even the "*unlimited power of one man*,"[64] as another possible incarnation of despotism— were, in this respect, the big obstacles to be overcome with the help of the education of the people and a number of institutions—municipal life, associations, freedom of the press, independence of the justice, and so on—which should work as antidote: a medicine against the damages the social democratic state is exposed to. Above all, in order to combat the problem of individualism, exercising political freedom was one part—the most important one—of the solution. This is so because political liberty draws men away "from the middle of their individual interests," lets every man see that he is not "independent of his fellows,"

60. *DA*, 160.
61. Quoted by James T. Schleifer, *The Making of Tocqueville's Democracy in America* (Indianapolis: Liberty Fund, 2000), 170. Accessed from http://oll.libertyfund.org/title/667/67141.
62. *DA*, 513.
63. *DA*, 891.
64. *DA*, 514.

arouses his disposition to cooperate, and makes him aware of "the value of the public's regard." This is, to a large extent, the grounding for Tocqueville's praise of the United States and the free institutions that Americans possess, which "recall constantly, and in a thousand ways, to each citizen that he lives in society." Tocqueville is sure that to combat the evils that development of equality may engender "there is only one effective remedy: political liberty,"[65] and such remedy has proved to be effective in the United States. Perhaps, this is the main lesson that the other countries may get, together with "these principles of order, of balance of powers, of true liberty, of sincere and profound respect for law," which he considers "indispensable to all Republics" and, consequently, they should be "common to all" so that they may survive and normally progress.[66]

To conclude, let us come back to Argentina. If those who believe that our republic has been kidnapped are not exaggerating, it will undoubtedly be difficult to rescue it, because such an enterprise needs a network of values and norms that are currently decadent, which, unless they are cultivated, cherished, and above all, internalized by people, they will become, such as many other things, unnecessary. That is the reason why, if seen from this perspective, the issue about reviving our civil responsibility to encourage the arousal of better politics will be inevitably transformed into a moral issue. Besides, it may also be inferred that the solution to be devised necessarily has to involve the awareness about the fact that good democracies cannot be built overnight and that we will have to gradually solve our insufficiencies, in order to shape, on more solid cultural bases, a firm and enduring institutional skeleton.

In any case, such undertaking should necessarily follow two directions. The first one will go against any sort of voluntarism and rationalistic utopia, and it will spring directly from the society itself, on prudential grounds and from the so-called conditions of possibility; the second one, which will be based on politics and its institutions, will be

65. *DA*, 889–94.
66. Advertisement to the twelfth edition of *Democracy in America,* printed in 1848 (*DA*, 1375).

capable of generating consensus and habits related to free institutions, thus favoring the advancement of our democracy: a system which might be slow, perhaps an enemy of perfection, but which—as Raymond Aron believed—is the best at limiting the margins for the rulers' activities and to which the acceptance of peaceful competition and freedom of discussion are inherent.[67]

This is, to the best of my understanding, the lesson we have to learn from an Argentine reading of Tocqueville. I hope someday, after so many comings and goings, we can achieve a harmonious array of customs and political institutions.

67. Raymond Aron, *Introducción a la filosofía política* (Barcelona: Paidos, 1999), 162.

14

Tocqueville and Eastern Europe

AURELIAN CRAIUTU

*I so often wonder whether that solid land we have sought for so long
actually exists, and whether it is not our fate to rove the seas forever!*
—Tocqueville, *Recollections*

In the Footsteps of Tocqueville

Since the end of the Cold War, Alexis de Tocqueville has been celebrated as one of the most original and relevant analysts of democracy.
Many of his key concepts such as social capital and civil society, pluralism and the art of association, self-government, the role of intellectuals
in politics, and the relationship between decentralization and political
freedom have been identified within the literature as crucially important for understanding the evolution of postcommunist politics and
democratic consolidation in Eastern and Central Europe.

In keeping with the general theme of the present volume—
explorations of Tocqueville's development of his ideas during his
American journey and discussions of Tocqueville's "voyage" beyond
his own time, and the dissemination of Tocquevillian ideas throughout
the world—I have chosen to highlight a few Tocquevillian topics that
seemed relevant when examining the current status of democracy and
democratic consolidation in Central and Eastern Europe. The countries of that region are confronted today with challenges that remind
one of those faced by Tocqueville's postrevolutionary generation: the
institutional and cultural legacy of the old regime; the uncertainties
and challenges of building a democratic and liberal society and a free
economy reconciling the demands of freedom, fairness, and equality;
citizenship, centralization, decentralization, and self-government.

Tocqueville's reflections on the pervasive effects of centralization and the tradition of paternalism in France are a gold mine for anyone interested in examining the challenges to democratic consolidation posed by the legacy of statism and weak civil society in Eastern Europe. While most commentators are inclined (for good reasons) to pay special attention to *Democracy in America,* I believe that Tocqueville's *The Old Regime and the Revolution* and his posthumously published *Recollections* are equally valuable in this regard and should not be ignored. Also relevant are Tocqueville's views on the virtues and limitations of democracy, the role of mores and civil society in promoting sound democratic institutions, the ambiguous effects of individualism, the complex relationship between market and the rule of law, and the compatibility between religion and democracy. As such, Tocqueville's writings invite us to reflect on seminal questions such as: How do historical legacies affect the evolution of new political institutions and political behavior? What is the relationship between equality, freedom, and democracy? How does centralization destroy the capacity for local initiative and self-governance, and what can be done to countervail this pernicious tendency? What kind of safeguards do we need in order to preserve freedom and prevent democracies from becoming unstable and unruly?[1]

Needless to say, this is not a case of identity but (at best) of similarity of situations. Tocqueville's writings, which attempted to make sense of the legacy of the French Revolution on the eve of the industrial revolution, can only have a *partial* applicability to the posttotalitarian context and a postindustrial and globalized world. It is anyone's guess what Tocqueville could have thought of our myopic, greedy, and overpaid bankers, our ineffective politicians and expensive bailouts, the stagnant real incomes and unprecedented levels of economic inequality, our anemic growth, high unemployment, and powerful lobbying groups and distributional coalitions, or the power of credit agencies and international corporations curtailing the authority of sovereign states. As

---

1. For an application of "Tocquevillian analytics" to the study of democracy, see Aurelian Craiutu and Sheldon Gellar, eds., *Conversations with Tocqueville: The Global Democratic Revolution in the 21st Century* (Lanham, Md.: Lexington Books, 2009). The book also contains a chapter on Russia ("Democracy in Russia: A Tocquevillian Perspective") written by Peter Rutland.

an analysis published in the *Financial Times* put it, modern economies appear to consist more and more of two widely different tracks: "a fast one for the super-rich and a stalled one for everyone else."[2] Not surprisingly, the Occupy Wall Street and the Tea Party movements reopened old questions about the fairness of the free market and its allocation of resources. Twenty-five years after the end of the Cold War, the debate focuses today again on the moral questions underpinning individualist capitalism and the free market economy.

Be that as it may, it is tempting to use Tocqueville as a "guide" (sui generis) for reflecting on democratization in Central and Eastern Europe. The Frenchman might be interpreted as an *anti-Marx* who had a better intuition about the course of history than the author of *Das Kapital*. To be sure, with the benefit of hindsight, it can be argued that Tocqueville's understanding of the sociological underpinnings of democracy was more profound and accurate than Marx's. Yet this would be a simplistic and inaccurate reading of Tocqueville's writings that would not render justice to the complexity of his thought and would make us lose sight of the ways in which Tocqueville attempted to create a new political science. Unlike Marx, Tocqueville rejected deterministic theories of history and had few "certainties" to share with his readers other than the inevitable progress of democracy and the decline of aristocratic privileges. What kind of democracy would emerge from the ruins of aristocratic societies was for him an *open* question depending on various political, economic, and cultural factors including political wisdom, capable leadership, and chance. Precisely because he lived in an age fraught with uncertainty and turmoil, Tocqueville was able to grasp the limitations of a rigid deterministic understanding of politics and history. He resisted the temptation of putting forward simplistic one-dimensional theories of social and political change and rejected abstract political models offered as panaceas. As Tocqueville himself acknowledged in *Recollections*, he detested "those absolute systems, which represent all the events in history as depending upon great first causes linked by the chain of fatality, and which, as it were, suppress men from the history of the human race. They seem

2. *Financial Times*, January 9, 2012, 5.

narrow under their pretence of broadness, and false beneath their air of mathematical exactness."[3]

Tocqueville emphasized in his writings the importance of the "point of departure" for the evolution of democratic institutions and practices in America. He also understood that some important political events could and should be explained only by accidental factors in which chance often plays a significant role, though institutions, political crafting, and historical legacies are also important. In the footsteps of Montesquieu, he recognized that all societies are diverse and pluralistic in composition, being influenced by history, physical environment, culture, and laws. As such, "antecedent facts, the nature of institutions, the cast of minds and the state of morals are the materials of which are composed those impromptus which astonish and alarm us."[4] That is why Tocqueville's greatness and relevance do not lie in any single doctrine he may have espoused (as was the case of Marx) but in the ambivalent—or critical—ways in which he analyzed the multiple facets of the emerging democracy at a point in time when its principles were not yet universally acknowledged or were flatly contested by radical critics.

Tocqueville's firsthand experience of living in an age of transition to democracy and profound social and political transformation makes him a valuable companion for any student of transition to democracy in Eastern Europe.[5] Tocqueville belonged to a whole generation of passage, born in the shadow of arbitrary power yet committed to liberty, a generation whose task was to end the Revolution that had started in the summer of 1789. He came of age during the Bourbon Restoration, which was the ground of an intense and protracted battle for power

3. Alexis de Tocqueville, *Recollections,* trans. A. Teixeira de Mattos, ed. J. P. Mayer (New York: Meridian Books, 1959), 64.

4. Tocqueville, *Recollections,* 64.

5. In the aftermath of the fall of the Berlin Wall, Tocqueville's works were the object of several colloquia titled "Tocqueville et la démocratie" organized in Eastern Europe and France from 1991 to 1994. For more information, see Françoise Mélonio, "Tocqueville à l'Est," *La Revue Tocqueville/The Tocqueville Review* 15, no. 2 (1994): 193–205. A thematic summary of these colloquia can be found in Alexandru Zub, *Reflections on the Impact of the French Revolution: 1789, de Tocqueville, and Romanian Culture* (Iasi: Center for Romanian Studies, 2000), 169–89.

between, on the one hand, inflexible prophets of the past who wanted to restore the political institutions of the Old Regime, and, on the other hand, forward-looking spirits who defended the liberties enshrined in the Charter of 1814.[6] Tocqueville's generation was called to settle fundamental questions such as creating appropriate political and economic institutions for dispersion of political and economic power, devising new electoral systems, promoting transparency and accountability, rethinking the nature of the state, rebuilding civil society and a new professional bureaucracy, and, last but not least, institutionalizing political contestation, free press, and freedom of association. In the writings of these French liberals—Benjamin Constant is a major example—one finds numerous references to key constitutional issues such as balance of powers, the proper relationship between the executive and the legislative power, the responsibility of ministers, the role of the head of state, the issue of neutral (moderating) power, or the nature of the constitution as a "guarantee" of rights and liberties.

The Legacy of the Old Regime and the Exit from Communism

All of these issues have become priorities on the agenda of liberals in post-1989 Eastern Europe. The process of democratization in the region has been made difficult by the complex legacy of the past, which includes the absence of a real middle class, little or no experience with political competition, weak civil societies, political and administrative centralization, and habits of dependency on the state. Soon after the fall of communism in Eastern Europe, Berkeley political scientist Ken Jowitt predicted that the revolutions of 1989 would usher in a world that will be "increasingly unfamiliar, perplexing, and threatening."[7]

6. On the importance of the Bourbon Restoration, see Aurelian Craiutu, *Liberalism under Siege: The Political Thought of the French Doctrinaires* (Lanham, Md.: Lexington Books, Rowman & Littlefield, 2003), 9–26. For a presentation of the new generation that came of age during the Bourbon Restoration, see Alan B. Spitzer, *The French Generation of 1820* (Princeton: Princeton University Press, 1987).

7. Ken Jowitt, "The New World Disorder," *Journal of Democracy* 2 (1991): 12.

He argued that we live in a moment of "mass extinction" of Leninist regimes and clearing away, that could be compared, mutatis mutandis, to a catastrophic volcano eruption. "It will be demagogues, priests, and colonels more than democrats and capitalists," Jowitt claimed in 1992, "who will shape Eastern Europe's general institutional identity."[8]

Although Jowitt's prediction has not been borne out by subsequent events, twenty-five years later the countries of Central and Eastern Europe are still facing important challenges that cannot be underestimated. If, as a political and cultural regime, Leninism is today extinct, the "Leninist/Stalinist model of the highly disciplined, messianic sect-type organization based on the rejection of pluralism and the demonization of the Other has not lost its appeal."[9] According to the conventional wisdom, the emergence and consolidation of political pluralism are to a great extent dependent on the strength of civil society. Equally important for the crystallization of institutional arrangements are the mode of extrication from the old regime and the existence of elite pacts and settlements. In some countries, such as Hungary and Poland, the transition to an open society had been initiated (before the fall of the Berlin Wall) through negotiations and roundtables, while other countries, such as Romania, witnessed a sudden collapse of their old regimes. As a result, in the latter case, there were few or no institutional arrangements capable of providing channels for collective action and bargaining in an uncertain and highly volatile environment. The lack of pacts and negotiations before 1989 could account for the rhetoric of intransigence and the winner-take-all mentality of the main political actors that emerged after 1989, which delayed the consolidation of the new democratic regimes.

Not surprisingly, the strong legacy of centralization and top-down power networks has proved to be a resilient relic of the old communist regimes after 1989. The emergence of clientelistic networks may explain the erratic pace of economic reforms in some countries like Russia, Ukraine, Romania, and Bulgaria where the exit from state

8. Ken Jowitt, *New World Disorder* (Berkeley: University of California Press, 1992), 300.

9. Vladimir Tismaneanu, Marc Morjé Howard, and Rudra Sil, eds., *World Order after Leninism* (Seattle: University of Washington Press, 2006), 21.

socialism led to a perverted form of political capitalism. In some cases, managers of former state enterprises created parasitic private firms by using state resources and personal influence, while in others they used their connections and networks to reap the benefits of early (flawed) privatization schemes.[10] What emerged from all this was an inefficient and corrupt system based on patronage networks, dominated by greedy managers with close ties to both the old and the new regimes. Cheap credits were generously given to unperforming economic agents that eventually came to count on the government to clear off their unpaid debts or give them cheap credit. By failing to place state-owned enterprises under tight budgetary constraints, the government allocated a large portion of the state revenue to subsidize inefficient units in obsolete industries. The process of privatization was overbureaucratized and often lacked transparency, allowing the appearance of overnight nouveaux riches who were highly successful at acquiring state assets at bargain prices.

At the same time, other countries, such as Czechoslovakia and Hungary, had a tradition of antipolitics that has not been particularly helpful after 1989 in fostering civic activism and political participation. In many cases, the skepticism toward parliamentary forms of politics has been fueled mainly by the erratic behavior of politicians and the corrupt nature of political institutions. Moreover, when confronted with the task of creating an open society in a free environment, some of the former opponents of the old communist regimes could not shed the oppositional language that had been appropriate to the period when they were constrained to speak against the practices of the communist regimes, but was no longer appropriate to the task of building free societies in which open political contestation is the universally acknowledged rule of the game in a new parliamentary setting.

The vexing issue of the state power added additional challenges to the new legislators. While former communist states had been politically strong, they were at the same time administratively weak, relying on a lax ad hoc application of rules that contributed to political arbitrariness and an inefficient allocation of economic and human resources.

10. On this issue, see Venelin I. Ganev, *Preying on the State: The Transformation of Bulgaria after 1989* (Ithaca, N.Y.: Cornell University Press, 2007).

Nonetheless, statism has not been the only significant threat to freedom in the region. The absence of proper democratic and legal mores and culture to sustain the new democratic institutions and laws has proved to be another significant challenge to democratic consolidation in the region. To these two factors, one can also add the absence of a tradition of publicity (openness) and political accountability, which strengthened the gap between elites and citizens and reinforced a culture of cynicism and apathy.

Not surprisingly, after the fall of communism, the apprenticeship of liberty has proven to be a difficult and protracted process, with significant differences in political outcome among postcommunist countries. Those states that have become members of the European Union have introduced significant economic and political reforms while the majority of the former Soviet republics (with the exceptions of the Baltic countries) have encountered significant economic and political problems, from pervasive corruption and low state accountability (Kazakhstan and Moldova), to judicial arbitrariness (Ukraine) and state authoritarianism (Russia). Commentators have attributed a good part of the political and economic problems plaguing some parts of Eastern Europe and the former Soviet states to the complex social, cultural, economic, and political legacy of their old regimes. To be sure, the resilience of communist "habits of the heart" did play a role in perpetuating authoritarian practices in the aftermath of the fall of communism, as did the force of tradition, cultural values, and social character.[11] Several decades of misallocation of scarce resources and political arbitrariness, the absence of the rule of law, and the lack of a genuine political competition could not have been written off overnight. They had a significant impact on the delayed or protracted liberalization of some of the former communist regimes in the early 1990s.

Had Tocquevillle visited Eastern Europe a decade ago or so, he would have not been surprised by these phenomena. In book 2 of *The Old Regime and the Revolution,* he commented on the difficulty of dismantling the tradition of statism and centralization, and examined the

11. For an application of this approach to southeastern Europe, see Stjepan G. Mestrovic et al., *Habits of the Balkan Heart* (College Station: Texas A&M University Press, 1993).

mechanisms and consequences of the atomization of society and the rise of individualism with regard to civil apathy and the lack of a proper public life. What Tocqueville described in his book was the emergence of a strong paternalistic power that eventually annihilated local institutions and contributed to the vanishing of intermediary bodies that had traditionally served as effective bulwarks against absolute and arbitrary power. Between individuals and the central power there was nothing left but an immense empty space devoid of any protective screens, as was also the case in Eastern Europe, where the monopoly of the party led to the annihilation or persecution of civil society. This, in turn, led to the further atomization of society—the metaphor of *la société en poussière* (atomized society)[12] appeared during the parliamentary debates during the Bourbon Restoration—and the emergence of a pernicious form of "collective individualism"[13] that facilitated the steady rise of the central power. The institutions of the Old Regime, Tocqueville wrote, "had previously created habits, passions, and ideas which tended to keep men divided and obedient."[14] Everyone lived in a little society, for himself, and was interested only in matters which directly affected his narrow circle. As a result, people had little or no political connections to each other and classes were deeply divided. On the eve of the Revolution, the French nation was, in Turgot's words, "a society made of different orders badly united, and of a people whose members have very few ties where, by consequence, no one cares about anything but his own personal interests. Nowhere is any common interest visible."[15]

This situation paved the way to despotism by furthering the rise of "an immense central power, which has devoured all the bits of authority and obedience which were formerly divided among a crowd of secondary powers, orders, classes, professions, families, and individuals, scattered throughout society."[16] All public works were decided upon and

12. See Craiutu, *Liberalism under Siege*, chap. 4.

13. Tocqueville, *The Old Regime and the Revolution*, ed. François Furet and Françoise Mélonio, trans. Alan S. Kahan (Chicago: University of Chicago Press, 1998), 1:163.

14. Tocqueville, *Old Regime*, 1:245.

15. I noted Tocqueville, *Old Regime*, 1:170. The similiarity with Eastern Europe on the eve of 1989 is striking in this regard.

16. Tocqueville, *Old Regime*, 1:98.

conducted solely by agents of the central power, which ended up having its intrusive hand in all types of local business.[17] As Tocqueville noted, there was no city or village, no local institution that could have an independent will in its own affairs or freely administer its own resources. The government kept its citizens under its absolute tutelage, dictating to them what to do and seeking to control any significant local initiative.[18] As a result, the practice of self-government gradually disappeared along with political dissent. "The smallest independent body," writes Tocqueville, "frightened the government"; "the tiniest free association, whatever its objects, disturbed it; it only allowed those which it had arbitrarily created and governed to exist."[19] Not surprisingly, "no one thought that any important business could be well managed without the involvement of the state."[20] Thus, self-government became an empty word, as the local interests of towns no longer seemed to concern their inhabitants; moreover, local government degenerated into small oligarchies that exercised power without accountability and were impervious to the eyes of public opinion.[21] The intrusive nature of central power gradually fostered a vicious circle that led to more requests for state intervention in local affairs. The government disliked interference by citizens in any way in the examination of their own business and preferred sterility and inefficiency to genuine political competition and publicity that would have improved the functioning of its institutions in the long run.

The outcome of paternalism was a nefarious mixture of political arbitrariness, civic apathy, indifference toward the common good, a highly inefficient allocation of scarce resources, and the absence of accountability and rule of law. Not only did the government of the Old Regime constantly intrude into the judicial sphere but also it "took equal pains to keep its officials from the misfortune of having to submit to the law like ordinary citizens."[22] Political arbitrariness and administrative incompetence often went hand in hand. "This is the old regime

17. See Tocqueville, *Old Regime*, 1:118–28.
18. Tocqueville, *Old Regime*, 1:131, 135, 137.
19. Tocqueville, *Old Regime*, 1:139.
20. Tocqueville, *Old Regime*, 1:143.
21. Tocqueville, *Old Regime*, 1:127.
22. Tocqueville, *Old Regime*, 1:134.

in a nutshell," Tocqueville summed up his description of the administration and politics of l'ancien régime: "a rigid rule, lax implementation."[23] Everyone asked for exceptions from the written rules, and the central power was all too ready to grant them.

The similarity with the experience of the former communist countries should not go unnoticed. During the communist regime, laws and constitutions fell into general contempt, and the implementation of rules, laws, and constitutions was extremely lax. Not only were civil freedoms (acknowledged on paper) ignored in reality but everyone was encouraged to seek to obtain various exemptions from the laws. Sometimes, new rules succeeded one another so quickly that officials, even when giving orders, often had difficulty figuring out how to obey them. Even when the law was not changed, the way it was applied changed daily or from region to region. As a result, there were in reality few laws and rules that did not incur a thousand modifications in practice.[24]

Finally, because the government had sought to keep society under strict tutelage, the latter did not feel part of a common project and often remained passive or divided. The deterioration of the mores reflected this situation. The similarity with post-1789 France is worth noting again. "The men of '89," Tocqueville wrote, "had knocked down the building, but its foundations had remained in the very souls of its destroyers and on these foundations it was possible to build again."[25] Past institutions created habits, passions, and ideas that tended to keep men divided and obedient. In Eastern Europe, these mores encouraged political apathy and indifference to the public domain, while creating a culture of suspicion and distrust that made dissent more difficult. When in 1789 and 1989, the master fell, "what was most substantial in his work remained; his government dead, his bureaucracy still lived, and every time that we have since tried to bring down absolute power, we have limited ourselves to placing liberty's head on a servile body."[26] It is no coincidence that fifty years after the Revolution, Tocqueville wondered if the Revolution could ever be brought to a peaceful end and worried that

---

23. Tocqueville, *Old Regime*, 1:142.
24. A similar point was made by Tocqueville; see *Old Regime*, 1:141.
25. Tocqueville, *Old Regime*, 1:145.
26. Tocqueville, *Old Regime*, 1:245.

his generation might be condemned to rove the seas forever in darkness. Much the same feeling seems to have inspired those analysts of postcommunism whose Cassandra-like voice denounced the chaos following the fall of the Iron Curtain and predicted that the "clearing away" effect of Leninism's extinction could not be effectively contained.[27]

Tocqueville's New Science of Politics

Another thing that makes Tocqueville relevant to Eastern Europe today is that, through his own works, he sought to contribute to a larger tradition of political engagement and political rhetoric in which the writer entered into a subtle and complex pedagogical relationship with his audience seeking to convince and inspire his readers to political action.[28] Many Eastern European writers such as Alexander Solzhenitsyn, Vaclav Havel, and Adam Michnik did the same in the last decades of the twentieth century. Despite Tocqueville's anxieties about the future of freedom in modern society (and in France above all), he never really lost faith in the possibility of educating democracy and displayed strong confidence in the power of his new science of politics, which was supposed to explain how democracy could and ought to be moderated and purified of its revolutionary elements and tendencies. As Tocqueville claimed in the Introduction to volume 1 of *Democracy,* "a new political science is needed for a world altogether new."[29] His book was supposed to offer the blueprint of precisely such a new science of politics adapted to the new world characterized by a growing equality of conditions.

27. See Jowitt, "The New World Disorder," 12.
28. Pierre Manent, "Tocqueville, Political Philosopher," in *The Cambridge Companion to Tocqueville,* ed. Cheryl Welch (New York: Cambridge University Press, 2006), 111; Laurence Guellec, "Tocqueville and Political Rhetoric," in Welch, ed., *Cambridge Companion to Tocqueville,* 170. Also see Eduardo Nolla's important introductory study in Alexis de Tocqueville, *Democracy in America: Historical-Critical Edition of "De la démocratie en Amérique,"* ed. Eduardo Nolla, trans. James T. Schleifer, 4 vols. (Indianapolis: Liberty Fund, 2010), xlvii–cxlix. This edition is hereafter cited as *DA.*
29. *DA,* 16.

What did Tocqueville mean when claiming that a new political science was needed for a world entirely new? To be sure, his political science offered no methodology or compendium of axioms and had no room for abstract thought experiments made by impartial observers behind a supposed veil of ignorance. On the contrary, Tocqueville's new political science was designed for a specific circumstance—the democratic world—and was meant to be of use in a new social and political world in which the irresistible democratic revolution gives a certain direction to public spirit, a certain turn to the laws, new maxims to those who govern, and particular habits to the governed. As Eduardo Nolla remarked, "[T]he objective that Tocqueville is fixed upon is above all *political*,"[30] and his method must *not* be interpreted solely in sociological terms. Twenty years after the publication of *Democracy in America*, Tocqueville took up the point again in a famous passage from the preface to volume 1 of *The Old Regime and the Revolution* in which he claimed that "today humanity is driven by an unknown force which we can hope to moderate but not to defeat."[31] Once again, his main concern was a political one: moderating, educating, and purifying democracy.

The key concept of Tocqueville's new science of politics was the *social state (état social)* seen as a product and cause of political institutions, laws, customs, and ideas. On several occasions, Tocqueville commented on the strong interdependence between social and political order, and stressed the centrality of mores to the functioning of a healthy and stable democracy. He started from what is already given—the irresistible democratic revolution, the development of the equality of conditions— and sought to understand all of its political, social, and cultural consequences. That is why Tocqueville's approach was never axiomatic or overly systematic, as some of his interpreters wrongly claimed.[32]

This is amply demonstrated by Tocqueville's preparatory notes and his dialogue with his family and friends, which can be found in Nolla's critical edition of *Democracy in America*. Sometimes, as James Schleifer

---

30. *DA*, 16*n*x.

31. Tocqueville, *Old Regime*, 1:87.

32. See, for example, Jon Elster, "Tocqueville on 1789," in Welch, ed., *Cambridge Companion to Tocqueville*, 64.

noted, Tocqueville sought to carry his readers along by the sheer force of logic, while at other times he relied on carefully chosen metaphors and examples, parallel structures and contrasting pairs, in order to make his points more persuasively.[33] Tocqueville carefully evaluated the merits of all these strategies in his unpublished notes, which constitute a fascinating dialogue with himself as well as with his closest friends and readers (his father and brother, and his friends Gustave de Beaumont and Louis de Kergorlay). In these notes full of queries that reveal a less moderate and guarded thinker than we might expect, and one endowed with an uncommon degree of self-awareness, Tocqueville drafted a clear writing strategy, summarized his findings, and paid specific attention to refining his writing style and method. To this effect, he painstakingly weighed his choices of words and spent a lot of time reflecting upon the definitions of the key concepts used in his works.

The contemporary relevance of Tocqueville's new science of politics must be duly underscored. Much like two centuries ago, we are witnessing today another irresistible revolution, this time under the guise of globalization linked to the progress of equality and democracy. Globalization, too, seems irreversible and unstoppable at the same moment when new critics of the capitalist model have emerged, raising concerns about the effectiveness of the invisible hand of the market. While it may be true that the era of free-market triumphalism has come to a halt for now, we still live in a society where nothing is fixed and in which everyone is tormented by the fear of falling and the desire to rise: "Money has acquired an astonishing mobility, . . . becoming the chief means by which to distinguish between people. . . . The desire to enrich oneself at any price, the preference for business, the love of profit, the search for material pleasure and comfort are the most widespread desires."[34] This, Tocqueville remarked, was no accident given the existence of a close connection between equality of conditions and materialism. "In a

---

33. James T. Schleifer, "Tocqueville's *Democracy in America* Reconsidered," in Welch, ed., *Cambridge Companion to Tocqueville*, 122–24.

34. Tocqueville, *Old Regime*, 1:87. Similar passages can be found in *Democracy in America*, for example, in the chapters "Of the Taste for Material Well-Being in America," "Of the Particular Effects Produced by the Love of Material Enjoyments in Democratic Centuries," and "Why the Americans Appear So Restless amid Their Well-Being," *DA*, 930–38, 942–47.

democratic society," he wrote in a note, "the only visible advantage that you can enjoy over your fellows is wealth,"[35] and the love of well-being eventually becomes a way of life and the dominant taste that can be pursued "without difficulty and without fear,"[36] even if it fosters restlessness of the heart and weak wills.

Hence, the new political science that might be needed for our fast-changing post–Cold War world[37] would stand to learn a great deal from Tocqueville's analysis of the virtues and prerequisites of democracy and freedom. For one thing, his writings invite us to go beyond the minimal procedural definition of democracy and the state-centered perspective that are still fashionable among contemporary students of comparative politics who have studied democratization in Central and Eastern Europe and who often draw on the works of Joseph Schumpeter, Samuel Huntington, and Robert Dahl. According to this view, the presence of elections and multiparty systems is the litmus test of democracy, and the key to assessing the viability of a regime lies in evaluating the capacity of the state to enforce rules of peaceful cohabitation and cooperation. In his work, Huntington justified using a minimal and procedural definition of democracy based on free, fair, and open elections as follows:

> To some people . . . "true democracy" means *liberté, égalité, fraternité,* effective citizen control over policy, responsible government, honesty and openness in politics, informed and rational deliberation, equal participation and power and various other civic virtues. These are, for the most part, good things and people can, if they wish, define democracy in these terms. Doing so, however, raises all the problems that come up with the definitions of democracy by source

35. *DA,* 934*n*g. In a previous sentence (not included in the final text), Tocqueville remarked: "It is not the wealth, but the work that you devote to obtaining it for yourself that encloses human heart within the taste for well-being" (*DA,* 933).

36. *DA,* 931.

37. On Tocqueville's new science of politics, see *Journal of Democracy* 11, no. 2 (January 2000). This issue was entirely dedicated to Tocqueville and brought together a diverse group of authors who reflected upon and updated Tocqueville's analysis of democracy.

or by purpose. Fuzzy norms do not yield good analysis. Elections open free and fair are the essence of democracy, the inescapable *sine qua non*.[38]

The existence of a growing number of illiberal democracies with varying degrees of inequality casts doubt on the accuracy of Huntington's methodology. As his critics have argued, the latter significantly limits our understanding of the state of democracy by making us lose sight of the complex ways in which powerful political and economic elites manage to use existing laws and regulations to promote their factional interests and employ state assets to consolidate their political domination.

Even if Tocqueville's vision was limited by his Western European perspective, it had, however, a profoundly comparative dimension that Huntington's analysis (among others) lacked. It will be recalled that, for Tocqueville, the principle of equality (of conditions) was neither limited to nor contained within the boundaries of one civilization, but it had a clear universal connotation transcending the borders between civilizations. Unlike Tocqueville, Huntington defined democracy primarily as a political system giving the people a voice in the circulation of elites rather than a mechanism for promoting self-governance and preserving liberty. His emphasis on the primacy of central institutions and national elites left little room for the people to manage their own affairs, an approach that parts company with Tocqueville's insistence on self-government as essential to genuine democracy and the most important safeguard against tyranny.[39]

Tocqueville identified several interdependent contextual, sociocultural, and political factors affecting the functioning of political institutions.[40] Among the *contextual* factors, he emphasized the impact of the physical environment in shaping political, economic, and social structures and relationships; the importance of history in shaping political

38. Samuel Huntington, *The Third Wave* (Norman: University of Oklahoma Press, 1991), 9.

39. The comparison between Tocqueville and Huntington is made by Sheldon Gellar in his chapter "Tocquevillian Analytics and the Global Democratic Revolution," in Craiutu and Gellar, ed., *Conversations with Tocqueville*, 34–38.

40. For a useful synthesis of the main elements of "Tocquevillian analytics," see Craiutu and Gellar, ed., *Conversations with Tocqueville*, 44–50.

institutions and national character; the importance of laws, especially property rights and inheritance laws in shaping political, economic, and social structures. Among *sociological* factors, Tocqueville focused on the following: the degree of social equality in society and the extent to which there is movement toward greater equality; the importance of mores, customs, and values (culture) in shaping political institutions and political behavior; the central role of religion and religious institutions in shaping political attitudes, institutions, and relationships. Finally, he highlighted the importance of purely *political* factors such as political sovereignty and constitutional choice in the design of institutions; the identification of the concentration of power in centralized governments and bureaucracies as factors restricting freedom and initiative and leading to despotism and dependency; local liberties and the constitution of self-governing communities; the crucial role of political and civil liberties, especially freedom of association and the press, as bulwarks against absolute power. If one were to contrast Tocqueville's multiple definitions of democracy with the current trend in comparative politics favoring a Schumpeterian, minimalist definition of democracy, one might be tempted to endorse Tocqueville's position that reflects his perceptive intention to offer a broad definition of democracy as a multifaceted phenomenon that eludes narrow categories and is not confined to its American version.

There is an additional aspect of Tocqueville's approach worth highlighting here because it is related to the issue of democratic consolidation in Central and Eastern Europe. He invites us to rethink whether democracy can be implanted first in the political sphere and, from there, as it were, "transplanted" into the mores of society. To be sure, Tocqueville was not particularly optimistic about the prospects of such a development in Europe, a continent that held little promise for liberty during his lifetime. Nonetheless, the recent successful transitions to democracy in various parts of the world prove that such a trajectory may be possible after all and that wise political crafting can make a difference if aided by other factors and favorable circumstances. In *Democracy in America,* Tocqueville reflected on the complex relationship between mores and laws, highlighting their reciprocal influence. Mores, he argued, contribute more to the maintenance of democratic regimes than both laws and physical circumstances. By *mœurs,* Tocqueville referred to "habits of the heart" as well as the various notions and opinions held by people. Commenting on the superiority of mores over laws, he noted:

> When I have spent a good deal of time carefully calculating what the influence of laws is, their relative goodness and their tendency, I always arrive at this point that, above all and beyond all these considerations, beyond all these laws, I find a power superior to them. It is the spirit and the mores of the people, their character. The best laws are not able to make a constitution work in spite of mores; mores turn to good account the worst laws.... Laws, however, work toward producing the spirit, the mores, and the character of the people. But in what proportion? There is the great problem that we cannot think about too much.[41]

In a letter to Francisque de Corcelle from September 17, 1853, Tocqueville emphasized again the priority of mores over laws: "Political societies are not what their laws make them, but what sentiments, beliefs, ideas, habits of the heart, and the spirit of the men who form them, prepare them in advance to be, as well as what nature and education have made them."[42] Finally, in *The Old Regime and the Revolution,* Tocqueville attributed a good part of the misfortunes of French postrevolutionary politics to the absence of genuinely democratic mores. People lacking the art of self-government, he argued, are badly prepared to act on their own and cannot attempt to reform everything at once without destroying everything.[43]

At first sight, by emphasizing the importance of democratic mores over laws, Tocqueville's writings seem to suggest that it would be virtually impossible for democracy to be implanted first in the sphere of politics and legislation and spread from there into society at large. Nonetheless, the recent experience of several East European countries, such as Romania and Bulgaria, might challenge (to a certain extent)

---

41. *DA,* 499*n*m. Also compare and contrast with *DA,* 497*n*g and 513*n*m.

42. Tocqueville, *Selected Letters on Politics and Society,* ed. Roger Boesche, trans. James Toupin and Roger Boesche (Berkeley: University of California Press, 1985), 294.

43. Tocqueville, *Old Regime,* 1:215–16.

this view. It suggests that political crafting—either at the national level or at the supranational level in Brussels—could, in fact, promote democratization practices even where mores are not yet fully democratic. I also believe that granting an all-powerful influence to mores would go against Tocqueville's deeper intentions and instincts that prompted him to reject unicausal theories of political change seeking to ascribe particular causes to historical events. Tocqueville always believed that history remained an open experiment that could end up in either freedom or despotism. As Eduardo Nolla remarked, "[F]or Tocqueville, man is above all a participant in history. He is part of a vast project that he himself must work on each day."[44] If Tocqueville thought that the gradual advancement of the equality of conditions constitutes the key feature of modernity, he did not have the pretension of having discovered a secret logic of history that allowed him to predict the course of the future. While many historical events can be explained only by accidental causes, with contingency playing a role in these occurrences, Tocqueville believed that chance often does nothing that has not been prepared in advance by the social state, the nature of institutions, and the mores of society.[45]

Tocqueville's nuanced account of freedom and determinism in history also invites us to rethink swift large-scale changes that defy conventional theories of democracy and (social and political) change. Although free elections, multiparty political systems, and separation of powers are important principles of all democratic regimes, they are only a part of the story and must be complemented by sound democratic mores, effective self-government, a free press, a functioning civil society, and the rule of law. That is why Tocqueville's rejection of unicausal and unidimensional theories of democracy and political change might also serve as an effective antidote to what Albert O. Hirschman once called *la rage de vouloir conclure*.[46] This is particularly important for political scientists who sometimes doubt individuals'

44. Eduardo Nolla, Editor's Introduction, *DA,* cxlviii.

45. For more details, see Tocqueville, *Lettres choisies: Souvenirs,* ed. Françoise Mélonio and Laurence Guellec (Paris: Gallimard, Quarto, 2003), 798.

46. See Albert O. Hirschman, *The Essential Hirschmann* (Princeton, N.J.: Princeton University Press, 2013), 144.

ability to modify their own fate and tend to subject them to blind determinism. Tocqueville reminds us that, given certain economic, cultural, and social conditions, we should think more in terms of what is *possible* than what is *probable* in politics. He insisted that for all the inevitable growth of the equality of conditions in modern society, democracy could follow two possible paths. On the one hand, equality might lead individuals to greater independence and freedom, while, on the other hand, it might also bring novel forms of servitude.[47] We should be prepared to admit that political crafting does matter and that political outcomes sometimes depend on subjective evaluations and personal choices as much as on objective structural conditions.

A further hint at what kind of new science of politics Tocqueville had in mind can be found in an important speech he gave in 1852 at the Academy of Moral and Political Sciences in Paris. In this text, he drew a seminal distinction between the *art* of government and the *science* of government, insisting on the scientific nature of his approach to the study of politics. The art of government, Tocqueville argued, closely follows the ever-changing flux of political phenomena and constantly fights daily challenges. As such, it varies according to the diversity of events and seeks to meet the ephemeral needs of changing political circumstances.[48] The true science of government, he added, differs from the art of government in many important ways. It covers the immense space between philosophy, sociology, and law, and uncovers the natural rights that belong to individuals, the laws appropriate to different societies, and the virtues and limitations of various forms of government. It is grounded in "the nature of man, his interests, faculties, and needs and teaches what are the laws most appropriate to the general and permanent condition of man."[49] As such, it does not reduce politics to a mere question of arithmetic or logic, nor does it attempt to build an imaginary society in which everything is simple, orderly, uniform, and in accord with reason. The science of government, Tocqueville concluded, is a powerful science that forms around

47. *DA*, 1193; also see 1205.
48. Tocqueville, *Oeuvres complètes*, vol. 16, *Mélanges*, ed. Françoise Mélonio (Paris: Gallimard, 1989), 230. My translation.
49. *Oeuvres complètes*, 16:230; also see 16:231–32.

each society an intellectual atmosphere in which everyone breathes and from which both citizens and their representatives derive their principles of behavior.

The Real Virtues and Limitations of Democracy

Much like Tocqueville two centuries ago, contemporary liberals in Eastern European feel today the irresistible force behind the progress of democracy, which they contemplate with a mixture of admiration, enthusiasm, anxiety, and concern. The latter is triggered by the emergence of a new world in which firm beliefs are dissolved to make way for a universal and relentless questioning of all dogmas, principles, and authorities. Some of them have begun to share Tocqueville's uneasiness toward the rise of the middle class to political power and fear that the advent of a new global civilization might bring new forms of servitude posing serious threats to freedom. In this regard, too, they would be well advised to reread Tocqueville, whose works challenge us to reconsider the virtues and the limitations of democracy as a social and political regime. Far from being a dogmatic partisan of democracy, Tocqueville expressed important reservations about the latter and emphasized the multifaceted nature of modern democracy, being fully aware that the instincts of democracy must be educated and properly constitutionalized before they can bear fruit and extend benefits to society at large.[50]

50. In a lesser-known fragment titled "My instincts, my opinions" (ca. 1841), Tocqueville described his political beliefs as follows: "I have an instinctual preference for democratic institutions, but I am aristocratic by instinct, that is I despise and fear the crowd. I passionately love freedom, legality, the respect for rights *but not democracy*. This is the base of my soul. I hate demagogy, the disorderly action of the masses, their violent and uneducated participation in affairs, the lower classes' envious passions, the irreligious tendencies. . . . I belong neither to the revolutionary party nor the conservative party. But in the end *I hold more to the latter than to the former*. For I differ from the second more by the means than by the end, while I differ from the former by both means and end. Freedom is the first of my passions. This is what is true" (*The Tocqueville Reader*, ed. Alan S. Kahan and Olivier Zunz [Oxford: Blackwell, 2002], 219–20; all emphases added). On this topic, also see Zub, *Reflections*, 182.

It is revealing that, unlike Marx, Tocqueville never provided a single univocal definition of democracy. Instead, he worked with multiple definitions of democracy (James T. Schleifer identified over ten meanings of this concept!) that have puzzled his interpreters over time.[51] If Tocqueville identified democracy with the rule of the people and popular sovereignty, he preferred to emphasize democracy as social condition (*état social*). Equally interesting is the way in which Tocqueville described the real strengths and virtues of democracy, an approach that should be of particular interest to any observer of the political scene in Eastern Europe. As Stephen Holmes, a perceptive student of both Tocqueville and Eastern European politics, noted two decades ago, "[T]oday, the justification of democratic processes by invoking side effects that are unnoticed and unintended by the parties involved seems deeply unsatisfactory."[52] This was, in fact, Tocqueville's choice. While many of his contemporaries and followers tended to praise democracy for its direct effects—prosperity, political participation, dignity, and respect—Tocqueville endorsed democracy for its indirect side effects. To understand why he chose this way of praising democracy's virtues we may want to look at his correspondence. As Tocqueville confessed in the letter to Eugène Stöffels from February 21, 1835, he wanted to speak convincingly to both the overzealous enemies of democracy and its most committed partisans. The critics of democracy, Tocqueville suggested, are often misguided because they mistakenly take for democracy's virtues and flaws what is only secondary to its nature. Nevertheless, Tocqueville also wanted to remind the friends of democracy that it would be a great error to try to offer a single definition of democracy and view it as a *passe-partout*, ready to be transplanted everywhere, regardless of local traditions, customs, mores, and the legacy of the past. The French thinker believed that only by resisting the temptation to simplify the nature of democracy

51. For more detail on this issue, see chap. 19 in James T. Schleifer, *The Making of Tocqueville's "Democracy in America,"* 2nd ed. (Indianapolis: Liberty Fund, 2000), 325–39.

52. Stephen Holmes, "Tocqueville and Democracy," in David Copp, Jean Hampton, and John Roemer, *The Idea of Democracy* (Cambridge: Cambridge University Press, 1993), 33.

the friends of democracy could better address the critiques put forward by their opponents.

This is no minor issue because the virtues of democracy are often *not* those that most people have in mind. I believe that this point is highly relevant to the current context of the growing disenchantment with democratic institutions (such as parliaments and political parties) in Eastern Europe. As Jan Zielonka has remarked, "[C]ynics often describe the recent history of Central and Eastern Europe in terms of moving from one union to another. The former is of course the Soviet Union and the latter the European Union."[53] Eastern European countries were presented with a long list of membership requirements for entrance that left little or no room for bargaining. There were also significant postaccession blues as demonstrated by a 2006 Euro barometer that found that in the new member states (admitted in 2004), the majority of citizens did not believe that they had a real voice in the governance structure of the European Union, so different from the *Europe des patries* model. On the contrary, they perceived politicians in Brussels as detached from their immediate concerns, and they expressed their desire to be able to exercise significant control over issues that are important to their daily lives such as education, health, and social security. As Larry Siedentop warned some time ago, "Democracy in Europe is in danger of being reduced to a competition between elites (alias parties) who manipulate consumer preferences in the fashion of companies,"[54] with decisions taken at the center seeking to meet abstract technocratic targets and criteria.

This is all the more worrisome because, as Tocqueville reminds us, people's choices and instincts are never infallible; in fact, they often choose mediocre leaders in free elections and sometimes even enthusiastically endorse disastrous policies. Democratic governments are, as a rule, more expensive than others are and do not know the art of being economical. Oftentimes, a good part of their enterprises are ill conducted or remain uncompleted, with expenditures being

53. Jan Zielonka, "The Quality of Democracy after Joining the European Union," *East European Politics and Societies* 21, no. 1 (2007): 162.

54. Larry Siedentop, *Democracy in Europe* (New York: Columbia University Press, 2001), 217.

disproportionate to the size of the intended aim or simply unproductive. Moreover, most democratic governments lack a clear perception of the future, based on judgment and experience, for people feel much more than they reason. As a result, the laws passed by democratic legislatures are often defective or incomplete because most people are subject to transitory impulses and often pursue shortsighted plans.

Nonetheless, in spite of so many defects, Tocqueville reminds us that democratic governments enjoy a privilege that is denied to all other governments: democracy allows individuals to make *retrievable* mistakes, and in so doing, provides them with valuable opportunities for effective political learning in both the short and the long run. Democracy, Tocqueville argued, never displays a regular form of government, even when it benefits from exceptional local circumstances. Furthermore, compared to despotism, democratic freedom does not carry through its undertakings as perfectly as an enlightened despot would do it. On the contrary, it often abandons them before reaping the benefits, or embarks on new and perilous projects without finishing the old ones. Nonetheless, Tocqueville added, in the long run democracy produces more than any other political regime; it does each thing less well than an enlightened despot or an absolute monarch, but all things considered, it does more things and raises the general intellectual level of the population. The citizens of a democratic regime are more enlightened and more alert than those of any other form of government. They display civic spirit, are aware of their rights and duties, and respect the laws because they tend to promote the general interest and because these laws can be changed peacefully.

> Under its dominion, it is, above all, not what public administration executes that is great, but what is executed without it and outside of it. Democracy does not give the people the most skillful government, but it does what the most skillful government is often impotent to create; it spreads throughout the social body a restless activity, a superabundant force, an energy that never exists without it, and that, if only circumstances are favorable, can bring forth marvels. Those are its true advantages.[55]

55. *DA*, 399.

Left to its own inclinations, democracy tends to run into extremes, oscillating between too much freedom and too much equality. That is why the cures for democracy's ills must be carefully weighed and chosen, and democracy must be educated, purified of its impure instincts, and moderated.[56]

Tocqueville was uniquely suited to the task of moderating democracy, a topic that retains a surprising relevance for students of contemporary Eastern Europe. He clearly stated his goals not only in the carefully crafted introduction to *Democracy in America* but also in an important passage from the preface to volume 1 of *The Old Regime and the Revolution* to which I have already alluded. "Today," Tocqueville wrote, "humanity is driven by an unknown force which we can hope to *moderate,* but not to defeat."[57] This force posed a number of significant threats to freedom, including an excessive preoccupation with private interests, narrow individualism, and isolation, all of which made possible the appearance of a new form of soft, democratic despotism. Hence, Tocqueville argued, the primary task of those who are called to govern modern society is "to *instruct* democracy, to revive its beliefs if possible, to *purify* its mores, to *regulate* its movements, to substitute little by little the science of public affairs for its inexperience, knowledge of its true interests for its blind instincts; to adapt its government to times and places; to modify it according to circumstances and men."[58]

Written two centuries ago, Tocqueville's words could be applied mutatis mutandis to our condition today. They remind us that, in practice, the task of moderating democracy is inevitably a difficult one, fraught with many hidden dangers and overt challenges. The natural instinct of democracy tends to subordinate equal individuals to the power of the majority and to favor the concentration of power in the hands of the state. In a democratic regime that is unable to moderate its natural instincts, the very idea of right is extinguished, because democracy tends to disregard and trample individual rights under

---

56. I discussed Tocqueville's ideas on moderating democracy in Aurelian Craiutu, "Tocqueville's Paradoxical Moderation," *Review of Politics* 67, no. 4 (Fall 2005): 599–629.

57. *Old Regime,* 1:87 (emphasis added).

58. *DA,* 16 (all emphases added).

its feet while simultaneously extending the influence of society and strengthening centralization. Hence, the importance of cultivating sound judicial habits, respect for legal forms, the custom of public hearings, and the taste for formal procedures that can act as effective barriers against arbitrary power, all of which are highly relevant to the consolidation of the new democratic regimes in Eastern Europe and the emergence of a genuine rule of law in the region.[59]

What Tocqueville wrote in 1835 to Silvestre de Sacy, who had published a review of volume 2 of *Democracy in America* in *Le Journal des Débats,* remains relevant today in the context of Eastern Europe. The new social democratic state that produces great goods is also likely to give birth to a number of dangerous tendencies that must be countervailed through wise institutional crafting. "These seeds, if left to grow unchecked," wrote Tocqueville, "would produce...a steady lowering of the intellectual level of society with no conceivable limit, and this would bring in its train the materialism of mores, and finally, universal slavery. I thought I saw that mankind was moving in this direction, and I viewed the prospect with terror. It was essential, I thought, for all men of good will to join in exerting the strongest possible pressure in the opposite direction."[60]

Tocqueville's musings about the instability of democracy are also relevant to our present concerns about the *quality* of democracy at a point in time when political alternatives to democracy have lost a great deal of their previous appeal. The new consensus among political scientists seems to converge around the view that the real question is about the quality of democracy and its promotion. As Jeffrey C. Isaac pointed out in a provocative piece, "[T]he current discussion of 'quality of democracy' seems driven by a sense that the 'third wave' of democratization is in the midst of a strong undertow which necessitates a rethinking and refinement of basic concepts."[61] Could Tocqueville help us in this regard?

59. See *DA,* 431–42; *Old Regime,* 1:177.

60. Tocqueville's letter to Sacy as quoted in André Jardin, *Tocqueville* (New York: Farrar, Straus and Giroux, 1988), 273. The full content of this important letter was reprinted as an appendix in Lucien Jaume, *Tocqueville* (Paris: Fayard, 2008), 448–50. For more information, see Jardin, *Tocqueville,* 260.

61. Jeffrey C. Isaac, "Thinking about the Quality of Democracy and Its Promotion" (unpublished MS), Indiana University, 2010, 2–3.

It is well known that the Frenchman expressed serious concerns about the quality of democracy, especially the cultural and intellectual effects of unchecked and uneducated democracy. He understood that the instability of the democratic social state tends to shrink our mental horizons by making us prisoners of the present moment. It also encourages us in our pursuit of material pleasures, without much concern for larger vistas. Tocqueville described the effect on those living in democratic regimes as follows: they take a "serious, calculating, and positive turn," which makes them pragmatic to the point of forgetting that there is much more to life than getting rich. Tocqueville was deeply concerned that democracy fosters homogeneity and monotony in the long run rather than diversity. Democratic individuals, he remarked, tend to be alike and do similar things. Consumed by the desire to improve their well-being and having the opportunity to do so, they have many passions and goals, but they all end in the love of wealth or issue from it. The highest price to pay is the homogenization of society, a price that Tocqueville (and other nineteenth-century liberals such as François Guizot and John Stuart Mill) was unwilling to accept.

The solution offered by Tocqueville, which contains an important lesson for Eastern Europe today, was a political one inspired by his American experience. He praised the Americans' propensity to form civil and political associations and regarded these associations as laboratories of democracy that taught citizens the art of being free and gave them the opportunity to pursue their own interests in concert with others. Tocqueville believed that the science of association could serve as an effective means of combating and neutralizing the consequences of individualism that threatens to break society into its bare elements. He also understood that civil and political associations could offer a powerful remedy against social anomie and isolation. The need for associations arises from the relative weakness of each individual, a feature that, Tocqueville remarked, is inherent in the nature of democratic societies in which people are no longer united by firm and lasting ties or by prominent aristocratic individuals.

Nonetheless, in Tocqueville's view, the art of association can have not only a salutary effect in terms of social cooperation, but also a significant impact on the mind and souls of individuals living in democratic times. Feelings and ideas are renewed and the heart itself expands as the result of social interaction and exchanges between equals. Through them, people lend themselves mutual assistance and combine their efforts and energies in the pursuit of common goals. Associations teach their members new ways of improving both the common property and their own lot. They increase their self-confidence and respect for others, impart new knowledge, and enlighten individuals while also cultivating the taste for greater enterprises.

Tocqueville's focus on the importance of intermediary bodies in a free and open society reminds students of Eastern Europe that an orderly and viable democracy ultimately depends on the existence of a vibrant associational life consisting of a multiplicity of social networks, associations, and groups. Indeed, it would be difficult to imagine the daily functioning of modern democratic societies without the existence of civil associations such as charitable foundations, trade unions, churches, business groups, and other voluntary associations. All of these are credited with enhancing the quality of democracy by cultivating citizenship and promoting open fora for public deliberation and self-government. Judging by the density of these civic associations in Eastern Europe, one might be led to conclude that it would take many decades for democracy to gain deep roots in the region.

Nevertheless, the real challenge lies perhaps elsewhere insofar as it has to do with the nature of social bonds. In *Bowling Alone: The Collapse and Revival of American Community* (2000), Robert Putnam distinguished between two forms of social capital: bridging (inclusive) and bonding (exclusive). To paraphrase Putnam, it is essential for democracy in Eastern Europe to foster those forms of social capital that are neither by choice nor by necessity inward looking and do not tend to reinforce exclusive identities.[62] As such, bridging social capital is more likely to have liberal effects than bonding capital, because it encompasses not only a set of viable social networks but also the set of attitudes and mental dispositions that promote social cooperation and toleration.[63]

Building such civic bridges is not going to be an easy task in a region fraught with distrust and that has yet to come to terms with

62. Robert Putnam, *Bowling Alone: The Collapse and Revival of American Community* (New York: Simon & Schuster, 2000), 22.

63. See Putnam, *Bowling Alone*, especially 22–24, 178–79, 357–63.

the powerful legacy of suspicion bequeathed by four decades of communism. The devastating revelations produced by the opening of the archives of the former intelligent services across the region are a telling proof of the deep rifts and wounds in the body of the former communist societies. Moreover, the Eastern European countries have yet to develop a tradition of participation in town hall meetings, must raise the level and intensity of civic engagement, ought to rebuild the depleted social capital, and need to cope with new phenomena such as moral relativism, asocial individualism, increasing privatism, and civic apathy, all of which were discussed by Tocqueville in his writings. In the eyes of many citizens, politics has become nothing else than a synonym for corruption, cynicism, and empty words and promises, and a new ethos of antipolitics seems to emerge among those dissatisfied with the traditional forms of parliamentary democracy and open political competition.

Tocqueville's suggestions to those disenchanted with the status of their democracies would probably be to get involved in civil associations at the local level. He reminds us that civil associations perform many functions in democratic societies, from serving as centers of oppression to tyranny (of the state or of the majority) and neutralizing the effects of social anomie and civic apathy to fostering necessary civil (bourgeois) virtues. As such, they help transform unenlightened self-interest into self-interest rightly understood, moderate the excesses of individualism, and promote civic solidarity by bringing people together and giving them the opportunity to act in concert, all of which are still greatly relevant in the current Eastern European context. In doing so, civil and political associations help heal the fragmentation created by conditions in modern society and generalize norms of reciprocity and informal norms of cooperation.

A Few Tocquevillian Prescriptions

Joining the European Union has arguably been the greatest achievement to date of the former communist countries in Central and Eastern Europe. Becoming members of this select club has helped and accelerated the process of democratization and democratic consolidation in the region, while the extension of NATO's security umbrella over Central and Eastern Europe had allayed the traditional fears regarding Russia's imperial designs. Nonetheless, recent economic and political developments in the region, most notably in Hungary, which until recently had been considered as a success story before the new government of Viktor Orban introduced several nondemocratic practices, call for prudence when it comes to assessing the success of democratization in Eastern Europe. One caveat is in order. It would be a mistake to speak of the former communist countries as a unified block and to ignore the major differences between their postcommunist patterns of political and economic development. As the editors of a special issue of the *East European Politics and Societies* pointed out, "[P]ost-communist countries can claim both the best and the worst record of transition from authoritarianism to democracy.... While some countries enjoy high-quality democratic institutions, others suffer under authoritarian regimes of various hues."[64]

Making sense of all these differences has been a challenge for political scientists in the last two decades.[65] Their favored paradigm was predominantly of Schumpeterian inspiration, interpreting democracy as a form of institutionalized elite competition legitimated primarily through electoral processes. Yet it is equally obvious that the really interesting question is no longer *whether* democracy will win over in Eastern Europe in the short run, but what *kind* of democracy will obtain there in the long run. Democracy has always been a qualitative concept whose main meanings are essentially contestable and open to interpretation. In other words, the question yet to be decided is whether the region shall have a vibrant and workable democracy based on genuine party competition, civil society, rule of law, democratic accountability, and separation of powers, or a weak democracy based on a cacophonic and incoherent public discourse, weak grassroots politics, dubious elite settlements, no rule of law, and a low level of social trust. To use Tocqueville's words, it is still an open question whether the new

64. Grzegorz Ekiert, Jan Kubik, and Milada Anna Vachudova, "Democracy in the Post-Communist World: An Unending Quest," *East European Politics and Societies* 21, no. 1 (2007): 10, 12.

65. On this issue, also see Ganev, *Preying on the State*, chap. 1.

civil societies and political elites in Eastern Europe will manage to educate and purify democracy and its instincts in such a way that the new democratic institutions and practices will promote freedom and justice rather than an oligarchic structure based on deep social and economic inequalities.

This open question prompts us to reevaluate the factors that play a key role in explaining the success and failure of democratization in the postcommunist world. The renewed attention paid to the quality of democracy is undoubtedly a symptom of the recent anxieties of transitologists regarding democratic consolidation. Moreover, the shift from a focus on transition to democracy and democratic consolidation to the "quality" of democracy reflects the new political landscape and the belief that illiberal and dysfunctional democracies will continue to coexist with liberal ones in the years ahead. It is therefore tempting to conclude this essay by offering, cum grano salis, a few tentative Tocquevillian recommendations to politicians and students of democracy in the region. What, if anything, can Tocqueville's *Democracy in America* and *The Old Regime and the Revolution* teach legislators in Eastern Europe?[66] Here are a few tentative conclusions.

1. *Democracy for a global world.* It is widely acknowledged today that no powerful new ideological competitor is likely to challenge democracy's supremacy at the beginning of the twenty-first century. Equality of conditions as a process toward more equality and inclusion will continue to spread to other parts of the world in spite of occasional setbacks and delays. In this regard, the inevitable advancement of equality of conditions resembles the concepts of globalization and modernization. Therefore, one of the main tasks facing all Eastern European democracies will be to adjust

66. On this topic, also see *Journal of Democracy* 10, no. 1 (January 2000), a special issue dedicated to Toqueville. The breadth of Tocqueville's interests and the comprehensiveness of his vision should also serve as a model to contemporary political scientists who would certainly be more persuasive and interesting (and less boring) if their writings, much like Tocqueville's works, combined insights from fields as different as history, law, religion, philosophy, and literature.

to the challenges of globalization while maintaining viable democratic institutions at home.

2. *Beware of transplanting the literary spirit into politics!* Tocqueville pointed out that intellectuals usually do not make good politicians and explained why this is the case by drawing on the example of the French *philosophes*.[67] Above the real society, they built an "imaginary society in which everything seemed simple and coordinated, uniform, equitable, and in accord with reason."[68] They developed a strong penchant for general theories and exact symmetry in laws, and displayed a disquieting propensity toward "the original, the ingenious, and the new in institutions; the same desire to remake the whole constitution all at once, following the rules of logic and according to a single plan, rather than trying to fix its various parts."[69] As a result, they lost touch with reality and failed in their attempt to successfully transplant their ideas into practice.[70]

3. *Educate democracy!* There is no better way of educating democracy than by promoting pluralism. Tocqueville disliked homogeneity and was deeply concerned that variety was disappearing from the modern world. He felt stifled in a world dominated by middle-class values that, in his view, tended to promote conformism and social homogeneity. That is why he never came to like capitalism and expressed

67. For a brief analysis of the predicament of Romanian intellectuals from a Tocquevillian perspective, see Sorin Antohi, "Une politique 'abstraite et littéraire': L'intelligentsia et la démocratie: Le cas roumain," *La Revue Tocqueville/ The Tocqueville Review* 18, no. 1 (1997): 99–106.

68. Tocqueville, *Old Regime*, 1:201.

69. Tocqueville, *Old Regime*, 1:201.

70. One might reply, however, that the "literary spirit" in politics can no longer be harmful today when technocrats, businessmen, and lawyers have become much more influential than intellectuals. Moreover, the current intellectual climate is influenced by liberal ironists and consumerist unbelievers who are no longer interested in playing the role of gadflies challenging public opinion. See G. M. Tamás, "Democracy's Triumph, Philosopher's Peril," *Journal of Democracy* 11, no. 1 (2000): 103–10.

serious concerns about the alleged vulgarity of democracy. Accordingly, he emphasized the need to "moderate," "purify," and "educate" democracy, being preoccupied with the quality of the human soul in democratic regimes. Tocqueville understood well the middling effects of democracy and was aware of the challenges posed by civic apathy, withdrawal, disenchantment with democracy, and the moral confusion brought by it. "Nearly all the extremes become softer and are blunted," he concluded in the last chapter of *Democracy in America*; "near all the salient points are worn away to make way for something middling, which is at the very same time less high and less low, less brilliant and less obscure than what was seen in the world."[71] To his credit, Tocqueville never succumbed to despair and pointed to a wide array of means of moderating and educating democracy. While criticizing the excessive love of material well-being that he believed fostered indifference and civic apathy, he also stressed the positive aspects of individualism and self-interest rightly understood (a virtuous form of materialism sui generis) as foundations for the art of association and self-government. He insisted (in an unpublished note that reminds one of Blaise Pascal) that, in the end, human greatness lies in finding a certain middle between the extremes: "It is necessary to find in some part of the work ... the idea of the middle that has been so dishonored in our times. Show that there is a firm, clear, voluntary way to see and to grasp the truth between two extremes."[72]

4. *Democracy as a "polycentric" system of self-governance.* Drawing on the work of Vincent and Elinor Ostrom, for whom Tocqueville was a constant source of inspiration, I would like to suggest that we consider a "polycentric" definition of democracy as a system that fosters a multiciplicity of decision-making units at different levels that are allowed to formulate policies based on diverse physical, socioeconomic, and cultural conditions

71. *DA*, 1281.
72. *DA*, 1281*ne*.

and contexts.[73] If we take this route that allows us to examine various levels of democratic governance, then we will be able to avoid working with a minimalist or purely formal definition of democracy based on elections, rule of law, and political competition that ignores the challenges posed by machine politics, money, and "boss rule" that have come to usurp the authority of citizens in stable democracies.

5. *Encourage self-government in order to foster "civic capacity."* The previous conclusion pointed to the multiplicity of forms and levels of self-governance, reminding us that one cannot become skilled at exercising liberty in great matters without first learning to use liberty in small ones. Tocqueville's lesson is that genuine democracy exists only where citizens learn how to effectively deal with public affairs at their local level. True democracy is not to be equated with elections and free competition among parties, and it is the opposite of a regime in which the center seeks to keep the nation in a semipermanent tutelage. Local institutions, Tocqueville insisted in *Democracy in America*, put liberty and rights within the people's reach, teaching them to appreciate their peaceful enjoyment and familiarizing people with them. At the local level, the individual remains the best and only judge of his own interest; local institutions combine independence and power and form strong attachments while promoting public spirit and fostering "civic capacity." If democracy at the local level remains weak, its institutions will not bear fruit and will lead to disenchantment.

Tocqueville's greatness lies precisely in demonstrating that building democracy always is an open task that requires prudence, wisdom, detachment, and enlightenment. In a famous 1837 letter to his English translator, Henry Reeve, he presented himself as an impartial observer

73. On the concept of polycentricity, see Vincent Ostrom's essay "Polycentricity," in *Polycentricity and Local Public Economies: Readings from the Workshop in Political Theory and Policy Analysis,* ed. Michael McGinnis (Ann Arbor: University of Michigan, 1999), 63–86.

placed at the center, in a perfect equipoise between past and future, aristocracy and democracy. He took to task not only those who tried to give different features to his works, according to their own political passions, but also those who wanted to make him a party man and alternately gave him democratic or aristocratic prejudices.[74] Having come into the world at the end of a long Revolution, which, after having destroyed the old state, had created nothing durable, Tocqueville felt that he belonged neither to aristocracy nor to democracy, so that his instinct led him blindly neither toward one nor toward the other. "In a word," he concluded, "I was so thoroughly in equilibrium between the past and the future that I felt naturally and instinctively attracted toward neither the one nor the other, I did not need to make great efforts to cast calm glances on both sides."[75] Tocqueville's desire to play the role of a detached observer reminds us that appreciating the true virtues of democracy is not an easy task, and that the apprenticeship of liberty is a long and arduous journey.

74. "I perhaps would have had one set of prejudices or the other," remarked Tocqueville, "if I had been born in another century and in another country. But the chance of birth has made me very comfortable defending both" (Tocqueville, *Selected Letters,* 115).

75. Tocqueville, *Selected Letters,* 115–16.

15

Tocqueville and "Democracy in Japan"

REIJI MATSUMOTO

Tocqueville never went to Japan. He had nothing to say about the country. He traveled in the United States and Canada to write *Democracy in America*. The only country or region other than Europe and North America that he saw with his own eyes was North Africa. On India, which he never visited, he carefully read available works and left unedited but interesting notes on them. In *Democracy*, we find a few significant references to some other nations of which he seems to have no profound knowledge: Egypt, Turkey, and China. But there is no reference to Japan, as far as I know, either in *Democracy* or in any of his other writings. Apparently the country occupies no place in his comparative perspective. The scope of his intellectual curiosity is narrower in this regard than that of Montesquieu.

China is a different matter. In *Democracy,* Tocqueville makes a few, but suggestive references to China. He sees in China a kind of egalitarian society, lacking feudalism or caste system, governed by a centralized and meritocratic bureaucracy in the name of the emperor. It is a well-ordered, stabilized, and prosperous society, but people are so obedient to authorities and cling so much to their ancestral laws and custom that they can't change anything. In short, according to Tocqueville, China represents a terminal stage of civilization deprived of any possibility of further change and development. One might say that he sees there "an end of history."

When the Europeans reached China three hundred years ago, they found all the arts at a certain degree of perfection, and they were astonished that, having arrived at this point, the Chinese had not advanced more. Later they discovered the vestiges of some advanced knowledge that had been lost. The nation was industrial; most of the scientific methods were preserved within it; but science itself no longer existed. That explained to the Europeans the singular type of immobility in which they found the mind of the people. The Chinese, while following the path of their fathers, had forgotten the reasons that had guided the latter. They still used the formula without looking for the meaning; they kept the instrument and no longer possessed the art of modifying and of reproducing it. So the Chinese could not change anything. They had to give up improvement. They were forced to imitate their fathers always and in all things, in order not to throw themselves into impenetrable shadows, if they diverged for an instant from the road that the latter had marked. The source of human knowledge had nearly dried up; and although the river still flowed, it could no longer swell its waves or change its course.

China had subsisted peacefully for centuries however; its conquerors had taken its mores; order reigned there. A sort of material well-being was seen on all sides. Revolutions there were very rare, and war was so to speak unknown.[1]

These comments are of course not a result of learned study but a stereotype of China prevalent in nineteenth-century Europe, the variations of which we could follow from Georg Wilhelm Friedrich Hegel's *Reich der Dauer* to Max Weber's *Rationalismus der Ordnung.* The image of China as an ultimate stagnation, however, had a wide resonance in modern Japan. Indeed, some of the early Japanese readers of *Democracy* took it seriously and tried to draw a sharply contrasting portrait of Japan as a dynamic country keenly reacting to the Western impact and transforming its old regime into the first modern state in Asia. This transformation was carried out by those who were deeply shocked at the news of the Opium War and who made every effort to escape the fate of the Chinese. One can say that the unexpected defeat of China drove the Japanese to abolish the old Tokugawa Regime. As a natural

1. Alexis de Tocqueville, *Democracy in America: Historical-Critical Edition of "De la démocratie en Amérique,"* ed. Eduardo Nolla, trans. James T. Schleifer, 4 vols. (Indianapolis: Liberty Fund, 2010), 786. This edition is hereafter cited as *DA.*

result of the historical process of the Meiji Revolution, China lost in the mind of the Japanese its traditional role as a model of civilization, a role that Europe would take over. Tocqueville did not cause this intellectual revolution, but he confirmed it.[2]

Then, is Tocqueville relevant for considering Japan itself, about which he says nothing? If so, how, why, and to what extent? This question of relevance is different from the question of reception, that is to say, the question of when and how Tocqueville was introduced to Japan and what influence he had on the Japanese people. In this chapter, I am mainly concerned with the first question, Tocqueville's relevance to Japan. But I would like to briefly address the related issue of reception, for his works, particularly *Democracy in America,* did find a significant audience in Japan in the early Meiji era, and they exerted a not negligible influence, which is now almost forgotten.

Democracy's First Voyage to Japan: Tocqueville and Fukuzawa Yukichi

Although Tocqueville never traveled to Japan, his works, in particular *Democracy in America,* did reach that country and were welcomed in the intellectual climate of enthusiasm for Western ideas aroused after the Meiji Revolution in 1867–1868.

The name of Tocqueville first became widely known to Japan through the Japanese translation of Samuel Smile's *Self-Help* published in 1870, in which he was described as a young man of ambition, who, throwing away his aristocratic background, sought in America his own fortune. The translator, Nakamura Masanao (1832–1891), also known for his translation of John Stuart Mill's *On Liberty* (1872), was a representative philosopher of the so-called Meiji Enlightenment and a member of *Meirokusha,*[3] the first important association of intellectuals in modern

2. It was not only Tocqueville who depicted China as an ultimate stagnation. Some English social theorists such as Thomas Buckle and John Stuart Mill were also influential in spreading in Japan the image of Chinese immobility.

3. For *Meirokusha,* see J. K. Fisher, *The Meirokusha* (Charlottesville: University of Virginia Press, 1974).

Japan founded in 1873, together with Nishi Amane (1829–1897), Tsuda Mamichi (1829–1903), Kanda Takahira (1830–1898), Fukuzawa Yukichi (1835–1901), Katō Hiroyuki (1836–1916), Mori Arinori (1847–1889), and others. Mori, who had studied several years in England and the United States and would later become the first minister of education, might have read earlier Henry Reeve's English translation of *Democracy* and drawn his colleagues' attention to the book.

The first Japanese translation of *Democracy* was also from the English version. Obata Tokujirō (1842–1905), Fukuzawa's primary associate at Keio Gijuku (now Keio University), translated and published in 1873 under the title of *Jyōboku jiyū no ron* (On freedom of the press) chapter 3 of part 2 of the first volume. Then, in subsequent years, he published three partial translations (always from Reeve's English version) of the First *Democracy*: chapters on public spirit, the idea of rights, and administrative decentralization. Apparently this choice of texts for translation met the intellectual demand of the time, for this was exactly the moment when, for the first time in the history of Japan, a democratic opposition movement was beginning to take shape.

The first declaration of political opposition based on democratic principles was the famous Memorial [i.e., Petition] on the Establishment of a Representative Assembly (*Minsengiin Setsuritsu Kenpakusho*) of 1874. Itagaki Taisuke, the leader of the group that addressed it to the government, had stepped down from the government the year before and returned to his home province, Tosa (now Kōchi Prefecture), and founded a political association (*Risshisha*), which would later develop into the first political party in Japan (*Jiyūtō*, the Liberal Party). So this opposition movement was born from a power struggle inside the oligarchic government. At its first stage it was mainly supported by frustrated former samurai, but it later spread widely among the common people. Indeed, in the late 1870s through the subsequent decade, it developed into a national opposition movement called the Movement for Freedom and People's Rights (*Jiyū Minken Undō*), or, more briefly, the Popular Rights Movement, which demanded the establishment of a constitution and an elected assembly.

Tocqueville's *Democracy in America* attracted the first Japanese audience in this political and intellectual context of the 1870s and 1880s. It goes without saying that Obata's choice of texts for his early translations was highly strategic.[4] Tocqueville's arguments for freedom of the press, individual rights, and the political effect of administrative decentralization provided a powerful theoretical basis for the agenda of the Popular Rights Movement. In a public speech commemorating the first anniversary of *Kōjunsha,* a voluntary association of intellectuals organized mainly by the alumni of Keio, Obata made a defense of party politics, drawing on Tocqueville's argument for the necessity of political associations for encouraging the activities of civil associations.[5] In the political upheaval and social confusion that was a natural consequence of the rapid transition of the country from a closed society to an open society,[6] Tocqueville was read as an intellectual guide to the democratic principle of free speech and voluntary association. When the complete translation of the First *Democracy* was published in 1881–1882, at the high tide of the Popular Rights Movement, the translator titled it *Jiyū genron,* that is to say, *A Fundamental Theory of Freedom.*[7]

Among various principles of democracy introduced to Japan at the time, particularly noteworthy was the issue of decentralization and local government, for it was a specifically Tocquevillian issue, while, on other issues such as freedom of the press and voluntary associations,

4. In 1875, two years after the publication of *Jyōboku jiyū no ron,* the government enacted the first legislation for restraining freedom of the press (*zanpōritsu* and *shinbunshi jyōrei*), which, as Tocqueville argues, had no effect but radicalizing political journalism.

5. Obata Tokujirō, "Kōjunsha Daiichi Kinenkai Hōkoku [Speech at the First Anniversary of Kōjunsha]," *Kōjunzasshi* 37 (1881): 6–8.

6. Drawing on Henri Bergson and Karl Popper, Maruyama Masao makes a brilliant analysis of the intellectual climate of Japan before and after the Meiji Revolution in the perspective of the abrupt transition of the country from a closed society to an open one. Maruyama Masao, "Kaikoku" [Open the country]. The essay was first published in 1959 and included in his book *Chūsei to hangyaku* [Loyalty and revolt] (Tokyo: Chikuma Shobō, 1992), and then in the collection of his entire writings, *Maruyama Masao chosakushū* [Collective writings of Maruyama Masao], vol. 8 (Toyko: Iwanami Shoten, 1996). There is a German translation of the essay "Kaikoku—Öffnung des Landes; Japans Modernisierung," in *Saeclum* 18, volume 1–2 (1967). For its main arguments in English, see the present author's review of *Chūsei to hangyaku,* in *Japan Foundation Newsletter,* 21–4 (December 1993), pp. 16–19.

7. *Jiyū genron,* trans. Koizuka Ryū from the English version (Tokyo & Osaka: Bararō, 1881–82).

not only Tocqueville but also other thinkers could be quoted for reference; John Stuart Mill or Herbert Spencer, for instance. The publication of Obata's translation of the chapter on "The Political Effects of Administrative Decentralization" was timely, and it was his mentor, Fukuzawa Yukichi, who made an original use of Tocqueville's argument in the political context of Japan at the time.

Fukuzawa read *Democracy in America* carefully in 1877. But already in his two famous works, *An Encouragement of Learning* (1871–1874) and *The Outline of a Theory of Civilization* (1873), he made certain arguments that would remind present readers of Tocqueville, although he gave no explicit reference to the French aristocrat: skepticism about governmental intervention, emphasis on private initiative, criticism at scholars' servility toward the government, and worry about people's tendency to always follow the trend of the time. These critical comments Fukuzawa made on the intellectual climate of Japan at the time showed certain affinities with Tocquevillian thinking about democracy. At a certain moment, his imagination went so close to Tocqueville's new concept of democratic despotism that he wrote as follows:

> In sum, the government of the past used force, but the present regime uses both force and intelligence. In contrast to the former, the latter is rich in techniques of controlling the people. Past governments deprived the people of power; the present regime robs them of their minds. Past government controlled men externally, the present regime controls their interior as well. The former was a devil to the people, the latter is now a god. Fear has given place to blind worship. If such abuses of the past are not reformed at this juncture, and the government undertakes something new, the form of civilization may seem to be gradually given shape, but in fact the people will lose all energy, so that the spirit of civilization will gradually wither away.[8]

8. Fukuzawa Yukichi, *Gakumon no susume*, trans. David D. Dilworth and Umeyo Hirano, *An Encouragement of Learning* (Tokyo: Sophia University, 1969), 31. For the essentials of Fukuzawa's thought, see Carmen Blacker's brief but brilliant study, *The Japanese Enlightenment: A Study of the Writings of Fukuzawa Yukichi* (Cambridge: Cambridge University Press, 1964).

Playing a leading role in enlightening the people about Western civilization, Fukuzawa had a certain skepticism about the rapid and undiscriminating westernization at the time. First, it was too much led and controlled by the government and too little promoted by private initiative. He deplored that governmental regulations extended to every sector of industry and commerce. "Schools are licensed by the government," he said, "as are preaching, cattle grazing, and sericulture. Almost seventy to eighty percent of private enterprises have some government connection."[9] Fukuzawa worried that the excessive leadership of the government in westernization would only aggravate people's traditional spirit of dependence. Worse, the scholars of Western learning, his colleagues and comrades in the intellectual mission of enlightenment, were pleased to be hired by the government and to lead the people from above. Provoking most of his friends, he declared his principle of doing things as private enterprise (*shiritsu igyo*). "I shall first take the position of private enterprise to lecture on the art of learning, go into business, discuss the law, write books, publish papers, etc. I should do any or all of these things within the limits of my capacities and without offending others. I should correctly manage my own affairs within the bounds of law. Should I suffer injustice due to bad government decrees, I should exhort the government severely without subservience."[10]

Generally speaking, the modernization of an underdeveloped country was usually started by governmental initiative, and one might refer to Japan as its first successful example. Indeed, the government played a leading role in the subsequent development of modern Japan and many scholars and intellectuals, Japanese as well as those invited Europeans and Americans called "*oyatoi gaikokujin*" (literally, "hired foreigners"), collaborated in it. But private scholars' effort to enlighten the people also brought about beneficial results, and Fukuzawa's warning against the excessive initiative of the government was not without meaning. Thanks to him, Japan took a course of modernization different from that of Muhammad 'Ali's Egypt depicted by Tocqueville as follows:

9. Fukuzawa, *An Encouragement of Learning*, 25.
10. Fukuzawa, *An Encouragement of Learning*, 26.

The Pasha who reigns today over Egypt found the population of the country composed of very ignorant and very equal men, and to govern it he appropriated the science and the intelligence of Europe. The particular enlightenment of the sovereign thus coming to combine with the ignorance and the democratic weakness of his subjects, the farthest limit of centralization has been attained without difficulty, and the prince has been able to make the country into his factory and the inhabitants into his workers.[11]

Fukuzawa's second reservation about the intellectual tendencies of the time consisted in his doubt whether the Japanese people's abrupt and holistic reception of Western civilization was spontaneous. Was their change of mind from cultural seclusion to westernization a resolute decision derived from critical reflections on tradition? He suspected that most people rather blindly obeyed the direction of the government and followed the current tendency of opinion. Then, if so, it was the same spirit of dependence that drove them to move in the opposite way. In spite of the collective conversion of the people from isolationism to internationalism, they did not acquire the spirit of independence any more than before. Thus, Fukuzawa did not fail to see in the changing attitude of the people an unchanged habit of mind. "They only believe in the new through the same faith with which they once believed in the old."[12]

Even if these arguments in *An Encouragement of Learning* revealed certain affinities with Tocquevillian thinking, they were not derived from Tocqueville's text. They rather showed that Fukuzawa had held Tocquevillian ideas before reading Tocqueville. A few years later, however, he began to read carefully *Democracy in America,* using first Obata's Japanese translation and then Reeve's English version. What he learned from the book was clearly seen in his tract of 1877, *Bunkenron* (On decentralization), and his reading notes contained in *Oboegaki* (Memoranda) of 1876–1878.[13] These writings clearly show that he read

11. *DA*, 1214–15.

12. Fukuzawa, *An Encouragement of Learning*, 95.

13. *Bunkenron* is included in *Fukuzawa Yukichi Zenshū* [Collective works of Fukuzawa Yukichi] (Tokyo: Iwanami Shoten, 1959), vol. 4, and "Oboegaki," in vol. 7.

Democracy in America in the political context of Japan in order to consider serious problems confronting the people at the time.

In spite of certain reservations and skepticism, Fukuzawa's main line of argument in *Encouragement* and *Outline* had basically been in accordance with the orientation of the government toward modernization. The two books were in a sense the product of his effort to collaborate in his own way with the government in leading the people to civilization. A few years later, however, the government's autocratic implementation of radical policies aroused among the people two significant opposition movements. One was the Popular Rights Movement launched by Itagaki and others, and the other was a series of military insurrections of frustrated former samurai, the last of which eventually developed into the *Seinan Sensō* (Southwest War) of 1877, the greatest civil war in modern Japanese history, started by the revolt of Saigō Takamori, the very hero of the revolution of 1867–1868 and one of the top leaders of the government until 1873.[14] Fukuzawa took this political situation

14. The radical policies of the government that deprived the great majority of former samurai of their social privileges and economic foundation drove them to desperate rebellion, and a series of military insurrections broke out in 1875–1877. The *Seinan Sensō*, marked in a sense the end of the Meiji Revolution. The rebel army, led by Saigō Takamori, was composed of more than forty thousand former samurai who had fought under his command against the *bakufu* in the civil war of 1868–1869. As a result of fierce battles over several months, it was defeated by the new conscript army mostly composed of peasants. Saigō committed suicide, and his old comrade now leading the government, Ōkubo Toshimichi, consolidated his leadership, but he was himself assassinated the next year by a former samurai.

The Meiji Revolution was a samurai revolution in the sense that it was carried out mainly by lower-class samurai, but its end result was the elimination of the whole class of samurai and the creation of an egalitarian and competitive society. The *Seinan Sensō*, with its more than thirty thousand casualties, tragically revealed this historical consequence of the revolution. The successive deaths of Saigō and Ōkubo, the two heroes of the revolution, enemies in their last years, marked the completion of the revolution's first task. Hegel would find there an example of the *cunning of reason* and Tocqueville would say, "Everywhere you saw the various incidents in the lives of peoples turn to the profit of democracy; all men aided it by their efforts: those who had in view contributing to its success and those who did not think of serving it; those who fought for it and even those who declared themselves its enemies" (*DA*, 10).

seriously and tried to alter it, proposing a strategy based on a socio-logical analysis of the opposition movements. Tocqueville's theoretical distinction of government and administration gave him a suggestion for this proposal.

In *Bunkenron*, Fukuzawa began his argument by saying that there were virtually no other people than former samurai (*shizoku*) who were capable of managing public affairs in Japan at the time. This view was based on his historical judgment that, in the Tokugawa Regime, only the class of samurai had been involved in politics, while other peo-ple, peasants, merchants, and artisans, had been preoccupied with their personal interests and lived in complete indifference to public affairs. Under this historical condition, Fukuzawa said, there was no important political change that was not caused by the power of samurai. The drastic political change triggered by the coming of Commodore Perry's squadron, which eventually resulted in the overthrow of the Tokugawa Regime, was a typical example. Indeed, the Meiji Revolu-tion was the destruction of a samurai regime by samurai themselves. Precisely because the samurai had formed in the old regime a politi-cal class and performed political functions, they could change it from within and finally transformed it into a totally new regime. This samu-rai capacity to change the system, Fukuzawa emphasized, was not a new power created at the time but the old capacity that they had exer-cised over two hundred years in the old regime. Only it was radically transformed and used for a totally different purpose. "Although that political change was caused by the power of samurai," he said, "it was not that they created a new power but that they transformed the old power of their own to do it."[15]

---

15. *Bunkenron, Fukuzawa Zenshū,* 4:238. This contrastive use of the words *shizō* (creation) and *henkei* (transformation) should be interpreted in reference to another contrast that Fukuzawa shows between creation and progress (*kai-shin*) in the famous preface to *An Outline of a Theory of Civilization.* In this pref-ace, written a year and a half before he wrote *Bunkenron,* he had emphatically underlined the novelty of the Japanese people's experience in absorbing Western civilization. The essence of Western civilization consists in development, and therefore every country in the West is always in movement and makes progress every day and every month. This development, however, is a gradual growth of the same elements and far from a creation of new things, which is an imminent

Scarcely a decade after the revolution, Fukuzawa found in no social class other than *shizoku* enough development of public spirit. In the rapid progress of social transformation under the new government, however, the class of *shizoku* was inevitably divided. Fukuzawa identified three subgroups of *shizoku:* those who were in the government or cooperated with it in leading the nation, those participating in the Popular Rights Movement, and the supporters of military rebellion. The first two were progressive or reformist, for they accepted Western civilization and enlightenment; the last was conservative, clinging to traditional values. Fukuzawa himself was one of the intellectual leaders of progress and enlightenment, but, as shown above, he distanced himself from the government and declared his position of private enterprise. As for the Popular Rights Movement, he was of course sympathetic to its project and even provided several basic ideas for it. To some extent, he can be regarded as one of the intellectual originators of the movement. However, Fukuzawa had some doubt about certain tendencies in the movement, for it seemed to him that it was too absorbed in acquiring governmental power and lost the spirit of independence from the government. In his eyes, many leaders of the movement appeared to be the same kind of people as those of the government, and he suspected that, once in power, they would have done the same thing as the latter were doing then and left few things for private citizens to do. In other words, Fukuzawa was critical of the Popular Rights Movement in the same way as Tocqueville was of opposition parties in the July Monarchy. The perspicacious observer of French politics remarked in 1840:

> In France where the revolution I am speaking about is more advanced than in any other people of Europe, these same opinions [in favor of the centralization of power] have entirely taken hold of the mind. When you listen attentively to the voices of our different parties, you will see that there is not one of them that does not adopt them.

----

task for the Japanese at the time. "Contemporary Japanese civilization," he says, "is undergoing a complete metamorphosis like that of fire into water, and a transition from nothing to something. This sudden change should not be called progress, but could be labeled creation." Bunmeiron no gairyaku, *Fukuzawa Zenshū,* 4:4 (translation mine, for the English translation referred to above contains an apparent error).

Most consider that the government acts badly; but all think that the government must act constantly and put its hand to everything. Even those who wage war most harshly against each other do not fail to agree on this point.[16]

In contrast to the political tendency of the Popular Rights Movement, which Fukuzawa thought was too much preoccupied with the acquisition of governmental power and too little concerned with restraining it, he found in the hopeless rebellions of the *shizoku* an eruption of independent spirit. He saw this as extremely important, particularly in the intellectual climate of conformity then prevailing. Being himself an eminent scholar of Western learning, Fukuzawa was skeptical of the collective conversion of the people to Western civilization, which seemed to him a result of their traditional spirit of conformity and dependence. In contrast, and quite paradoxically, he placed a high value on the moral energy that drove frustrated *shizoku* to revolt against the government. Just after the *Seinan Sensō* and in the midst of the storm of condemnation against Saigō, he wrote the famous treatise *Teichū Kōron* [*A Public Discourse in the Year of 1877*], a hidden tract not published until his death, in which he dared to defend Saigō and praised the rebellion as a manifestation of "the Japanese people's spirit of resistance."[17]

It is not that Fukuzawa supported the uprising of Saigō's troops. Nor was he in sympathy with the latter's political ideals. He regarded the rebellion as reactionary and destined to fail. But he found in the last samurai revolt an invaluable spirit of resistance, which was, to his regret, withering in the course of government-directed modernization. Considering people's general tendency toward conformity and dependence at the time, Fukuzawa thought it essential to maintain the ancient samurai spirit and to apply it not to a desperate armed revolt but to a more constructive project. The power of the samurai was indispensable for the preservation of the moral energy of the people, but it needed to be "transformed" into the modern ethos of independence.

16. *DA,* 1198.

17. *Fukuzawa Yukichi Zenshū,* 6:533–53. For the meaning of Fukuzawa's paradoxical praise of Saigō's spirit of resistance, see Maruyama Masao's insightful analysis in "Chūsei to hangyaku," lead article of the book *Chūsei to hangyaku.*

Saigō was only to be blamed because of his lack of thought for the future.

For this project of transforming the power of samurai, Fukuzawa found an appropriate solution in Tocqueville's praise of local liberties based on the theoretical distinction of government and administration. As a nationalist, he was in full agreement with the French aristocrat that governmental centralization was indispensable for national independence and acknowledged from this viewpoint the historical legitimacy of the Meiji Revolution that abolished the polygovernmental Tokugawa Regime. In contrast, he was deeply impressed by Tocqueville's argument against administrative centralization: "I think that administrative centralization is suitable only to enervate the peoples who submit to it, because it constantly tends to diminish the spirit of citizenship in them."[18] Finding in Tocqueville's argument an important suggestion for resolving the political crisis caused by the successive *shizoku* rebellions, he proposed to create a system of local administration and to involve the *shizoku* in it. Probably, Fukuzawa was thinking of transforming the class of the *shizoku* into something like English gentry, which played an important role in English society as the guardian of local liberties, and apparently Tocqueville was an intellectual origin of this idea.

So much for the Japanese reception of Tocqueville in the early Meiji era. In the latter part of this chapter, I shall consider the other aspect of the problem, the relevance of Tocqueville to Japan: how and to what extent are Tocqueville's ideas useful for understanding modern Japan? What new perspective would his theory of democracy provide for reconsidering its history and society? In this theoretical examination, I shall discuss the two central issues of Tocquevillian thinking about democracy, equality and revolution, and give some reflections, in the light of these two problems, on the historical development of modern Japan. In this consideration, however, I shall be more concerned with revolution than with equality, for I have already discussed general tendencies toward equality in Japanese society elsewhere.[19] The

18. *DA*, 147.

19. I have fully discussed the historical tendencies toward equality in Japanese society in "Tocqueville and Japan," my contribution to *Conversations with Tocqueville: The Global Democratic Revolution in the Twenty-first Century*, ed. Aurelian

next section on equality is a supplement to my preceding argument, which takes into account the recent debate on the new inequality. After these reflections, I would like to conclude by suggesting a possibility of writing *Democracy in Japan* from a certain Tocquevillian viewpoint.

Equality and Egalitarianism

A basic reason for Tocqueville's relevance to Japan is that its society is democratic. In spite of the recent debate[20] on the new inequality, or "disparity" (*kakusa*), it is impossible to regard Japan as a relatively less egalitarian country in the present world. It is true that there has been a remarkable increase of economic inequality in the last two decades and Japanese society has undergone a considerable change since the 1980s, when the economy was at its zenith and 90 percent of the people considered themselves to belong to the middle class. But the similar phenomena of inequality, the increasing differentials of income and the appearance of a new underclass, have also been observed in other advanced countries, to a greater degree in the United States and perhaps less in several European countries. They should be considered as a natural result of neoliberal economic policies and global financial capitalism since the 1980s.

In 2008, the new publication of the classical novel of proletarian literature, *Kanikōsen* (*The Crab Canning Ship*), written in 1929 by Kobayashi Takiji, made an extraordinary success, with the sale of a million copies. A new film based on the story was made after an interval of more than half a century since its first version of 1953. This small book, a masterpiece, once widely read but forgotten for a long time, of the communist writer who had been tortured by the police to death in 1933 at the age of twenty-nine, unexpectedly caused a big sensation, which was not limited to Japan but spread in Europe. After the Spanish and Italian

---

Craiutu and Sheldon Gellar (Lanham, Md.: Lexington Books, 2009), chap. 13. The following argument is just a brief depiction of the present state of society, touching upon the contemporary debate about the new inequality.

20. Miura Nobuo, *Karyūshakai: Aratana kaisōshūdan no shutsugen* [Lower society: The appearance of a new group of class], (Tokyo: Kōbunsha, 2005); Tachibanaki Toshiaki, *Kakusashakai: Nani ga mondai ka?* [Society of disparity: What is the problem?] (Tokyo: Iwanami Shoten, 2006).

versions, the French translation published in 2009 under the title of *Le bateau-usine* found a tremendous resonance in the atmosphere of growing worry about the global economic crisis.

These recent phenomena clearly show that there does exist among common people a serious concern for the future of the global economy, in which poverty and inequality might prevail more widely than ever before. The protestation of Wall Street "occupants" has proved that those frustrated people found a target for attack in the alleged center of global financial capitalism. In the rise of various types of protest movements of "the multitude," in Antonio Negli's use of the term, some people call for the return of Marx instead of Tocqueville.

In the 1960s, Raymond Aron wrote that Marx's apocalyptic vision of capitalist society, that of growing inequality and inevitable class conflict, which had in fact seemed relevant to the world of the 1930s, was at the time being replaced by Tocqueville's vision of egalitarian democratic society.[21] Are we witnessing the reverse replacement?

In any case, it is true that the growing crisis of global economy induces us to reconsider Tocqueville's notion of equality and inequality in democratic societies.

The Tocquevillian notion of democracy does not mean a completely egalitarian society in which no kind of inequality exists. This is not merely to say that perfect equality is not attainable in the real world. Tocqueville apparently admits that there is a certain inequality in democracies. "It is not that there are no rich in the United States," he says, "as there are elsewhere; I do not even know of a country where the love of money holds a greater place in the human heart and where a deeper contempt is professed for the theory of the permanent equality of property. But wealth circulates there with incredible rapidity, and experience teaches that it is rare to see two generations reap the rewards of wealth."[22] So the decisive criterion of democracy consists not in the equal distribution of wealth but in the everlasting vicissitude of fortune in which no one is bound to his or her present status in society.

Moreover, Tocqueville also sees the possibility of the impoverishment of the working class in democratic societies. In the famous chapter

---

21. Raymond Aron, *Main Currents in Sociological Thought*, trans. Richard Howard and Helen Weaver (London: Weidenfeld & Nicolson, 1965), 1:192.

22. *DA*, 85.

on "Industrial Aristocracy," he shows the alienation of workers as an inevitable result of industrial capitalism and describes the portrait of the new aristocracy of wealth. Indeed, he regards this manufacturing aristocracy as "one of the harshest that has appeared on the earth." But it is also, according to him, "one of the most limited and least dangerous."[23] Why? He gives two reasons: first, however sharply employers and employed may be divided in the manufacturing industry, this class distinction is a particular phenomenon limited to a partial sector of society; and second, although factory workers cannot expect to escape their condition, factory owners may be forced or pleased to quit business at any moment, so that they don't form a stable class of aristocracy.

So the existence of inequality in our society does not make Tocqueville irrelevant. At issue is the question of whether the increasing inequality or disparity in the contemporary world will in fact bring about, as Marx predicted, the consolidation of class structure and the bipolarization of society as a whole into a small number of the wealthy and a great majority of the poor. This is a big question not easy to answer. Without getting into further consideration on this challenging issue, however, I would like to say that we need both Tocqueville and Marx for reference, and at the same time I suggest that neither nor both would be sufficient for us to find a plausible solution to our contemporary problems.

In any case, considering those qualifications which Tocqueville himself adds to the notion of democratic equality, it would be too early to conclude that the recent increase of economic disparity in Japanese society diminishes the relevance of his theory of democracy to the country. Even if the growing number of the "working poor" raises a serious problem, there is no reason for anticipating the return of aristocracy in Japan. The rise of the issue itself shows that equality is recognized as a basic social value. The passion for equality is still dominant, and it drives more and more people, rich or poor, to the pursuit of happiness. It is true that the present global crisis of finance and credit is jeopardizing the prospect of the economy, but it is an inevitable consequence of "mass capitalism," which involves the common people in speculative investment. Even if the neoliberal economy and market fundamentalism may have a tendency to increase inequality,

23. *DA*, 985.

it is a result of the explosion of the market's own egalitarian principles and of everybody's democratic passion for enrichment. Under the influence of a kind of Social Darwinist rhetoric of popular journalism, which classifies people into the two groups of winners and losers, most of the Japanese are frightened of being defeated and are driven to restless competition. In this competition, both winners and losers are obsessed by the same fear and greed. The former is never free from the anxiety of losing its present status, and the latter is always envious for the fortune of others. They shared the same passion for wealth and material well-being, which Tocqueville considers as originating in the middle class and spreading through the rest of society.

So however different the present economic situation of Japan and the world is from that of the 1980s, when the country was applauded as "number one," the Japanese people do not seem to have remarkably changed. Although not so many people are complacent enough to regard themselves as belonging to the middle class and not a few feel deprived of hope for the future, the prevailing passion is still that of acquiring wealth and most people are busy pursuing their own personal happiness. They are still "democratic men" in the Tocquevillian sense of the word, people who are devoted to the pursuit of happiness and material well-being, isolated in their private lives without interest in the outer world, and are, therefore, unless habituated to the exercise of political liberty, easily inclined to obey the order of authority. Thus, recently, Sasaki Takeshi, the former president of the University of Tokyo and a leading political philosopher in Japan, recommended Tocqueville's *Democracy in America* as a rare example among Western classics that gives useful suggestions for thinking about the problems of contemporary Japanese politics.[24]

Revolution and Revolutionaries

Tocqueville's notion of democracy is not always one and the same. It is not only that his notion can be interpreted in various ways. Tocqueville

24. Sasaki Takeshi, "Kotenteki Meicho ga tsukitsukeru sengonihon no genjitsu" [A great classic facing us with the realities of postwar Japan], *Ekonomisuto* [Economist], Mainichi Shinbunsha, August 19, 2008.

himself consciously makes a distinction among several types of democracy. The clearest one is that of the American type of liberal democracy and the French type of revolutionary democracy. Jean-Claude Lamberti considers this distinction a leading idea of *Democracy* and argues that Tocqueville's primary concern was to explore the possibility of and the condition for the transition of the latter to the former.[25]

Apart from institutional differences, Tocqueville gives two explanations for the contrast of the two kinds of democracy. First, Americans were born equal and had a democratic social state already in their original position, while the French had to endure a long and bitter class struggle before approaching democracy. In America, democracy has naturally developed without an enemy since the Revolution, in the process of which Tocqueville finds nothing revolutionary except the abolition of primogeniture. By contrast, French democracy had to march through chaos and tumult, always struggling against its enemies, so that it has never been separated from revolutionary violence in the political confusion of the postrevolutionary era. Compared with the revolutionary nature of French democracy, he emphasizes, "this country [the United States] sees the results of the democratic revolution that is taking place among us, without having had the revolution itself."[26] So the French case shows a transitional phase of democratization, in which remaining aristocratic forces are still continuing a desperate struggle against democracy, whereas the American scene represents a fully developed democracy. This is the second explanation that Tocqueville proposes for the difference between the two democracies.

If the social and political confusion of postrevolutionary France represents a transitional stage on which democracy is fighting the last battle against aristocracy, then, will the confusion disappear when the battle is over and the resistance of aristocracy dies out? If Jacksonian democracy, which Tocqueville finds working and stable despite all its defects, reveals the nature and essence of democracy itself, then, can the French also expect to live in a similar orderly and legitimate society

---

25. Jean-Claude Lamberti, *Tocqueville et les deux démocraties* (Paris: Presses Universitaire de France, 1983).

26. *DA*, 26–27.

in the future? This is the basic question that he asks himself through studying America.

His answer is positive. It was inevitable that French democracy marched through the muddle of anarchy and gained power through violence, for it had been born in a feudal and aristocratic society and grown up in the turmoil of struggle with its enemies. Even after the French Revolution, it was attacked everywhere by men and groups filled with resentment against the Revolution and nostalgia for the Old Regime, those who "had learnt nothing, forgotten nothing." Tocqueville's worry about the future that France was going toward another bigger revolution was widely shared by his contemporaries. After several years' thoroughgoing study on America, however, he reached an encouraging conclusion: judging from the stability of American politics, an established democracy will make an orderly and regulated society, in which most people absorbed in the pursuit of material well-being dislike social confusion and revolutionary violence; the violent oscillation of French politics is not the necessary consequence of democracy, but a posteffect of the French Revolution. So, once the French accept democratic equality as just and legitimate and properly distinguish the passion of democracy from that of revolution, they will also, like Americans at the time, live in an orderly society, which may be not so brilliant and exalted as aristocratic societies in the past but more peaceful and prosperous. So however chaotic and unstable French politics may seem at present, it is a transitional aspect of democracy that will be replaced by a more tranquil state of society.

In chapter 21 of part 3 of the second volume of *Democracy,* titled "Why Great Revolutions Will Become Rare," Tocqueville tries to give a theoretical foundation to this conjecture about the future of democracy. He begins his argument by the statement that all historical revolutions were made either to consecrate equality or to destroy it. Once the equality of conditions is firmly established, however, most people, especially those belonging to the middle class and engaged in commerce and industry, tenaciously cling to their property and seek nothing but to maintain and increase it. As a result, they are afraid of all the commotions that might endanger their business and possessions, and try to evade revolutions as much as possible. Tocqueville does not deny the existence of revolutionaries in democracy. But they are in a decided minority and will have little prospect of leading the majority of people to revolutionary uprisings, for they struggle against the general spirit of their age and country. Not categorically excluding the possibility that the small minorities might bring about a revolution in a democratic society, he concludes that great revolutions will be rare in the future. "Democratic peoples, left to themselves, do not easily become engaged in great adventures; they are carried toward revolutions only unknowingly; they sometimes undergo revolutions, but they do not make them. And I add that, when they have been permitted to acquire enlightenment and experience, they do not allow them to be made."[27]

This prognosis or expectation of Tocqueville in 1840 was not confirmed in the subsequent commotions of French politics during his lifetime. In 1848, he encountered another revolution and tried as a leading politician to stabilize its result, the Second Republic, but in vain. In compensation for his failure, however, he left us one of the most brilliant eyewitness histories of a revolution ever written, *Souvenirs.* His last book made a profound analysis of the causes and background of the French Revolution and persuasively explained how the revolutionary spirit had been born in the process of centralization under the Old Regime and survived the Revolution, always agonizing the French people. Lamberti, reinterpreting *Democracy in America* in the context of the development of Tocqueville's theory of revolution, argues that he abandoned the above-mentioned thesis of transitional democracy. According to Lamberti, to expect a stable democracy in the future of France is the error of confusing a pure type with historical existence, and Tocqueville himself, aware of that, changed his view and became more afraid that the overlapping effects of centralization and revolutionary spirit would recurrently make French democracy insecure. What is anticipated for the near future of France is not a stable democracy but the alternate danger of revolution and despotism. The notion of democratic despotism featured in the closing chapters of *Democracy,* according to Lamberti's reading, is quite different from the prospect of the arrival of a liberal and egalitarian society at the end of the transitional phase of revolutionary confusion, which is based on the optimistic hypothesis of the separation of democracy and revolution. He

27. *DA,* 1142.

goes as far as to say that *Democracy in America* should be clearly divided at the end of the third section of the second volume and that the last section is not a continuation of the precedent arguments but an anticipation of later works, *Souvenirs* and *The Old Regime*.[28]

Although I don't fully agree with Lamberti in too sharply cutting *Democracy* into two parts, it is true that Tocqueville gives two different predictions for the future of democracy: the prospect of a stable democracy free from revolutionary confusion and the fear of democratic despotism resulting from the alternate danger of revolution and anarchy. In the light of his own historical experience after the publication of the Second *Democracy,* it is very natural that he should abandon the first vision and take the second more seriously and concentrate on the historical explanation for the persistence of the revolutionary spirit in France. But, if we take a longer-term perspective on history, taking into account the later development of French democracy after his death, we don't find the first vision completely falsified.

After the tragedy of the Commune was over and as the political institutions of the Third Republic were established, parliamentary democracy gradually began to work in France. The revolutionary spirit did not disappear completely and caused political turmoil from time to time, but it could not successfully arouse the whole nation to a great revolution as before. It is true that the radical chic of the Left Bank attracted admirers from all over the world in the postwar era and still does to some extent. But those Left intellectuals seemed to be absorbed in "arguing revolution" rather than carrying it out.[29] After 1917, the real center of revolution was not in Paris but in Moscow. In twentieth-century France, no revolutionary change of political regime and society occurred except as the result of war. Even the crisis of May 1968 ended in the peaceful retirement of Charles de Gaulle, not in the overthrow of the Fifth Republic.

This stabilization of French democracy means neither the French assimilation of American democracy nor the fusion of the two. In spite of the weakening of the revolutionary spirit in France, there are certain

---

28. Lamberti, *Tocqueville et les deux démocraties,* chap. 9, 271–99.

29. Sunil Khilnani, *Arguing Revolution: The Intellectual Left in Postwar France* (Cambridge: Cambridge University Press, 1994).

continuing differences between the French and American democracies. Indeed, the end of the Cold War and the subsequent progress of globalization once again brought out the contrast between the French republican model of democracy and the American liberal or libertarian model.[30] The differences were observed in many areas: the economy, diplomacy, social welfare, educational system, religion, immigration, and so forth. So in spite of the great metamorphoses that the French and American models of democracy have undergone since his time, Tocqueville's comparison of the two models is still relevant in the present world. What should we say, then, about Japanese democracy? To which type is it closer?

Apparently Japanese people were not all born equal in the sense that Tocqueville says that Americans were. At the starting point of modern Japan, equality of conditions was not a given but something to be acquired through revolution. The Meiji Revolution, which abolished class distinctions and declared the equality of the four peoples [*shimin byōdō*], samurai, peasants, artisans, and merchants, was a typical democratic revolution in the full sense of Tocqueville's use of the term and therefore comparable with the French Revolution.[31] As a social revolution, it gave birth to far greater consequences than the latter, and

30. The difference between the French and American types of democracy was one of the main issues discussed at the Tokyo conference on Tocqueville in 2005. See the proceedings of the conference, *La France et les États-Unis, deux modèles de démocratie? Actes du colloque international commémoratif du Bicentenaire de la naissance d'Alexis de Tocqueville* and its published version in Japanese, R. Matsumoto, S. Uno, and N. Miura, eds., *Tokuviru to demokurashii no genzai* (Tokyo: University of Tokyo Press, 2009).

31. Watanabe Hiroshi, a leading scholar of the history of Japanese political thought, drawing on some arguments of *The Old Regime and the Revolution,* discussed historical parallels between the two revolutions in his paper presented to the above-mentioned Tokyo conference. See the paper included in the proceedings, Watanabe Hiroshi, "The Old Regime and the Meiji Revolution," and its enlarged Japanese version, "Anshan Rejiimu to Meiji Kakumei," first published in *Shisō,* 979 (November 2005): 51–70, and then included in the book *Tokuviru to demokurashii no genzai.* See also my own argument, drawing on Watanabe, in "Tocqueville and Japan," chap. 13 of Craiutu and Gellar, *Conversations with Tocqueville.* There is also a long history of debates among Japanese Marxist historians on the comparison of the two revolutions.

with far less violence. Indeed, throughout a quarter century of revolutionary turmoil, the Japanese experienced a fundamental change in almost all spheres of social and cultural life: law and political system, socioeconomic structure, manners and customs, even language and vocabulary. This rapid and total change of all the aspects of society made a deep impression on foreign observers without exception. Basil Hall Chamberlain, who lived in Japan for over thirty years, wrote in 1891, "To have lived through the transition stage of modern Japan makes a man feel preternaturally old; for here he is in modern times, with the air full of talk about bicycles and bacilli and 'spheres of influence,' and yet he can himself distinctly remember the Middle Ages. The dear old Samurai who first initiated the present writer into the mysteries of the Japanese language, wore a queue and two swords. This relic of feudalism now sleeps in Nirvana.... Old things pass away between a night and a morning."[32] L. I. Mechinikov, a Russian *narodnik* revolutionary, who came to Japan in 1874 and lived two years there, teaching Russian, was astonished at finding that his ideal of revolution had been realized in this small island country.[33] Seeing this deep rupture of a revolution, Tocqueville would find it difficult to apply to the case of Japan his thesis of continuity from the Old Regime through the Revolution to the Modern.

The reason for this rapid and radical transformation of society caused by the Meiji Revolution is that it was not only a social and political revolution but also a turning point at which the Japanese people as a whole started to learn and absorb the Western civilization that had been almost totally unknown to them. It was at the same time the abolition of the status system of the past and the beginning of the national project of westernization. This rupture with the past and leap

32. Basil Hall Chamberlain, *Things Japanese* (Kegan Paul, 1891), quoted in Andrew Gordon, *A Modern History of Japan, from Tokugawa Times to the Present* (Oxford: Oxford University Press, 2003), 61.

33. L. I. Mechinikov, *Kaisō no Meiji Ishin: Ichi Roshiajin kakumeika no shuki* [The Meiji Revolution in reminiscence: Memoirs of a Russian revolutionary], ed. and trans. Watanabe Masashi (Tokyo: Iwanami Bunko, 1987). This is the Japanese translation of a series of essays published in a Russian journal in 1883–1884 as *Vospominaniya o dvukhletnei sluzhbe v Yaponii* [Recollections of two years' service in Japan].

into the future were regarded as necessary for the independence and survival of the nation in the imperialist world at the time. The Meiji Revolution was the political consequence of the country's reactions to the Western impact, and the international context in which it broke out inevitably gave it a nationalistic character. Historians considering that context define it as a nationalist revolution.

The international environment of East Asia, then, was an important factor causing the Meiji Revolution. But it also imposed constraints on further revolutionary development, for, insofar as people were conscious of an external threat to national independence, whether real or imaginary, they would tend to regard any radical opposition to the government as dangerous and detrimental to the national interest and security. It is often said that the Popular Rights Movement was not defeated by governmental repression but faded away in the rise of popular nationalism. The keen consciousness of external threat had a lingering effect on people's mind even after the Russo-Japanese War and transformed the early nationalism of Meiji Japan into an excessive expansionism, which would lead the country to the invasion of China and eventually to the desperate war against the United States.

What influence did these conditions have on the development of democracy in Japan? Generally speaking, it is safe to say that the excessive fear of an external threat and the consequent obsession with national security don't provide a favorable condition for liberal democracy. Even in the United States, democratic liberties have been greatly restricted in periods of fear and insecurity, as shown by the McCarthyism of the 1950s and again, to some extent, in the contemporary "war on terror." The history of modern Japan seems to give another example supporting the theory. State building under the Constitution of 1889, based on the Prussian model and rejecting the alternative of British parliamentary politics, which was strongly recommended by Fukuzawa, was a natural choice of the "founding fathers" of modern Japan, who were preoccupied with national independence and international hegemony, and had little concern for the freedom of the people. As the country established its status as an international power, parliamentary democracy and party politics were introduced under the restraint of the Constitution and began replacing the autocratic rule of the Meiji government. Unfortunately, however, the so-called Taishō democracy enjoyed just a short life of barely a decade. With the Japanese invasion of China and the growing crisis of the economy, democracy and party politics were severely attacked and then totally replaced by military dictatorship through the 1930s.

As for revolutionary democracy, the existence of an external threat has a contradictory effect on it. On one hand, the persistent fear of an external threat and the struggle for hegemony in international politics naturally led a nation to strengthen governmental authority and to impose controls on the rights of the people. The people themselves, at least the great majority of them, tend to refrain from criticizing the government and to regard dissidents as subversive of national unity. The government, for its part, takes full advantage of jingoistic patriotism to repress revolutionary minorities. One of the reasons for the gradual disappearance of the French revolutionary tradition in the Third Republic, in my opinion, was the national fear of Germany, for, after the German Unification of 1871, the French were afraid that another revolution in Paris would have revealed the weakness of the nation in the face of the powerful neighbor to the east. In the same way, the first revolutionary elements in modern Japan, born from the Meiji Revolution and the Popular Rights Movement, were increasingly marginalized in the Meiji State. Some of the radicals of the Popular Rights Movement, like Ōi Kentarō (1843–1922), out of despair at the political situation of Japan, tried to join hands with Korean revolutionaries. In later years, not a few political adventurers, both on the Left and on the Right, left Japan to join the movement of revolutionary nationalism in China. The most famous was Kita Ikki (1883–1937), a kind of revolutionary national socialist who became a friend and supporter of Song Jiao-ren and was later involved in the abortive coup d'etat of February 26, 1936, and was executed as the guru of the young officers leading the coup.

However, an autocratic government continuously exposed to an external threat sometimes provokes a revolutionary crisis owing to its own conduct, for its excessive repression of revolutionaries drives them to intransigent resistance and even earns them the sympathy of the people. This happens in particular when a national crisis discredits an oppressive regime among the people. The situation will be further exacerbated if the crisis develops into a war. Indeed, the two great revolutions in the twentieth century, the Russian and the Chinese, were products of a war and defeat. In Japan, the revolutionary Left, Communists and anarchists, remained a small minority even in the 1920s and the 1930s, at the high tide of the international communist movement. They were held to deny the National Polity (*kokutai*) of Japan, that is to say, the Emperor System. So they were feared by the common people and repressed by the police without mercy. Nevertheless, this small illegal minority never ceased its desperate resistance to war and the invasion of China, which aroused to some extent sympathy among the people, in particular, the intellectuals and educated people.

More remarkable was the rise of right-wing revolutionaries in the same period. They called for the emperor's direct rule, excluding the "liberal" establishment composed of higher bureaucrats, party politicians, and business elites, and acquired supporters and sympathizers in the army. The group of radical young officers called *kōdō-ha* [the Imperial Way faction] and their civilian allies caused a series of assassinations and violence culminating in the coup d'état of February 26, 1936, which was suppressed by the command of the emperor himself. After this failure, the group was disbanded and its members were ousted from their positions, but their radical program itself, later adopted by the leaders of the army and the government, played an important role in militarizing the country.

Considering this historical process of the militarization of Japan, Tocqueville's worry about the penetration of the revolutionary spirit into the army is particularly suggestive. In the last chapters of the third part of the Second *Democracy,* he discusses the democratic army and war, and points out that the revolutionary and the military threaten democracy with similar dangers.[34] Both are disturbing elements in democratic societies. In the general spread of the democratic passion for order and stability, he anticipates, the revolutionary spirit will weaken but never disappear completely. He finds, however, a greater danger in the military ambition than in the revolutionary, for the former has the legitimate receptacle of the army, while the latter is shared only by a small number of political radicals. When the army of

---

34. *DA,* 1153–86. See my argument on Tocqueville's view of the army, "Is Democracy Peaceful? Tocqueville and Constant on War and the Army," *Tocqueville Review* 28, no. 1 (2007): 153–65.

a peaceful democracy can't satisfy every member's democratic ambition for upgrading, frustrated officers and soldiers anxiously wait for a war, which would provide for them a chance for advancement, and if it is impossible to wage a war, they would cause domestic social confusion, from which a military despotism might emerge. In a stable democracy, in which it is always difficult for a small number of revolutionaries to arouse the people to a revolutionary uprising, the penetration of the revolutionary spirit into the army would pose a real danger. It is not a revolution but revolutionary militarism that democratic peoples should fear in their future.

Thus warning against military despotism, apparently Tocqueville had in mind French Bonapartism. But his argument is also worth reconsidering in the political context of the twentieth century in which various kinds of revolutionary militarism, including that of Japan, rose and fell.

The postwar reform, eliminating the residues of social inequality and encouraging the political participation of the common people, including women, to say nothing of the effect of demilitarization, provided a solid basis for democracy in Japan. Parliamentary politics under the new constitution gradually restored political stability, and the remarkable growth of the economy brought about a prosperous and stable society, in which every individual is absorbed in the pursuit of happiness and material well-being. It is true that there was a certain period of political passion and enthusiasm, in which the opposition parties, the Socialist and the Communist, successfully mobilized many people to their radical movement against the government. But there was no real possibility of revolution except in a short period immediately after the defeat of 1945, and a main reason for the success of the opposition movement consisted in that it appealed to the pacifism and anti-Americanism of the people in the Cold War era. In the trend of growing social stability and economic prosperity, the political radicalism of the Left gradually lost popular support, and Japanese society in the 1980s, as I have already suggested, showed many features of Tocqueville's ideal type of democratic society.

Looking back over the development of democracy in modern Japan since the Meiji Revolution, I can't help saying that it basically confirms

Tocqueville's main arguments about democracy: almost all great revolutions in history were carried out for the purpose of either consecrating or destroying equality; if a democratic revolution establishes equality of conditions in a society once and for all, it will be difficult to make a fundamental change in that social state, for a democratic people will try to preserve equality at any cost; and a democratic people in a transitional stage, however bitterly troubled they may be by political disturbances and social confusions at a particular moment, can entertain the hope of a more stable democracy in the future. The history of Japanese democracy can be roughly interpreted in the light of these statements. What should I say, then, about Tocqueville's final worry that an excessive fear of revolution may lead a democratic people to intellectual stagnation? Does the following remark have no relevance to our present state of society at all?

> If citizens continue to enclose themselves more and more narrowly within the circle of small domestic interests and to be agitated there without respite, you can fear that they will end by becoming as if impervious to these great and powerful public emotions that disturb peoples, but which develop and renew them. When I see property become so mobile, and the love of property so anxious and so ardent, I cannot prevent myself from fearing that men will reach the point of regarding every new theory as a danger, every innovation as an unfortunate trouble, every social progress as a first step toward a revolution, and that they will refuse entirely to move for fear that they would be carried away. I tremble, I confess, that they will finally allow themselves to be possessed so well by a cowardly love of present enjoyments, that the interest in their own future and that of their descendants will disappear, and that they will prefer to follow feebly the course of their destiny, than to make, if needed, a sudden and energetic effort to redress it.[35]

The present stability of democracy in Japan, however, does not mean that it is coming close to the American type of liberal democracy. Most democratic reforms introduced to Japan under the Occupation were based on the American model. The prewar system *à la française* of

35. *DA,* 1150–51.

local administration was transformed into the American system of self-government. The school system was also renewed after the American model. The new constitution defines exactly the same system of judicial review as the U.S. Constitution does. Labor legislation and the Antimonopoly Act were also influenced by U.S. legislation. The consequence of these laws and institutions *à l'américaine*, however, is different from that of their originals in the United States. Some of those institutional reforms, like the decentralization of police administration, regarded as alien to Japan, were renounced immediately after the end of the Occupation. Indeed, legal and institutional Americanization in postwar Japan shows the limited effect of introducing foreign laws and institutions to a different culture.

Let me just give a remarkable example, which is concerned with a core issue of Tocquevillian thinking about American politics: judicial review. As mentioned above, the Constitution of 1946 introduced the same system of judicial review as that of the United States, although the way of the nomination of Supreme Court judges is different. However, the Japanese Supreme Court, which has been in general reluctant to pronounce the sentence of unconstitutionality, has never enjoyed that important role which its U.S. counterpart plays in American political life.

The most imminent constitutional issue now at stake is the problem of disparity in the relative weight of voting. Repeatedly since the 1970s, constitutional lawsuits have been brought over the unequal apportionment of seats at each election, yet these inequalities have not been corrected. After a series of decisions declaring various apportionments unconstitutional, the Supreme Court judged the general election of August 2009 (to have been conducted) "in the state of unconstitutionality," as violating the principle of equality before the law (Art. 14), but it did not go so far as to nullify the election itself. This means that the Japanese people have been, since the Hatoyama Ministry, under a government that lacks constitutional legitimacy.

Unless a drastic reapportionment has been done by the time of the next general election, which must be held as late as summer 2013, the Supreme Court will inevitably give another sentence of unconstitutionality. Indeed, it is possible for the Court to declare the election to be nullified, which would cause a terrible political confusion. If not, and if the democratic principle of one person, one vote continues to be violated, then serious doubt will be cast on Japanese politics: is it really constitutional and democratic? Nevertheless, neither the legislative nor the executive has taken initiative to drastically change the present system of apportionment. Even public opinion and political journalism seem to keep silent about this issue. This state of affairs would be incredible in the United States.[36]

American rules and American-modeled institutions operate so differently in Japan than in America; this question of judicial review (and the related matters of balance among political institutions, and the roles of a free press and of public opinion) is just one example of that. Another interesting example is the paradoxical consequences of the postwar reform of local administration based on the American model which I have discussed in another work.[37] No wonder that many students of comparative politics, in particular the so-called revisionists of Japanese studies, have repeatedly emphasized the difference between American and Japanese politics.[38] An American sports journalist living a long time in Japan once wrote an amusing book about Japanese baseball,[39] saying that the Japanese people have developed a very different style of playing baseball even under the American rules of the game. This difference, he also says, is to some extent a reflection of the cultural differences between the two peoples.

Similarly, just as in baseball, we have developed our own play style of politics under the same American rule of democracy. But is there

36. In the latest two national elections, which were conducted with a minor change of apportionment on November 16, 2012 (the House of Representatives), and on July 7, 2013 (the House of Councillors), several court decisions have already been made. Although a couple of lower courts dared to declare them void, the Supreme Court did not go so far as to change the former judgment of "the state of unconstitutionality." But the serious doubt of the constitutionality of the Japanese government has not been cleared up.

37. See my "Tocqueville and Japan," chap. 13 of Craiutu and Gellar, *Conversations with Tocqueville*.

38. The most conspicuous is Karl van Wolferen, *The Enigma of Japanese Power: People and Politics in a Stateless Nation* (New York: Knopf, 1989).

39. Robert Whiting, *The Chrysanthemum and the Bat: The Game Japanese Play* (Tokyo: Permanent Press, 1977).

nothing to worry about in the cultural variety of play styles in politics? Is it just as amusing as in baseball?

In any case, the paradoxical consequences of legal and institutional Americanization in postwar Japan remind us of Tocqueville's argument that the same law works differently when transplanted to a different culture and that mores are more important than laws as the determining factor of social behavior. To write "Democracy in Japan" from Tocqueville's viewpoint would be possible and interesting, but the book would be different from *Democracy in America*.

Index

293; property rights of, 280, 296; racial status of, 249; relationship with the French, 13–14, 14n55, 262, 262n53, 262n55, 281, 283, 283n25; relocation of, 294; reversal by Tocqueville in view of fate of, 280–84, 290; social state of, 151, 249, 284; Tocqueville's view of, xx, 24, 81, 282; treatment as administrative units under Federal supervision, 256; treatment in Central and South America, 261n51; and westward expansion of white America, 256–58. *See also specific tribes*

NATO, 419

natural religion, 196

natural rights, doctrine of, 114–19, 117n17, 119nn21–22, 123, 124n33, 136n50, 137, 141

nature. *See* state of nature

Negli, Antonio, 439

Negroes, 46–47; segregation and limited rights of, 266–67. *See also* race prejudice *for segregation*

neologisms, use of, 18

New England: colonists settling, background of, 74, 152–53, 167; Tocqueville's focus on, 18, 132–36; Tocqueville's travel to, 263; Tocqueville's view of America colored by, 80; township model in, 50. *See also* Puritan New England

New Orleans, 19n102, 80, 86, 263

new political science, xviii, 95–96, 115, 142–76, 346–53; basis for, 208; framework of, 144–45, 348–49; history of movement toward greater equality of conditions, 145–49, 214–15; intimations of, in *Democracy in America*, 206–7, 215; and liberty in democratic social state, 158–76; meaning

of, 144n11, 178–79; and mores, 163–76; and practical popular political education, 160–63; and providential history, 148; relevance to Eastern Europe, 401–10; and social state, 145, 150–57, 221, 223

New York (western), 257

New York City, 36, 83, 98–100, 266, 267

Niagara Falls, 36, 98

Nietzsche, 191

Nishi Amane, 428

Noailles, Enrique Valiente, 373

Nolla, Eduardo, xvi, xvii, xviii, xx, 1, 43, 105, 142, 165n52, 185, 258, 281n18, 345, 402, 408. *See also Democracy in America*

North Africa, French conquest of, xxi, 305–7; arguments for empire, 313–21; bringing civilization to conquered population, 318–21; impact on domestic French politics, 315–16; legacy of, 274; lessons for democratic founders from, 321–25; mistakes in, 308, 318, 320n42, 322, 333–34; moral disaster in, 334; and reclaiming France's rightful place in Europe, 314–15; Tocqueville's personal account of, 307–12, 425; Tocqueville's support for French emigration to, 309. *See also* Algeria

North American Review, 91

Northern states: disagreement of Northern and Southern whites, 82, 268–73; freed Negroes in, 21; work ethic of, 272. *See also* New England

nullification, 107, 271, 359

Numa, 114

Obata Tokujirō, 428, 429, 430, 432

Occupy Wall Street, 392

The typeface used for this book is ITC New Baskerville, which was created for the International Typeface Corporation and is based on the types of the English type founder and printer John Baskerville (1706–75). Baskerville is the quintessential transitional face: it retains the bracketed and oblique serifs of old-style faces such as Caslon and Garamond, but in its increased lowercase height, lighter color, and enhanced contrast between thick and thin strokes, it presages modern faces.

The display type is set in Didot.

This book is printed on paper that is acid free and meets the requirements of the American National Standard for Permanence of Paper for Printed Library Materials, z39.48-1992. ∞

Book design by Rich Hendel, Chapel Hill, North Carolina

Typography by Brad Walrod/Kenoza Type, Inc.

Printed and bound by Worzalla Publishing Company, Stevens Point, Wisconsin